The Man Who Stopped
the Trains to Auschwitz

D1557668

Religion, Theology, and the Holocaust
Alan L. Berger, Series Editor

The Man Who Stopped the Trains to Auschwitz

George Mantello, El Salvador, and Switzerland's Finest Hour

David Kranzler

With a Foreword by
Senator Joseph I. Lieberman

Syracuse University Press

The paper used in this publication meets the minimum requirements of the
American National Standard for Information Sciences — Permanence of
Paper for Printed Library Materials, ANSI Z39.48-1984.∞™

Library of Congress Cataloging-in-Publication Data

Kranzler, David, 1930–
    The man who stopped the trains to Auschwitz : George Mantello, El Salvador, and
Switzerland's finest hour / David Kranzler ; with foreword by Joseph I. Lieberman.
        p.   cm. — (Religion, theology, and the Holocaust)
    Includes bibliographical references (p.) and index.
    ISBN 0-8156-0644-3 (alk. paper)
    1. Mantello, George. 2. Jews—El Salvador—Biography. 3. World War,
1939–1945—Jews—Rescue—Hungary. 4. Diplomats—El Salvador—Biography.
5. Righteous Gentiles in the Holocaust. 6. El Salvador—Ethnic relations.
7. Switzerland—Ethnic relations. I. Title. II. Series.

F1497.J48 M365 2000
972.84'004'924'0092—dc21
[B]

                                                                00-029158

With a dedication by Harold Grinspoon

To
my wife
Diane Troderman
who often finds herself
in the right place at the right time
to become a
"charge agent"
for our Jewish community
and who understands that transformation
is made possible
by caring passionately
about human potential
With my deepest love and profound admiration

David Kranzler, historian and retired professor at the City University of New York, is the author of nine books and numerous articles on rescue and rescue attempts during the Holocaust. These include *Japanese, Nazis, and Jews: The Jewish Refugee Community of Shanghai; Heroine of Rescue*; and *Thy Brother's Blood: The Orthodox Jewish Response During the Holocaust.* He contributed two chapters to the Goldberg Commission Report on American Jewry During the Holocaust and is a contributor to the *Encyclopedia of the Holocaust, The World Reaction to the Holocaust*, the forthcoming *Yale Encyclopedia of the Holocaust*, and the *New Dictionary of National Biography*.

Contents

Contents

Illustrations

Foreword

Senator Joseph I. Lieberman

Once unimaginable crimes against humanity were systematically devised, implemented, and accelerated against Jews by Nazi Germany and its collaborators during the Second World War. It was a Holocaust against a people, a faith, and every dimension of human decency from which our civilized world is still recovering, and for which the testimony of survivors has steeled a resolve to remember the heroism of those who fought evil against all odds of success.

In recent years, the world has taken to heart brave persons such as Raoul Wallenberg and Oskar Schindler, who saved thousands of Jews from the gas chambers in the final months of the war. Others, such as Protestant Rev. Martin Niemoller, have long been famous for personal revelations that turned indifference into German resistance against the Nazis: "When Hitler attacked the Jews, I was not a Jew, therefore, I was not concerned. And when Hitler attacked the Catholics, I was not a Catholic, and therefore I was not concerned. And when Hitler attacked the unions and the industrialists, I was not a member of the unions and I was not concerned. Then, Hitler attacked me and the Protestant church—and there was nobody left to be concerned."

Switzerland has become a focal point of Holocaust research. Policies of the Swiss government against Jewish refugees and those of Swiss banks against the holdings of Jewish depositors have been rescued from the shadowed whispers of the guilty by individual acts of conscience and heroism in our time. What is new, thanks to the work of Dr. David Kranzler in this powerful and moving book, is the discovery and documentation of heroic efforts made in Switzerland during the Second World War.

The ancient Mishna, a time-honored expression of Jewish law, says, "Whoever saves one life, it is as if he saved the entire world" (Sanhedrin

4:37a). In 1944, many worlds were saved in the darkest hours of humanity by acts begun in Switzerland. Theologians such as Karl Barth, Paul Vogt, and Adolphe Koechlin helped George Mandel-Mantello—the first secretary in the Consulate-Gerneral of El Salvador in Geneva—create a press and church campaign that informed Switzerland and the world of the horrors of Auschwitz and the deportation of Hungarian Jewry to certain death. The campaign not only evoked the first public outcry by world leaders such as the pope, Roosevelt, Eden, and the king of Sweden (who then dispatched Wallenberg to Budapest) but it also reached deeply into the Swiss conscience, and the resulting pressure forced an indifferent Swiss government and its International Red Cross to help rescue the remaining 140,000 Jews in Budapest.

The poet Carl Sandburg wrote, "A baby is God's opinion that life should go on." Fortunately, there have been many such births since the Holocaust, many born to those who survived because of the bravery of individuals they would never know. But perhaps the greatest birth has been the truth—in all its dimensions, good and bad. Dr. Kranzler offers us another part of that truth, a hopeful and inspirational passage of which the Swiss people and good people everywhere can be very proud.

Acknowledgments

One of the pleasures of completing the final chores on a nonfiction manuscript, especially one that took more than fifteen years to research and write, is the opportunity to express my appreciation to the many persons whose crucial involvement permeates every facet of this work. These special people include survivors and rescuers who shared their memories of and insights into a fascinating, but relatively little-known area of rescue and rescue attempts during the Holocaust, as well as colleagues and friends who have assisted, supported, and encouraged my work over a long period of time.

I am profoundly grateful to have made the acquaintance and enjoyed the friendship of the late George Mandel-Mantello, the prime hero of this saga. When I first met him, many years ago, I found his story hard to believe, for I had not seen his name in any of the literature. Even after extensive research, I was able to cite only two insignificant mentions. It took many years of intensive digging in both public and private archives (throughout the world) to unearth the thousands of documents that would substantiate almost every one of his contentions. I am also grateful for the more than eighty hours of taped interviews, and for his private papers, which include the original Swiss newspapers.

I am honored by the gracious foreword by the distinguished Senator Joseph Lieberman, the conscience of the Senate, and for the kind words for the book by Professor Franklin H. Littell, the foremost scholar in the field of churches and the Holocaust. Likewise, I thank the brilliant theologian Dr. Hans Schaffert of Zurich. As the sole surviving participant of this heroic Swiss epic, his commendation adds a poignant authenticity. It is my pleasure to express my deep gratitude to Harold Greenspoon for his gracious dedication of this work to Diane Troderman, his extraordinarily dynamic wife.

Acknowledgments

This book is also my personal tribute to the interviewees from all over the world (most of whom are no longer alive) who had been involved in various aspects of rescue. They not only elucidated their particular areas of activity during the Holocaust, but they also added a personal and human dimension.

I sincerely appreciate the assistance of the following staffs: of the Franklin Delano Roosevelt Library, the American Jewish Archives, the American Jewish Historical Society, the National Archives, the archives of Agudath Israel, the Joint Distribution Committee, the Jewish Labor Committee, and YIVO, in America; of Yad Vashem, the Zionist Archives, Moreshet Archives, Haifa University Archives, and Machon Lavon Institute in Israel; the Archiv fur Zeitgeschichte ETH Zentrum and the Zentralbibliothek in Zurich and the Schweitzerisches Bundesarchiv in Bern, Switzrland. I must highlight the assistance of the indefatigable archivists L. Kohler and Dr. Daniel Bourgeois.

Because my research involved documents in several languages, mostly German and French, but also Hungarian and Spanish, I was fortunate in having several colleagues and close friends help with the translations. I thank my dear friend Ernest Seewald, who provided encouragement as well as much help with the translation of the most difficult official German and Swiss documents. For the French documents, I was fortunate to have had two pros: Ruth Neuberger, who had known Mantello in Switzerland, did a superb job on the first set of French-language documents, and Dorothy E. Johnson did an equally outstanding job with the more recent, newly opened Swiss documents. My colleague at CUNY, Professor Catherine Sestay, translated the Hungarian documents, and my friend Dr. David Cymet transformed the Spanish into good English. Finally, I wish to thank Sherry Schwartz for her general inspiration and assistance in every phase. Naturally, I am solely responsible for any possible errors resulting from these translations.

I would also like to express my great appreciation to the scholars who reviewed my manuscript at various stages. These include Dr. Robert Rozett, Director of the Yad Vashem Library and one of the few scholars with direct knowledge of many of the events; Professor Franklin H. Littell; and Dr. John Conway. They provided much constructive criticism and prevented some real bloopers. My good friend Dr. Melech Press helped find some obscure Jewish sources, and Feigie Silverman helped shape the first draft of the manuscript.

Throughout the long period of the manuscript's "gestation," I learned to appreciate the true value of the very talented and ever-helpful staff of the Syracuse University Press. My special thanks to its director, Dr. Robert Mandel, for his early interest in the subject and his steady encouragement at every stage of the manuscript's development, and to my exacting copyeditor, Tom Seller, and to the rest of the staff of Syracuse University Press.

I was blessed with a warm and loving family, who provided constant material and emotional support. I thank them for their deep and abiding faith in me, and for tolerating my erratic schedule through the long years. They rejoiced in my accomplishments, and by so doing, gave me the strength to strive for even more. A very special debt of gratitude, more than words can describe, is due my dear nephew Dr. Gerald Weisfogel, whose loving support and encouragement through some difficult moments spurred me onto completing the work. From the past I acknowledge my dear parents, the late Yerachmiel and Chana Kranzler, O'H, who instilled a love of Jews and Judaism into all seven siblings, and who thankfully left Germany in time to avoid the coming Holocaust; and my in-laws: the late Rabbi Yaakov and Anna Bein O'H, whose rescue efforts in Hungary during the war inspired many ideas in this work. In the present, I would like to respectfully acknowledge the contribution of my dearest Judy, my lifelong helpmate and inspiration; my eldest son, Moshe, and daughter-in-law, Faigie; my daughter, Shani, and son-in-law, Shaye, whose love of Eretz Israel made them settle there, and my youngest, Yaakov Meir, who has read all my works. I humbly thank them for their steady encouragement during the seeming endless years of research and writing.

And to those of my family, who represent the future, my four wonderful grandchildren, Aliza, Yonatan Boruch (named after the hero of this work), Elisheva Kranzler, and Dena Bracha Greenwald. I pray they will learn to appreciate and draw inspiration from the great deeds of the heroes and heroines in this work and my other works, who created the glimmer of light during this indescribably dark and tragic era.

Last, but not least, my sincerest appreciation is extended to the the Guido Jarach Committee at the Hebrew University, for awarding the summary article on this work, the 1991 Guido Jarach Prize for the best article on a rescue by a diplomat, and more recently, EGIT Grant Committee of the Histadrut, in Tel Aviv, who awarded this manuscript with the 1998 Egit Award for the best manuscript on the Holocaust.

Introduction: Switzerland's Finest Hour

One cannot attribute the paucity of press coverage on Hungarian Jews to skepticism. . . . *It is possible that if the press had raised a major outcry, nothing would have happened.* The Allies were as intent on adhering to a policy of rescue through victory as the Nazis were intent on destroying the remnants of European Jewry before their defeat. But the press does not decide how it will treat a story on the basis of whether attention to a topic will effect a change in policy. . . . For much of the American press this news was still a minor "sidelight." (emphasis added)
—Deborah E. Lipstadt, *Beyond Belief: The American Press and the Coming of the Holocaust*

As a relatively independent Axis satellite governed by Regent Admiral Horthy, Hungary was the last reservoir of Jewry during the Holocaust. Some 800,000 Jews lived there in relative peace for the first five years of the war.[1] This tranquility would come to an end by mid-March of 1944, when the Germans, in the face of the advancing Russian army, marched into Hungary. Eichmann was anxious to complete Hitler's Final Solution in that country; assisting him, with Horthy's complicity, were German ambassador Veesenmayer and their Hungarian cohorts.

Hungarian Jewry was totally unprepared for the speed of this onslaught. A relatively small contingent of SS Gestapo men, with the help of the Hungarian gendarmerie, systematically plundered the Jewish community of all its assets, herded the Jews into ghettos, and finally dispatched them to Auschwitz on specially prepared railway lines at the rate of more than 10,000 per day. These mass deportations began on May 15, 1944, and one month later more than 400,000 Hungarian Jews had already been dispatched to Auschwitz.

Reports about the earlier mass murder of 1.765 million Jews in Auschwitz had already circulated, based on the experience of several escapees from Auschwitz and pleas sent out by Rabbi Michael Ber Weissmandl and Gisi Fleischman, heads of the Slovakian Jewish underground, to all Jewish organizations in Switzerland; but despite these messages, nothing seemed able to stop the completion of this "greatest crime in human history," as Churchill later described it. Leaders of all Jewish factions in occupied Hungary pessimistically concurred that there was no way to halt the trains to Auschwitz. They expected the deportations of the remaining 250,000–300,000 Jews in and around Budapest to be completed within several weeks.

We now know that ever since mid-1941, Western intelligence had been fully aware of the mass murder of Jews taking place in Europe, but despite an early warning from Roosevelt in April 1944, prompted by the War Refugee Board,[2] the Allies essentially chose to remain silent. Their standard response to the many requests for help, especially to Weissmandl's plea that the Allies bomb the railroads leading to Auschwitz, was that the best way to save Jewish lives was to win the war as quickly as possible.

This virtual silence was maintained until the end of June 1944. Then, suddenly, seemingly out of nowhere, there erupted an incredible series of protests against Admiral Horthy and the deportation of Hungarian Jews. These came from the pope, President Roosevelt, Churchill, and the king of Sweden, who then dispatched the dauntless Raoul Wallenberg to Budapest. Horthy had abandoned his authority in the face of Hitler's insistence on completing the Final Solution in Hungary, but finding himself under sudden and intense international scrutiny, he reasserted his authority and halted the deportations to Auschwitz on July 7.

In a remarkable policy reversal, Horthy began to seek ways to protect the Jews. He even made an unconditional offer to permit the exit of 10,000 Jewish children from the country, which, sadly, was never seriously taken up by the Allies. Linked to this offer, he also said that he would protect all Hungarian Jews with "foreign" papers. Despite a pro-Nazi coup that deposed him, and despite continued pressure from Eichmann and the new Hungarian regime to destroy the Jews in Budapest, the deportations in the form of a "death march" were eventually resumed on a much smaller scale. Aiding in the protection of the Jews were a number of courageous diplomats from neutral countries who were stationed in Budapest, including representatives of Switzerland, Sweden, Spain, and Portugal, as well as the papal nuncio and officials of the International Red Cross. Because of the concerted efforts of these previously indifferent parties, about 140,000 Budapest Jews survived until the liberation.

At the heart of this miraculous turn of events lay a man named George Mantello, a Jew who served as first secretary of the El Salvador consulate in Geneva, Switzerland, from 1942 to 1945. With bold initiative, he disclosed to the press two vitally important atrocity reports. The first, better known as the Auschwitz Report, was a six-page summary of a larger document detailing the mass murder of close to two million Jews between April 1942 and April 1944, in the greatest of all death factories.[3] The second report, also a six-page document, described the Hungarian deportation of over 400,000 Jews to Auschwitz since mid-May 1944.[4]

It was not easy for Mantello to obtain these reports; he met at first with a wall of silence on all sides. Most Jewish organizations in Switzerland had already obtained copies of the two reports by May 16 or 17, and all of them gave copies to Roswell McClelland, the American representative of the War Refugee Board, sent to facilitate rescue. Tragically, even with blatant evidence in his hands, McClelland did very little to fulfill his task. Furthermore, the Jewish organizations did not do much better in informing the world or even most of the Jewish organizations of the horrific information they had obtained. After the German occupation of Hungary, the Nazis had drawn an iron curtain of silence around their activities, and only hints and rumors of their atrocities against the Jews reached Switzerland.[5] Mantello wanted to help, but to do so, he needed an authentic survey of the Jewish situation in Hungary—and so he sent a courier, his friend Dr. Florian Manoliu, the Romanian commercial attaché.

Berlin provided Manoliu only with a transit visa straight to Bucharest via Hungary, but he risked his life by disembarking in Budapest and going directly to the Swiss legation to begin his quest for information. There he met with Carl Lutz, the Swiss consul in charge of foreign interests, who took him to meet Moshe [Miklós] Krausz, head of the Palestine Office, who was hiding in the Swiss compound. Krausz gave Manoliu copies of the two atrocity reports, as well as a letter that Krausz himself had written, expressing abject despair about the fate of Budapest Jewry.

Instead of going on to Bucharest as his visa dictated, the courageous Manoliu defied Nazi instructions and returned immediately to Switzerland with the devastating news of the nightmare of Auschwitz. He became the bearer of traumatic personal news as well, forced to tell Mantello that his own large, extended family had been among the deportees to Auschwitz.

Instead of giving in to despair, Mantello determined to alert the world about the mass deportations in order to prevent the total annihilation of Hungarian Jewry. With the help of his well-placed connections in the American and British intelligence forces, and a strong letter of support from four of the leading Swiss Protestant theologians, Mantello sent a summary of the two atrocity reports to all diplomatic circles in the West. The head of the British News Exchange cabled Roosevelt, Churchill, the archbishop of Canterbury, and Francis Spellman, archbishop of New York. He also made the summaries available to more than 120 Swiss newspapers, which resulted in more than four hundred articles, many of them featured on the front page. Full of moral indignation, these articles condemned in the fiercest terms the German mass murders in Auschwitz. Among the headlines were these: "Gassed and Burned," "The Horror and Disgust of the Entire World," "The Butchery of Men," "The Assassination of Jews," "Silence Is Complicity," and "Mankind, How Low Have You Fallen?"

Under Mantello's inspiration, the Protestant theologians, led by Pastor Paul Vogt, performed three important services during the press campaign. First, they instructed all their pastors to hold special services dedicated to the plight of the Hungarian Jews; Vogt himself gave the first stirring sermons from the pulpits of Switzerland's largest churches. Second, the Protestant leaders reproduced thousands of copies of the Auschwitz atrocity reports and distributed them to all university faculty members, students, and political figures, thereby spreading the news of the Jewish tragedy to every part of Switzerland. He also enlisted the help of three other great Swiss theologians, Carl Barth, Emil Brunner, and (the Dutchman) Visser't Hooft, to support Mantello's efforts to inform the world about Auschwitz and the deportation of Hungarian Jews. Under their moral leadership, every newspaper published front-page articles on this tragedy, while every church rang with sermons condemning the German atrocities and the Hungarian complicity. Third, they created a campaign of relentless pressure on the highest level of the Swiss government and the International Red Cross (IRC) to get involved in rescue efforts.

This press campaign not only created a radical change in Hungary's policy toward the Jews, but also completely altered the long-standing anti-Jewish climate of opinion in Switzerland itself. Swiss antipathy toward the Jews had been buttressed by ten years of anti-Semitic German propaganda and reenforced by a fear of a German invasion. Such an atmosphere fostered a strict censorship that did not permit any criticism of Germany, making Mantello's press campaign all the more startling a phenomenon. The articles also created an uproar in a country known for its staidness and imperturbability, and provoked a series of mass demonstrations on behalf of the Jews by women's groups, labor organizations, and university students. Even members of the Swiss government challenged their own government and the International Red Cross, criticizing their indifference, if not hostility, to the Jewish tragedy. The indignant Swiss reaction spread, sparking an outraged response from Western leaders and affecting Admiral Horthy so strongly that he ordered the mass deportations in Hungary to cease. This turned into what must surely be considered Switzerland's finest hour.

The astonishing interruption in the appalling fate of Hungary's Jews should have evoked the great interest of historians. Somehow, however, historians of the Holocaust have either taken this dramatic change of events for granted, or have explained Horthy's attempt to reassert his authority without thoroughly investigating the underlying causes. Documents from the German foreign office give direct evidence of Horthy's transformation, the German and Hungarian reactions, and Veesenmayer and Eichmann's ongoing struggle to counter this new "benevolence" toward the Jews and to press for the Final Solution. The documents also point directly to the cause of these unusual developments: Mantello's extraordinary Swiss press and church campaigns. The details of this complex and widely effective public outcry offer an additional revelation, shedding light on one of the war's best-kept secrets—the Swiss people's heroic rescue efforts.

Mantello was also at the helm of another rescue effort that had saved approximately 20,000 to 30,000 Jews throughout German-occupied territories the year before. He accomplished this by issuing approximately 10,000 Salvadoran citizenship papers, each good for an entire family, to Jews and to many endangered non-Jews as well. In fact, such papers could be obtained from any of the Latin American consuls in Switzerland.

While citizenship papers issued by these other consuls cost anywhere from 500 to 3,000 Swiss francs, Mantello's were free. He gladly provided them to Jewish organizations or to individuals who offered him lists of their friends and relatives. At the outset, there was much skepticism about the efficacy of these Salvadoran papers because there was not a single "real" Salvadoran citizen in Budapest, but they turned out to be the most valuable protective papers of all. During the crucial final months before liberation, Mantello was receiving fifty-page cables from Romania, replete with hundreds of names of friends and relatives requesting these valuable papers.

Much of the credit for this amazing enterprise must go to Mantello's Salvadoran supporters: Col. José Castellanos, the Salvadoran consul general in Geneva; José Gustavo Guerrero, a former president of El Salvador and former judge at the International Court at the Hague in Holland, who was then residing in Geneva and offered Mantello much moral support; and the government of El Salvador itself. Without their help, Mantello could not have accomplished anything.

Who was this George Mantello, and why did he involve himself so extensively in rescue?

Mantello had been a very successful financier and textile manufacturer in Bucharest before the war. He had met and befriended Consul Castellanos in the thirties, and had used his business connections to help him purchase goods for El Salvador at a competitive rate. In 1939, Castellanos appointed Mantello El Salvador's honorary consul for Czechoslovakia, Yugoslavia, and Romania, though he was based primarily in Bucharest. After most Latin American countries declared war on Germany in January 1942, Mantello obtained a Salvadoran passport and secured an official appointment as first secretary to the Salvadoran consulate in Geneva. He made a miraculous escape from Nazi hands in Yugoslavia, fleeing into Switzerland in August 1942, where he took up his official position in the Salvadoran consulate.

Mantello could then have chosen to relax and enjoy the exquisite and serene beauty of Switzerland, in the company of his fellow diplomats, far from the tragedy enveloping his fellow Jews. Yet his Jewish and Zionist instincts impelled him to utilize his position for the best possible purpose, fully devoting his time, money, connections, and creativity to assisting his unfortunate brethren. Because of his foresight, he and his brother and business partner, Josef Mandl,[6] had been able to bring much of their considerable fortune to Switzerland and therefore had a ready supply of capital to invest in rescue. From 1942 until the end of the war, Mantello never took a penny from anyone for any of his rescue activities, including assistance to Allied intelligence personnel. Moreover, he paid out more than 100,000 Swiss francs from his own pocket to set up an office for the production and distribution of the Salvadoran papers.

Tragically, Mantello's rescue efforts were recognized neither by his contemporaries nor by historians. In fact, because of informers who accused him of profiting from the distribution of the Salvadoran papers, he was held in detention by the Swiss authorities for sixteen days in May of 1944, during which time he was unable to continue his rescue activities. Such charges continued to haunt him even after the war, prompting him to ask for a public inquiry presided over by three prominent Swiss-Jewish jurists. Anyone who wished was invited to testify, and a number of prominent personalities did so on Mantello's behalf, including the Swiss consul in Budapest, the head of the British News Agency, and the head of the Relief Committee for the war-stricken Jewish population, commonly referred to as RELICO, headed by Dr. Abraham Silberschein, a representative of the World Jewish Congress (WJCong) and former senator of the Polish Parliament. The inquiry lasted a year, and at the end Mantello was acquitted of all the charges.

A few years later the Swiss government dropped all its charges against him as well; yet the rumors and innuendo persisted, thrusting Mantello and his rescue efforts into almost total oblivion. Some writers barely mention his work in their postwar memoirs, or omit him altogether; others claim credit for his accomplishments. To cite but one example, Andre Biss, a major rescue activist in Budapest and an assistant to Kastner in his negotiations on behalf of Hungarian Jewry, wrote an unsolicited letter to Mantello in early February 1945, shortly after the liberation of Budapest. In this Hungarian-language letter (cited in its English translation), Biss thanked Mantello profusely and credited him for both his Salvadoran papers and the efficacy of his extraordinary press campaign. Yet, in his published account of his and Kastner's efforts, entitled *A Million Lives to Save,* Biss ignores Mantello and his rescue activities completely. Thus, historians have had little to go on in comprehending his outstanding role in rescue—and the available primary sources have been largely ignored.

I first discovered Mantello quite by accident. More than twenty years ago I visited Jerusalem on a research trip, in search of material on rescue during the Holocaust. An acquaintance directed me to an elderly gentleman with a beret who turned out to be (Matthieux) Maitre Muller, a French lawyer and a refugee who had fled to Switzerland during the war. He headed Mantello's office in Geneva, which was devoted solely to the production and distribution of Salvadoran papers. Muller gave me the first inkling of the extent of Mantello's rescue efforts and told me that he was still alive in Rome. Because Mantello came to the United States twice a year on business, I left Muller my phone number.

The next time Mantello came to New York, he called me and agreed to meet with me at his hotel. He related to me extraordinary tales of rescue on a large scale, especially in Hungary. As a trained historian, I was naturally quite skeptical, especially because I had specialized in research on Holocaust rescue for many years and had neither read nor heard about him. After meeting him, however, I began to delve into the existing literature in this area and finally found one reference to Mantello and the Salvadoran papers in an early article on Latin American papers entitled "The Rescue of Jews with the Aid of Passports and Citizenship Papers of Latin America."[7] The writer, Nathan Eck, mentions Mantello favorably: "We must place on record a Mr. Mandel-Mantello,[8] then an official employed in the consulate of San [*sic*] Salvador,[9] who issued [citizenship] documents free of charge, even covering part of the expenditure involved out of his own pocket."[10]

Subsequently, during a lengthy search among the voluminous papers of the War Refugee Board, I found an even more reliable document authored by John Winant, the American ambassador to Britain. This was a confidential memo to the State Department about the Swiss investigation of Latin American consuls' "sale" of their countries' passports in the winter of 1943. In it, Winant made a pointed observation: "The average price paid for a passport was approximately 700 Swiss francs. On the other hand, the consul of San [*sic*] Salvador has acted from purely humanitarian motives and has charged no fee at all.[11]

At that point I began to take Mantello's stories seriously, and to search for the complete, documented history of his activities, however fantastic they may have appeared. The journey led me through eighty hours of taped interviews conducted with Mr. Mantello before his passing in 1992; thirteen years of research in public and private archives in Israel, England, Switzerland, and the United Sates, and the photocopying of thousands of documents, including hundreds of articles from Mantello's Swiss press campaign. The result was a fantastic saga that substantiated about 95 percent of Mantello's claims. The remaining 5 percent, which includes many aspects of Mantello's personal life, are presented as his recollections.

The information that turned up along the way illuminated many other facets of the Hungarian tragedy. These included the so-called Kastner Train to Bergen Belsen and the eventual liberation of its passengers in Switzerland, the "Horthy offer," and negotiations with the Nazis conducted by Kastner, Mayer, and Becher, as well as those by Sternbuch, Musy, and Schellenberg.

Mantello was not the only unheralded hero who emerged from these forgotten files. There were other outstanding personalities, mostly non-Jewish, without whose dedicated efforts Mantello's campaign to save the remnant of

Hungarian Jewry would not have succeeded; all of these people deserve Jewry's gratitude. Among them, one must single out Dr. Florian Manoliu, the Romanian commercial attaché who risked his life to obtain the Auschwitz atrocity reports from Hungary; Pastor Paul Vogt, who helped galvanize the Swiss churches into supporting the Jewish cause; the Protestant theologians Carl Barth, Emil Brunner, Visser t' Hooft, and Alphons Koechlin, whose moral authority and wholehearted support enabled Mantello to break through the censorship of the Swiss press and the indifference of the Swiss bureaucracy and the International Red Cross; Allen Dulles and Freddie West of the Allied intelligence and Walter Garrett of the British Exchange Telegraph, all three of whom helped Mantello prepare the first reports for the newspapers and who immediately cabled the Western leaders; and the Salvadoran government, represented by the consul general Col. José Arturo Castellanos, and the former president, José G. Guerrero.

The courageous neutral diplomats, who held their ground during the dangerous last months of the Nyilas regime, must also be mentioned: the well-known heroic and tragic figure of Raoul Wallenberg; the virtually unheralded Swiss Carl Lutz; the Spaniard Angel Sanz-Briz; the Italian Giorgio Perlasca; the Portuguese Liz-Texaira Branquinho; and the papal nuncio Angelo Rotta.

Finally, one must also salute the countless, nameless Swiss people themselves, who rallied to the pastors' call in their finest hour, venting in street demonstrations their moral outrage at the murder of the Jews, condemning not only German barbarity and Hungarian complicity but their own government's indifference to the fate of the Jews. All these combined to enable Mantello to fulfill his impossible dream of halting the trains to Auschwitz and saving the remnant of Hungarian Jewry.

One can only imagine how many more tens, if not hundreds or thousands, of Jews could have been saved had the Jewish organizations in Switzerland shared the atrocity reports with Mantello when they received them, six or seven weeks before he obtained them himself. The saga of Mantello's extraordinary rescue efforts goes far to disprove the notion held by historians and the public alike that no one could have made a major difference in its outcome. [12]

The Man Who Stopped
the Trains to Auschwitz

1

Background

In mid-June of 1944, 12,000 Hungarian Jews were being deported daily from Budapest to the death camp Auschwitz. Miklós (Moshe) Krausz, head of the Palestine Certificate Office, smuggled out a desperate letter from the Swiss compound where he was hiding. Dated June 19, 1944, it read in part:

> 335,000 Jews have been deported up to June 7 and since that date, another 100,000. In the provinces, there are only four towns left that still have Jews. . . . It will soon be Budapest's turn. The number of Jews in and around Budapest is 350,000. The ghettos, which were set up in Budapest on June 16, are due to be terminated by June 21.
>
> The entire Jewish people is condemned to death. There is no possibility of hiding, and we must face our fate. . . . We do not even have the chance of escaping to a neighboring country. There are only two possibilities: suicide, or the acceptance of our fate. The Swiss Legation in Budapest . . . has done its best, but unfortunately without any success whatsoever. HELP! HELP! HELP![1]

About this time, Rudolph Kastner, a Zionist leader in Budapest who was negotiating with the Germans to save at least a portion of Hungarian Jewry, wrote, "Only a miracle can save us."

A miracle did happen; its messenger was George Mandel-Mantello, first secretary of the El Salvador consulate in Geneva. Who was this person? How did he accomplish such a miracle—and why is it that virtually no one seems to know of him?

Until 1942, Mantello had been a successful Romanian businessman and financier who had traveled all over the world. He had been in Vienna when the Germans marched into that city in 1938; in Prague when the Germans overran it in 1939; and in Belgrade when the Germans invaded in 1941. Long before many others, Mantello realized the viciousness of Hitler's army, the brutality of his anti-Semitic policies, and the extremity to which they might extend. Mantello pledged to himself that he would do whatever was in his power to help his fellow Jews escape from that barbaric regime.

In 1939, Mantello took a step that would gain him some measure of safety against the Nazis. During the course of his business travels, he had befriended José Arturo Castellanos, the Salvadoran consul general in Germany, and helped his consulate purchase items at a low rate. Small countries such as El Salvador, which could not afford an extensive staff of diplomats, typically offered positions to local businessmen. Using his influence with Castellanos, Mantello became honorary attaché of the El Salvador legation in Bucharest and honorary consul of El Salvador in Yugoslavia and Czechoslovakia.

At that time, he changed his name from Mandl to Mantello. His new name was pronounced Mantellyo, but because people in Switzerland would later call him Mantello, he adopted that pronunciation.

In early 1942, Castellanos appointed Mantello first secretary (second in line only to the vice consul) of the Salvadoran consulate in Geneva. Now he was a full diplomat, with the privileges of diplomatic immunity and a diplomatic passport, which would allow him to travel freely.

Soon after this, Mantello engaged in his first act of rescue. Upon Mantello's request, Wilhelm Filderman, head of the Union of Romanian Jews, gave Mantello a report describing the deportation to Transnistria, Ukraine, of Galician Jews who lacked Romanian citizenship. On his first trip from Romania to Switzerland under his Salvadoran passport, Mantello delivered Filderman's report to the Jewish organizations stationed in Switzerland: the Joint, the Jewish Agency, the World Jewish Congress, and others. Mantello appended to this report a proposal that he and his brother Josef had worked out, detailing a plan for the systematic delivery of relief shipments to the Jews.

But Mantello's information and proposals met with barely any response. For instance, his report was conveyed to the World Jewish Congress headquarters in New York only at the end of 1942; and he learned of that only incidentally, while listening to a lecture in 1944 by Dr. Arye Kubowitzki, the American representative of the World Jewish Congress, who was then in Geneva.

In 1942, Mantello decided to liquidate his business affairs in Bucharest and move to Switzerland. He divided his assets in Romania, leaving his factories to his partners and turning many other items into cash. He also engaged in a series of currency exchanges, trading English pounds for Swiss francs and Swiss francs for Romanian lai, ending up with more than 140 million lai. With this money he bought sixty train carloads of cotton from the Romanian finance ministry, shipped them to Switzerland, and sold them at a good profit.[2]

While Mantello was still settling his affairs in Romania, the United States entered World War II on December 8, 1941. El Salvador, together with most Latin American countries, declared itself part of the Allied powers and broke off relations with the Axis, which included Romania. Because Mantello held a Salvadoran diplomatic passport, he was now the subject of an enemy power. Switzerland immediately took over the protection of most Latin American consuls in Axis lands, including El Salvador, and Mantello therefore came under Swiss protection.

Because diplomats of hostile countries were allowed to travel home safely, Mantello left Bucharest by train, in the company of a number of Swiss and Latin American diplomats, all headed for Switzerland; but at the Swiss-Italian-Yugoslav border, two Nazi guards, suspecting Mantello of being George Mandel, a French-Jewish minister, ordered him off the train. Pointing to the suitcase above his head, one of the Nazis ordered, "Take your suitcase!" This valise belonged to the wife of one of the Swiss diplomats. Mantello, knowing that she would not say anything, pulled down her suitcase, and the two Nazis arrested him and took him to the Gestapo office in nearby Zagreb. There, one of the Nazis ordered him to open the suitcase.

Mantello said, "I can't. I don't have the key."

"Why not?"

"Because it's not my suitcase."

The officer was enraged. "Then why did you bring it?"

"Because you told me to."

The Nazi forced open the suitcase. When he saw that it was filled with women's clothing, he grew so incensed that he picked up a chair and slammed Mantello across the face, breaking two teeth and part of his jaw—an injury from which he suffered for the rest of his life. Enraged, Mantello responded by punching the Nazi in the face. Years later, he commented, "I don't know how I managed to do that—the audacity of hitting a Gestapo officer. I could have been shot." However, he was protected to a degree by his diplomatic status.[3]

Mantello was summoned to Col. Edmund Veesenmayer, a major general in the SS who was attached to the German legation at Zagreb. Veesenmayer was a central German diplomat in Yugoslavia who would later become Hitler's plenipotentiary and minister in charge of Hungary, as well as a collaborator with Eichmann in the Final Solution.[4]

Mantello told Veesenmayer, "The Salvador government is keeping track of my whereabouts. If you make any problems for me, I assure you that my government will bar Germans from leaving El Salvador." He added, "If I am harmed in any way, the Swiss consul will find out about it. And if any charges are brought against me, the Swiss consulate will testify for me."[5]

Veesenmayer treated Mantello courteously, as one diplomat to another. He let Mantello go and register at a hotel, but warned Mantello not to communicate with anyone about the arrest and placed him under the constant surveillance of the Ustasha, the Croatian Nazi police. This was how Mantello lived for the next three or four months—under unofficial house arrest, in constant uncertainty and danger.

One day, Mantello was approached by one of his Romanian business partners, who proposed a daring getaway scheme. A pilot was traveling from Milan to Bucharest with a stopover in Zagreb; Mantello could escape from the hotel and fly to Bucharest disguised as a copilot. From Bucharest, he would have to make his own way back to Switzerland. Mantello agreed to the plan.

The pilot, well paid for his work, visited him in the hotel with a copilot's uniform that he had smuggled in. Mantello put on the uniform and left the hotel. When they arrived at the airport, Ustasha soldiers approached Mantello. Thinking him to be a pilot, they demanded, "Where is the man, Mantello?" Apparently, the Nazis had discovered his escape and were looking for him. Mantello pointed to two young *Volksdeutsche* (ethnic Germans) who were standing nearby. The Ustasha approached the young men to arrest them, and a fistfight broke out. The Ustasha finally subdued them, and in the meantime Mantello and the pilot slipped away.

They registered in another hotel, and the pilot instructed Mantello to stay put in his room for eight days until their next opportunity to escape. But Mantello could not bear being cooped up and he went outside, where he came across the two young *Volksdeutsche*. They told him that the Ustasha had been searching for a man named "Mangello" and that they had cleared their own identity at the police station.

A few days later, Mantello and the pilot flew out of Zagreb to Belgrade, and from Belgrade to Budapest. Mantello was now faced with the task of traveling across Romania and entering Switzerland incognito. One of his business partners was Captain Vasilescu, the Romanian military attaché, whose brother-in-law, General Dragenescu, was the head of Romania's secret police. Mantello went to see them, and after much negotiating, they came to an arrangement whereby Mantello would travel to Switzerland via Yugoslavia disguised as Vasilescu, who held a transit visa. It would have been preferable for Mantello to travel via Hungary because, among other things, he spoke Hungarian; but he had to follow the itinerary of Vasilescu's visa.

Mantello donned a Romanian army officer's uniform and boarded a train with his falsified papers, traveling first-class, while Dragenescu and Vasilescu, the latter under an assumed name, traveled in a separate car for their own purposes. Mantello had wanted to stop in Budapest to visit his wife, son, and inlaws, but he was instructed not to get off the train. At the train station, his family walked onto the platform, and all that they could do was wave to each other. Mantello barely ate or slept for days as the journey continued. So frightened was he of arrest that he hardly ever took off his uniform. In Bucharest, he had worn it even when he went to bed.

At last, the train reached Milan. From here, its route would take it through the longest tunnel in the world, from which it would emerge onto Swiss territory. Fearing a last-minute search and arrest, Mantello made his way to the locomotive and told the engineer that he was a Romanian officer who would like to see the tunnel. The engineer invited Mantello to sit next to him. By this time, after eight days of travel, Mantello was nearly delirious from sleep deprivation. At last, he arrived at the Swiss border and debarked from the train. Amid telephoning his brother Josef, he collapsed. When he regained consciousness, he found himself in a Swiss police station. Still posing as Vasilescu, whose visa permitted him to enter Switzerland, Mantello was allowed to proceed to Geneva.

In Geneva, he registered at an affluent hotel called the Hotel DeBerg, where he had to borrow 2,000 Swiss francs from one of the porters. He immediately made his way to his lawyer, George Brunschvig, who was head of the Swiss Jewish community (the Schweizer Israelitische Gemeinde—SIG). At last, Mantello was able to shed the role of Vasilescu.

Mantello, a very wealthy man, could now have attended to his own comfort and ignored the horrible fate of his fellow Jews. He could have lived on the fortune that he had transferred to Switzerland, which amounted to several million Swiss francs; but he was haunted by the tragedy that threatened the Jews of Europe. He later stated, "The terrible thing that I had experienced left a mark on my soul. Although I felt safe in Switzerland, I always saw before me heartrending scenes of the terrible Jewish martyrdom in Nazi-occupied Vienna and Prague. The moment that, with the help of God, I had escaped this fate, I promised myself to do everything to save my fellow Jews from their fate and to improve their lives."

On August 25, 1942, Mantello was appointed first secretary of the El Salvador consulate in Geneva, a post in which he continued to serve without remuneration, as he had done during his years as honorary consul. Mantello now carried out a series of rescue activities that used his business acumen, personal financial resources, and driving sense of urgency. In all that he did, he cooperated fully with the representatives of all the Swiss-Jewish organizations and the local representatives of world Jewish organizations that were drawing global attention to the situation of the Jews in Nazi-dominated lands.

In 1942, Mantello conceived of a joint trust company that would achieve two important goals: one, the Jews in Nazi-occupied countries could safeguard their money for themselves or their heirs; and two, Jewish organizations could use that money for rescue work. According to Mantello's idea, Jews in occupied countries would bring their assets to the local Swiss embassy or consulate and receive a receipt. A copy of that receipt would be sent to the joint trust company in Switzerland, which would guarantee postwar repayment in dollars. In the meantime, these assets would be made available for rescue work.

Ordinarily, Jewish organizations sent money to Jews in occupied countries via couriers. These couriers kept 20 to 30 percent of the money as their payment; but with a joint trust company, all of the money could be used for rescue. Also, this venture would be entirely legal, a factor that was important to relief organizations such as the American Jewish Joint Distribution Committee, better known as the Joint, which had a great fear of engaging in any illegal activity. Thus, this scheme was superior to ideas such as sending money directly from America, which would have contravened the Trading with the Enemy Act, a legal enactment forbidding communication with the enemy or the sending and using of American or Allied money within the Axis-dominated territories.[6] The trust fund also contributed to Mantello's overall effectiveness; the fact that he was attempting to set up a legal framework with Swiss cooperation made him appear trustworthy and dependable in the eyes of the British and Americans, whose aid was to prove crucial in his later rescue work.

Mantello envisioned that the trust fund would function as a center of harmonic cooperation, connecting a wide range of Jewish organizations, such as the Jewish Agency, the World Jewish Congress, the Joint, the Palestine Certificate Office, and the Orthodox Agudath Israel. It would have a legal department and also a press department, the latter operating under the cover of the

Salvadoran consulate. The trust fund would purchase its own building in Geneva, which would house the offices of the various organizations as well as the Salvadoran consulate. To this end, Mantello pledged to buy stock and give credit in the amount of 300,000 to 500,000 Swiss francs, which would be returned to him within one year after the end of the war. To ensure his disinterest, he pledged to remain unconnected to the administration or management of the trust fund.

Mantello presented this idea to a number of influential men, among them Saly Mayer, representative of the Joint; Dr. Abraham Silberschein, head of RELICO; Dr. Samuel Scheps and Dr. Chaim Posner, representatives of the Palestine Certificate Office; Rabbi Dr. Taubes, chief rabbi of Zurich and head of the Swiss Rabbis' Committee; Rabbi Dr. Lewenstein of Agudath Israel and former chief rabbi of Holland; Rabbi Yisroel Chaim Eis of the Agudath Israel; and Dr. Gerhard Riegner of the World Jewish Congress.

To his dismay, his idea, which had the potential of saving tens of thousands of lives, met with failure—not because it was wrongly conceived but because of the distrust and jealousy that divided the members of rival organizations. He could not, for instance, persuade the organizations to meet together on the same day, because Saly Mayer refused to sit at the same table with Gerhart Riegner. Not even the Nazi threat to the survival of European Jewry was enough to make these representatives set aside their deep-seated ideological rivalries.[7] (Mantello also believed that the representatives rejected his plan because they had not conceived of it themselves.)

But Mantello's energy and resourcefulness did not flag. In the autumn of 1942, he created a lobbying committee called the Swiss Rabbis' Committee (Schweizer Rabbinerverband), which allowed the religious leaders of Swiss Jewry—about a dozen rabbis who had until now played a feeble public role—to speak in a powerful and united voice. Mantello intended this organization, which was modeled along the lines of non-Jewish religious groups, to serve as an efficient, nonpolitical body whose mission would be to intercede with the Swiss authorities, church bodies, and foreign missions to protect and rescue Jews. To ensure its independence, Mantello laid the condition that the organization would not be financially beholden to other Jewish groups.

Mantello was supported in this venture by Rabbi Dr. Zvi Taubes, chief rabbi of Zurich, who became president of the organization. Other supporters were Dr. Abraham Silberschein and Dr. Scheps, chief of the Palestine Certificate Office. But the organization was opposed by George Brunschvig, head of the

SIG, who protested to Rabbi Taubes that the job of the rabbis—who were employees of the SIG—was to discuss Judaism, not to engage in politics, and Brunschvig considered rescue to be in the realm of politics.[8]

Upon learning of this, Mantello grew incensed. He called Brunschvig on the telephone and subjected him to a blistering lecture. "I have come from hell," he said, "and I know what's going on. The Germans are criminals straight out of hell." Mantello won the argument. With the wholehearted backing of the rabbis, he was able to deflate Brunschvig's opposition.[9]

The Swiss Rabbis' Committee proved to be an extremely effective lobbying group, particularly in its ability to gain access to Protestant theologians and other non-Jewish religious leaders. Perhaps the most important contact was Pastor Paul Vogt, a good friend of Taubes and one of the most popular religious leaders in Switzerland; his associate, another important leader, was the influential Prof. Alphons Koechlin, president of the Swiss Federation of Evangelical Churches. Through Rabbi Taubes, Mantello established a personal relationship with Vogt, which he cemented by supporting the volunteer relief agencies with which Vogt was involved. Subsequently, Vogt would play a crucial role in the global press and church campaigns that Mantello mounted.

Throughout this period, Mantello forged relationships with people on all levels. For instance, he subsidized the activities of non-Jewish university students, many of them children of the Hungarian nobility who had fled to Switzerland. Later, their help was of great importance in publishing and distributing reports about the plight of the Jews.

In all the liaisons that Mantello cultivated, he never requested payment for his services, even when compensation would have been considered reasonable. An outstanding example of the success of his approach was his close relationship with members of the American and British intelligence forces. As a diplomat, Mantello attended many social functions, where he met, among others, the British commercial attaché. The attaché began requesting favors of Mantello, which at first were quite minor. For instance, he asked Mantello to accept mail at the Salvadoran consulate in order to circumvent the German spy system, which was intercepting all mail to the British consulate; he also asked for advice on how to best trade in currency. Mantello began lending considerable sums—100,000 to 200,000 francs—without interest to the British embassy, which frequently did not receive needed money on time from its London headquarters.

In 1942, the attaché came to Mantello with an urgent request: Could Mantello help acquire a thousand chronographs, watches, and other instruments urgently needed by the Royal Air Force? Mantello agreed. He went to a factory and ordered production; then he purchased many of the instruments with his own money, charging no fee. The British were able to obtain the chronographs immediately, without waiting for money to arrive from their home office. In addition, Mantello arranged the circuitous delivery route necessary to avoid German interception. This shipment was sent to New York, and from there to England. (According to Mantello, he engaged in a number of such deals; at times the instruments were relayed by Latin American couriers via Bermuda.)[10]

In this way, Mantello earned a good reputation with members of the British and American intelligence community. In particular, he became a friend of Commodore Freddie West, who proved to be one of Mantello's most important contacts, especially in the press campaign (see chapter 7). Through West, Mantello also came to know Allen Dulles of the Office of Strategic Services (OSS) in Switzerland.

Mantello, who had been a brilliant, shrewd businessman, now moved beyond the orbit of his financial interests. He applied himself with single-minded fervor to preventing the impending doom of the remaining Jews in Hungary, employing his ingenuity and all the resources at his command—chief among these, the contacts he had formed. Ultimately, tens of thousands of Jews owed their lives to his impassioned activity, innovation, and application. In subsequent historical records, the figure of Mantello receded into obscurity, and what little information there was about him was tainted with intimations of impropriety. With the collation of thousands of documents and testimonies, there now emerges a portrait of a man who was arguably the greatest hero of this tragic era of Jewish history.

What sort of background had nurtured the personality that so successfully orchestrated these herculean rescue efforts?

George Mantello was born as George Mandl on December 11, 1901, in Lekence, Transylvania. His father, Baruch Yehudah Mandl, had been born in the same town on November 20, 1878. His mother's name was Ida—in Yiddish, Yenta—Mandl (née Spitz). Mantello's paternal grandfather, Yitzchok Yaakov Mandl, was related to Rabbi Yekusiel Teitelbaum, the great Hasidic Admor (grand rabbi) known by the name of his magnum opus, the *Yeteiv Lev.* Rabbi Yitzchak Yaakov Mandl had come to Transylvania from Alsace in the middle of the nineteenth century and served as the chief rabbi of Beszterce, in an area of Transylvania called the Siebenbergen, or the seven mountains.

Mantello's family was well-to-do; his father owned a mill and held an appreciable number of shares in a bank in Beszterce. He had two brothers and three sisters (another two brothers and a sister died in infancy). One of the brothers, Josef, who was his elder by two years, later played an important role in his rescue work.

Although Mantello's grandparents had been pious, he did not grow up in an exceptionally religious atmosphere. He received a basic Jewish education in Cluj (also known as Kolozsvár, and to Jews as Klausenberg). Afterward, he attended a commercial high school in Budapest for three years, and then, during World War I, he attended a military school. One of his military instructors, General Dragenescu, who had been a Romanian hero in World War I, was later to become Mantello's business partner; and still later he would help him escape from Nazi-dominated Romania.

In his youth, Mantello cut a debonair figure, always dressed in well-tailored, dapper suits. Although no longer identifying strongly with Orthodoxy, Mantello became a Jewish nationalist. He was actively involved with the right-wing Revisionist Zionist movement, and in 1922, he joined a group of young Revisionists traveling to the land of Israel. There, he recalled in later years, they made a pilgrimage by foot from Haifa to Jerusalem.

During these years, Mantello was developing his skills in his natural brilliance: business. From 1921 to 1924, he worked for a bank in Vienna. At the same time, he became the proprietor of a textile mill in Bucharest. In 1924, he became deeply involved in his father's granary business, and in 1926, he engaged in the first great financial deal of his life. Characteristically, he displayed great verve and bravado, risked failure by his brinkmanship, and succeeded to an astonishing degree.

Mantello's father had delegated him to acquire one hundred train carloads of grain, but instead he obligated himself to purchase five hundred. To get the money he needed to finance the purchase, Mantello applied to a bank in Craiviova, Romania. The bank director agreed to advance the money on the condition that Mantello purchase the grain from a bank customer named Klein, which he did. When he returned home, his father and uncle were upset, in particular his uncle, who thought that he had engaged in a disastrous deal, a pipe dream. Where were they going to find customers for an extra four hundred carloads of grain? Mantello's business judgment was soon vindicated when grain prices rose by 50 to 60 percent. The grain had been purchased at a very opportune time, and the family made a fortune on that shipment.

When the bank director saw how well Mantello had done and how expeditiously he had repaid the loan, he offered him a job. Upset with his father and uncle's criticism, Mantello left home and began a new career at the bank in Craiviova. He now engaged in two lines of endeavor, working in the grain business on projects such as the financing of grain deals and supervising currency deals.

George Mantello. Geneva. The Jewish first secretary of the
El Salvador consulate in Geneva. 1942–45. From Jeno Levai,
Zsidosors Europaban (Budapest, Magyar Teka, 1948).

From the beginning of his banking career, Mantello demonstrated financial genius. One of the keys to his success was his extensive use of the telephone. In the early twenties, when telephones were not as widely used as today, he hired three operators to connect him to London, Zurich, and New York. He thus received instantaneous information on the changing prices of foreign currencies in various foreign exchanges, and with his excellent math acuity, he very profitably bought and sold currencies.

Mantello worked at the bank from seven in the morning until two in the afternoon, and then spent the rest of the day socializing. He mixed very little with the Jews where he was living; they were mostly Sephardim of Spanish origin who spoke Ladino with one another, and he experienced them as insular and uninviting. Instead, he befriended wealthy Romanian Gentiles. Mantello was well liked by these Romanians, despite the anti-Semitic atmosphere of the time. They called him Georgio, a gentile name, although he did not conceal his Jewishness.

Within a relatively short time, Mantello attained the post of bank director. In 1927, he traveled to Switzerland on business. A Swiss banker he met expressed his astonishment at Mantello's youth; in his country, he said, a man had to work at least twenty years before attaining such a post. Mantello took a romantic interest in the daughter of this man, who was an assimilated Jew and who approved of the courtship. The girl, however, had absolutely no sense of her Jewish identity. For this reason, Mantello's father objected strenuously to the match for this reason, and so his son withdrew from the relationship.

Having rejected the bank director's daughter, Mantello was now in an awkward position professionally. He therefore resigned his post and moved to Budapest, where he engaged in various financial deals. This work necessitated constant travel to Budapest, so he maintained apartments in both cities. So regular were his visits to Vienna, in fact, that in 1932 he obtained Austrian citizenship.

At this time, Mantello met the young woman whom he was to marry. Her name was Iréne Berger, a dancer who had been born in 1906 to a wealthy family in Beregszás (which had been incorporated into Czechoslovakia in 1918). Her family stemmed from Sabbatarians, members of the Transylvanian branch of the Magyars who had adopted a Sabbath-observing form of Judaism in the nineteenth century. Known as the Szekelys, they had later fully converted to Orthodoxy. Iréne's grandfather had converted to Judaism about 1860 and sent his pious son—her father—to a yeshiva in Bratislava (Pressburg). In 1928, the couple married. A year later, they moved to Cluj, where Mantello had spent his youth, and in 1930, she bore their only child, Enrico, called Imrei in Hungarian and Zvi in Hebrew.[11]

Meanwhile, Mantello pursued his prodigious business activities. In 1933, for instance, he created a corporation together with General Dragenescu, his former military instructor, and Captain Vasilescu, a law officer in the Romanian military schools and later a Romanian military attaché.

Josef Mandl. Brother of George Mantello and his business partner. He not only helped his brother, but he also initiated a number of important rescue efforts, including the Swiss-Romanian Committee to help refugees who fled to Romania. His close relationship with Florian Manoliu, the Romanian commercial attaché in Switzerland, facilitated this diplomat's heroic mission to Budapest. From Jeno Levai, *Zsidosors Europaban* (Budapest, Magyar Teka, 1948).

Mantello was a robust and courageous man whose very presence was powerful. "The fact is," his son, Enrico, later summed up, "the man had no physical fear." In 1936, Mantello embarked with the six-year-old Enrico to visit relatives in a rural section of Transylvania. As they were about to leave their hotel in Cluj, Mantello learned from his chauffeur that their car had broken down, and he decided to travel instead by bus. On a country road in the midst of rolling hills, when the bus was halfway to its destination, a tire blew out. While the driver changed the tire, the other passengers, most of them rugged mountain peasants, came down from the bus. Meanwhile, behind a flimsy wooden fence, a bull glared at them, snorting angrily.

Suddenly, the bull broke through the fence and charged at the bus, ramming its horns repeatedly into the side of the vehicle. Some of the passengers scrambled back into the bus, while others hid behind it. Mantello glanced nervously at his watch. Enrico heard him tell the driver, "This can go on for the rest of the day, and I have to be back in Cluj by this evening." He stepped down from the bus, walked over to the bull, and began talking to it until the animal quieted down. Finally, he took it by the horn and led it back to the pasture. The animal trod back behind the fence and walked away to the farmhouse in the distance. When Mantello came back onto the bus, the other passengers applauded him and shook his hand.[12]

Mantello's business dealings took him through all of central Europe. He owned a prosperous textile manufacturing plant in Bucharest, Romania, in partnership with his brother, Josef Mandl, General Dragenescu, and Vasilescu; but primarily he was a financier.

Let us go now to Switzerland, Mantello's eventual battleground for rescue, and see how this small, neutral country became involved in the fate of European Jewry.

2

Switzerland as an Information Center

Information

Switzerland, a neutral country in the heart of Europe, was a primary center for gathering information about the Jewish situation in Nazi-occupied countries. One reason for this was that Switzerland was a hotbed of espionage for all sides during World War II. But more importantly, Switzerland was a focal point for major Jewish organizations across the world, all of whom had representatives there. On the whole, these representatives did a very creditable job of gathering and analyzing information obtained from their contacts in occupied countries.[1]

These organizations can be divided into Zionist and non-Zionist groups. The Zionist groups were the Palestine Certificate Office (called Palestina Amt or Palamt), RELICO, the Jewish Agency, and Hehalutz. The non-Zionist groups were the Joint, the Jewish Labor Committee, Agudath Israel, Vaad Hatzalah, and HIJEFS.

The Palestine Certificate Office was a Palestine-based organization represented in Geneva by Dr. Samuel Scheps and his assistant, Dr. Chaim Posner.[2]

RELICO was a small but highly effective relief organization established and run by Dr. Abraham Silberschein.[3] After attending the Zionist Congress in Switzerland in August 1939, Silberschein remained in that country and set up RELICO. This organization specialized in distributing food parcels and, after 1941, providing Latin American protective papers—passports that the Nazis honored—to members of Silberschein's Labor Zionist group in Poland.[4]

The Jewish Agency was represented in Geneva by Richard Lichtheim, a highly intelligent observer whose stream of pessimistic reports to Jerusalem was highly accurate, though not much heeded.[5]

Hehalutz, the umbrella organization for Socialist-Zionist pioneer youth groups, including Hashomer Hatzair, was headed by Natan Schwalb (whose last name in Hebrew is Dror). In 1939, Schwalb initiated highly successful rescue and relief efforts throughout much of Nazi-occupied Europe. He developed what was probably the most efficient courier system among Jewish organizations, connecting him to Hehalutz underground contacts in Nazi-dominated countries. Even those not of Schwalb's ideological persuasion, such as Rabbi Weissmandl and Gisi Fleischman in Hungary, sent him many pleas for help, knowing that he routed his information to seven or eight contacts in Jerusalem, London, Istanbul, and New York.[6]

The World Jewish Congress was represented in Geneva by Dr. Gerhard Riegner. This was an American-based but world-wide, Zionist-oriented organization that had been headed since its establishment in 1936 by Stephen S. Wise, an outspoken Reform rabbi and one of the first Jewish-American leaders to support Zionism. A great orator, he led numerous liberal causes in a public career that spanned more than half a century and also headed a number of other organizations, including the American Jewish Congress (AJCong). Wise was American Jewry's foremost leader and the only one with relatively open access to President Roosevelt.[7]

The most influential organization was undoubtedly the Joint, a huge, non-Zionist rescue and relief organization that had spent tens of millions of dollars aiding Jews throughout the world since World War I. It was represented in Switzerland by Saly Mayer. Unlike most of the other representatives, who were employed by their organizations, Saly Mayer was a retired businessman who spent virtually all his time working gratis on behalf of the Jewish community. During the twenties and thirties, he had been active in fighting anti-Semitism in Switzerland, and he headed the Federation of Swiss Jewish Communities (SIG) until 1942. Mayer was regarded as a principled individual whose word was entirely trustworthy.[8]

In the minds of not only Jews but most non-Jews—including the Germans—the Joint represented an alleged block of American Jewish, and even world Jewish, financial power. What helped promote this view was the fact that most of the activities of the American and Yishuv-based organizations were financed by the Joint.[9]

Another group represented in Switzerland was the non-Zionist Jewish Labor Committee,[10] whose contact in Switzerland was Dr. Emanuel Sherer. The JLC had been founded in 1934 by Baruch Charney Vladek, the prominent Socialist labor and political leader, and was a highly effective rescue and relief organization. In New York City, it was headed by Adolph Held and Jacob Pat, who represented the 500,000 members of the Jewish-dominated unions (e.g., amalgamated unions, needleworkers) in the city's garment industry.

The Jewish Labor Committee branch in Switzerland obtained much first-hand information about the slaughter of Jews in Poland through its connections with the Jewish Bund's (socialist) underground in Poland and the general Polish underground, both of which were in radio contact with the Polish government-in-exile in London. The Jewish Labor Committee not only provided information to its members through constant news briefs, but also informed other Jewish organizations. For instance, it was responsible for publicizing the Bund Report in June 1942, the first major report on the annihilation of Polish Jewry.[11]

In the middle of 1940, after the fall of France, and with the help of the American Federation of Labor, the JLC initiated the very valuable program of Emergency Visitors' Visas, also known as "above-quota visas." These were issued to endangered Jewish and non-Jewish European labor and intellectual leaders, above the established visa quota. This program, one of the rare humanitarian rescue efforts approved by the Roosevelt administration, was subsequently used by Zionist and other organizations to rescue their foremost leaders. With the help of its contacts in the Soviet Union, the JLC also sent food packages to its friends in Siberia, Shanghai, and Nazi-occupied Europe.[12]

Since 1941, Agudath Israel and the Vaad Hatzalah—two small, New York-based Orthodox rescue organizations—had had their own contacts in Switzerland.[13] The Vaad Hatzalah used the services of Recha Sternbuch in Switzerland; she had been active on her own since 1938, helping bring in many hundreds of Austrian and German Jewish refugees who had come to Switzerland illegally, or providing them with transportation to other safe havens. She organized border guards and even humanitarian police officials, such as Dr. Stocker and Paul Grüninger, to spirit refugees out of Austria and later out of France, legalized them, and organized ships sailing for Palestine. For such activities, she was arrested in 1939, and Paul Grueninger was deposed. Although eventually the case was dropped against Recha Sternbuch, Grüninger lost his position and pension and was only recently (1997) rehabilitated by the Swiss government.[14]

In 1941, Recha and her husband, Isaac, and brother-in-law, Eli Sternbuch, founded a broader-based organization called HIJEFS, Relief Organization to Help Jewish Refugees in Shanghai, to assist Rabbi Abraham Kalmanowitz, one of the Vaad Hatzalah's three-man presidium, in transferring Swiss francs to the approximately five hundred rabbis and talmudic scholars in Japanese-occupied Shanghai.[15] Also in 1941, Eli Sternbuch initiated the use of Latin American passports as protective papers, a valuable rescue tool that was quickly imitated by some other Jewish representatives.[16]

Eli soon transferred the Latin American paper project to Dr. Julius Kuhl, a friend of the Sternbuchs, who was in charge of the Jewish Section of the Polish legation of the Polish government-in-exile in Bern. Kuhl was instrumental in obtaining for the Sternbuchs a number of valuable resources of the government-in-exile, whose headquarters was in London;[17] among these was the use of the Polish diplomatic cable, a coded telegraphic service. In his strategic position, Kuhl became one of the most important sources of information on the fate of Jews, especially those in Poland. He obtained information that was reported by foreign diplomats and secretly transmitted by the Polish underground to the Polish government-in-exile in London and Switzerland. The Polish legation also obtained information from people who had escaped from Poland to Switzerland, and from Swiss businessmen returning from Poland, and passed it on to Kuhl.[18] Kuhl in turn made all this information readily available to people such as Saly Mayer, the Sternbuchs, Dr. Silberschein, Dr. Lichtheim, and Dr. George Brunschvig, the prominent lawyer and head of the Bern Jewish community, who succeeded Saly Mayer as head of the Swiss Jewish community in 1942.[19] Kuhl was also the intermediary between the Polish legation and the Paraguayan consul, a Mr. Huegly, who, for a large sum of money, provided the Paraguayan passports that the Sternbuchs and others sent to Jews in occupied countries.[20]

Although Recha and Isaac Sternbuch were members of the Agudath Israel World Organization, the American branch of Agudath Israel preferred to use as its representative in Switzerland Yisroel Chaim Eis, a businessman, writer, and Agudist from Poland.[21] Eis served in this position until his death in the fall of 1943.[22] Eis and the Sternbuchs, who belonged to different factions of the small but fragmented Swiss Agudath Israel, were generally at odds with one another.

After Eli Sternbuch told Eis about the efficacy of the Latin American papers as rescue tools, Eis too began to use them. He cooperated closely with George Mantello, who provided him with the earliest Salvador protective papers.[23] A colleague of Eis who worked with him on the Latin American papers project was Maitre (Matthieux) Muller, a refugee from France and long-time head of the French Agudath Israel. Eis introduced Muller to Mantello, and after Eis's death in the fall of 1943, Mantello hired Muller to work full-time for him on the Salvadoran papers program.[24] At that point in time, American-based Orthodox rescue efforts greatly broadened in scope, and Jacob Rosenheim, president of World Agudath Israel, who was then in New York, designated Sternbuch and HIJEFS as the Agudah representatives to replace Eis in Switzerland.[25]

The Two Cables

Switzerland's importance as a center of information on the fate of European Jewry is exemplified by two cables that informed the free world of the plans and implementation of Hitler's Final Solution. These are the well-known Riegner cable and the lesser-known Sternbuch cable, which were sent in the fall of 1942.

Even before this, information about Nazi atrocities had been published in the West. For example, on May 21, 1942, the Bund (Jewish Socialist Party in Poland) transmitted to London the Bund Report on the mass murder of more than 700,000 Polish Jews. This report was broadcast by the BBC on June 2.[26] In addition, on July 22, the Jewish Telegraphic Agency (JTA) published a report, based on the same source that provided the information in the Sternbuch cable, about the mass deportations from the Warsaw Ghetto.[27] Five days later, on July 27, the JTA reported that Ignacy Schwarzbart, a Jewish member of the Polish government-in-exile in London, sent yet another cable from London to the New York office of the World Jewish Congress that began: "The Germans have begun the mass murder of the Warsaw Ghetto."[28]

The Riegner cable of August 1942, however, was the first dispatch that not only described atrocities, but also reported the vastly more horrific plan: the so-called Final Solution. It announced Hitler's scheme to murder the Jews by means of prussic acid and was based upon information supplied by two Germans: Eduard Schulte, an industrialist, and Artur Sommer, a lieutenant colonel in the Wehrmacht, attached to Admiral Canaris's counterintelligence division. The cable read:

RECEIVED ALARMING REPORT THAT IN FUHRER'S HEADQUARTERS PLAN DISCUSSED AND UNDER CONSIDERATION ACCORDING TO WHICH ALL JEWS IN ALL COUNTRIES OCCUPIED OR CONTROLLED GERMANY NUMBERING 3½ FOUR MILLION [excluding Soviet Jewry] SHOULD AFTER DEPORTATIONS AND CONCENTRATION IN EAST BE EXTERMINATED AT ONE BLOW TO RESOLVE ONCE FOR ALL

THE JEWISH QUESTION IN EUROPE STOP ACTION REPORTED PLANNED FOR AUTUMN METHODS UNDER DISCUSSION INCLUDING PRUSSIC ACID STOP <u>WE TRANSMIT INFORMATION WITH ALL NECESSARY RESERVATION AS EXACTITUDE CANNOT BE CONFIRMED</u> STOP INFORMANT STATED TO HAVE CLOSE CONNECTIONS WITH HIGHEST GERMAN AUTHORITIES AND HIS REPORTS GENERALLY SPEAKING RELIABLE (emphasis added)

RIEGNER[29]

Schulte and Sommer sent this information to Dr. Benjamin Sagalowitz, head of the Swiss-Jewish news agency in Zurich. On August 1, Sagalowitz passed the news on to Dr. Gerhart Riegner.[30] A week after receiving this cable, Riegner cabled the information to two important Jewish leaders, Rabbi Stephen S. Wise in New York and Sidney Silverman in London. Silverman was a member of Parliament and chairman of the British section of the World Jewish Congress.

The cable intended for Wise never reached him, because the State Department held it back on the grounds that it was "unsubstantiated." This excuse was probably based on the cable's admission that the information was transmitted "with all necessary reservations as exactitude cannot be confirmed." Undersecretary Sumner Welles, one of the few State Department officials considered friendly to Jews, was the signatory to that order. Tragically, this was not the sole instance in which such reservations hampered rescue efforts.[31]

However, Riegner's cable to Silverman did get through; and because Riegner had thoughtfully added the words "Inform and consult New York," Silverman dispatched a copy to Wise by the ordinary Western Union route. This arrived on August 28.

Wise was shocked at the information and shared it with several close friends, including the Jewish leaders Felix Frankfurter, Maurice Perlzweig, and Nahum Goldmann. None of them, however, informed the president or called for public demonstrations. Instead, after a hiatus of five days, Wise informed Sumner Welles, who had seen and suppressed the original cable weeks earlier. Welles persuaded Wise to maintain silence until the State Department could verify the information independently. Despite the earth-shattering nature of this news, Wise complied with Wells's request, exhorting the Jewish leaders with whom he had shared this news to maintain silence until the State Department gave its approval.[32]

On September 3, 1942, a second cable from Switzerland containing tragic news about the fate of European Jewry arrived in the office of Jacob Rosenheim at the Agudath Israel office in New York: the Sternbuch cable. This cable eluded State Department censorship because the Sternbuchs sent it via the secret Polish cable, with the cooperation of the Polish embassy in Washington.[33]

This cable described the Final Solution in progress: the first mass deportation and murder of Jews from the Warsaw Ghetto. This news had been reported to Dr. Kuhl by two eyewitnesses, escapees from Poland, and Kuhl reported it to Jewish organizations in Switzerland. In line with his policy, Kuhl made available any information he obtained to the Sternbuchs, his close friends, and to representatives of other Jewish organizations.[34] Although Riegner had obtained this information from Kuhl by August 14, he inexplicably did not forward a cable to Wise or to anyone else. Perhaps he felt that his own earlier cable was far more important, although the present one could have been used as confirmation. Lichtheim, on the other hand, cabled the news of the Warsaw deportations to the Jewish Agency in Jerusalem.[35]

The Sternbuch cable ultimately became the basis for the public outcry and demand for action in America, and it served as the foundation for the "Crimes Against Humanity" concept used at the postwar Nuremberg trials.[36] In contrast to the wavering stance of the Riegner cable, this one was unequivocal, and it differed radically in its conclusion. It read as follows:

ACCORDING TO RECENTLY RECEIVED *AUTHENTIC* INFORMATION THE GERMAN AUTHORITIES HAVE EVACUATED THE LAST GHETTO IN WARSAW STOP BESTIALLY MURDERING ABOUT ONE HUNDRED THOUSAND JEWS STOP MASS MURDERS CONTINUE STOP FROM THE CORPSES OF THE MURDERED SOAP AND ARTIFICIAL FERTILIZERS ARE PRODUCED STOP THE DEPORTEES FROM OTHER OCCUPIED COUNTRIES WILL MEET THE SAME FATE STOP IT MUST BE SUPPOSED THAT ONLY ENERGETIC REPRISALS ON THE PART OF AMERICA COULD HALT THESE PERSECUTIONS (emphasis added)[37]

DO WHATEVER YOU CAN TO CAUSE AN AMERICAN REACTION TO HALT THESE PERSECUTIONS STOP DO WHATEVER YOU CAN TO PRODUCE SUCH A REACTION STOP STIRRING UP STATESMEN THE PRESS AND THE COMMUNITY STOP INFORM [Stephen S.] WISE [Abba Hillel] SILVER [Jacob] KLATZKIN [Nahum] GOLDMANN THOMAS MANN AND OTHERS[38]

Wise had a history of protecting the president from Jewish pressure at all costs, but Rosenheim had no such compunctions. On September 3, the very day he received the Sternbuch cable, he transmitted it to Roosevelt, adding, "I dare, in the name of Orthodox Jews all over the world, to propose for consideration the arrangement by American initiative of a joint intervention of all neutral states in Europe and America expressing their moral indignation."[39]

The next day, September 4, Rosenheim and Kalmanowitz met with James MacDonald, chairman of the President's Advisory Committee on Political Refugees, who was close to the sympathetic Eleanor Roosevelt. MacDonald sent her a copy of the cable and requested that she bring it to her husband's attention. She complied, but the president never responded to this information. Not only that, it took him three weeks before he even forwarded it to the State Department.[40]

On the same day, under pressure from Rosenheim and Kalmanowitz, Stephen Wise called for an emergency meeting of thirty-four national American-Jewish organizations, to be held in two days' time. At that meeting, although Wise privately informed a few of those present about the Riegner cable, he focused publicly on the Sternbuch cable; but it became evident that the meeting delayed intervention rather than facilitated it. Instead of promising action, Wise impugned the veracity of the Sternbuch cable and condemned Kalmanowitz and Rosenheim for spreading *Greuelmaerchen,* atrocity tales.[41]

Wise did not mention that this cable was the third of three major, independent revelations of Nazi mass murder, the first two of which should have confirmed the accuracy of its contents. These were the reports of the Bund and the JTA; in addition, Schwarzbart's private cable had undoubtedly reached Wise's attention.[42]

Following Welles's suggestion, Wise directed everyone at the meeting to maintain silence until the State Department verified the matter independently.[43] It took the State Department until November to gather enough outside evidence to permit Wise to publicize the tragic information. Included in the evidence were two remarkable letters in code detailing the mass deportations from Warsaw, which the Sternbuchs had shared with Riegner; he in turn forwarded them to the State Department.[44] Not until November 24, 1942, did Wise finally announce the appalling news of the Final Solution at a press conference.

Although hobbled by the secrecy imposed upon it, the meeting of the thirty-four Jewish organizations did result in the formation of an ad hoc committee called the Special Conference on European Jewish Affairs. This committee comprised American Jewry's sole united front on behalf of rescue, but lasted only until a delegation met with the president in December 1942. At that time, it was dissolved by Wise.[45]

The Jewish Organizations as Conduits for Relief and Rescue

The representatives of Jewish organizations in Switzerland served as active conduits for relief and rescue, transferring money, packages, and Latin American papers, and at times providing resources of their own.

These representatives sent messages to their parent or sister organizations or both in the United States, Britain, Turkey, Palestine, and Sweden, requesting—at times, demanding—help, money, papers, or lobbying efforts on behalf of rescue.[46] They also regularly sent out updated information on the constantly changing situation and frequently intervened directly on behalf of European Jews with representatives of the Allied governments, the War Refugee Board, the Vatican, and the International Red Cross (IRC) in Switzerland.

The Joint provided financial support for most rescue efforts. As a result, contacts throughout occupied Europe, as well as other organizations' representatives in Switzerland, sent their requests and reports to Saly Mayer (or "Uncle Saly," as he was called, with a broad allusion to rich "Uncle Sam"). This made the Joint a major repository of information on the growing Jewish tragedy in Europe.

Perhaps the most important source of information, particularly in Slovakia and Hungary, was the "Working Group," (known as the Pracovna Skupina in Slovakia). This was the Slovakian Jewish underground, which operated out of Bratislava and was headed by Rabbi Michael Ber Weissmandl and Gisi Fleischmann.[47] Weissmandl was not only the creator of the Working Group, but also the originator of most of the ransom and rescue plans for Slovakian and Hungarian Jewry. He is best known as the author of the plea for the Allies to bomb the rail lines to Auschwitz and the death camp itself.[48]

Weissmandl and Fleischmann sent a constant stream of cables and letters appealing for money and other rescue assistance to most of the representatives of the Jewish organizations—particularly to Saly Mayer and Natan Schwalb, as well as to the Sternbuchs. They also frequently sent their messages to the Moetza in Istanbul, which represented the Jewish Agency's Vaad Hahatzalah, the Jerusalem-based rescue committee, headed by Chaim Barlas. Weissmandl often sent copies directly to his friend, Dr. Jacob Griffel, a member of the Moetza, because he knew that Griffel acted more immediately and flexibly than did the bureaucratic Barlas. As for Fleischmann, she had the advantage of being the only Jew to whom the Slovakian authorities permitted direct phone access with the Jewish organizations in Switzerland.[49] This enabled her to speak to and plead with them directly.

Many contacts in occupied countries, such as Rudolph Kastner and Zvi Szilágyi in Budapest, sent their reports to Natan Schwalb. They frequently also sent copies to Saly Mayer, which they noted in their correspondence with Schwalb. Schwalb did a superb job of providing Swiss francs and Latin American protective papers to members of his Hehalutz movement in occupied countries, using a well-developed cadre of couriers. These couriers also brought Schwalb the most recent information about the Jews' situation from his contacts.[50]

Because of his long experience and wide web of contacts, Schwalb was surely one of the best-informed persons on the Jewish condition in Slovakia and Hungary. To assure that Saly Mayer was aware of Jewish needs, Schwalb would usually send or personally deliver him a copy of reports he received, translated from the Hebrew or other languages, on his own stationery and with his imprimatur.[51]

Mayer supported Schwalb's rescue work liberally, and he was not alone. Roswell McClelland, the representative of the War Refugee Board (WRB), admired Schwalb for his work with the Yishuv pioneers and supported his rescue efforts with more than $110,000 from the WRB's little-used discretionary funds.[52] As the representative of the mighty United States and its great liberal president, McClelland was thought to be the ultimate source of aid. Anyone with information tried to enlist his help, which undoubtedly made him the best informed of all the elite rescue delegates.[53]

Failure in Cooperation

Although the Swiss-Jewish organizations did forward the information they received to other organizations, governmental bodies, and sometimes colleagues, their representatives made little effort to share this data as broadly as possible with one another. Indeed, there was little cooperation among the organizations in pooling resources, information, and ideas for rescue. On the contrary, the tragic reports in the letters and cables were often treated secretively, rather than as vital information to be shared by all Jewish organizations, the Allies, and the neutral states.

In some cases, this was due to major ideological differences between organizations, such as those between the Joint and the Jewish Agency, or between the Agudath Israel and all the other groups; but in addition, there were personality conflicts that splintered virtually all the organizations. Thus, representatives often did not share information even with colleagues of their own ideological group, making Jewish cooperation for the sake of rescue impossible. For instance, Shwalb was close to Saly Mayer and provided him with copies of all messages he received from abroad, but he never provided information to Richard Lichtheim, representative of the Jewish Agency, nor to Riegner of the World Jewish Congress.[54] Riegner, in turn, did not extend information to Silberschein, a fellow member of the WJC.

This problem also existed among members of the Zionist groups, such as Chaim Barlas, head of the Jewish Agency's Immigration Department and later of the Moetza. In a comment to Eliyahu Dobkin of the Jewish Agency in Jerusalem, Richard Lichtheim expressed dismay at the lack of coordination within the Zionist camp. Lichtheim wrote:

> There are no real differences between myself and other members of our movement here . . . but I have to deal here with undisciplined people who are driven by good intentions, but partly also by personal vanity. . . . Nathan [Schwalb] and Henryk [Chaim Posner of Palamt] are working quite independently . . . (backed by Barlas) . . . do what they like. . . . You would be surprised if you heard what institutions like the Red Cross think of this behavior of our various groups. The outside world is not accustomed to this sort of disorder and disorganization and are already making jokes about it. What shall a man like Schwartzenberg of the Red Cross think . . . if Schwalb and Henryk [Chaim Posner] are paying visits to them without informing me . . . the representative [of the Jewish Agency] and [M.] Kahany, the secretary-general.[55]

An equally frank assessment of the discord was expressed by Arye Kubowitzki, the American representative of the World Jewish Congress, who visited Europe during the final months of the war and noted that "the rivalries and jealousy of the various rescue bodies was such that it was quite impossible to get an unbiased report on any social worker or social organization."[56] In addition, even the tiny Agudath Israel in Switzerland consisted of several independent factions that had nothing to do with one another.[57]

Into this conflict-riddled environment Mantello entered, the lone voice of a nonestablishment Jew seeking to cement Jewish unity for the sake of rescue. With such projects as the Rabbis' Committee and the distribution of Salvadoran protective papers, he set an example for unified action; but tragically, his example was rarely followed.

3

Early Salvadoran Papers

Mantello's failure to achieve greater cooperation among Jewish organizations in Switzerland might have forced him into inertia. He could then have used the prerogatives of his wealth and diplomatic status to hobnob with the diplomatic corps and foreign social elite; he could have enjoyed life in a scenic country that retained its serene neutrality amid the growing inferno of Nazi-dominated Europe, satisfying his conscience by donating some money to help Jews and rationalizing his relative inaction. This, in fact, is what most of the Jews in Switzerland did, including some representatives of the Jewish organizations. They asserted that nothing could be done to save a substantial number of Jews, an assertion that has been echoed by many postwar historians.

However, Mantello's early failure to achieve cooperation did not discourage him from using his diplomatic status and resources to help his fellow Jews. At the beginning of 1943, about a half a year after he had arrived in Switzerland, he began a new enterprise: the use of Salvadoran protective papers.

The scheme to rescue Jews by using protective Latin American passports and citizenship papers had been initiated in 1941 by Eli Sternbuch, brother of Isaac Sternbuch and brother-in-law of Recha. The Sternbuchs had learned that a Jew in Warsaw with a foreign passport had been permitted to remain outside the ghetto without having to wear the yellow star. They began to purchase Paraguayan and other Latin American passports from Latin American consuls in Switzerland and sent them to their friends and relatives in Poland.

Although these passports were extremely expensive, they were considered well worth the money. Prices ranged from 500 to more than 3,000 Swiss francs, which had to be raised either by the holders' relatives in the free countries, particularly the United States, or by Jewish organizations.[1] Eli Sternbuch focused much of his attention on obtaining such papers for Orthodox Jews in Poland

and elsewhere, mostly friends and members of the Agudath Israel or related circles. Among the first to receive a paper was his future wife, Guta Eisenzweig, and her mother in the Warsaw Ghetto. To take the place of her deceased father, she added another person, Dr. Hillel Seidman, to her passport, changing his name to Eisenzweig-Seidman.[2]

Soon after the Sternbuchs began their rescue efforts, they were followed by Yisroel Chaim Eis, a member of another faction of the Swiss Agudath Israel, who sent Latin American papers to his circles in Poland. This rescue tool was soon used by representatives of other Jewish organizations as well.

Although the Sternbuchs did not hesitate to use illegal and semilegal avenues of rescue, not everyone was ready to follow suit. Particularly adamant against anything that smacked of illegality was the Joint Distribution Committee and its representatives throughout the world, notably Saly Mayer in Switzerland. Similarly, Richard Lichtheim, the Swiss representative of the Jewish Agency, stated, "I have always carefully abstained from having anything to do with the 'visa business.'"[3] This legalistic stance was supported by Roswell McClelland.

Others, however, were quick to seize this opportunity for rescue. Among the first was Dr. Abraham Silberschein, who was followed by many organizations, both Jewish and non-Jewish, and eventually by statesmen, neutral countries, and even the Holy See.[4]

Although everyone was aware of the dubious legality of these Latin American documents, the Germans chose to recognize them, motivated by their concern for the several hundred thousand German nationals residing in Latin America. As Martin Luther of the German Foreign Office wrote to his superior, Joachim Ribbentrop, on December 4, 1941, "Special consideration was generally only granted to Jews of Latin American citizenship because these states may possibly take reprisals against Reich Germans."[5] Half a year later, in June 1942, Theodor Dannecker, chief of security police and SD (Sicherheitsdienst, the Nazi party intelligence) in France, issued instructions regarding deportations that included exceptions for "Jews . . . subjects of . . . Mexico, belligerent enemy countries of Central and South America, neutral countries, and the Allied Powers."[6]

In the words of the American ambassador to England, John Winant, "The German authorities seem to have cherished the hope that the persons with these South American passports might constitute a basis for the exchange of German nationals in South American countries."[7] Nazi authorities either protected the Jewish bearers of these Latin American papers or sent them to internment camps such as Tittmoning, Vittel, or special sections of such camps as Bergen Belsen, holding them for eventual exchange until mid-1943, when the validity of the papers was thrown into question.

When Mantello realized how much money Jewish organizations were spending for Latin American papers, he resolved to provide as many Salvadoran papers as he could gratis, in most cases paying all expenses himself, or, at the most, accepting payment only to cover his costs.[8] He began by issuing a few Salvadoran papers to friends or organizations in Switzerland who wanted them for their relatives in Poland. For instance, a friend of his who had relatives in the Warsaw Ghetto asked him to provide them with papers. Mantello made out these papers and sent a letter to the relatives in Warsaw, which was still receiving mail from neutral Switzerland, requesting a photo and other necessary data to fill out the document. After receiving these, he sent the completed citizenship papers by courier. Not only were the man and his family permitted to leave the ghetto, but they were also allowed to remove their yellow stars. In this modest fashion began Mantello's series of rescue efforts, which would eventually save tens of thousands of Jewish lives.[9]

Mantello's first Salvadoran papers went to Holland, Belgium, France, Poland, and Slovakia, and a few were even dispatched to Germany.[10] After processing the first few papers on his own, he realized that he would require the permission of the El Salvador Consulate and made his request of the consul general, Col. José Arturo Castallanos. Castallanos first required that Mantello gain the approval of Gustavo Guerrero, former president of El Salvador and former chief justice of the World Court at the Hague. Guerrero, who had escaped from Holland to Switzerland after the German invasion, readily gave his assent, and Mantello pushed forward with his plans. Still, their assumptions at first envisioned but a few such papers. However, although the numbers mushroomed arithmetically and eventually geometrically, Castellanos and Guerrero, and later the government in San Salvador, never wavered in their complete support.[11]

The Salvadoran consul general permitted Mantello only to issue citizenship papers and not passports, which would have enabled the bearer to travel and were more highly valued. Mantello's papers simply declared the bearer and his family to be citizens of El Salvador. The condition limiting travel had arisen from the fear that spies might use passports against Allied interests;[12] but the

CONSULADO GENERAL
DE LA REPUBLICA DE EL SALVADOR, C.A.
GINEBRA
SUIZA

Dos. W. 3573/942.

Certificat de Nationalité.
================================

        Le Consulat Général à Genève de la République de
Salvador (amérique Centrale) confirme par ces présentes que

Monsieur le Docteur WEINER Paul né le 28/1 1904 à Kunszentmiklos

est reconnu comme citoyen de la République de Salvador
avec tous les droits et devoirs inhérents à cette nationalité.

        Si,l'intéressé voulait envisager une émigration,
il lui appartiendrait d'aviser ce Consulat Général en temps
utile de son intention à ce sujet,en envoyant en même temps
une photographie de date récente pour passeport.Cette photographie devrait porter au verso une certification légalisée
par une autorité compétente ou un officier ministériel.

Ginebra,le 18 décembre 1942.

PREMIER SECRETAIRE
DU CONSULAT GENERAL.

Original Salvadoran citizenship papers made out by Mantello.

fact that Jews in Hungary with citizenship papers could not travel later turned out to be a blessing in disguise, for it assured that they would not be deported to Auschwitz.[13] Another disadvantage of passports was that they would have had to be signed by the consul himself, an inconvenience that would have eliminated any chance of rescue on a large scale. For that reason, Mantello preferred to deal with citizenship papers as opposed to passports.

At first, few Jews had much confidence in these Salvadoran papers. They assumed that a real passport, however fraudulently obtained, would serve them better than a citizenship paper, especially one that looked flimsy and was distributed free of charge.[14] To transform the papers into impressive-looking documents that would influence German, and later Hungarian, officials, both of whom revered ornate government stamps, Mantello transformed the simple single sheet into a three-page document on Swiss-taxed and stamped paper. The first page was written in French, with a German or Hungarian translation attached, executed and stamped by an official translator.[15] The paper was usually predated by two years, especially when intended for use in Hungary, for the Germans had announced that they would not recognize any change of citizenship after 1942.[16] As a safety measure, Mantello sent out notarized photostatic copies and retained the originals;[17] in mid-1944, however, Roswell McClelland reversed this procedure by demanding that the originals be sent out.

Along with the documents, Mantello wrote instructions for the recipients in Hungary. He advised them what to say if they were arrested; they were to claim, for instance, that the certificate had been obtained through the efforts of relatives and friends in Latin America.[18] Because a single document covered an entire family, people would sometimes claim nonrelatives as part of their family.

The Jewish organizations or individuals requesting the papers for their friends or relatives had to provide both the photos and necessary vital statistics.[19] Mantello would, when possible, attach photos and vital statistics to the papers and then send them out; otherwise, the photos and statistics had to be sent for, which wasted precious time. Therefore, by mid-1944, Mantello decided to send out prestamped and signed documents, allowing the recipient to add the photos and data himself (see chapter 5).

As word circulated about the Salvadoran papers, demand began to build, particularly because Mantello charged no fee, or only a minimal fee, to cover costs, in contrast to the other consuls. In his memoir, Joel Brand recalled:

There was a certain Georges Mantello who worked in the Geneva Consulate of the Republic of San [*sic*] Salvador. . . . If anyone wrote to him, sending his description and photograph, he would be sent a passport [i.e., citizenship paper] as a national of the Republic of San [*sic*] Salvador and thus would become, as far as the Hungarians and Germans were concerned, a neutral alien. We sent a courier [in 1943] to see Mantello, and he declared himself ready to give us hundreds of passports, all duly stamped and signed. We only had to supply him with the names. San [*sic*] Salvador's colony of nationals in Budapest increased enormously at this time [in 1944]—its numbers exceeded those of all foreign groups put together.[20]

In contrast to the careful discrimination and regulatory procedures of the Jewish organizations and individuals distributing such papers, Mantello made no distinctions of any kind. Any Jew or Jewish organization that requested help, whether for family or friends, was accommodated unconditionally. Thus, representatives of all the Jewish organizations in Switzerland—Zionist, non-Zionist, Orthodox, Reform, Agudath Israel, Mizrachi, Hashomer Hatzair, and Revisionist—received as many papers as they requested. Eventually, even the Vatican, the Swiss legation in Budapest, and Jewish organizations in Romania requested and received papers en masse.

At first, Mantello's papers were typed up by a secretary at the El Salvador General Consulate, but as demand grew, he devised new arrangements for distributing them. He had become very friendly with Eis, who had been among the first to request Salvadoran protective papers. Sometime in mid-1943, Eis introduced him to Dr. Matthieux ("Maitre") Muller, a lawyer and fellow Agudist who was a refugee from France, and who was assisting Eis in making out Latin American papers. After Eis died in early November 1943, Mantello put Muller in charge of his Salvadoran papers project, and as demand continued to grow, he gave Muller a separate office and eventually provided him with a secretary. Volunteers also pitched in whenever emergencies arose.[21]

After about a year, Muller took over almost the entire operation, under the auspices of the Swiss section of World Agudath Israel, which paid his salary. The price charged for those who could afford the expenses of translation, notarization, taxes, and so forth, rose to 25 Swiss francs, 10 francs above cost, which enabled Muller to subsidize those who were unable to pay anything. Mantello also signed and distributed letters for the Swiss Hungarian Committee, which also charged an average of 25 Swiss francs per document; here, too, he paid the basic expenses. Most of the Salvadoran papers were dispatched by courier to German-occupied countries, especially Hungary.

Some Jewish rescue organizations used Nazis as couriers to transmit messages and money, a course Mantello declined to follow. He correctly suspected that, although these couriers would deliver the documents and money, the Gestapo would cull the information and use it for its own purposes. Instead, he used diplomats from Portugal, Romania, El Salvador, the International Red Cross, and the Vatican to deliver the papers. He also sent documents via regular Swiss mail through the services of a notary in Geneva.[22]

Once the papers arrived, the recipient would contact the Department of Foreign Interests at his local Swiss embassy or consulate, because Switzerland acted as the protective power, or intermediary, between most Nazi-occupied countries and many Latin American countries. Swiss representatives would issue the recipients a Swiss protective document stating that the bearer was a bona fide Salvadoran citizen subject to Swiss protection. This meant, among other things, that neither he nor his family could be deported.[23]

This entire operation was fraught with obstacles. For instance, the Swiss could not always be relied on to provide protective papers to bearers of Latin American papers, especially during the latter part of 1944. In particular, problems arose concerning the issuance of documents in Hungary and Romania, which were satellites and for a long time were not considered occupied. Mantello and others exerted much effort to persuade the Swiss to extend their protection in these countries as well (see chapters 10–11). Also, the fact that no genuine Salvadorans lived in Hungary made the recognition of such papers additionally problematic;[24] they were not accepted at all in Slovakia.

Even before Switzerland's assumption of the role of protective power in Hungary in the fall of 1944, most countries provided some degree of protection for Jews holding Salvadoran papers. However, a series of problems had threatened the use of the papers even then. At the end of 1943, as will be discussed later in this chapter, Germany temporarily withdrew recognition of these papers. To compound the tragedy, other Jewish intermediaries who were distributing Latin American papers lost much of their business because Mantello was giving them away free, and they denounced him to the Swiss government with the false charge that he was profiteering from his Salvadoran papers. The Swiss detained him for sixteen days in May 1944, preventing him from issuing his life-giving documents during this time. In addition, obstacles were placed in his way by organization officials who resented the interference of a nonestablishment Jew in rescue affairs.[25]

In the fall of 1943, the Swiss launched an investigation into the entire issue of the sale of Latin American papers, which were generally considered fraudulent. John Winant, American ambassador to Britain, reported on the results of this investigation to the State Department on March 2, 1944. The report highlighted the illegal intervention of several Latin American consulates, but praised Mantello:

> There has been a large trade in passports. It is estimated that 4,000 have been issued from Switzerland; it is known that others have been issued from other neutral countries, including Sweden. Some informants estimated the total number to be as high as 9,000 to 10,000, but some thought that it did not exceed 5,000. In Switzerland it was organized by private individuals and reached such proportions that the Swiss Federal Government had to intervene. . . . Legal action was taken against several of the organizers. . . . [For example,] the Honduras Consul . . . issued 400 passports. . . . The consuls in Switzerland for Haiti, Paraguay, and Peru had been dismissed. The average price paid for a passport was approximately 700 Swiss francs.
>
> The consul [*sic*] of San [*sic*] Salvador [Mantello] has acted from pure humanitarian motives and *has charged no fee at all.* (emphasis added)[26]

Winant was not the only person who recognized Mantello's disinterested motivation in issuing the Salvadoran papers. Even before the occupation of Hungary, there were several individuals who were well aware of the invaluable and selfless service that he performed. Letters from three prominent Swiss rabbis stand as testimony. The first is from Rabbi Dr. Tuviah Lewenstein of Agudath Israel, former chief rabbi of Holland. On February 18, 1944, he wrote to Mantello:

> At the risk of detracting from your well-known modesty . . . It is almost two years since our organization was able to take note, on many occasions, of your unstinting efforts on behalf of those who were close to death: thousands of men, women, and children in Belgium, France, Holland, Poland, Romania, and Slovakia. Not only were you able to save them from terrible deportation, but your charges have been given a ray of hope for the future and immediate moral support. . . . Contrary to the dealings of many others, you have not only

rejected the idea of personal gain, but you have made great personal sacrifices. . . . Please be assured not only of our highest respect, but also of divine reward by the Father of all.[27]

About the same time, Rabbi Armin Kornfein of the Zurich rabbinate gratefully responded to Mantello on a more specific issue:

> It behooves me to thank you with all my heart for the help you have given my parents, who were in great danger in France. I am even more grateful in view of the fact that you were unaware of my relationship with those unfortunate victims of Nazism. I have also heard from many sides of all the help you have given to other people, without expecting anything at all in return. I know that you have used your own money to defray costs. There is nothing as beautiful as the act of saving a human life. Only God can reward you for your acts. Nonetheless, as the undersigned rabbi, I would like to thank you in the name of all those whom you have helped and to assure you of the total gratitude reserved for you by all of Jewry, as well as by men of good will, whatever their religion.[28]

The third rabbi was Dr. Zvi Taubes, chief rabbi of Zurich, who wrote to Mantello on December 16, 1943:

> Dear Mr. Mantello,
>
> Very often in the past few months, your name has been mentioned to me by our fellow Jews. I have learned that you have participated on a totally selfless basis to save the remnants of European Jewry from under the Nazi heel. I deem it my duty to express to you my gratitude, in the name of all those who have benefited from you and who are not able to express their gratitude directly to you.[29]

Despite the obstacles in his path, Mantello kept expanding his protective papers distribution. As will be detailed further on (see chapters 10–11), after the Szalazi coup in Budapest on October 15, 1944, these papers inspired the issuance of tens of thousands of additional protective papers by the consuls of other neutral countries, such as Switzerland and Sweden, as well as the International Red Cross and the Vatican.[30]

Vittel

At the outset, Latin American protective papers seemed to fulfill the expectations of those in need, but things were not to remain so hopeful. In the middle of 1943, Germany withdrew its recognition of the papers, threatening the entire rescue effort. The Jewish organizations and government groups in Washington, Bern, and the capitals of virtually all the Latin American countries quickly interceded, but it would take more than a year before the matter was resolved. The stakes were high. As time passed, especially after Germany's occupation of Hungary, an ever growing number of Latin American papers had been issued; by the latter half of 1944, when the Hungarian tragedy was at its height, their number reached many thousands. Let us focus now on the early stages of the problem and the attempted solutions.

Less than a year after Latin American papers were first used in 1941, hundreds of Jews in occupied Poland held passports, most issued by the Paraguayan consul. This group of protected individuals, who neither had to move into the ghetto nor wear the yellow star, even included a few real American citizens. One was an American-born sixteen-year-old girl, Mary Berg, who had been visiting relatives in Poland with her mother, Sylvia, when the war broke out. In her diary, she expressed her amazement at the papers' efficacy:

> It was clear that many Jews could be saved from the ghetto with the help of South American passports. The Germans recognize the validity of such passports, although their possessors can speak neither Spanish nor Portuguese. It seems that the Germans need human material for exchange against the Germans interned in the American republics. How can the world be informed that human lives can be saved with these little slips of paper?[31]

The recipients of the first Latin American passports were interred in Pawiak Prison in Warsaw beginning on July 17, 1942, only five days before the Germans began the first of their mass deportations from the Warsaw Ghetto to Treblinka. They included Guta Eisenzweig, her mother, Sarah, and Dr. Hillel Seidman, Guta's former classmate at Warsaw University.[32] Bearers of Latin American papers were brought to Pawiak prison from other parts of Poland. Ironically, whereas the Germans recognized the papers of "enemy nationals"—Latin American countries that had broken relations with Germany—papers from Latin American countries friendly to Germany, such as Argentina and Chile, were not accepted. This was because Germany's sole interest was to expedite an exchange of nationals.

Of the Pawiak inmates, 238 were sent to the Vittel detention camp in France in the winter of 1943.[33] This detention camp was set up at the former resort town of Vittel in northeastern France. There, the Germans also held several thousand Americans, British, and Poles for possible exchange. Although only a small percentage of the British and American prisoners were Jewish, the Polish group was almost entirely Jewish and was generally kept apart from the others. Although the Vittel camp was surrounded by layers of barbed wire, it was quite different from the usual concentration camp, and even from other camps used for exchange purposes. It consisted of a number of former French resort hotels set within a park, and the inmates were treated relatively decently.[34]

However, this security was not to last long. As long as no one had raised a voice against these passports, everyone could choose to ignore their dubious legality, but this silence was soon broken. Paraguay, whose consul in Switzerland was the first to sell passports, took action that undermined the viability of the protective papers. The Sternbuchs had obtained information from the papal nuncio, Filippe Bernadini: it seemed Paraguay had discovered that a list of its own citizens scheduled for exchange with German nationals in Paraguay included Jews who had purchased Paraguayan passports. Because these Jews' papers had been obtained illegally, Paraguay refused to recognize them as citizens. Once the Germans learned of Paraguay's refusal, it had to respond; it did so by withdrawing its recognition of the papers and suspending the right of Spain, the protective power for Paraguay and Bolivia, to grant protection to the bearers.[35]

On December 1, 1943, a German commission arrived in Vittel, confiscated all Latin American passports from the Jewish inmates, and sent the passports to Berlin for verification. The Jews assumed that all these inmates would be killed. Because they were able to communicate with Switzerland through the IRC, they immediately contacted the Sternbuchs, who had long been in touch with friends and relatives in Vittel. On December 15, four days after the visit of the German commission, the Sternbuchs sent an urgent cable to Jacob Rosenheim of the Agudath Israel and the Vaad Hatzalah in New York, demanding immediate intercession with the State Department and the War Refugee Board to persuade the Latin American countries to recognize these papers officially.[36]

Vaad Hatzalah and Agudath Israel representatives immediately met with the State Department, which promised to send cables to this effect to each of the Latin American countries. These could have been quite helpful, as the United States had tremendous influence in the affairs of Central and South American states during those years;[37] but, as the Vaad Hatzalah discovered more than four months later, the State Department never sent the cables. On April 5, the

Sternbuchs sent another urgent cable to the Vaad Hatzalah, saying that, based on the information contained in recent appeals from Vittel inmates, the entire group would be sent to their deaths unless the United States took immediate action.[38]

The next day, April 6, which was Passover, three rabbis from the Vaad Hatzalah traveled by train to Washington to meet with Henry Morgenthau Jr., the Jewish treasury secretary and head of the War Refugee Board.[39] Also present were members of the State Department. The rabbis' objective was to persuade Morgenthau to pressure Secretary of State Cordell Hull to send the vital cables to all the involved Latin American countries and pressure them to recognize these papers officially. After the three rabbis spent the entire day pleading with Morgenthau, he persuaded Hull to send the cables that same evening. The next morning, April 7, Morgenthau noted the following to his assistants: "Nothing has pleased me more than being able to get the State Department to send out this cable [to all the Latin American countries] in regard to Camp Vittel. It just shows [that] if we put enough heat in the right place it can be done, and believe me we have put plenty of heat on Mr. Hull."[40]

In its cables, delivered by the American embassies in each Latin American country, the State Department allayed any fear of a flood of Jews entering their countries, either in exchanges or in postwar immigration. For instance, in its cable to the American embassy in Paraguay, the State Department asked the American ambassadors to give the following assurance:

In the event of exchange, Paraguay will not (repeat, not) be expected to grant physical admission to any of the persons concerned even on a temporary or tentative basis.

In light of these assurances, please impress upon the Paraguayan government the extreme urgency of acquiescing to our requests and of acting upon them without delay. You should impress upon Paraguayan officials that since failure to act would almost certainly spell death for the persons involved, and that since no (repeat, no) responsibilities or obligations would result for Paraguay from acquiescence to our requests, we would be sorely disappointed if Paraguayan authorities would not (repeat, not) wholeheartedly cooperate with our efforts to save these people.[41]

The cable also informed the American ambassadors of the rationale behind the request, which was a radical departure from normal protocol. It clarified the role of the War Refugee Board, and its objectives and limitations, noting, for example, that given the priority of winning the war, "the WRB aims at helping rescue . . . to perform [what is] essentially an emergency life-saving task—aiding people to get out of Nazi-dominated countries." The board was not concerned with the ultimate destination of these people, but their immediate safety.

To accomplish this objective, the cable continued, the board would rely largely on the cooperation of private organizations and other governments. These organizations would be able to use the United States secret cable and other communication facilities; they would be able to count on American intervention with other governments to help Jews escape; and the War Refugee Board, despite its limited funds, would provide financial help (which it sometimes actually did). Finally, the cable urged the Jewish agencies to cooperate in this common goal.[42]

This important message should have put to rest any doubts of the Latin American countries involved, the protective powers and the personnel serving the War Refugee Board, especially in Switzerland. Tragically, these critical issues were not to be so easily resolved.

The cables came too late for the inmates of Vittel. Except for three persons who had hidden during the roundup in April, the rest were deported to their deaths in Auschwitz. Moreover, the issue of official recognition of Latin American papers in general, and El Salvadoran papers in particular, involved a number of individuals and agencies in different countries that often obstructed the process. It would take the intervention of many parties before the holders of Salvadoran and other papers, especially in occupied countries, were able to use them successfully.

In addition, even in June of 1944 and later, the State Department reiterated its desire, already expressed in April, to have all the Latin American countries recognize their Jewish holders in Nazi-occupied territories with some measure of protection. It was ready to cooperate with Switzerland and Spain, the two primary countries who represented the interests of the Latin American countries to the Axis. It even assured them that the United States was responsible for their upkeep if any of the holders made it to neutral countries. Eventually, this American assurance became an important factor in the protective roles played by the various neutral countries in the fall of 1944, after the pro-Nazi Szalasi coup on October 15, 1944.[43]

At the same time, America made an unsuccessful attempt to request Switzerland to take over the representation of El Salvador and other Latin American countries in Hungary. No doubt, the fact that Roswell McClelland, the American representative of the War Refugee Board in Switzerland, who had been sent to facilitate rescue, was a rather reluctant advocate for rescue in general and for the use of Latin American papers in particular, did not help matters. This superlegalist found the entire matter of the use of "false papers," to use his phrase, so distasteful that even the State Department had to remind him of the value of these papers as rescue tools.[44]

Enrico's Entry into Switzerland

At the close of 1943, while Mantello was involved with the Salvadoran papers, he devoted a measure of his energy to a personal problem: spiriting his son, Enrico, out of Hungary and into Switzerland. Enrico had been living in Budapest with his mother and maternal grandparents. At first, he had been the only Jewish boy in a general school; later, he attended a Jewish school. When he visited his grandparents in Transylvania, he saw that the lower class of Hungarians had become officers and now strutted about like conquerors, humiliating the Jews; later on, these were the men who collaborated with the Nazis. An atmosphere of hatred was building, and Enrico decided that he wanted to get out.

In helping his son, Mantello had to use as much ingenuity, effort, and reliance on important connections as he needed to help Jews with the Salvadoran papers. He had grown close to Commodore Freddie West, the British military attaché, and one day he approached West and told him that he wanted to get his thirteen-year-old son, Enrico, out of Hungary. (His wife had chosen to remain in Budapest to care for her elderly parents.)

General West contacted a delegate of the International Red Cross, Narciso Freire de Andrade of Portugal, and asked him to act as an escort to Enrico. Fortunately, at this time of declining German fortunes, the Portuguese were very amenable to requests for assistance from the Allies. In fact, Mantello himself had dealings with the Portuguese; it was through Portugal that he was shipping chronographs to the Royal Air Force, and in the process he had become close to some of the members of the Portuguese legation in Bern.[45] As a result of this rapport, de Andrade readily agreed to escort Enrico. He traveled to Budapest on the pretext of visiting the Hungarian Red Cross, and was received there by important politicians, including Admiral Horthy.

Enrico now had a chance of getting out of Hungary, but Mantello still had to persuade the Swiss authorities to allow his son to enter Switzerland. He sent the lawyer Jean Brunschvig to contact the Swiss Alien Police, which was headed by Dr. Heinrich Rothmund.[46] Brunschvig informed them that Mantello had Salvadoran papers for Enrico and was requesting a visa for him, but the treatment he received was nowhere near as clement as that of the Portuguese. Rothmund himself replied that if Enrico came to the Swiss border, he would be sent back to Budapest and told to straighten out his papers there. When Brunschvig reported this, Mantello was furious. "Is that all you accomplished?" he asked.[47]

He then tried a second approach. He went to the Italian ambassador and asked him to help arrange for Enrico to be allowed into Switzerland at the railroad station on the border of Switzerland and Germany.[48] At that time, Mussolini had fallen and the Germans occupied Italy. The ambassador told Mantello, "I don't favor either the Germans or the British. I'll be glad to help you." Mantello arranged a luncheon meeting at the Hotel Schweitzerhoff in Bern with the Italian ambassador and representatives from the American and British embassies. He knew that the Swiss police, who were stationed throughout the hotel, would report this meeting to Rothmund's office; his objective was to impress Rothmund with his high-placed connections, hoping to convince him that he could not simply dismiss the request to allow Enrico entry.

At the meeting, Mantello loudly expressed his anger at Rothmund. As he had anticipated, the police reported to Rothmund's office that Mantello was liable to cause a scandal. A short while later, a call came from the Swiss Alien Police informing Mantello that they had given orders to the police in St. Gallen to allow Enrico to enter the country, and that they would take care of the visa at the border.

Enrico received a message from his father that somebody would be coming to get him. Soon thereafter, de Andrade arrived in Budapest with his secretary, and Enrico received a Hungarian passport that omitted the *J* for *Jude*. Next, de Andrade needed to secure for Enrico a German exit visa, and he took advantage of the present climate in German-Portuguese relations. The Portuguese were now in a strong bargaining position with the Germans, who were trying to endear themselves in an attempt to persuade the Portuguese to stop letting the Americans use their military base in Lisbon. Counting on this vulnerability, de Andrade arranged to be invited to lunch at the German ambassador's home, where he successfully persuaded him to grant Enrico a German exit visa. Apparently, he claimed that Enrico was his illegitimate child or the child of someone higher up in Portugal.

Having attained the necessary papers, de Andrade and Enrico got on a train and headed for Vienna. The train was fully equipped with a luxurious dining car, as though it were still peacetime; but when they entered Austria, conditions changed radically. Soldiers boarded the train—soldiers who had not seen any good food in a long time. The atmosphere was tense, and it was apparent that they had entered a war zone.

On December 18, 1943, de Andrade and Enrico spent the night at a hotel and returned early the next morning to the train. When they arrived in Innsbruck, Austria, about 200 kilometers from the Swiss border, the train began to engage in various maneuvers because the Allies had bombed the railroad lines. At one point the train could not proceed any farther, and all the passengers—about 150 people—were told to board a series of buses that would eventually take them to another rail line farther on. De Andrade had to attend to the luggage and temporarily lost contact with Enrico. They wound up on separate buses.

Enrico's bus, which was filled with young Germans, took a detour of about fifty miles. One of the young men said to him in German, "Where are you coming from?"

"From Budapest."

The German youth said, "Then you'll enjoy the sea with us."

"What sea?"

The boy explained that they were going to build defenses on the Atlantic. When the bus arrived at a small train station and the passengers got back on the train, an official told Enrico that he was not to leave the group, but Enrico replied, "I don't belong with them." He showed his passport, but to no avail; he had to return to the bus. By the greatest good fortune, the seaside post was only one stop on the bus's itinerary, and all the original passengers of the train did meet again, as they had been promised, at a rail point farther ahead. Here, de Andrade and Enrico found each other again, but much time had been lost along the way.

Meanwhile, Mantello had arrived at St. Gallen, where Enrico's train was scheduled to arrive at four in the afternoon. But it never arrived, and there was a report that there had been a bombardment on the tracks. Mantello stayed up waiting all night in the train station, but his son never came. A Swiss official advised him to go back to the hotel "because the Germans and the Swiss are here, and it won't be good for you to be on this side of the border, near the control." Mantello retorted, "I've got one son; I can't sit there in a hotel. I'm going to stay here." The person replied, "Do what you want; but just don't stand outside where all the guards can see you. Stay inside the station." Finally, General West informed Mantello that he had received good news: de Andrade and Enrico had been cleared and were all right.

The train finally arrived at the Swiss border at four or five the next morning. To enter Switzerland, one had to walk through a building with one's passport and emerge on the other side. The platform was divided between Germany and Switzerland, with two German soldiers on one side and two Swiss soldiers five meters farther on. As the train pulled into the station, Enrico looked up and saw his father waiting for him. He jumped off the train, ran desperately between the two German soldiers, and leaped into his father's arms. Seeing that he was a youth, no one interfered with him; but as father and son were heading toward the hotel, guards stopped them and said, "Wait. We have to clear your papers."

Mantello replied, "Not here. If you want, you can come with us to the hotel." By the time Mantello and Enrico arrived at the hotel, it was nine in the morning. An hour later, St. Gallen's chief of police brought Mantello a bottle of champagne to celebrate Enrico's return.

As for Rothmund's attempt to obstruct Enrico's entry, Swiss files show that he subsequently "took energetic steps" in protesting to Consul Castellanos that Mantello had "circumvented the visa regulations" by "giving [Enrico] a Salvadoran diplomatic passport at the border" without "a formal request for permission to immigrate." This, Rothmund said in self-justification, "was approved reluctantly as an exception, for humanitarian reasons."[49]

Meanwhile, there would be a lull of several months in the lives of Hungarian Jews, who were hoping that the advancing Soviet army would bring the war to a close and spare them any further travails; but this was not to be. The Germans seized Hungary and occupied it, an invasion which turned into a major catastrophe for the Jews, and which presented Mantello with the greatest challenge of his life.

4

Jewish Rescue Efforts in Hungary

$\mathbf{A}$s soon as Hitler's troops marched into Hungary on March 19, 1944, Jewish individuals and organizations disseminated information on the broadest possible scale about the status of Hungarian Jews. Leaders of the Working Group, the Slovakian Jewish underground, sent a spate of reports, plans, and pleas out of Bratislava to Jewish organizations in Switzerland, who in turn communicated with their contacts back in Slovakia and Hungary. They also informed their associates in Istanbul, which was a center of Jewish rescue activity, and their parent bodies in Jerusalem, New York, and London. The information they shared concerned such matters as the ghettoization and deportation of Hungarian Jews, Weissmandl's plea to bomb Auschwitz, and the Brand affair.[1] The news network was created in the hope that these associates would pass the information on to the Allies, who were expected to act on it,[2] but such faith in Allied help was rarely gratified.

In Switzerland, Jewish organizations frequently interceded with the Swiss representatives of the IRC, the papal nuncio Monsignor Bernadini, the American ambassador Lelland Harrison, and, after April, Roswell McClelland, who became the representative of the influential War Refugee Board (WRB). The organizations expected that these prominent men would inform and influence their governments, the IRC, and the Holy See to act swiftly to avert total disaster for the Jews in Hungary; but these men did very little until they were at last forced into action by Mantello's press and church campaigns in the summer of 1944.

As for the modus operandi of the Jewish organizations, occasionally several Jewish representatives would intercede as a delegation,[3] but on the whole, because of ideological and personality differences, rescue efforts were fragmented, involving neither mutual consultation nor the sharing of crucial information on Jewish conditions in Hungary. For example, the same material was frequently sent to Jerusalem at different times by different individuals, each unaware of the others' dispatches.

Several rescue efforts, in which Mantello had no part, took place in Switzerland during the first three months of the Hungarian occupation, mostly involving information sent to Jewish organizations in Istanbul, Jerusalem, New York, and London, as well as to Allied governments. We will now briefly examine the reactions these messages elicited and their practical outcomes. The reader will then be better able to appreciate the circumstances within which Mantello's rescue activities took place, the methods he used, and the results he achieved.

Hungarian Jewry on the Eve of the Occupation

The Jewish population of Hungary before the war was approximately 450,000, a little more than 5 percent of the general population. In 1939–40, when Hungary reacquired many of the areas earlier ceded to Czechoslovakia, Romania, and Yugoslavia, the number of Jews jumped to approximately 735,000.[4] There were also tens of thousands of Jews who had converted to Christianity and whose numbers increased appreciably after the German occupation.[5] Besides these residents, there were approximately 15,000 Jews without Hungarian nationality, primarily refugees of German, Austrian, Polish, and Slovakian origin. In 1941, these nonnationals were deported to Kamenets-Podolsk in the Ukraine, where most of them were murdered.[6] Of the 2,000 survivors, some fled to Hungary, where their harrowing stories helped put a stop to the massacres.

As Germany's ally, Hungary promulgated a spate of anti-Semitic laws before the German invasion, calling up many Jewish men into the labor battalion that acted as an auxiliary to the Hungarian army on the eastern front. Thousands of these young men died or were wounded as human minesweepers. Nevertheless, compared with the Jews in Nazi-occupied countries, Hungary's Jews lived in relative peace until the country was occupied in March 1944.

Hungarian-Jewish Organizations

In Hungary, several Jewish organizations dedicated their resources to helping the Jews, providing relief and housing, for example, to the refugees in Budapest. Principal among these groups were the Neolog (Reform), Orthodox, Zionists, and the local branch of the Joint.[7]

Neolog

The Neolog, or Reform, wing of Hungarian Jewry, which represented the largest and wealthiest segment of Budapest Jewry, was headed by the banker Samuel (Samu) Stern. As proponents of assimilation, the Neolog refused to engage in illegal or semilegal activities, fearful of raising the specter of dual loyalty. Their highest priority, to be accepted as equals in their adopted countries, ranked far above particularist Jewish interests, including survival. For example, in 1942 Samuel Stern refused to contribute to Weissmandl's efforts to raise $25,000 (in U.S. currency) to complete the ransom negotiations for the 25,000 Jews remaining in Slovakia.[8]

Zionists

In opposition to the Neolog policy, the Zionists and Orthodox produced and made available false papers.[9] The small Zionist party was technically headed by Otto Komoly, but was run in reality by Rudolph (Rezsö) Kastner, a brilliant journalist from Cluj. In 1941, Kastner, together with two men named Joel Brand and Sámuel Springman, created "Operation Tiyul," illegally smuggling hundreds of Zionists from Poland into Hungary. This action laid the basis of the Waada Ezra WeHazala, the Zionist party's relief and rescue committee, popularly known as the Vaada,[10] over which these three men presided.[11]

Sámuel Springmann was a diamond merchant who had known Brand from their youthful days in Hachsharah (youth camp designed for preparation in settling on a kibbutz). By 1941, he had established many good connections with foreign embassies in Budapest, and with German and Hungarian secret police. As for Joel Brand, he became the central figure in the negotiations with the Germans and Allies for the rescue of Hungarian Jewry in May and June of 1944.[12]

In December 1942, the Istanbul branch of the Jewish Agency's rescue agency, Vaad Hahatzalah, designated the Vaada as its financial conduit for relief and made Kastner the official representative of Vaad HaHatzalah headquarters in Jerusalem. Kastner thus controlled the finances from both Jerusalem and Istanbul.[13] Until the German occupation, the Vaada specialized in bringing refugees from Poland, Slovakia, and Germany into Hungary. One of those groups consisted of some six hundred members of the Zionist youth movements, who eventually formed the basis for the so-called Kastner Train.[14]

The Vaada developed into a highly efficient vehicle of communication, particularly with the Working Group (Slovak Jewish underground), which was sending out information on an almost daily basis. The Vaada used many couriers to transmit information to its colleagues in Geneva, Istanbul, Jerusalem, London, and New York; the colleagues then relayed these messages to all their contacts in the free world.[15] The Vaada also helped refugees flee from Hungary to the relatively safer terrain of Slovakia. Its German connections included agents of the Abwehr, the Wehrmacht's intelligence division,[16] who provided a courier service for the Jews between Budapest, Bratislava, and Istanbul. These agents reliably transferred cash, albeit for a 10 percent cut, but they also transmitted to the Nazis copies of all correspondence, such as the documents involving Weissmandl's Europa plan.[17]

During the German occupation, the Vaada used all of these connections. In helping the refugees, its members, by careful interrogation, learned much about conditions in the ghettos and camps.[18] It sent this information to its contacts in Geneva, Istanbul, and Jerusalem.

An additional Vaada rescue effort included the use of Latin American passports, which were readily available for purchase in Switzerland from most Latin American consuls or their contacts. In 1943, the Vaada found its work in this field greatly eased when it discovered a Latin American diplomat, George Mantello, who was providing such protective papers for free.[19]

Closely related to the Zionists' rescue efforts were those of the Palestine Certificate Office (Palestina Amt or Palamt). This office was headed by Moshe (Miklós) Krausz, who was both a member of Mizrachi, the religious Zionist party, and a representative of Hashomer Hatzair, the extreme-left Zionist group.[20]

Krausz distributed the valuable Palestine certificates, which enabled their bearers to enter Palestine. The distribution of these certificates, at the rate of fifty per month in Hungary, was controlled by Jerusalem's Jewish Agency and had to be approved on a case-by-case basis by the British government. Holders of the certificates were among the quota of 75,000 Jews that Britain's White Paper of 1939 permitted entry into Eretz Israel during the next five years.[21]

Some of these certificates were known as "capitalist certificates." They required evidence of a bank account with a thousand pounds sterling (about $5,000 U.S.) and were distributed without regard for party affiliation. Most certificates, however, were apportioned strictly according to Zionist party membership, which served as a constant source of friction among Zionist factions vying for the lifesaving certificates.[22]

Orthodox

The leader of the Orthodox rescue committee was Philip Freudiger, head of Budapest's Orthodox Jewish community. He was assisted by Alexander Diamant, deputy chairman of the Budapest Orthodox community, Samuel Kahan-Frankel, head of the Hungarian Orthodox community, and Gyula Link.[23] In addition, Chaim Roth, head of the Chevra Kadisha (Holy burial society), was active in providing false papers to incarcerated refugees that enabled them to reside in Hungary.[24] They did this by bringing the Jewish chaplain at Budapest's house of detention large metal cans of kosher soup, in the hollowed bottoms of which were secreted false gentile identity papers.[25]

Hungarian Jewish Equanimity

In comparison with the Jews of other countries that were allies of, or occupied by, the Nazis, Hungarian Jews enjoyed a measure of relative security. This was principally a result of two factors: the intertwining of many Jewish concerns with the Hungarian economy and the benign rule of the Kallay regime. As a result, Jewish leaders and laity assumed that Admiral Horthy, Hungary's regent, would never allow Hitler's barbaric treatment of Jews in other countries, especially Poland, to take place in their land.

Even the Hungarian Jews who believed the atrocity stories told by refugees from Poland and other countries did not believe that such a fate could befall them. One example is the reaction to the graphic description given by Rabbi Boruch Rabinovich (admor of Munkács, also known as Mukacevo) of the 1941 massacres in Kamenets-Podolsk, from which he had escaped. The proud, patriotic Hungarian Jews refused to believe that this could happen to them, assuring themselves that they were protected by their Hungarian citizenship.[26]

Indeed, the actions and attitude of the Hungarian government seemed to indicate a continued regard for the safety of the Jews. On April 30, 1943, Edmund Veesenmayer, Hitler's expert on east central Europe and later his plenipotentiary and minister to Hungary, reported the following to his superiors:

> The Hungarian population is marked by a fundamental, intense defeatism, if not cowardice. *The fear of bombing is so acute as to penetrate deeply, affecting even national opposition circles. The strong participation and significance of the Jews is thus regarded as the best guarantee and protection against serious air raids.* . . . In return for their hospitable attitude to Jewry they expect to be spared

and guaranteed benevolent treatment; they look upon the Jews as a guarantee for the protection of "Hungarian interests" and believe they could produce through the Jews evidence to confirm that they have been virtually compelled to enter this war on the side of the Axis powers, but have in actual fact indirectly promoted the cause of the enemies of the Axis powers by latent sabotage. This explains why the position of the Jews is greatly strengthened, particularly since Kallay has come into office. . . . [T]he [Fascist Nyilas] Szalasi movement—which formerly aroused some hope—has sunk into utter insignificance. . . . In Hungary, the partisanship of a cunning Jewish-plutocratic system by latent sabotage, espionage, and creation of a defeatist atmosphere threatens to grow into a serious danger for Axis policy. (emphasis added)[27]

Not until sometime in early June did Hungarian-Jewish leaders realize that a terrible fate awaited their community. When the Nazis entered Hungary, they almost immediately created a Judenrat (Jewish council) to be able to deal with a central Jewish body representing the Neolog, Orthodox, and Zionist factions. By the end of May or the beginning of June, Freudiger, the Orthodox representative of the Judenrat, showed the other Judenrat members a copy of the Auschwitz report. Now they realized to what extremes of depravity they, too, were vulnerable.[28]

Then, suddenly, the Jews' integration into Hungarian life, and its attendant promise of safety, began to dissolve. Professor Braham writes in his authoritative work on the destruction of Hungarian Jewry:

When disaster struck with the German occupation of Hungary on March 19, 1944, the Jews discovered that they were no less vulnerable than their brethren elsewhere in Nazi-dominated Europe. One by one, the major pillars upon which they based their hope collapsed. The conservative-aristocratic faction of the Hungarian Right, on which they counted so heavily for their continued protection, was eliminated; the leftist and progressive opposition which they expected would take a stand against the Nazis remained . . . an impotent shell. Finally, the Christian neighbors with whom they thought they had shared a common destiny for over a thousand years remained basically passive. This was especially true in the provincial communities, where the ghettoization, concentration, and deportation of the Jews were carried out extremely rapidly.[29]

The German Occupation of Hungary

To understand Germany's decision to occupy Hungary in March 1944, it is important to take note of the causative military and political factors. For almost two decades, Hungary had been unhappy with the Trianon Treaty of 1920, which had significantly reduced its size and population. In the years 1938 to 1941, with the direct help of the Germans, Hungary regained much of this territory at the expense of Czechoslovakia, Romania, and Yugoslavia. As a result, Hungary eagerly entered the Axis Alliance in 1940; and in June 1941, the country joined Germany's war against Russia, hoping to further expand its territory.

But these hopes were dashed in the wake of Hungary's great losses on the eastern front in 1942, and the major German defeats in North Africa in 1942 and at Stalingrad in the winter of 1942–43. Fearing a process that might lead to ruin, Hungary grew increasingly interested in a separate peace with the Anglo-American Alliance.[30]

In fact, throughout its term, the Miklós Kallay government (1942–44) had been engaged in continuous secret negotiations with British and American contacts in neutral countries. Hungary's interest in a possible accommodation with England and the United States was fueled by its great fear of the Bolsheviks, a fear arising from the memories of the brief but bloody Communist regime led by Béla Kun in 1919, which had engendered the even more bloody repression of Admiral Horthy's "white terror."[31]

The Germans, who had infiltrated Hungarian intelligence, were fully aware of Hungary's incipient attempts to disengage from the Axis. German concern about a Hungarian defection grew acute in the summer of 1943, when Italy pulled out of the war, providing Hungary with an impetus to follow suit. This delicate situation was exacerbated by the Kallay government's insistence, as late as February 1944, that surviving Hungarian forces return from the eastern front to protect the homeland.[32]

In addition, the Germans were irked by Kallay's benign policy toward the Jews and his refusal to expel them. A number of Hungarian officials were well disposed toward the Jews, one of the most outstanding of whom was the anti-Nazi minister of the interior, Ference Keresztes-Fischer. In the words of Philip Freudiger, "[Keresztes-Fischer] somehow had found ways and means of carrying out the anti-Jewish measures in such a way that the living conditions of Jews in Hungary—compared to conditions prevailing in other spheres of interest—were among the best."[33]

This cluster of factors impelled Hitler to order the invasion of Hungary in March 1944. The Jews' relatively tranquil situation was to change as a result of Hitler's personal summons of Horthy on the heels of the German invasion.[34]

By February 1944, the advancing Russian armies were at the Dniester, and the arrival of an American mission to Budapest to arrange for Hungary's surrender was imminent. Hungary's collapse would expose the valuable Romanian Ploesti oil fields and the German army on the eastern front to encirclement by the Russians, and would undoubtedly lead to a total collapse of the Axis. These factors convinced Hitler of the need to act immediately to stave off Hungary's surrender.

On March 12, 1944, Eichmann informed his experts on Jewish affairs about the upcoming German occupation of Hungary; on March 15, Hitler summoned Horthy for a "conversation."[35] At that meeting, which took place on March 18, Hitler expressed his displeasure concerning Hungary's independent aspirations and informed Horthy that Germany would take over Hungary, with Horthy remaining the nominal regent under a new government.[36] Hitler also made clear his intention to "solve the Jewish problem" and pressured Horthy into concessions that doomed Hungarian Jewry, one of which was an agreement to permit the delivery of a few hundred thousand Jewish workers to Germany as slave labor for war-related projects. Although Horthy never signed deportation and other anti-Jewish orders, they were carried out by the new Sztojay pro-German government that was formed shortly after his return to Budapest on March 19.[37]

Thus, with only about 150 SS men and full Hungarian complicity, Eichmann was able to carry out his Final Solution with a speed unheard of in the other German-occupied countries. Veesenmayer himself pointed out after the war that without the complete cooperation of the Hungarian government and gendarmerie, the Germans could never have carried out the deportation and murder of close to half a million Hungarian Jews. When the Horthy regime did take a strong stand against deportations later on, noted Veesenmayer, it was successful.[38]

At eleven P.M. Friday, March 18, 1944, the day after the Jewish holiday of Purim, while Hitler was lecturing Admiral Horthy, eleven German divisions under Field Marshall von Weichs, spearheaded by the elite parachute regiment of the Brandenburg Division, marched into Budapest.[39] So unprepared was Horthy that he had not even left any contingency plans should he not return on schedule.

Jewish groups in Hungary, Slovakia, and the free world reported on the occupation to Jewish organizations and Allied governments. Foremost among them was the Working Group, the Slovakian Jewish underground, which informed Jewish leaders of the latest developments and spread its ideas for rescue, in which it had been actively engaged even before the German invasion of Hungary.

By the time of Hitler's invasion, the Working Group's courier service to Budapest arranged for an almost daily delivery of messages. For example, at the end of April, the Working Group had discovered the agreement between the Slovakian and Hungarian rail lines to begin deporting the 320,000 Jews of Carpatho-Ruthenia by mid-May on 180 trains, and immediately informed the Jews of Budapest (see chapter 5).[40]

An episode recorded in *Min Hametzar*, Weissmandl's profound, incomplete memoirs, illustrates one of his earliest attempts to warn Hungarian Jewry about the Nazis' impending Final Solution. This episode highlights the great difficulty he had in persuading Hungarian Jews of the veracity of the Nazis' genocide plans.

Shortly after the German occupation of Hungary, Weissmandl met a Jew from Ungvár, who had come to Hungary to get his father and return with him to Slovakia, which was then relatively safe. Weissmandl immediately saw this as an opportunity to send an urgent warning to the Jews of Hungary. He composed scores of letters as though they were from inmates of various ghettos and camps, describing their brutal treatment.[41] In addition, he wrote to the Jewish leaders of Ungvár about the Nazi plans for the destruction of the Jews, warning that they were doomed and that ghettoization was merely the prelude to Auschwitz. Under no circumstances, he counseled, should they ever enter a ghetto. If ghettoization had already taken place, he advised them to fight their way out, noting that although some would get killed, many more would be saved. Weissmandl suggested that they petition Horthy, who might be able to halt the deportations, because the Germans did not have a large enough number of troops in Hungary to enforce the Final Solution on their own.[42]

The young man went to Ungvár with Weissmandl's documents and handed them to one of the representatives of the newly established Judenrat. In disbelief, the well-meaning representative took the material to the Germans and asked whether the detailed atrocities and Nazi plans for mass murder were true. The Nazis denied it; then, to prevent this information from spreading, they shot about thirty Jews.[43]

All of this activity aimed at rescue was in sharp contrast to the stance taken by many other Jewish representatives. For instance, even after Kastner received the Auschwitz Report, he saw no threat to the Jews of Hungary and consequently informed no one outside the Vaada.[44] In fact, Kastner, Brand, and other members of the Vaada had been aware of the impending occupation of Hungary five days before it occurred, and about six weeks before they obtained a copy of the Auschwitz Report.

On March 14, Kastner and Brand were summoned to an urgent meeting with Dr. Joseph Schmidt, the head of a negotiating committee of the Abwehr, and his colleague, Josef Winninger. For months the Vaada had been dealing with Winninger, who, in return for bribes, had promised to help smuggle Jews across the border. At this meeting, Schmidt delivered an optimistic report on the Jewish situation. He declared that the Abwehr had won its long battle with its rival, the SS, in regard to the "Jewish problem," and he promised a new, humane policy, which included the cessation of deportations and cruel treatment in the concentration camps and death camps. In an obvious ploy to provide himself and his friends with a postwar alibi, he gave Brand and Kastner a list of Abwehr officers and asked that they transmit it to their colleagues in the Moetza in Istanbul, so that the Jews would know that some members of the Abwehr were "trying to fight the war in a more civilized manner."

Winninger then revealed: "I'll tell you something that would cost me my neck if you gave me away. Next week, Budapest is to be occupied by German troops. The decision has been taken. Hungary will cease to be an independent country."[45]

After the meeting, the Vaada called all its members and apprised them of this astounding news. They decided to transmit the details immediately to the Moetza in Istanbul, so that it would inform Jerusalem—which in turn was expected to warn the Allies. But there is no known record of any response to this incredible news; apparently, the Allies never received this information.[46]

Shortly after the occupation of Hungary, Kastner and Brand engaged in negotiations with Schmidt and Winninger over a plan to ransom the Jews of Hungary. Earlier, Schmidt had been involved in the Europa Plan, the Working Group's unsuccessful attempt in 1943 to ransom all Jews under Nazi control for $2 million. At that time, in transmitting the Vaada's documents to Istanbul, Schmidt had made copies of them for the Wehrmacht. He now presented this plan as his original idea.

Meanwhile, the SS, rival to the Abwehr and thus to Schmidt and Winninger, was interested in conducting its own deals with the Jews. One of the SS principals was Dieter Wisliceny, who had negotiated with the Working Group, especially Weissmandl, since 1942 for Slovakian Jewry and who had also been involved in the Europa Plan. After Wisliceny, Hermann Krumey and other SS officers in Eichmann's Sonderkommando entered Budapest on March 19, but they did not immediately begin their negotiations for the sale of Hungarian Jews. Instead, as mentioned earlier, they first created a Jewish Council (Zsido Tanacs, or Judenrat), so that they would be able to deal with a central body representing the Neolog, Orthodox, and Zionist Jews. Samuel Stern of the Neolog was appointed head of the Jewish Council, while Philip Freudiger represented the Orthodox, and Nissan Kahan the Zionists.

From the outset, Wisliceny promised the Jews that no harm would befall them if they cooperated fully.[47] He returned to Berlin on March 24, stopping off in Bratislava to obtain several letters of recommendation that he could present to the Jewish Council to gain its members' trust. Weissmandl provided Freudiger with such a letter, while Nissan Kahan wrote to Kastner and the Zionists, and a third member of the Working Group prepared a letter for Stern.[48]

Weissmandl sent two letters to Freudiger. One was a brief letter intended to be seen by Wisliceny, recommending him as a negotiating partner. The other, longer letter, dispatched with great haste via courier, was meant for Freudiger's eyes only. In it, Weissmandl detailed the history of negotiations with Wisliceny and warned of possible dire consequences. He directed that the Jews absolutely refuse to accept the establishment of ghettos, let alone enter them, for ghettoization was the first step to Auschwitz—whose workings he then graphically described. If the Jews were caught in a ghetto, he suggested that they escape or even revolt; although many might die, many others would survive. Weissmandl also advised Freudiger to emulate the Slovakian Working Group, which was a generally united effort of all Jewish factions.[49]

Upon his return from Berlin to Budapest, Wisliceny showed the open letter to Freudiger and told him, "Now we can reap the results of our earlier labor." But instead of asking for the $2 million that had been required by the Europa Plan, he demanded $12 million, of which $10 million was slated for the SS.[50]

Meanwhile, Schmidt's attempt to make a deal was discovered by the SS after Eichmann's men searched his home, where they found copies of the original Europa Plan. As a result, Schmidt and his colleagues were arrested by the SS and ousted from the negotiations.

Rivalry existed as well among the Jewish Budapest leadership. Kastner and Brand managed to push Freudiger out of the negotiations, evidently persuading Wisliceny that their connections with "world Jewry," through the Jewish Agency in Jerusalem and the Joint in the United States, made them better suited to carry out negotiations.[51] Similar rivalry existed between Kastner and Brand, as well as between Kastner and Krausz.[52] Whereas Kastner's approach to rescue was through direct negotiations with the Nazis, Krausz focused on dealing through neutral countries, especially Switzerland (see chapters 10–11).[53]

Kastner and Brand's negotiations with Wisliceny soon grew complicated and ultimately met with only limited success. The result was that Weissmandl's original "Europa Plan" of ransom for several million dollars was eventually transformed into the so-called Brand Mission of "Goods for Blood," or "10,000 Trucks for One Million Jews." On May 15, the day all preparations had been completed for the mass deportations of Hungarian Jewry, Brand was informed by Eichmann about his mission, for which he departed the next day.

On May 16, after the mass deportations had begun, Brand set out to meet his "companion," Bandi Grosz, in Istanbul; from there they were to travel together to Eretz Israel to meet with the Jewish leaders. Bandi Grosz was a Jewish triple agent whom Eichmann sent along with Brand on an independent assignment—to establish contact with the Americans and British. This was probably the primary objective of this "dual mission" and was directed by Himmler himself.[54] Grosz's assignment in Istanbul, where he first met up with Brand, was to speak to Allied intelligence officers to discuss the possibility of a separate peace between Germany and the Western Allies. Brand had actually been assigned to be a cover for the more important mission of Bandi Grosz.

Brand and Grosz arrived in Istanbul on May 19 and were received by members of the Moetza and the American ambassador to Turkey, Laurence Steinhardt, to whom Grosz disclosed his mission. British officials, however, were very unhappy about the proposed negotiations for Jewish lives, fearing a mass influx of refugees into Eretz Israel. Despite their full awareness of Grosz's mission, which was largely beneficial for the Allies, they quickly arrested him. Brand, meanwhile, who had hoped to discuss his mission with the Jewish leadership in Jerusalem, was "invited" to go down to the Yishuv via Syria. However, as soon as he stepped into Aleppo, he too was arrested by the British, who took him to Egypt instead of Jerusalem. Only through pressure from the War Refugee Board was Ira Hirschmann, its activist representative, able to interview

Brand and to arrange for his release several months later. In October, Brand was permitted to travel to Eretz Israel, by then a frustrated and dejected man.

The British were adamantly opposed to any discussion of Brand's mission of negotiating with the Germans to save Jews. They publicly refused it through an airing on the BBC on July 19, decrying the "monstrous offer" as a means of blackmailing the Allies. The Americans, on the other hand, were more amenable to negotiating with the Germans to save Jews, an attitude that we will explore further in chapter 10.[55]

The Kastner Train

Kastner's first negotiation with Eichmann involved permission for a group of six hundred Zionist certificate holders in Budapest to travel to Palestine. Many of these Jews had been rescued from Poland by the Vaada on the basis of Zionist party membership. Each local Zionist party leader, together with a committee from his party, had submitted a list of names to Kastner and his group. Kastner himself selected a few hundred friends and members of his family from his hometown of Cluj, whose ghetto contained a population of 18,000 Jews. He also included the families of members of the Vaada and the Jewish Council, among them Andreas Biss, Joel Brand, Otto Komoly, Sándor Offenbach, and Samuel Stern.[56] In all, Kastner selected 388 Jews.

On June 10, the Jews from Cluj were brought to Budapest and housed in special barracks on Columbus Street, soon dubbed the "privileged camp." In addition, Kastner added several hundred more prominent Jews, such as intellectuals, scientists, and artists, based on lists from different factions submitted by Otto Komoly and Zvi (László) Szilágyi. The number of Jews now came to 750.

Because Eichmann, through his associate Kurt Becher, demanded $2 million to allow these Jews freedom, additional train seats were sold to anyone who could pay the price of approximately $2,000 per seat. Of these, Freudiger paid for eighty Orthodox persons and their families, including Rabbi Joel Teitelbaum, admor of Satmar. By the time the train was set to travel at the end of June, the number of passengers had reached 1,200 (see chapter 7). Much, if not most, of the money was paid to Becher in the form of gold, silver, and jewels, delivered in several suitcases.[57] In addition, Kastner was also negotiating with Eichmann for about 15,000 Jews to go to Vienna and remain there, pending future negotiations.[58]

Early Information about Hungary's Occupation Reaches the West

The press kept American Jewry informed about the occupation of Hungary and the tragedy of Hungarian Jewry. Although Americans would not be aware of Auschwitz for months, they were fully cognizant of the fact that the German occupation of Hungary in March 1944 represented a threat to the lives of its nearly one million Jews. This is evident from the front pages of the Yiddish press and several major general newspapers, chief among them the *NYT,* as well as the reports of the JTA—the last two of which circulated among the editors of virtually all Anglo-Jewish newspapers.

Representative was a front-page article on March 22 in the Yiddish *Morning Journal* under the headline "One Million Hungarian Jews Frightened for Their Lives after Nazi Takeover." This was immediately followed by a proclamation: "[I]n the past, United States Jews have been negligent in saving Jews, especially from Hungary, where rescue opportunities existed but were not exploited. But even now, it is not completely too late. Many can yet be saved."[59]

Two days later, on April 24, President Roosevelt sent a stern warning to the Hungarians (albeit in a watered-down version of the original warning suggested by the War Refugee Board), strongly advising Germans, Hungarians, and other Europeans against cooperating with the Nazi crimes against humanity in general.[60] After calling attention to the postwar crimes trials that would be held, he mentioned the particular plight of Hungarian Jewry: "That these innocent people, who have already survived a decade of Hitler's fury, should perish on the very eve of triumph over barbarism, which their persecution symbolizes, would be a major tragedy." Although Roosevelt listed the Jews at the end of a roster of other suffering nations, this statement was significant, for it marked the first time that he officially referred to the Jewish tragedy. Nevertheless, although several newspapers and periodicals waxed poetic over the president's positive remarks, especially Stephen Wise's *Opinion,* others were more skeptical, hoping for action rather than words.[61]

The subsequent Allied bombing of Budapest, which was not done to help the Jews—nothing was ever done militarily to rescue Jews—was believed by both the Hungarians and Germans to have been carried out on their behalf.[62] The Hungarians, no less than the Germans, attributed to the Jews enormous influence on the American government.

The tightening of the noose around Hungarian Jewry was revealed publicly in a series of articles in the Jewish Telegraphic Agency and in the *New York Times*. The measures they reported included the following:

April 14: The establishment of a Judenrat (a central Jewish Council), to speed up anti-Jewish measures.

April 16: Confiscation of Jewish property.

April 17: The beginning of deportations.

April 19: Dissolution of Zionist and other organizations.

April 24: Transfer of Budapest Jews to "closed districts."[63]

As early as April 4, Gerhart Riegner, who had first alerted the world to the Nazi plans for genocide in 1942, sent a desperate cable to Rabbi Stephen S. Wise regarding the unfolding Hungarian tragedy. He wrote:

It is reported reliably that the government of Germany is planning . . . for the destruction of 800,000 Jews within six months. . . . [T]hese plans should be vigorously and repeatedly denounced by radio. . . . [T]he Jews should be told to seek shelter in all conceivable ways outside or inside of Hungary . . . to destroy all relevant lists . . . and avoid registration. Encourage officials of Hungary and the populace to help the Jews.[64]

Riegner's report was confirmed in a *New York Times* article of May 10, date-lined Istanbul, which revealed that the Hungarian government "is now preparing for the annihilation of Hungarian Jews."[65] Articles in the *New York Times* and the *Jewish Telegraphic Agency* confirmed these reports, offering the following facts:

May 18: 80,000 Jews already deported.

May 26: Germans reported that "there are still about 500,000 Jews to be dealt with in Hungary."[66]

Yet, all this information about the Hungarian-Jewish tragedy did not produce a major reaction in America, even though it came at the height of Roosevelt's election campaign for an unprecedented fourth term—a time when American Jews held real political power, had they chosen to use it.

Symptomatic of the American-Jewish lack of focus on rescue was the Madison Square Garden rally held on March 21, attended by more than 20,000 people, whose objective was to push for the implementation of a "Congressional Resolution on Postwar Palestine." The rally's program and speeches, protesting the British White Paper's immigration restrictions that were due to go into effect in ten days, had been prepared long in advance, and no changes were made to accommodate the tragic new dimension of the Holocaust—even though the NYT reported on the Nazi occupation of Hungary on that same day.

In fact, American Jews never pressured the American government regarding either Palestine or rescue work in Europe.[67] They found it easier to rail against Britain than to pressure their beloved FDR, in this election year, to pursue the rescue of Hungarian Jewry.[68]

On May 18, three days after the start of mass deportations from Hungary, Joseph Levy, the *NYT* reporter stationed in Istanbul, sent a report noting that the initial steps in the destruction of Hungarian Jewry had been completed. "The first act in the program of mass extermination of Jews in Hungary is over, and 80,000 Carpathian Jews have already disappeared. They have been sent to murder camps in Poland." He added, "Unless drastic measures are taken immediately to put an end to the Hungarian government's brutality, 1,000,000 Hungarian Jews are doomed." Levy's dispatches to Istanbul were among the most accurate and frightening in the entire press;[69] his accuracy was due to his ready access to Dr. Jacob Griffel, who in turn obtained this information from Weissmandl.[70]

As the above examples demonstrate, much public information on the ongoing tragedy of Hungarian Jewry was available. In addition, there was a wealth of firsthand accounts of the Germans' activities, numerous pleas for rescue to the Allies, the Vatican, and the International Red Cross from many Jewish organizations, and the efforts of the War Refugee Board; yet by early June, most of Hungarian Jewry had been openly deported.

Berlin suggested to Edmund Veesenmayer that he camouflage the forthcoming Aktion against Budapest Jewry,[71] but on June 8, Veesenmayer confidently replied in a secret cable: "World public opinion will not be shocked greatly by the proposed measures against the Jews in Budapest, since outside opinion paid very little attention to the 'evacuation measures' [i.e., deportation] undertaken against the Jews until then."[72]

However, unknown to Veesenmayer, Jewish and non-Jewish organizations, and even the Allies, George Mantello had initiated a series of actions that would radically change not only the methods of rescue, but also the results.

The following chapter will examine the early period of the German occupation of Hungary and the steps that Mantello took to rescue his brethren.

5

Mantello's Early Rescue Efforts

On March 20, one day after German troops marched into Hungary, Mantello and his brother Josef Mandl rushed to Zurich. There they met with several prominent personalities in an attempt to foment action that might hold back the disaster engulfing the last intact Jewish community under the Nazis.

Mantello first went to see Dr. Zvi Taubes, chief rabbi of Zurich and head of the Swiss Rabbis' Committee. Dr. Taubes agreed to call on a number of influential persons for a meeting on the twenty-third, in the home of Mrs. Lajos Buchwald. This meeting was chaired by Michael (Mihály) Bányai, a well-to-do Swiss of Hungarian origin. Other participants included Rabbi Armin Kornfein, Maitre Muller, Mrs. D. Lewenstein (wife of Rabbi Tuviah Lewenstein), Geza Pallai, Ferenc Schlesinger, Ferenc Tauszky, Lajos Sonnenfeld, Josef Mandl, and Bányai's daughter, Dr. C. Bányai, who soon became committee secretary.

At this initial meeting, the participants planned to form an organization that would focus solely on the plight of Hungarian Jewry.[1] The organization was officially called the Schweizerisches Hilfskomitee fuer die Juden in Ungarn, the Swiss relief committee for Jews in Hungary. It was also referred to by the abbreviation SHC and popularly known as the Bányai Committee, after its chairman.[2] As its title indicated, the SHC originally saw its role as a relief society with the primary aim of collecting money; but Mantello, with his diplomatic vision, well-placed connections, and long experience in rescue efforts, pressed it to adopt a much broader rescue approach.

The SHC quickly adopted the rescue policies advocated by Mantello and pursued them throughout the Hungarian tragedy, thus becoming a valuable rescue lobby. It represented Hungarian Jewry to the Jewish organizations, the Swiss and Allied governments, and international bodies, especially the International Red Cross. The SHC was particularly effective in two areas: gathering information about the situation of Jews in Hungary from various sources, including the Hungarian media, and translating it into German and English; and initiating rescue proposals, which it distributed to representatives of the Jewish organizations, the IRC, and the Allied governments.

The SHC's first step, however, was to achieve legal status, no small feat in a country that had a policy of abstention from conflict. Switzerland, because of its fear of German sensibilities, maintained very strict censorship in favor of its historic neutrality. In practice, for example, this meant that no anti-German articles could be published unless they had previously appeared in the publication of another neutral country.[3] Also, Switzerland allowed only Swiss citizens to engage in political or relief and rescue activity.[4] Thus, when the SHC went to the Cantonal Police to establish its legality, the police approved every member of Swiss-Hungarian origin except Geza Pallai, who, although on the board of a prominent export-import company, was not a Swiss citizen. Only after Roswell McClelland personally intervened on his behalf was Pallai allowed to participate.[5]

After attaining legal status, the SHC had to establish its credentials in rescue among the representatives of the Jewish organizations, as well as the Allied and neutral governments. Above all, the SHC desired to create good relations with the War Refugee Board, a connection that represented the best hope for facilitating the rescue of Hungarian Jewry. This was so not merely because of the WRB's actual power and prestige, but because of its tremendous potential influence on Swiss authorities.

Under Mantello's relentless pressure, the SHC quickly swung into action.[6] Within a week or so, it presented itself and its rescue program to most of the Jewish organizations, such as the SIG and the Joint, and to non-Jewish bodies as well. Mantello attempted not merely to make the Jewish organizations aware of the SHC, but to seek a reasonable level of cooperation and even unity among them. He arranged for two emergency meetings in Geneva, to be held on March 27 and 28, with representatives of most of the Jewish organizations. (Two meetings were necessary because personality and ideological clashes prevented everyone from sitting together at the same table.) Participants included Riegner of the World Jewish Congress, Lichtheim of the Jewish Agency, Dr. Samuel Scheps of Palamt, Silberschein of RELICO, Dr. Solomon Ehrmann of Agudath Israel, Dr. Rom of Mizrachi, and a representative of OSE (Oeuvre de Secours aux Enfants, a worldwide Jewish children's health organization).[7] At these meetings, Mantello reiterated his policy of distributing as many Salvadoran papers as possible, and he asked that the other representatives provide him or the SHC with any news they obtained regarding the Jewish situation in Hungary.

Despite his appeal, other representatives' previous lack of cooperation in sharing information with Mantello did not improve. They kept asking for citizenship papers but ignored his requests to share news about Hungarian Jewry. For example, at this time (April 27, 1944), Schwalb sent Mantello a letter in which he "urgently requested" that Mantello sign and stamp the enclosed Salvadoran papers and return them immediately with a courier who stood ready to take them in an attached envelope. Schwalb concluded, "We recently obtained very bad reports from Hungary. Deportations have already begun," but he never provided copies of this or any other report to Mantello.[8]

With the help of several trustworthy couriers, such as the attachés from Turkey and Portugal, Mantello sent hundreds of Salvadoran papers to Hungary. To save the recipients valuable time, these papers were already filled out and signed. However, because Hungarian Jewry had already been sealed off by the Germans, Mantello was unable to get any response from the recipients.[9]

At the time of the occupation of Hungary, Mantello wrote a proposal that described the rescue role he envisioned for the SHC, as well as his rescue ideas in general. All of his points became part of the official program that the SCH offered to the various international bodies, including the War Refugee Board and the IRC.[10] In the proposal, Mantello expressed his belief that the WRB should play a key role because it would be able to contact all other governments, even enemy governments, through protective powers (i.e., neutral countries that undertook to represent one of the warring sides. An example of this would be Switzerland's representation of most Latin American countries). Because it represented America at the height of its power, the WRB had the most influence with American governmental agencies, including legations and embassies.

Among the ideas Mantello suggested was that the WRB use its all-encompassing power to persuade the members of the United Nations, primarily the Latin American countries, to confer temporary citizenship on Hitler's most vulnerable victims, especially if there would be an opportunity to evacuate children. The IRC would convey the necessary information and photos that needed to be attached to the Salvadoran citizenship papers. In line with his global perspective, Mantello also suggested that Jewish organizations in the neutral countries such as Turkey, Sweden, and Portugal emulate the SHC and make use of their common fate by utilizing their influence with their own governments. Another clause that he stressed again was the great importance of continuous collection and dissemination of information on the German-Hungarian persecution of the Jews.

Finally, Mantello's proposal lauded President Roosevelt's founding of the War Refugee Board in January 1944. He pointed out the United States' moral stature as Hitler's archenemy and leader of the world's democracies, and, above all, he emphasized that the president and the full might of his government now stood firmly behind the efforts to rescue European Jews.[11]

Mantello then wrote a second essay, entitled "Exposé," in which he provided the latest information about the Jewish situation, including the ghettoization of much of Carpatho-Ruthenian Jewry in primitive camps surrounded by barbed wire. At this point, he was not privy to Weissmandl's warnings about the Germans' series of steps leading to the implementation of the Final Solution; he therefore warned only about the impending death of thousands from malnutrition and disease in these camps. He appealed to the IRC to do something to thwart this catastrophe, for it was the only agency that could make its way into the camps to observe, report, and demand amelioration of the wretched conditions. Because these Jews had been deprived of their rights as Hungarian citizens, Mantello begged the Allies to place them under the category of "prisoners of war" and have the IRC treat them in a manner equal to internees from other countries. He also suggested that, to counter Nazi-Hungarian anti-Semitic propaganda, the IRC should use the radio and leaflets to present a true picture of Nazi objectives and methods, as well as to warn the Nazis and their accomplices that retaliatory measures would be taken if the offenses continued. This step would be particularly effective if the Allies were to persuade the Soviet Union to issue a Roosevelt-like warning in favor of protecting the Jews, for the Soviet Army's military advance would put teeth into that warning.[12]

At the same time, Bányai wrote to the American legation in the hope that it would cable the State Department concerning the worsening situation in Hungary. Klahr Huddle, counselor of the American legation, responded on behalf of Ambassador Lelland Harrison that the legation was aware of the situation and would cable Bányai's urgent message to the State Department. However, he made it clear that the SHC would have to pay for the telegram. Bányai immediately responded that the SHC would be glad to pay these and other rescue-related expenses. Apparently, the War Refugee Board had not allocated any money for such crucial rescue tools as cables.[13]

Bányai set up two additional meetings, one with the sympathetic papal nuncio Filippe Bernadini, and one with the Joint. He met with Bernadini on March 29 to introduce the SHC and describe the current Hungarian situation, in the hope of reaching the influential but quiescent Holy See. The SHC wanted the Vatican to use its considerable influence with the Hungarian Church—especially its primate, Cardinal Jusztinián Serédi—to help the Jews. Bányai asked Bernadini to instruct the clergy to shelter Jews in the monasteries and convents, and especially to help secure the lives of children and spiritual leaders. Bernadini promised to convey these suggestions to the Holy See.[14]

The next day, March 30, Bányai met with Saly Mayer of the Joint. Although Bányai had met Mayer almost a week earlier and had sent a written request regarding the IRC, he wanted to engage in a more detailed discussion, for the Joint's financial support for any rescue scheme was crucial for success. (As had everyone else, Mantello and the SHC provided Mayer with all reports and rescue suggestions but received little response.)[15]

Among the most important tasks performed by the SHC was the compilation of information concerning the situation of the Jews in Hungary. This was carried out by scanning the Hungarian radio and press for details relating to anti-Semitic decrees, laws, Hungarian propaganda, speeches, and statements by political figures, especially the viciously anti-Semitic Baky and Endre. The SHC also dispatched specific news items to McClelland as early as May. Besides this, Bányai sent McClelland a series of background reports. One of these was a nineteen-page series of reports on different facets of the ongoing Hungarian-Jewish tragedy derived from the Hungarian, and occasionally foreign, media. These concerned anti-Semitic propaganda and information regarding anti-Jewish measures taken by the Hungarian government during the first two months of occupation.[16]

The first report was a compilation of extracts of public statements beginning on March 20 and concluding on May 16, the day after mass deportations had begun. One excerpt cited the April 9 edition of the Budapest paper *Nemzetti Ujsag,* which detailed the appointment of a Jewish Council (Judenrat), relating its duties and the names and identification of its members.[17] Still another excerpt listed all Jewish authors whose works were henceforth banned,[18] and a third, from a May 12 newspaper, reported on László Endre's trip through the provinces of Carpatho-Ruthenia, detailing the ghettoization of thirty-four towns.[19] Quoting the newspaper *Magyarsag* of May 16, the report cited a speech by Endre Baky in an article entitled "On the Territories East of the River Tisza [i.e., Carpatho-Ruthenia] 320,000 Jews Have Been Shut into the Ghettoes." Baky declared, "First and foremost, we must rid the Hungarian people of Jewry . . . we must remove every Jew of [*sic*] the country; not a single one is going to stay here."[20] The SHC sent entire issues of Hungarian newspapers, especially the German-language *Pester-Lloyd*, previously the foremost Hungarian newspaper and widely read by foreigners, to influential people such as Pastor Vogt.[21]

By mid-April, as conditions in Hungary worsened, the Swiss government carried out its first foray into internal Hungarian anti-Jewish policy. Hungary had frozen all Jewish assets, confiscated all Jewish businesses, and forcibly replaced their management. On the suggestion of Bern, the Swiss legation in Budapest informed the Hungarian Foreign Ministry that these measures were adversely affecting Swiss businesses with Jewish partners, and demanded that the Hungarian government take all precautions necessary to avoid harming any of its interests. To add an edge to its demand, the Swiss threatened that if Hungary should fail to comply, it would take retaliatory measures against Hungarian interests in Switzerland; it might, for instance, suspend "the agreement about the exchange of goods and money between the Kingdom of Hungary and the Swiss Federal Republic . . . which would remain in effect until there was full clarification that all Swiss claims were secured."[22] In addition, within days, the Swiss legation in Budapest provided letters of protection for those Swiss businesses with Jewish partners—making them, in effect, Swiss property. By April 26, a response from Hungary settled the matter to Switzerland's satisfaction.[23]

It is debatable whether Ambassador Jäger in Budapest merely reflected the reluctance of the Swiss government to get involved in rescue efforts, or whether he was, in the words of one Hungarian diplomat, "a timid man, and not what one would call a forceful personality." Jaeger played no role in the rescue efforts until he was pressed into service after the transformation of Swiss public opinion through the press campaign (see below).[24]

One manifestation of Swiss indifference to the Jewish fate before the press campaign involved the use of Salvadoran citizenship papers. In response to a plea from Bányai to transmit a number of Salvadoran papers to Jews in German-occupied territories, the IRC refused to provide any assistance. The IRC was joined in its negative policy by the Swiss government, which threw its diplomatic weight against any participation in such efforts. Thus, on June 7, 1944, Mr. Pury of the Division of Foreign Affairs wrote the following letter to Minister B. Bona, head of the Department of Foreign Affairs, in which he noted,

> We are pleased to send you a copy of two letters. . . . We sent to the Swiss legation in Berlin and in Budapest about a matter concerning representation of El Salvador interests.
>
> The instructions we are giving to Minister Feldscher [in Berlin] are intended to prevent our representatives in Germany from intervening in favor of Salvadoran nationals who are not recognized by their government.
>
> Moreover, since Switzerland is not responsible for representing the interests of El Salvador in Hungary, we are warning Minister Jaeger about requests which could be made to him by *so-called Salvadoran nationals.* (emphasis added)[25]

As late as July 5, the Swiss legation in Budapest remained hesitant to provide letters of protection for holders of Palestine certificates, on the following bureaucratic grounds: Because these persons were not officially protected by Switzerland, the legation did not want to weaken the value of its genuine protective papers in the eyes of the Germans by processing papers of dubious validity. Moreover, it did not want to have thousands of its letters in the hands of people who, properly speaking, had no claim to them.[26]

The IRC had likewise refused to transmit such documents. Interestingly enough, the author of this letter noted correctly that Mantello must have sent these documents through another channel. He then suggested to the Swiss ambassador that if any Jews were to show up with such papers, copies should be made and sent to Bern. Officials there would ask the El Salvador government directly whether Bern should take action. A copy of this letter from the Department of Foreign Affairs was also sent to Ambassador Jaeger in Budapest.[27]

The IRC had access to much information concerning the fate of Hungarian Jews from numerous Jewish sources and from its own delegates, yet until mid-July, after Mantello's press campaign, and pressure by the Swiss public, it took a cold and narrow stance.

On May 2, the War Refugee Board sent a memorandum to the IRC, which read in part, "It is urged by the WRB that the International Red Cross, through considered approaches to the German authorities and the authorities of the occupied areas and through any other possible means, do all that is possible to facilitate the departure of the refugees in question to neutral countries which may receive them. . . . The WRB is ready to collaborate with the International Red Cross in every way."[28]

In reply, Max Huber, president of the IRC, defended his organization's long-standing refusal to deal with the persecution of Jews. Huber stated:

> Steps of this nature by the ICRC [*sic*] would go so far beyond the limits of their tradition . . . and . . . the government to whom such a request might be addressed would not fail to view this proposal from that particular angle.
>
> In the provisions of the International agreements the ICRC [*sic*] have only a slender basis upon which to found their humanitarian activities. The latter are, therefore, dependent upon [the] goodwill of belligerent states and can only take practical shape insofar as they are accepted or solicited by the government concerned.
>
> Consequently, the ICRC [*sic*] might lay themselves open to the objection that they were going beyond the limits of their competencies, and trespassing upon the internal concerns of a state should they act on behalf of certain categories of persons [i.e., Jews] whom that state [i.e., Germany] considered to be subject exclusively to its domestic legislation.[29]

On the same day, the IRC responded similarly to Bányai's poignant plea for assistance to its delegate, Jean Schwartzenberg, saying that "any intervention on its part did not come within the scope of its mandate."[30]

Bányai also appealed for aid to the WRB in Washington. In a cable of May 2, sent via Ambassador Harrison's good offices, he informed the WRB of Hungary's most recent confiscatory laws, specifically the expropriation of virtually all of Hungarian Jewry's businesses, properties, and bank accounts. He suggested that America inform the Hungarian population of this latest barbarity through radio broadcasts and leaflets dropped over major cities, impressing upon them that anyone holding Jewish property was guilty of possessing stolen goods and would be prosecuted after the war.[31]

Bányai approached Swiss theologians as well, this time in the company of Rabbi Taubes. Although he usually acted as the SHC's sole representative to organizations, he would sometimes make visits together with others, particularly Rabbi Taubes; in his role as head of the Swiss Rabbis' Committee, Taubes had already formed good connections with members of the clergy, especially the influential Pastor Vogt. True to his humanitarian nature, Vogt not only received the two men with the greatest sympathy, he also immediately contacted several important Protestant leaders, such as Dr. W. A. Visser't Hooft (the Dutch secretary of the nascent World Council of Churches), Dr. Alphons Koechlin, president of the Swiss Protestant Churches, and Prof. Emil Brunner.[32]

Taubes's objective was for Vogt to use his contacts among other church leaders, especially within the Evangelical Church, which had a Hungarian counterpart.[33] However, the extraordinary rapidity of events far outstripped the slow process of meetings and discussions intended to halt the ongoing tragedy of Hungarian Jews. On May 2, news arrived that Carpatho-Ruthenia and North Transylvania had been declared out of bounds to all travelers. It is now known

Dr. W. A. Visser't Hooft. Dutch theologian and
secretary of the nascent World Council of Churches.
One of the four signers of Vogt's letter of July 4.
Courtesy of Ringier Pressehaus.

that this development presaged the next stage of deportation and annihilation, which were accomplished with such speed that they left even the most seasoned rescue activists in shock and in despair.[34]

Despite numerous snippets of information gleaned from news clippings and the hints in hundreds of postcards from Hungary, no solid information about the deteriorating Jewish situation in Hungary was available to the SHC.[35] Almost daily, detailed letters and reports on the worsening situation were being sent to Schwalb, Mayer, McClelland, and others,[36] but neither Mantello nor the SHC were privy to them. Throughout May and the first half of June, he and his brother remained ignorant of the fate the Germans were preparing for Hungarian Jewry by enlarging the death camp Auschwitz.

The Auschwitz Protocols

Rescue efforts until this point were too often desultory and halfhearted, but developments were taking place in Auschwitz whose consequences would soon push the forces of rescue to a new intensity.

In February and March, the Nazis had engaged in elaborate, feverish work to enlarge the death facilities of Auschwitz, to efficiently murder the approximately 800,000 Hungarian Jews. An SS officer is supposed to have remarked to some Jews in Auschwitz, "We will soon eat fine Hungarian sausage."[37] Then, in April and May, several inmates escaped from the camp, seeking to inform the free world of the horrors of Auschwitz and to warn them of Hungarian Jewry's impending doom. The Western public, including virtually all of Hitler's potential victims, still naïvely believed in the existence of a "world opinion" or "collective liberal conscience" that would be the Jews' ultimate salvation. One inmate expressed this hope succinctly: "If only somebody would succeed in escaping and contacting our free Jewish brethren and alerting . . . the powerful [world] leaders and the press, they would arouse world opinion against the Nazi atrocities, and people would pressure their governments to save the Jews still in their homes and to stop the daily mass murder we are witnessing here."[38]

To move this "world conscience," the underground in Auschwitz assisted Walter Rosenberg and Alfred Wetzler, two courageous young Jews from Slovakia, who were determined to escape. (During their escape, the two assumed the Slovakian-sounding names of Rudolf Vrba and Jozko [Josef] Lanik respectively, and were subsequently known by these pseudonyms.) In their daring escape, they were aided by the underground in Auschwitz. The two escapees had been clerks in crucial locations in Auschwitz-Birkenau since 1942 and had enjoyed relative freedom of movement. This had enabled them to observe the arrivals of the new transports and other vital information.[39]

They escaped from Auschwitz on April 7 and reached Zilina, in Slovakia, on April 25, where they were put in touch with Andre Steiner, a member of the Working Group. They were joined at his house by Dr. Oscar Neumann, who was soon followed by Oskar Krasznyansky from Bratislava. For two days, Krasznyansky interrogated the two escapees, checking much of their information against previously known facts.[40]

Based on this data and with the two men's help, Krasznyansky compiled a twenty-six-page German-language report (typed up by Steiner's wife, Tova), known variously as the "Auschwitz Protocols," the "Protocols," or the "Auschwitz Report." Besides describing the extraordinary atrocities and cruelties that were taking place in this death camp, the report listed all the transports to Auschwitz from the various countries and the number of those who had been murdered from April 1942 through April 1944—a total of 1,765,000.

The details of the dispatching of this report to various Jewish contacts are still not entirely clear. Different versions of the Protocols, of various lengths and with various additions, were sent out.[41] Within a day or so, a copy was given to Kastner, who had come to Bratislava at about that time. Kastner asked Krasznyansky to prepare a Hungarian translation for Horthy,[42] but he showed the document only to his friends in the Vaada.[43]

In addition, within a few days, both Freudiger and Schwalb obtained copies. Schwalb dispatched them to his contacts in Istanbul, Geneva, London, and Jerusalem, and then called a meeting of four Jewish representatives, including Mayer, Lichtheim, and Riegner; together they presented this horrifying news to McClelland.[44]

In his postwar memoirs, Vrba notes that by April 26, Krasznyansky and Neumann had assured him that a copy of the report had been dispatched to the Hungarians—that is, the Vaada. However, as Braham has pointed out, most of the people who were supposed to have received copies do not mention them in their postwar memoirs or oral recollections. Freudiger, who recalled having obtained a copy from Weissmandl sometime between the end of May and early June, was the the only one who showed the report to the other members of the Jewish Council.[45]

Besides composing various versions of the report, Weissmandl attached the pleas to bomb the Auschwitz rail lines to every copy of his version of the Protocols, as well as to scores of cables and letters that he dispatched to all Jewish organizations and contacts in Switzerland and Turkey. These organizations, in turn, relayed them to their contacts in Jerusalem, London, and New York.

A second series of the Protocols and warnings was dispatched by the Working Group on May 16, the day after the start of the mass deportations of 12,000 Jews per day from Hungary. This series reached even more destinations in the free world than the first. One of the recipients was Natan Schwalb, who received his thirty-three-page version on May 17, twenty-four hours after it was sent. That same day, Schwalb had copies made on his Hechalutz stationery, which he immediately dispatched to his contacts abroad. For example, on May 19, he sent a copy to Eliyahu Dobkin, cochairman of the Jewish Agency's Aliyah Department and head of its Youth and Pioneer Department. In the letter he attached to the report, Schwalb wrote: "Upon return from yesterday's phone conversation concerning Ella [i.e., Slovakia] and its Mazaf [sic] [i.e., the situation of its Jews] I am sending you urgently . . . this very important report and beg you to read it immediately together with David B[en] Gurion and Mosche Czertok [sic], and undertake urgent steps. . . . I'll phone again in two days."[46]

Weissmandl also created a five-page summary and his extraordinary plea as a companion piece to the Protocols. He began, "We are sending you a special courier about the terrifying situation. . . . Yesterday, at the rate of 12,000 per day, began the deportations of Hungarian Jews from Carpatho-Ruthenia— the beginning of the end for its 320,000 Jews." In a page and a half of very clear points, Weissmandl provided the essence of the Protocols and the background to the developing Hungarian tragedy. He then added the following:

> And you, our brothers in all the free lands, and you, the governments of all the countries and states, where are you? What are you doing about the extermination, which long ago consumed over six million Jews, and which still today swallows 10,000 a day! In the name of all those murdered and those still condemned to death, we call upon all of you! Remain silent no longer! Do not associate with those resting their hands in their laps! Have no doubts about the accuracy of the atrocity reports, especially now, when we are dealing with our last remnant. We plead with you in the name of the blood of thousands and in the name of the tears of additional thousands, we demand immediate help![47]

Weissmandl then presented a series of seven concrete suggestions, including three detailed points about the bombardment of the rail lines to Auschwitz and the camp itself. He demanded that Jews send money—not trifling sums, but millions—to save those who could still be saved, through various means. From the depths of his heart, he sought to shake the Jews out of their lethargy:

> Brothers, don't you realize in what hell we are living! And all our pleas are worthless, even less than the supplications of a beggar! You throw us a few pennies along with a questionnaire. Are we dealing with a charity case? For whom is it easier, you, the dispenser of pennies, or we, who are providing the blood and tears in the valley of hell! Who nowadays demands an accounting! At the very least, deal with us with no less alacrity than do the murderers! . . . We've already informed you a number of times about the tragic situation. Do you have greater faith in the veracity of the murderers than in the victims! Is this really possible! May the dear God open your eyes and give you the opportunity and right, during this last hour, to rescue our remnant!

Weissmandl's final paragraph reiterated the key rescue points and the plea to bomb the primary rail lines to Auschwitz, and concluded,

> Writing from the sea of tears, and in anticipation of your help and rescue, for today the deed is of primary concern, we remain with best wishes.

Signed,

M[ichael] B[er Weissmandl]
G[isi] Fl[eischman]
(Hebrew signatures)

Weissmandl's frantic attempts to inform the world about Auschwitz and his plea for the Allies to halt the mass extermination took several forms. Besides sending out copies of both the complete and brief versions of the Auschwitz Report to as many Jewish leaders as possible, he sent out scores of cables and letters. His messages were sent to at least five sources in Switzerland: Natan Schwalb of Hechalutz, Saly Mayer of the Joint, Gerhard Riegner of the World Jewish Congress, Sternbuch of the Vaad Hatzalah in New York, and Boruch Meshulem Lebovitz, Weissmandl's boyhood friend. Lebovitz, in turn, dispatched Weissmandl's messages to Rabbi Solomon Schonfeld in London, where he headed the Chief Rabbi's Council, a very active rescue organization. Schonfeld was greatly inspired and influenced by the rescue plans of Weissmandl, his former teacher. Moreover, in Hungary they were usually sent to Freudiger, in the form of coded letters sent by courier.[48]

Two recipients of these cables sought to convey his plea to the American

government. The first was Sternbuch, who had received numerous cables start-
ing May 16 and brought to McClelland to relay to the Vaad Hatzalah in New
York. By June 22, Sternbuch noted to McClelland in great frustration that all
this time he had never received a response. However, ten days earlier, on May
12, Sternbuch had sent this same message to the Vaad Hatzalah in New York,
via the illegal, secret Polish cable, which bypassed the State Department's censorship. This reached Jacob Rosenheim of World Agudath Israel, the home of
the Vaad Hatzalah, the following day; and by the eighteenth, Rosenheim
implored John Pehle of the War Refugee Board to take action as soon as possible. He added that the paralysis of the rail traffic to Auschwitz would at least
slow down the annihilation process.[49] Pehle, not thoroughly convinced of the
efficacy of this plan, made a halfhearted and unsuccessful attempt to persuade
the War Department to act on this request.[50]

The second attempt to reach the American government through the Jewish
circles was made by Yitzchok Grünbaum, head of the Jewish Agency's Vaad
Hahatzalah in Jerusalem. On June 2, he arranged for L. C. Pinkerton, the
American chargé d'affaires in Jerusalem, to cable the WRB in Washington.
While his message did go through, nothing seems to have occurred.[51] There
were a few further attempts by various parties to awaken the American government to halt the mass murders in Auschwitz, but no concrete action was
ever taken to accommodate this plea.

Beyond the indifference of the American government, the American Jewish establishment never used its political power to pressure Roosevelt amid his
election campaign for an unprecedented fourth term. He would have had no
choice but to respond to an outcry at such a politically sensitive time, but none
was forthcoming. This lack of response was especially poignant during the critical month of June 1944, when appeals to the government to bomb the
Auschwitz rail lines were made by several Jewish and non-Jewish sources. This
relatively minor military intervention could easily have been carried out had
the president so desired, for the Allies controlled the skies then, and its armies
were advancing on every front; the successful D day invasion of France was
only one indication of their progress. The fact is that the Allies twice (August
20 and September 13, 1944) bombed Auschwitz, or better the Buna plants and
other "war-related" targets, manned by Auschwitz inmaters, only a few miles
from the crematoriums. During these bombings, accidental bombs dropped
on Auschwitz itself, killing both SS guards and inmates. One of my key interviewees, concerning Auschwitz, was Mrs. Rivka Paskus. She was working in

the Gestapo office when these "accidental" bombs fell and her friend was killed. Several other inmate interviewees, including Rabbi Menachem Rubin, also noted how they all wished that the bombs would fall on the entire camp despite their being killed.[52]

However, for most American Jews, the rescue of European Jewry was not their highest priority. The American Jewish community and its foremost leader, Rabbi Stephen S. Wise, worshiped their beloved president, the architect of the New Deal, the welfare state that represented their dreams for the messianic era; they did not want to pressure Roosevelt in any way or take any action that might cast a shadow on his good graces. Indeed, Roosevelt was revered by European Jews as well, who considered him the best friend the Jews had.[53]

Mantello's Arrest

Amid this stage of the Hungarian tragedy, while Mantello was seeking to rescue as many Jews as possible, he suddenly found himself under house arrest. On May 3, as he later recalled, Heinrich Rothmund, head of the Swiss Alien Police, entered his hotel suite, accompanied by several officers. Rothmund had previously attempted to keep Mantello from bringing his son to Switzerland (see chapter 3), and he was trying once again to obstruct his activities.

When Mantello was brought to Rothmund's office, he angrily demanded, "Are you the Gestapo? What justification do you have to arrest me?" Rothmund said, "Do you think you're in Palestine?" Mantello responded, "I'm not in Palestine, I'm in the heart of Switzerland. But do you think you are in the middle of Berlin?" Rothmund did not offer Mantello a seat until several minutes into this heated exchange, and when he finally did so, Mantello refused. "The time to offer me a seat was when I came in, not now. Now it's too late." He repeated, "I'm in Switzerland, but you're in Berlin. Some day, you'll get your punishment—not from me, but from the One Above."[54]

Mantello was not released until sixteen days later, on May 19, during which time he was unable to issue or sign any Salvadoran papers. He was charged with black-market activities in regard to the chronographs and other instruments he had helped the British acquire (see chapter 3). It is clear from the Swiss interrogation records that he had purchased at least a thousand chronographs, watches, and watch parts; according to Mantello, they were sent to New York on behalf of British intelligence, which had requested them as necessary for the pilots of the fighter planes, and had nothing whatsoever to do with the black market. The details concerning the involvement of intelligence personnel in the watch transactions cannot be verified either by the Swiss interrogation documents or from the postwar testimony that Walter Garrett, head of the British Exchange Telegraph, offered on Mantello's behalf; any intelligence activities would obviously have been kept secret. Nevertheless, intelligence officials Allen Dulles and Commodore Freddie West, as well as Garrett himself, later extended their full support to Mantello in his press campaign, underlining the veracity of his claim that he had assisted Allied intelligence (see chapter 7).[55]

Although the formal charge against Mantello involved the chronographs, he was questioned more extensively concerning the Salvadoran papers, and was accused of selling them for an unconscionable profit. The baselessness of that charge has been demonstrated (chapter 3). Although the matter would follow him into the early postwar years (see chapter 12), Rothmund's charge was now dropped when Mantello deposited 2,000 Swiss francs to cover any fines for the possible violation of police regulations. It seems that the accusation had originally been made by an informer who sought to get Mantello into trouble.

Desperate Letters

By late June, the Jewish leaders in occupied Hungary and Slovakia had heard the news that the deportation of 320,000 Jews from the provinces had been completed. Carpatho-Ruthenia was completely Judenrein; all its Jews had gone to Auschwitz. Apparently, the only surviving enclave were the 250 to 300,000 Jews in and around Budapest. A sense of despair and hopelessness arose within the ranks of the Jewish leaders, for they saw no way of halting the rapid conclusion of the Final Solution in Hungary. This was apparent in letters sent out from Budapest and Bratislava.[56] Although the capital city appeared outwardly calm and the general Jewish populace was unaware of the immediacy of the danger, the leadership clearly saw the Nazis' preparations as the beginning of the last act of the Final Solution in Hungary.

The letters from Budapest, which reached Natan Schwalb, Saly Mayer, and Roswell McClelland, provided independent, reliable, and firsthand accounts of the tragic situation in Hungary and the danger to Budapest Jewry in particular. In addition, information was transmitted by non-Jewish sources, including Nazi sources, that confirms these letters for the historian. Tragically, none of the letters were made available to Mantello, who did not learn about the situation in Hungary until weeks later, when tens of thousands of Jewish victims were on their way to Auschwitz.

In May, Friedrich Born, the sympathetic delegate of the IRC in Budapest, described the situation in the city in a report to Max Huber, head of the IRC.[57] This letter, mentioned earlier, was written by Moshe Krausz, who had intended it for Chaim Barlas in Istanbul.[58] Edouard de Haller, the Swiss federal government's delegate for Mutual International Aid and a member of the IRC, got hold of this report ("owing," wrote Haller, "to an indiscretion"), and a few days later forwarded it to Huber.

The essential portion of Krausz's message read as follows:

> It would seem that 300,000 [Jews] from Hungarian provinces have been interned in concentration camps; 170,000 of them, according to the information received through discreet channels, have been deported to the Auschwitz destruction camp, while the remaining 130,000 are being deported now. Also, 200,000 Jews have been concentrated in provincial ghettos to be transported to Auschwitz. The Jews of Budapest, numbering about 300,000 in round figures, are to be sent to the Auschwitz destruction camp beginning June 8. Every effort to save them has failed.[59]

Ben-Tov, the authority on the IRC and Hungarian Jewry, has found no comments from either the IRC or the Swiss government relating to this report.

An exchange of Nazi memos on June 6 and 7 confirms the tragic facts in Krausz's letter. Eberhard Thadden, legation counselor and expert in Jewish affairs in Section Inland II of the German foreign office, suggested to Horst Wagner, his chief at Inland II, that it would be a good idea for the Germans to time the deportations of Budapest Jewry to coincide with the Allied invasion of France on June 6, for "it would cause the world press to ignore the former because of the overwhelming importance of the military operation."[60] In response, Veesenmayer dismissed Thadden's idea of "'camouflaging' the Aktion against the Jews of Budapest" because he felt that *world public opinion will not be shocked greatly by the proposed measures against the Jews of Budapest, [since] outside opinion [has] paid very little attention to the 'evacuation measures' undertaken against the Jews until then*" (emphasis added).[61]

On or shortly after May 22, Czech ambassador Jaromir Kopecky obtained important information from Weissmandl, which had come from his contacts among the railroad workers. On June 19, he transmitted this information to

McClelland, stating that "5,000 Jews were deported daily to Poland, probably to the camp of Oswiecim, and 7,000 through sub-Carpathian Russia." McClelland appended a dry, cold note to this letter: "The source is reliable but the figures are high, although lower than the 15,000 daily over the Kaschau-Preschov line received by Sternbuch from Bratislava. *Am doing utmost to check these figures*" (emphasis added).[62]

On June 12, in two separate letters, Freudiger and Josef Blum, the Joint's representative in Budapest, provided Hugo Donnebaum (Sternbuch's HIJEFS colleague in charge of dealing with Hungary) with virtually the same dismal picture of the Hungarian Jews' fate. They each wrote, "To date, 400,000 people have been deported. . . . As far as Budapest is concerned . . . we are expecting the worst. . . . Every day another 12,000 Jewish people are being taken. . . . There is no point in even hoping for a general halt to deportations."[63]

This desperate situation is confirmed in a June 13 dispatch from Veesenmayer to Ribbentrop. Veesenmayer explained that by mid-July, "the last zone [i.e., Budapest] would be *cleared*" (emphasis added).[64] On June 14, Rudolph Kastner wrote:

> Up to today, 400,000 have been deported. . . . As far as Budapest is concerned, we should not depend on useless hopes. . . . We are expecting the worst. . . . It is admitted by Ashkenaz [i.e., the Germans that] Group Three [i.e., those not selected for labor] will be destroyed in the infamous Auschwitz [camp]. . . . Every day another 12,000 Jewish people are being taken. . . . There is no one talking about a general stop of deportations. . . . What we can negotiate now is the rescue of a small number of the people here.[65]

Several days later, Bányai submitted another equally devastating report to McClelland and Schwalb. This report had been written by a non-Jewish Swiss woman, obviously well connected, who had recently returned from Budapest, and described the situation there before June 15. This humanitarian woman vented her disappointment at the members of the Swiss consulate in Budapest, describing one of them as a "convinced Nazi"; of another, Minister Maximilian Jäger, she wrote that he "is married to a German and his sympathies lie in that direction." The IRC delegates, she claimed, were no better. The only person for whom she had kind words was a Dr. Kilchmann, whom she considered a "decent man" who "refuses to mix into any political matters" out of fear. She added that while many Jews were talking about the gas chambers and about suicide, they did not want to believe it, saying, "Such brutalities are inconceivable."[66] Schwalb wrote to McClelland on June 20:

> At the beginning of this week [June 13], we received from our friends in Slovakia several items concerning conditions in several extermination camps. Despite the fact that *you have already seen the report [a week earlier] on Auschwitz and Birkenau* [i.e., the Protocols] at Dr. Kop[ecky]'s in Geneva, I take the liberty of enclosing it to you.
>
> In addition, I am sending you photocopies [i.e., stats] of three sketches [of the camp and its installations] attached to this report. I also enclose a photocopy of the Hebrew letter [i.e., Weissmandl's] from Jewish quarters in Bratislava concerning the situation in Hungary, as well as various proposals and requests. In order to avoid any delay, I translated literally the last [Hebrew letter] for your convenience. The copies [of reports] from May 17th are also included.
>
> Hopefully, the appeals of thousands of suffering . . . Jews facing destruction will find an empathetic ear and immediate, practical help.[67]

On June 10, a colleague of Kastner's named Perez Revesz wrote to Schwalb from Budapest, "Still under the impact of the terrible events, I am sitting down to write to you. I do not know how to start. . . . The most terrible thing [concerning] *Mazav Klali* [i.e., the general situation]. There are no words for it. The tempo is unbelievable, and the prospects inconceivable. This week the third *Meah Elef* [hundred thousand] was deported and the Carpathians [Carpatho-Ruthenia] are just about *Judenrein*."[68]

On June 23, the Judenrat, by now fully aware of the fate awaiting the Jews in the capital, entreated Regent Horthy to halt the impending deportations, providing him with detailed statistics of the number of Jews deported from each of the Hungarian towns. The Judenrat officials had a three-word evaluation of the situation that said everything: "All is lost."[69] The regent did not even respond.[70]

On June 14, Kastner dispatched a report to Schwalb which read in part, "The deportations are in full swing. . . . If this procedure is not stopped at the last minute, Hungary will be without Jews in a few weeks. There are already no Jews [left] in the Provinces. The Red Cross, the foreign representatives, the churches, have at best made some very weak attempts to alleviate the process but they found no willing ears. . . . These are the bitter and stark facts."[71]

In the later report of June 24, Kastner's colleagues, Perez [Revesz], Zvi [Szigeli], Eli [Sajo], and Yehuda,[72] added the following:

> We are in the midst of a most frightful tragedy. The stream of trains to Auschwitz cannot be delayed or halted. Deportations are in full swing. There are no words for it. The tempo of [the deportations] is unbelievable, and the prospects are terrible. Nowhere is there anybody who can do something for us. The Church is evading its responsibility! We want to try something, but it is as if the earth would be opened up before us. [On June 24] the concentration of Jews in the capital has been completed. The last act of the drama begins. . . . Five days were given for the transfer of 250,000 Jews, and three more days were added. . . . The deportation of the so-called Motherland . . . will probably be completed in two weeks. . . . If there is no miracle, the process will be completed by August.[73]

In another letter to Schwalb, Kastner's colleagues confirmed his pessimistic outlook and also described the frustrations involved in their rescue efforts. These included the so-called Kastner Train, which they hoped would soon leave Budapest:

> The general situation [is] unfortunately very bad. . . . We have tried through our work to save at least the pioneers [i.e., the seven hundred Palestine certificate holders], *the most valuable part of our people,* in conjunction with our larger approach [i.e., the Brand negotiations of a million Jews for ten thousand trucks]. Our rescue has four categories: Return flight to Slovakia . . . flight to Rumania [*sic*] . . . preparing documents [i.e., Palestine certificates and Latin American papers] . . . and [preparation for hiding] in caves. . . . I went to visit there [Slovakia] and brought Naomi [Gisi Fleischman] some money and Salvador papers. . . . Believe me, we are frequently desperate. (emphasis added)

Unsure of the reliability of their plans, they added, "Will it be a real aliyah? Can we have faith in the Germans? And in the end, will this be a deportation? . . . We have nothing to lose."[74] Schwalb provided McClelland with this and numerous other such letters.

On June 25, the situation looked graver than ever for the Jews of Budapest. The government declared a curfew for all the Jews in the capital, and they were required to wear the dreaded yellow star. For the first time, the rumors and fears of ghettoization and mass deportations that had been circulating for months began to assume a frightening reality not only for the Judenrat leaders, but also for all the city's Jews.[75]

At the same time that the Swiss Hungarian Committee dispatched these desperate letters to Schwalb, Mayer, and McClelland, it also made constant appeals to the War Refugee Board. However, neither Mantello nor the SHC were privy to the wealth of information that had been pouring into the Jewish organizations in Switzerland since the end of May—information with which McClelland was being inundated. This included many copies and versions of the Protocols or letters from Weissmandl and Kastner, which provided the latest details on the deportations along with pleas for the Allies to bomb the rail lines to Auschwitz.

Until late in June, Bányai of the SHC possessed nothing more than "strong rumors" and "hints" in letters about the ghettoization and deportation of Hungarian Jewry. On June 18, he wrote:

> Unfortunately, terrible reports about Hungary are increasing day by day. Although there are no concrete reports that people are being deported abroad, it has been proven that in many areas of Hungary, Jews are being sent in railroad cars, in great masses, to unknown destinations. Very strong rumors [indicate] that these people [exist] under the most dreary conditions. . . . Today I received from my niece . . . the following report: "Uncle Gyula and Kalman are now in . . . a metal factory, but will soon be traveling. My sister Edith and I will go in the next few days to the company Deutsch [in Germany] to work there." . . . It is really a question of thousands of innocent young girls. . . . Can we look at this without doing something? Should we not call out to the entire world and shake up the conscience of human beings and demand quick assistance before it is too late? I know that you, Mr. McClelland, want to help quickly. . . . Please help those few who are left.[76]

But McClelland never responded to any of this news.[77] In addition, McClelland received information from D. W. Maher, one of the assistants at the American legation in Bern. Maher had just conferred with an attaché to the Swiss legation in Budapest, who pointed out that he had obtained information from the head of a Jewish organization in Budapest [i.e., Freudiger]. The Swiss attaché told Maher that all the Jews [450,000] east of the Danube had been deported to Poland. He added, "It is reported that they are now dead." Moreover, although the Jews west of the Danube had not yet been deported, the Jews of Budapest were being assembled in special Jewish houses, and will be taken away at night to "extermination camps." Maher noted that the attaché had "added some lurid details of which he had no actual knowledge," and assured Maher that he did not trust his source, especially because he had been requested [by Freudiger] to go to the head of a Jewish organization [Vaad Hatzalah] in St. Gallen [i.e., Sternbuch] to pass on the information. [Freudiger] also requested that the Swiss attaché bring half a million Swiss francs from this organization for the Jews of Budapest. Neither McClelland nor the Swiss attaché followed up the tragic information emerging from Budapest.[78]

At the same time, the Yishuv conveyed much of this terrible information about Hungarian Jewry to Stephen S. Wise in the United States, through the office of the World Jewish Congress. The first message came from Yitzchok Grünbaum of the Jewish Agency's Vaad Hahatzalah in Jerusalem, who sent a cable in early June that reached the WJCong by the nineteenth. This cable undoubtedly reflected Schwalb's earlier reports from Weissmandl. Grünbaum requested that Wise "contact the War Refugee Board stop according to just received information 12,000 Hungarian Jews deported daily unknown destination during first decade [i.e., days of] May."[79]

The second message came on June 26 from Lichtheim, the Jewish Agency's representative in Geneva, who sent it after receiving a copy of Mantello's reports (see chapter 6). In his letter to Yitzchok Grünbaum of that date, Lichtheim reported:

> Meanwhile we have received most distressing reports about the situation in Hungary; the process of destruction is proceeding there even more quickly than was the case in the other countries. . . . The Provinces are already "Judenrein" and even in Budapest . . . there is no longer any hope. . . . I have informed our offices in London and New York, and various suggestions have been made . . . but there is very little hope that anything substantial will be achieved because the only method which could be effective has so far never been used: reprisals.[80]

By July 19, Dr. Leon Kubowitzki of WJCong had conveyed this concern about the Hungarian Jewry situation to Miss Florence Hoddel and Mr. J. Lesser of the War Refugee Board, but no public outcry was initiated by Wise. He did not even try to arrange a meeting of Jewish leaders with the president regarding these tragic circumstances, even though such action would have had a considerable effect on Roosevelt, as we have mentioned, during the heat of the 1944 election campaign.[81]

Non-Jewish sources in Budapest were also aware of the impending danger. After the war, Friedrich Born, a delegate of the IRC, reported to his organization that by the end of May 1944, there were already rumors of deportations in the capital, circulated especially by refugees from the provinces. Soon, most Jews in Budapest were divided into two groups, those who had converted to Christianity and those who had not, and were transferred to yellow-star houses throughout the city. Especially terrifying were the rumors of the ghettoization and deportations, which could no longer be denied; the Jews now knew that they would all be deported to Germany, and that they were totally helpless.

The Judenrat could do absolutely nothing to change the course of the German plan. All the humanitarian organizations and leaders had been made impotent by the Gestapo. The Hungarian Church was not able to manage a collective appeal to the government, and even the Hungarian Red Cross did nothing. Within weeks after the German occupation, more than 400,000 Jews were driven out of their homes and country.

Both Mantello and his brother Josef remained an important influence on the Swiss Hungarian Committee and a source of its ideas and rescue activities. However, they stayed primarily in the background, directing most of their energy toward rescue opportunities the SHC could not approach. Bányai usually represented the committee in person and in correspondence. Mantello, on the other hand, preferred to use his diplomatic status and connections to make personal contact with individuals, organizations, and governmental bodies, while Josef used his close relations with members of the Romanian legation and other bodies to pursue other rescue tracks. The brothers' efforts usually, though not always, coincided.

6

The Manoliu Mission

As noted earlier, Mantello was unaware of the massive amount of evidence on the Hungarian tragedy—in particular, the Auschwitz Report—that had been available for weeks to the American legation, virtually all the Jewish organizations in Switzerland, and many Jewish organizations abroad. As far as he was concerned, the Nazi curtain of silence surrounding Hungarian Jewry had been ruffled only by hints, rumors, and scraps of information culled from Hungarian papers. Such sources were insufficient to mount a rescue campaign, for they could readily be denied even by well-meaning persons.

Mantello decided that, to obtain authentic information, he must send a courier directly into Hungary. He and his brother searched for the right person for this dangerous mission, which would require both courage and trustworthiness. They selected a longtime friend and business associate of Josef's, Dr. Florian Manoliu, the commercial attaché at the Romanian consulate in Bern.

Manoliu had a reputation as a liberal and an anti-Nazi. He was a good friend of Grigore Gafencu, who had been Romania's foreign minister before the takeover of his opponent and head of the Iron Guard, Ion Antonescu. After withdrawing from the government, Gafencu had moved to Switzerland, where he continued to retain some measure of influence. Manoliu was also a friend and relative of another opponent of Antonescu, Iuliu Maniu, the former prime minster, who had remained in Bucharest. During the war, Manoliu had been acting as an intermediary between Gafencu and Maniu. Now both men encouraged Manoliu in his mission on behalf of the Jews. Along with his mission of mercy on behalf of Mantello, he would also be carrying messages from Gafencu to Maniu.[1]

Manoliu went not only to collect information about the Jews, but also to help them. Mantello provided him with a thousand completed and stamped Salvadoran citizenship papers, an undisclosed sum of money, and a supply of medications for the Jewish community.

The first stop on Manoliu's mission was to be Bistrice, Mantello's hometown, where his parents and their large extended family were among the city's 8,000 Jews. His relatives, along with other Jews, were to receive one hundred of the Salvadoran protective papers. Because each certificate was made out for an entire family, it would be easy to claim nonrelatives as family members. Months earlier, Mantello had provided his wife with a regular Salvador passport which had since expired, and Manoliu was now bringing her an updated one.[2]

Manoliu then planned to meet with Moshe Krausz, head of the Palestine Certificate Office in Budapest. To assure that Krausz would talk freely to Manoliu, whom he did not know, Josef Mandl tried to obtain a signed visiting card from Krausz's friend and counterpart, Dr. Samuel Scheps, head of the Palestine Certificate Office in Geneva. However, Dr. Scheps was unavailable because he was serving as a reservist in the Swiss army. Instead, Josef obtained a visiting card from Scheps's assistant, Dr. Chaim Posner, which stated in Hebrew that Manoliu was fully trustworthy. Mantello did not see the necessity for this proof; certainly Krausz, who was stranded in Nazi-occupied Hungary, would trust a diplomat who provided him with one thousand Salvadoran citizenship papers, money, and medicine. Nevertheless, he did not contest Josef's cautious measure, and indeed, the visiting card turned out to be a very helpful item.[3]

Mantello's role as initiator of the Manoliu mission is found in two crucial sources. The first is the notes taken by Wilhelm Filderman, head of the Romanian Jewish community, on his conversation with Dr. Florian Manoliu on August 21, 1944. Filderman wrote: "His Excellency [Manoliu] informed us that he is the author of the press campaign against Hungary, having passed through Budapest, from where he brought reports to Switzerland concerning the atrocities committed [by the Germans and Hungarians]. He [Manoliu] added that his [press] campaign was not instigated by himself but by Mr. George Mantello, alias George Mandl, a Romanian originally from Transylvania and the brother of Josef Mandl."[4]

This was further confirmed by Manoliu. In an interview a number of years after the war, Manoliu described the origin of his mission: "Upon the request of Mr. Mantello, I traveled to Budapest on May 22, 1944, with a number of El Salvador papers. George Mantello and his brother, Josef Mandl, gave me the assignment to ascertain the exact nature of the events [regarding the Jews] in Hungary. They also asked me to help their parents in Bistrice."[5]

Before Manoliu could leave, there was a delay of several weeks to prevent his departure, owing to efforts of the German embassy in Bern, which was aware of his anti-Nazi and liberal leanings. The Germans were particularly secretive at this time, for they were adamant that no one, not even their allies, witness the implementation of the Final Solution of Hungarian Jewry. In the end, they allowed him to travel but forbade him to debark in Budapest.

On May 22, Manoliu finally departed on his mission. As a diplomat, he was aware that the Swiss-Austrian border would not provide any obstacles, because the border guards would be unlikely to look beyond his diplomatic passport. He was more concerned about his first stop in Vienna. Therefore, he arranged for the Romanian consul in Vienna to meet him at the train station and take his diplomatic pouch, which contained the money, medicine, and Salvadoran papers into safekeeping.[6]

As he had expected, Manoliu's reputation as a liberal made him suspect, and he was quickly sent from Vienna to Berlin to be interrogated about the objective of his trip. Fortunately, the diplomatic pouch, with its incriminating evidence, was in safe hands. Manoliu complained to his German interrogators, "Aren't we allies? Why are you questioning me? Any questions about my trip should be addressed to the Romanian ambassador." Only after the strong intervention of officials in Bucharest was Manoliu permitted to return to Vienna— and then, only upon his written assurance that he would go straight to Bucharest and not debark in Budapest. In Vienna, Manoliu retrieved his diplomatic pouch before continuing on his journey.[7]

After leaving Berlin on or about June 3, Manoliu must have gone to Bucharest to deliver Gafencu's message to Maniu, remaining there until June 10. Then, instead of returning to Switzerland as his German-authorized transit visa dictated, he traveled to Bistrice in search of Mantello's family.[8] When he arrived, however, he found neither the Mandl family nor any other Jews. All he saw was a small white flag—which, a local official informed him, indicated that Bistrice was "Judenrein"; two days earlier, all the Jews had been loaded onto wagons and sent to the train station to be taken to the East. Though he did not know what "East" meant, Manoliu realized that this news did not augur well. Not to arouse any suspicion, he pretended to be pleased with the official's response and replied, "Good; we must do the same in our own country."

For several days, Manoliu traveled to various towns in Transylvania such as Kolozsvár, Satu-Mare, and Des. In all of them, he found the same white flag and the same ominous explanation: "Judenrein."[9] To find out what was happening to the Jews, he finally decided to travel to Budapest, paying no heed to the danger in which he was placing himself by contravening the Nazis' orders. Without hesitation, he set out on the eight-hour train ride to Budapest, arriving on the morning of June 17 or 18.[10]

Manoliu entered a city whose silence was ominous. It seemed that something too awful for words was about to happen. In fact, as he was soon to discover, the city's Jews were in the grip of a nameless fear, uncertain what the next hour would bring them.

Swiss consul Lutz, in the report that he wrote immediately after the war, described the fear of the Jews in the capital during this period. By the end of May, rumors of deportations had already been spreading, based on information from refugees from the provinces, or the rural Carpatho-Ruthenia area, who described the early ghettoization and deportations of Jews in their own towns. Within weeks after the German occupation, more than 400,000 Jews had been driven out of their homes, and out of the provinces altogether. The Jews of Budapest now began to realize that they would all be deported to Germany, and that they were totally helpless. The Judenrat could do nothing; under the Gestapo's pressure, all humanitarian organizations and leaders were silenced. Even the Hungarian Red Cross did nothing, and the Hungarian Church was unable to manage a collective appeal to the government.[11]

A sincere humanitarian under the most trying circumstances, Lutz sought to alleviate the Jews' vulnerability. He protested to the Hungarian Foreign Office, which responded by blaming the Germans. He then complained to Dr. Theodore H. Grell of the German Foreign Office, who at first denied the meaning of the deportations, claiming that the deportees were only going to join a Hungarian workforce. When Lutz pointed out that older people and children were hardly good "worker material," Grell responded that the Jews worked better when their families were with them; the deportees would be going to keep their relatives company.

By mid-June, extraordinary measures were being taken against the Jews in Budapest. Most were transferred to twenty-three hundred yellow-star houses throughout Budapest, with one room per family. The Jews were divided into two groups: those who had not converted to Christianity and those who had. They were also deprived of their hospitals, asylums, and other institutions, and were now waiting in a paralytic state for some kind of final blow.[12]

Manoliu did not yet know any of this, but he sensed that his mission in Budapest was an urgent one. He showed the authorities his personal suitcase, but the incriminating package of money, medicine, and citizenship papers remained safely in his diplomatic pouch. Realizing that he was under surveillance by the Gestapo, he went as quickly as possible to the Romanian consulate at 15 Horánszky Street. There he conferred with the consul general, Joachim Daianu, explaining his mission and itinerary in case the Nazis or their Hungarian allies should create any difficulties. Consul Daianu assured Manoliu of his full cooperation and offered to help him meet with anyone he wished to see; he also suggested that they discuss sensitive matters in privacy at his apartment at 50 Nürnberg Street.[13]

Still holding on to the stack of Salvadoran papers and other items, Manoliu proceeded to the Swiss compound in the building that had formerly housed the American embassy, on 12 Szabatsagter Street. Here he met with the sympathetic Carl Lutz, head of the Swiss Division of Foreign Interests, which served as the protective power for many countries that had broken off relations with the Axis. Manoliu related his mission and gave him most of the Salvadoran papers. Lutz, however, had only limited knowledge of the Jewish situation and believed that the deported Hungarian Jews had been sent to a labor camp in Germany. He added that Miklósz Krausz, who was hiding out in the Swiss compound, could provide him with the latest information on the Jewish situation.

Krausz, head of the Palestine Certificate Office, had sought refuge in the compound at the time of the German occupation a few months earlier. Because the Swiss were handling British interests, Lutz had good reason for taking him in, as the handling of Palestine certificates was under British auspices.[14] However, even though Krausz was right there on the premises, it is unclear why Lutz, by his own admission, had less information than Krausz.

In any case, Lutz took Manoliu to Krausz's hideout. At first Krausz, who knew neither Manoliu nor Mantello, was hesitant to talk; he had learned that the courier system used by the Jewish organizations for sending messages from Nazi-occupied countries to the free world had been penetrated by the Germans, and he was afraid that Manoliu was part of a Gestapo trap to determine how much the Jews knew about the last phase of the Final Solution.[15] Only after Manoliu handed him Posner's visiting card, with its reassuring Hebrew message, did Krausz feel secure enough to speak with him.

He then tried to explain the desperate Hungarian Jewish situation, especially in regard to the remaining 250,000 Jews in and around Budapest. However, because Manoliu was not fluent in Hungarian and Krausz did not know French or Romanian, Manoliu suggested that Krausz write a summary of his report in a letter that he would bring take to Geneva. Krausz agreed to this and added, "Please take two important reports that spell out all the horrible details of Auschwitz and the Hungarian situation, plus a brief message to Dr. Posner." Krausz added that he had only recently obtained these reports; how he obtained them is unknown.

The two men agreed to meet the next day at Manoliu's hotel rather than at the Romanian consulate, which would have been too dangerous for Krausz. Krausz's wife typed copies of the two reports and his letter,[16] and the next day, despite the danger, he himself delivered the material in person to Manoliu at the Romanian legation at 15 Horánszky Street.[17]

The first report was a five-page abridgement of the original thirty-three-page Auschwitz Report, concluding with a list of deportations by country and the total of 1,765,000 Jews murdered. This summary also contained the abridged version of additional testimony by Arnost Rosin and Czeslaw Mordowicz, two men who had escaped from Auschwitz in May 1944; this was about a month after the first pair of escapees had provided the information for the original Auschwitz Report. The testimony of this second pair provided corroborative information, including statistics on the continuing mass murder of Hungarian Jews from early April until late May. Very likely, this summary version of the Auschwitz Report, as most, had been authored by Weissmandl.[18]

The other document that Krausz gave Manoliu was the Hungarian Report, which was about six pages long. It detailed the ghettoization and deportation of Hungarian Jews, town by town, to Auschwitz. The ghettoization had begun in some areas of Carpatho-Ruthenia in April, where the first few small transports were deported at about that time. Then the first full-scale deportation began on May 15, and within three weeks—by June 7, 1944—more than 335,000 Jews had been deported to Auschwitz. Krausz's letter added that, from June 7 to 19, when he gave Manoliu the reports, an additional 100,000 Hungarian Jews were turned into ashes in the furnaces of Auschwitz.[19]

Krausz's letter, dated June 19 and addressed to Dr. Chaim Posner, read as follows:

Dear Sir,

I have just received your visiting card and take advantage of the opportunity to send you the enclosed two reports concerning the situation here. As you will see from the reports attached, the deportations from Hungary began on May 15th and within a period of three weeks—i.e., up to June 7th—335,000 Jews have already been deported, approximately 90% of them to Poland, Birkenau-Auschwitz, and the remainder to Germany.

As far as the situation in Hungary is concerned . . . the passive attitude of the [non-Jewish] population . . . encourages the government to act with increasing cruelty, and the Hungarian government even endeavors to surpass the demands of the German authorities in every respect. . . . Many Jews have fallen victim to the above-mentioned treatment in the ghettos, and most of them are loaded halfdead into the wagons. We have tried various ways of saving these people, but unfortunately until now all our attempts have been unsuccessful. . . . [T]he whole Jewish race in Hungary is condemned to death. There are no exceptions, there is no escape, there is no possibility of concealment, and we have to face our fate. We have not even the possibility of escaping to a neighboring country. . . . There are only two possibilities left to us: suicide or the acceptance of our fate. The Swiss legation in Budapest . . . has done its best, but unfortunately without any success whatsoever.

Dear Dr. Posner, I really do not know what to ask of you. I see no possibility of escape, as we have only a few days before us. . . . I do not know whether I will have another opportunity of writing to you. It would, however, be a satisfaction to me if you could publish this letter and the enclosed reports either now or at a later date, so that the world may learn of the cruelties committed in the twentieth century in so-called civilized countries.[20]

When he was alone, Manoliu took these reports apart and placed the pages between the pages of Romanian diplomatic documents so that they should not appear as distinctive reports in the event of a search.[21]

When Manoliu had first met Consul Lutz, he had mentioned that he also wished to get in touch with Mantello's wife, Iréne, and her parents' family in Budapest. Lutz told Manoliu that he had assigned her to care for Jewish children who were in the protection of the Swiss compound, and that her father lived not far away. Although Manoliu was unable to get in touch with Mantello's wife, Lutz helped him locate Iréne's father, Ignaz (Yitzchok) Berger. Berger arranged to meet Manoliu on June 19 at his hotel, rather than at the Romanian consulate, which would have aroused suspicions. There, besides money and medicine, Manoliu gave Berger the new passport for his daughter and a Salvadoran citizenship paper for himself and his family.[22] He also showed Krausz's letter and reports to Berger, who decided to enhance their sense of urgency by adding a note to Mantello in Yiddish, addressing his son-in-law by his familiar Yiddish name, Bandi (diminutive of Boruch Bendit):[23]

My Dear Bandi!

I am sending you the letter of M[oshe] K[rausz] plus two reports.

You can imagine what we have to endure. I beg of you, do whatever you can. Don't delay!

Best regards once again,

Yours,
Yitzchok[24]

With the reports in his possession, Manoliu had completed the most crucial aspect of his mission; but his return to Switzerland, with these revealing documents in his diplomatic pouch, put him in an even more dangerous position. In addition, there was a good chance that, even without a search, he would be stopped at the Hungarian-Swiss border, where the Hungarian guards might challenge him: "Based on your transit visa, your destination was Bucharest. Why did you return from Romania to stop off in Budapest?" If he were caught, he would surely be shot; but in his desperate mission to return to Switzerland as quickly as possible with the horrific reports, he completely disregarded this danger.[25]

At about eleven P.M. Tuesday evening, June 20, the phone rang in the living room of George Mantello's hotel suite in Geneva, where Mantello and his brother were anxiously awaiting Dr. Manoliu's return from Hungary. More than four weeks had passed since Manoliu had set out on his mission on their behalf to obtain precise details about the fate of Hungarian Jewry.

The call was from Manoliu. "George," he said, "I've just arrived at the border, and I have some very bad news. I'll see you as soon as I get to Geneva." Mantello understood that Manoliu was reluctant to speak further on the telephone, given the constant monitoring of the Swiss censorship police.

Manoliu finally arrived at two in the morning and told the two brothers all that he had learned. With great sadness he described the immensity of the national tragedy, as well as the brothers' personal loss; more than two hundred members of their own close-knit extended family in Bistrice had been deported. As he related the incredible details, the sheer vastness of the numbers of the men, women, and children involved, the brothers sat and listened in profound shock.

Manoliu ended by delivering the note from Mantello's father-in-law, which Josef read aloud as tears streamed down his cheeks. With that, Manoliu got up, embraced the two brothers, and left the room. He had completed his mission and was drained, both physically and emotionally. The responsibility for carrying on the struggle for the rescue of the remnants of Hungarian Jewry would now rest on the brothers' shoulders. Manoliu did, however, meet with a few members of the Swiss Hungarian Committee the next morning.[26]

When Manoliu left the apartment, the two brothers embraced and gave vent to their anguish, trembling with rage and fear at the news of the deportation of their parents and family to Auschwitz. Sobbing for their murdered parents, they tore their lapels in the Jewish mourning ritual performed upon hearing tragic news. Soon afterward, they collapsed in exhaustion; but after half an hour of silence, Mantello rose, still speechless at the thought of the monstrous Nazi murder of almost two million of his fellow Jews, but now determined.

Mantello and his brother Josef resolved to accomplish the impossible: they would do whatever they could to save the remaining 300,000 or so Jews in and around Budapest, the last remnant of Hungarian Jewry, before Eichmann's SS and Horthy's gendarmerie murdered them as well.[27]

Mantello's anguish was now transformed into a demon that would not let him rest until he had accomplished his goal. For the next week or so, neither food nor sleep were of consequence to him; he caught short naps and occasionally grabbed something to eat, rushing about as if in a frenzy. No one dared interfere with his monomaniacal determination to inform the world about the tragedy of Hungarian Jewry. Against all odds, against all logic, against the opposition of bureaucrats, petty officials, and gainsayers, both Jewish and non-Jewish, Mantello intended to break the world's silence in the face of Hitler's Final Solution. So extraordinary did his campaign appear that Rabbi Taubes, who worked closely with him, recalled after the war that "he was so filled with determination and worked so feverishly, we simply couldn't understand him. We felt that he had within him the soul of a Maquis [French underground fighter] or a Serbian guerrilla fighter."[28]

For the few remaining hours of that Tuesday night, June 20, the two brothers worked feverishly to plan a series of steps toward their goal. Josef made calls to the various members of the Swiss-Hungarian Committee for an emergency meeting in Zurich the following morning, and Mantello got in touch with the leaders of Swiss-Hungarian university students. His objective was to start work immediately on translating the two reports into several languages so that they could be disseminated to the foreign press and to as many circles as possible in this multilingual country.[29]

During his two years in Switzerland, Mantello had established good relations with diplomatic, religious, and social circles. He had also befriended Hungarian students by subsidizing some of the needy individuals among them, and by financing their club. This club consisted primarily of non-Jewish Hungarian sons of émigrés and nobility who had left Hungary during the short-lived Communist revolution of 1919 in Hungary, or who had sent their sons to Switzerland for higher education and safety during the Second World War.[30]

The first five or six students to show up very early that Wednesday morning were assigned the task of providing a German-language version of the two reports and of Krausz's letter. To assure efficiency, Mantello divided the group into three pairs, each of which translated several pages; the groups then checked each other's work. In this way, within several hours, a reasonable German translation was completed. That same morning, Mantello looked about for a Gestetner mimeograph machine to run off the first fifty copies. He gained access to one in a hotel, where he sent two students with the completed version. In all, about thirty students, proficient in several languages, worked on all the translations. It took another day to complete the English, French, and Spanish versions.[31]

To make Krausz's letter a more effective rescue tool, Mantello made a number of textual changes. First, he changed the name of the addressee from Posner to his own, for he himself was better known in Swiss diplomatic and governmental circles. Moreover, because Krausz had ended his letter on a despairing note, Mantello added a few lines that encouraged rescue. The revised paragraph concluded with the assurance that help was still possible and that there were those willing and able to give it. As will be seen, he had specific British and American personalities in mind when he wrote these lines. His addition read as follows: "Please use every opportunity to establish contact with all authorities and sympathetic people. We are certain that the Americans and English will help. Help! Help! Help!"[32]

The students made a minor error in the text of the Auschwitz Report that turned out to be a boon for historians. In their rush to complete the translation, they omitted one of the Nazi-occupied countries, Lithuania, and the number of its Jews murdered in Auschwitz (50,000). Thus, instead of the total of 1,765,000 Jews gassed, as found in every other version of the Auschwitz Report, Mantello's copies cited the figure of 1,715,000. This makes it easy for the historian to trace the global dissemination of Mantello's versions.[33]

On Thursday morning, June 21, with copies of the reports in hand, Mantello joined the members of the Swiss Rabbis' Committee and Swiss-Hungarian Committee for an emergency meeting in Zurich to inform them of the tragic news. The tense meeting lasted all day and long past midnight. The dozen or so members who listened to Mantello read some passages of the reports and Krausz's letter sat in silence and dismay. Finally, Rabbi Kornfein declared, with tears streaming down his face, "This is like the destruction of the Second Temple. We must sit shiva." He fell to the floor and ripped the lapel of his jacket in the Jewish mourning ritual, with the rest of the group following suit in an outpouring of sobs and groans.[34]

The news was so horrendous that one member of the SHC, most likely Pallai, found it difficult to believe. He stood up and shouted, "This is nothing but Romanian propaganda," echoing the age-old ethnic rivalry between Hungarians and Romanians. An angry Mantello jumped to his feet and demanded, "Throw him out; I don't ever want to see him again. We've got too much at stake to listen to fools like him." Pallai left the organization soon after.

Mantello then issued a series of commands that took even his close associates by surprise. "You, Rabbi Kornfein, get hold of Pastor Vogt so that we can obtain the backing of the Church. And you, Michael Banyai, take a copy to the American representative of the War Refugee Board. We have no time to lose! As for me, I'm going to see Commodore Freddie West of British Intelligence."[35]

As soon as he left the meeting, Bányai composed a handwritten note to McClelland in German, rather than waiting to have his secretary translate and type it. He delivered it personally to the American legation the next day, June 22. In this note, Bányai sought to convey the urgency of the situation:

> June 22, 1944
>
> My Dear Mr. McClelland,
> Since I am so completely distraught, I am unable to think straight and send you in a hurry this [*sic*] enclosed report[s]. My worst fears have been exceeded. The accompanying letter is dated June 19, a completely new date, and it was brought yesterday by a diplomat. He [Krausz] sent us the report, whose name

I only give to you personally on a separate paper, and I ask you for the strictest discretion in order not to endanger this man's life. The report contains such terrible news that further commentary is unnecessary. We have to leave it to you and your government [to determine] what remains to be done. At present there are about 300,000 Jews in Budapest. Most of the Jews have already been deported from the Provinces. If the remainder are to be saved, no time must be lost. I ask you to excuse me for being unable to write more about this matter, and I put this matter in all confidence in your hands.

That same day, Bányai spoke to Manoliu, after which he dashed off another hurried note to McClelland:

Please excuse me, since I have no other paper at my disposal. . . . I have spoken today personally with a diplomat who came back from Hungary yesterday, and who brought the reports. He makes an absolutely reliable and serious impression. *He had to look for Krauss* [sic] *in Budapest for a very long time, since he [Krausz] was afraid to talk with any stranger.* If you want to talk to the diplomat in Bern yourself, he will gladly make the introduction. (emphasis added)[36]

In the meantime, Imre (Georges) Tahy, the first secretary of the Hungarian legation in Geneva, had returned from Budapest just two days before Manoliu. Tahy, who was an anti-Nazi, kept Mantello informed of developments in Hungary and was to continue to be of assistance later in the crisis. He now declared his willingness to tell McClelland his own views of the desperate situation of the Jews in Budapest.

In one of his two letters of June 22, Bányai had informed McClelland of Tahy's offer to talk with Hámori, McClelland's Hungarian-speaking assistant. This was an especially urgent offer because Tahy was leaving Switzerland for Budapest in several days.[37]

The next day, in a third letter to McClelland, Bányai added the following important points, which he had previously omitted in his agitation: "The Rumanian [sic] diplomat . . . told me that the Jewish Transports go in the direction of SNYATIN, CERNOWITZ, via MARMAROS-SZIGET and KOROS-MEZO. Furthermore, he told me that the Rumanians [sic] are quietly permitting all [Hungarian] Jewish refugees to cross the border into [Romania]" (capitals in original).[38]

McClelland's long-delayed responses to Bányai's urgent pleas made it clear that he never took the opportunity to speak either to Manoliu or to Tahy. In fact, it took two weeks, until July 7, before he even responded to Bányai. By that time, Horthy had halted the deportations to Auschwitz, and McClelland had received several additional copies of the Auschwitz and Hungary Reports, including one with an accompanying letter from the four leading Swiss theologians. In this important letter, these outstanding men of the cloth authenticated the reports and requested that they be widely disseminated.[39] When McClelland finally did respond, he thanked Bányai for the reports and added a condescending note: "You have certainly been untiring in your efforts on behalf of persecuted Jewry in Hungary, and even though the results are discouraging, in the last analysis you can feel that you have done everything within your power."[40]

Not until about June 24 did McClelland send any word to Washington about Auschwitz or the tragedy of Hungarian Jewry. At that time, he dispatched a brief cable summarizing several earlier versions of the Auschwitz Report and the plea to bomb the rail lines to Auschwitz. McClelland commented skeptically: "This [plea] is submitted by me as a proposal of these agencies and I can venture no opinion on its utility." Even this cable he sent only after Czech ambassador Jaromir Kopecky, along with Fritz Ullmann and Gerhard Riegner, provided him with a more complete version of the Auschwitz Report. It took another two weeks, until July 6, before McClelland cabled an abridged version of the Auschwitz Report to the United States, and an additional five months before he finally transmitted the complete, detailed version of the report.[41]

Fortunately, McClelland's efforts to obstruct the rescue effort were more than offset by Pastor Paul Vogt, who was to help Mantello bring the Swiss community to its finest hour in his quest to save the remnant of Hungarian Jewry.

7

The Beginning of the Swiss Press Campaign

Driven by a desperate sense of urgency, Mantello used a variety of means to inform the world of the plight of the Jews in Hungary. In some areas, such as his distribution of the Auschwitz Report and press articles, he worked alone; in others he was assisted by key individuals such as Rabbi Zvi Taubes, head of the Swiss Rabbis' Committee, and Pastor Vogt, the influential Protestant theologian. Most important, he was a motivator behind the scenes, inspiring his collaborators, orchestrating the activities of individuals and organizations. Virtually every venue of rescue that he explored proved productive, several effective beyond anyone's imagination. His initiatives not only helped transform the prevailing climate of opinion in Switzerland, but also affected the Allies and, even more important, changed Hungary's Jewish policy.

Mantello's primary goal was to break through Swiss censorship and awaken the world to the immensity of the tragedy that awaited the Jews. He realized that to accomplish this, he would have to obtain the support of outstanding personalities in both the political and religious arenas. In the political arena, he required the support of the American and British legations, and especially the intelligence community, with which he was already on good terms.[1] He hoped to persuade the British Exchange Telegraph, a news agency that worked closely with the foreign press and with British intelligence, to publish his information and thus bring it to the attention of the Swiss and international press.

In the religious arena, Mantello sought the support of outstanding Swiss church figures to sway the skeptical Swiss press and an unsympathetic nation influenced by ten years of German anti-Semitic propaganda. In fact, despite some outstanding humanitarian Swiss public figures, there were several pro-Nazi groups and publications that influenced negatively on the Jewish Question.[2]

In addition, since the start of the war, out of fear of a German invasion, Switzerland had reenforced its historic policy of strict neutrality in general and in the media in particular. Its church figures faced the task of breaking through the wall of silence on German atrocities imposed by this stringent censorship.[3]

On Thursday evening, June 22, Mantello met with Commodore Freddie West, a military attaché and high-ranking member of British intelligence.[4] As soon as he presented the Auschwitz and Hungary Reports, West agreed to urge Walter Garrett, director of the British Exchange Telegraph, to create a press release. West cooperated readily not only because of his confidence in Mantello, but also because he was already familiar with much of the content of the reports from his own intelligence work.[5]

After leaving West's house, Mantello went to see Garrett, taking along Dr. Max Kimche, a lawyer and friend of Garrett. Although West had introduced Mantello to Garrett earlier, the two men had had no dealings as yet.[6]

By the time Mantello and Kimche arrived at Garrett's house, it was almost midnight on Thursday, but under the circumstances, Mantello had no compunctions about waking him. Although Garrett considered the reports that Mantello showed him persuasive, he hesitated to act, questioning their veracity in the eyes of the Swiss and the British.[7] He also cautioned that a summary of the reports would fill three to four long cables, the cost of which would run to thousands of francs. "Don't worry," Mantello assured him. "Whatever the cost, I'll pay for it."

"And before I do anything," Garrett continued, "I have to get approval from Bern."

"Who in Bern?"

"I can't tell you."

"Do you mean West?" said Mantello. "He already knows about the reports. You can call him right now."

"At this hour? It's already past two in the morning. I'll see him first thing tomorrow and get his approval."

Mantello insisted, "No, right now. There's no time to lose. West gave me permission to call him at any hour. You dial the number and I'll speak to him."[8]

As soon as Garrett finished dialing, Mantello picked up the phone and said, "I'm here with Walter Garrett and I've explained the situation to him, but he wants your approval before he does anything." He handed Garrett the phone and heard him respond, "Okay, okay, okay. Good night." As soon as Garrett hung up, he said, "Everything has been approved. The cables won't cost you a cent. The money will come out of our budget. Leave me the material, and by tomorrow night I'll have the summaries ready in cable form." Evidently, West must have convinced Garrett of the importance of these reports, and emphasized that Mantello was owed a favor.[9]

By late Friday night, Garrett finished summarizing the Auschwitz and Hungarian Reports and the Krausz letter, incorporating all three into four long cables dated Saturday, June 24. Because the Hungarian Report lacked authentication, Garrett added that a neutral diplomat had vouched for its truth; and when the Americans later requested the identity of the diplomat, he named Mantello.[10] An excerpt from the cables read:

NEUTRAL DIPLOMAT AND CATHOLICCHURCH HUNGARY VOUCH ABSOLUTE TRUTH FOLLOWING DETAILED REPORT REVEALING FATE HUNGJEWS CONCENTRATION HUNGJEWS BEGAN APRIL 16 FORTYSIX COMMUNITIES . . . TOTAL 335000 HUNG-JEWSDEPORTED CHIEFLY UPPER SILESIA . . .

CONCENTRATION JEWS BUDAPEST BEGAN JUNE 16 . . . JEWS OFFICIALLY INFORMED DEPORTATION BEGINNABLE [*sic*] END NEXT WEEK WHICH UNDOUBT-EDLY MEANS JOURNEY TO DEATH STOP . . . DIPLOMAT SANSALVADOR [*sic*] WITH SPECIAL AUTHORIZATION PRESIDENT SANSALVADOR UNDERTOOK ONLY WAYOUT SAVE LARGE NUMBER FAMILIES . . . BY GRANTING THEM NATIONALITY CERTIFI-CATESSANSALVADOR . . . MAYBE EMPHASIZED SANSALVADORS [*sic*] ENDEAVORS MERELY DICTATED UTMOST NECESSITY RENDER IMMEDIATE HELP AND <u>WITHOUT SLIGHTEST REMUNERATION</u>. (emphasis added)[11]

FOLLOWING DRAMATIC ACCOUNT ONE DARKEST CHAPTERS MODERN HISTORY REVEALING HOW ONEMILLION 715 THOUSAND JEWS PUT DEATH ANNIHILATION CAMP AUSCHWITZ BIRKENAU . . . REPORT COME EXTWO JEWS WHO ESCAPED BIRKENAU CORRECTNESS WHEREOF CONFIRMED RESPONSIBILITY THEREFORE ACCEPTED EXONE NEUTRAL DIPLOMAT TWO HIGH FUNCTIONARIES STOP

FROM BEGINNING JUNE 1943 NINETYPERCENT INCOMING JEWS GASSED DEATHSTOP . . . THREE GASCHAMBERS FOUR CREMATORIUMS BIRKENAU-AUSCHWITZ STOP EACH CREMATORIUM . . . TWO THOUSAND CORPSES DAILY.

With the support of British intelligence, Garrett lent his own credibility to the veracity of the reports in his conclusion:

GARRETT ADDS ABSOLUTE EXACTNESS ABOVE REPORT UNQUESTIONABLE AND DIPLOMAT CATHOLIC FUNCTIONARIES WELLKNOWN VATIKAN [*sic*] DESIRE WIDEST DIFFUSION WORLDWIDE END EXCHANGE (emphasis added)[12]

Although the identity of the "well-known Catholic diplomat" is not certain, it can reasonably be assumed that this was György Barcza, former longtime Hungarian ambassador to the Holy See, who resided in Switzerland.[13] Barcza had long publicly supported the Jews in their plight. On June 3, for instance, he had joined seven other former Hungarian diplomats, including Baron Gábor Apor, in an appeal on behalf of the Jews.[14] Barcza was on good terms with Mantello and his group; for example, Bányai of the Swiss Hungarian Committee had tried to introduce him, although unsuccessfully, to McClelland and Saly Mayer.[15] There is little doubt that Barcza received Mantello's package of reports on the twenty-third, either from Mantello himself or from Bányai. The following day, he sent a strongly worded cable to the pope requesting urgent intervention to end the persecution of the Jews in Hungary. This cable was no doubt a major impetus for the pope's first response to the persecution (see below).

To ensure that the editors of the important Swiss and foreign newspapers obtained their copies of these summaries in time for the morning editions, Garrett delivered the first two dozen or so copies late that same Friday night. Although Zurich was under curfew out of fear of air raids, Garrett bicycled through the darkened streets to drop the summaries off personally.[16]

Later that night, Garrett went to see Allen Dulles, head of the European Theater of the Office of Strategic Services (OSS). Although Dulles, like West, had access to much secret information concerning Nazi atrocities against the Jews, he was shocked when Garrett showed him Mantello's material. Perhaps these detailed reports put the Jewish plight into a more complete and horrifying perspective than the previous bits of information he had received, most of which were incomplete and unauthenticated; or perhaps Dulles's sympathetic response was based on his gratitude for Mantello's aid to American intelligence. In any case, he immediately cabled the summaries to Washington, in care of Secretary of State Cordell Hull. According to Garrett, responses came within a day.[17]

Meanwhile, Garrett cabled his summaries of the Mantello material to other major Allied figures, including President Roosevelt, Prime Minister Churchill, British Foreign Minister Anthony Eden, the archbishop of Canterbury, Queen Wilhelmina of Holland, and Archbishop Francis Spellman.[18] He added an Ankara dispatch to the cables, indicating that they had originated in a neutral country (Ankara, Turkey) and thus avoiding Swiss censorship regulations.[19]

As for Mantello, as we have mentioned, he had earlier enlisted the help of the Swiss-Hungarian Students' League to make approximately fifty mimeographed copies of the combined reports, translated into several languages; by June 23, he had distributed them to key people in the Swiss government and foreign service, and to representatives of all the Jewish organizations in Switzerland. Within a few days, the students reproduced thousands of copies of the reports, which they immediately distributed to all university students and faculty, and to political personalities, including members of Parliament. Thus, from the very beginning, Mantello spread the knowledge of the Nazi atrocities and the danger to Hungarian Jewry to everyone, Jew and non-Jew, instead of hushing up the reports, as virtually every other recipient had.[20]

Besides West and Garrett, Mantello personally delivered copies to the papal nuncio, Filippe Bernadini, who promised to send them immediately to the Holy See.[21] Mantello provided Posner, of the Palamt, with a copy of the letter Krausz had written to him, along with copies of his own version of the two reports. Another recipient was Dr. Samuel Scheps, Posner's superior at the Palamt, who had returned by now from his tour of duty in the Swiss Army Reserve.[22] The following day, Scheps and Posner mailed a copy of the Mantello package to McClelland, attaching a note expressing the hope "that you, my dear and honored Mr. McClelland, will do something to save the oppressed remnant of Hungarian Jewry."[23] This was only the first step that Posner took to spread Mantello's information to his connections in Istanbul, London, and Jerusalem.[24] Mantello and Bányai also provided copies to Saly Mayer in the hope that he would get directly involved, especially by helping pay for various rescue plans.

Mantello then asked Rabbi Taubes and the Swiss Rabbis' Committee to contact three influential American religious figures. Two were Zionists, Rabbi Stephen S. Wise and Rabbi Abba Hillel Silver, a Reform rabbi who was Wise's competitor for leadership of the American Zionist movement. The third figure was Dr. Louis Finkelstein, president of the Jewish Theological Seminary, head of the American Jewish Conservative movement, and an active member of the American Jewish Committee, an anti-Zionist defense organization.[25] Taubes attached a letter to the copies he sent to these leaders, which read in part:

> According to a report from Hungary dated June 19, the situation has drastically deteriorated and taken on a frightful dimension. . . . In three weeks over 400,000 Jews have been deported to Poland—over 90% to Birkenau-Auschwitz . . . [and] were gassed. . . . The Hungarian people stands by, further

encouraging their government even to exceed the German orders. . . . By now the Provinces are virtually *Judenrein*. In and around Budapest, ghettoization has already taken place in scattered neighborhoods, as a deterrent to [Allied] air raids. The remnant of Hungarian Jewry is condemned to death.

Make sure the American government intervenes immediately via Bern and have the IRC support far-reaching [rescue] efforts. Switzerland should also accept the role as protective power in Hungary for the holders of Salvadoran and Paraguayan papers. . . . Deal with Catholic circles so that the Hungarian cloisters and clergy take in these people. This worked well in France, where tens of thousands were saved, and could succeed equally well in Hungary if preceded by Vatican intervention. . . . [Official] resolutions don't reach the Hungarians. Drop millions of flyers over Hungary, warning the people that they bear personal responsibility and punishment for every war crime committed.

Signed,

Dr. [Zvi] Taubes
The [Swiss] Rabbis' Committee[26]

On that busy Friday, Bányai informed McClelland of two developments in the Hungarian situation that he had discovered in his talks with Manoliu. The first involved the exact railroad route used by the Germans to deport Hungarian Jews—a fact of which McClelland had been aware much earlier, through the Weissmandl cables and reports. The second piece of news was that the Romanian government, without fanfare, was permitting the entry of refugees from Hungary.[27]

Taubes's next target was Prof. Carl Barth, the world-renowned Protestant theologian in the Reformed Church in the Calvinist tradition. Barth responded to this emergency with alacrity. On June 25, the same day he received the reports from Taubes, Barth sent them to Ernst Nobi, the president of the Federal Council (Bundesrat*), accompanied by a letter in which he noted in part:

The enclosed reports from Hungary were sent to me . . . [indicating that] 10,000 a day are being murdered. . . . The threat is that it will all be finished within two to three weeks. Is there any chance for an outside intervention to save at least some people? . . . Perhaps temporary havens can be provided, or

---

*The Bundesrat, or Federal Council, is the highest Swiss political body. It comprises seven members, all heads or ministers of major cabinets, who annually rotate the presidency of Switzerland.

protection provided by means of foreign passports. . . . [Perhaps it is possible that] the Swiss government, together with the IRC and the embassies of the cooperating [neutral] countries, can accept this assignment. . . . I don't think it is necessary for me to go into the motivation that moved me, since I am sure that you realize fully well the urgency of the matter.[28]

The pressure on the president of the Federal Council continued with a similar plea on the following day from Alphons Koechlin, president of the Federation of Swiss Protestant Churches, which read in part:

In the name of the executive body of the Swiss Evangelical Church. . . . We come to you to intervene with the Hungarian Government and empower the Swiss Embassy [in Budapest] to make an all-out effort to save the Jews, and, together with the International Red Cross and officials from Sweden and Switzerland, take common action to impress upon Hungary that they must halt their action [i.e., deportations]. . . . [He concluded with] the assurance of complete support by the entire Swiss Evangelical Church.[29]

Koechlin wrote a similar letter to Federal Councillor Pilet-Golaz, the minister of foreign affairs, which concluded, "I am sure you will do everything in your power to bring a stop to the horrors before it is too late to do anything about them."[30] This was only the beginning of a steady campaign of pressure applied by the influential Protestant church figures on the foremost Swiss political body.

When Mantello's reports and news releases were distributed to all legations, newspapers, and Jewish organizations that Friday, they created a flurry of activity that eventually evolved into the press campaign. In addition, they spurred a number of individuals to act more quickly and effectively. For example, on this same day, June 23, Ambassador Kopecky, together with Riegner and Fritz Ullman, Kopecky's adviser for Jewish affairs, went to the IRC with a complete copy of the Auschwitz Report and Weissmandl's brief version. Kopecky had received the brief version from Weissmandl himself, and he had been holding both copies for almost a month, while Riegner and Ullman had had them since June 10.[31] Weissmandl's version contained his description of the deportations from the provinces and his demand that the Allies bomb Auschwitz and the rail lines leading to it.[32]

Unfortunately, their urgent plea to the IRC made no impression. Later that day, Mantello's own copies reached this organization and also without effect. It took another three days for IRC representative Jean Schwartzenberg to forward Krausz's copy of June 5 to Nicholas Burkhardt, the IRC delegate in London; and even then, instead of urging Burkhardt to act, Schwartzenberg sent specific instructions not to forward the report to Jewish organizations.[33] This attitude lingered another few weeks, at which time the IRC was shaken from its lethargy by the impact of the Swiss press and church campaigns and the vehemence of the protest by the Swiss people.

Jewish representatives who received these reports were devastated. For example, Arye Kubowitzki, an important Jewish rescue activist for the World Jewish Congress in the United States, responded in shock: "How thunderstruck were we when we heard on June 24th that 335,000 Hungarian Jews had already been deported." He conveyed the information to Stephen Wise, head of the WJCong, who did nothing to influence Roosevelt at least to bomb the rail lines to Auschwitz.[34]

The next day, June 24, Kopecky, Riegner, and Ullman visited McClelland and delivered to him the same material they had given the IRC. McClelland had received copies of other reports and pleas on behalf of the Jews, including those from Baron György Bakách-Bessenyey, former ambassador to Bern, and György Barcza, former ambassador to the Vatican; in fact, cables had been accumulating in his office since May.[35] However, it was undoubtedly Czech ambassador Kopecky's visit to McClelland on June 24 that finally spurred McClelland into notifying the War Refugee Board in Washington of the mass deportations and murder of Hungarian Jews.

Although McClelland did not provide much detail in his cable to Washington and did not convey the urgency of Krausz's desperate letter, he did give information on the deportation of most Hungarian Jews gleaned from both Weissmandl and Mantello's version of the Hungarian Report. From the report, he noted that the "concentration of Budapest's 350,000 Jews had already begun on the 16th and is expected to be completed by the 21st." In a single sentence, McClelland mentioned the Auschwitz Report and its estimate of "over 1,500,000 Jews killed since early summer 1942," and he also cited Weissmandl's plea to bomb the rail lines in Hungary, which were carrying 12,000 people per day to Auschwitz. He added that this plea, supported by many sources, "is submitted by me as a proposal of these agencies and I can venture no opinion on its utility."

McClelland would wait until October 12, nearly four months later, to send the WRB the complete version of the Auschwitz Report and Weissmandl's five-page summary, including his pleas to bomb the rail lines to Auschwitz; and even these he sent by regular surface mail, which assured that they would not arrive in Washington before November 1.[36]

After this, it took more than three weeks, until November 26, before the first account of the mass murder of Jews in Auschwitz, authenticated by the WRB, made the front page of the *New York Times* (and other major newspapers), in an article entitled "U.S. Board Hears Atrocity Details Told by Witnesses at Polish Camps."[37] This long-delayed article made such an impression that more than four hundred Jewish organizations requested copies of the complete reports.[38]

McClelland's and Dulles's cables to Washington were apparently intercepted by the Hungarian secret police; their knowledge of Weissmandl's request to warn the Hungarians helped reinforce the deep Hungarian fear of an alleged Jewish power that could pressure the Americans into bombing the Jews' enemies. (As noted above, America's subsequent heavy bombardment of Budapest on July 2, although unrelated to the Jewish situation, became one of the factors in Horthy's later decision to halt the deportations.)[39]

Mantello's campaign inspired a number of spin-offs by persons who used his material to alert others. These included Dr. Riegner, Dr. Lichtheim, and especially Dr. Posner. As noted earlier, Riegner and Czech ambassador Kopecky engaged in a sudden rush to bring copies of the Auschwitz Report to the IRC on June 23, and to McClelland on the following day. Although Posner did not have anything to do with Manoliu's mission to Budapest other than providing Mantello with his calling card for Moshe Krausz, he afterward made some valiant contributions to the rescue effort. After Mantello provided him with copies of the two reports and the Krausz letter on June 23, he sent a cable to Chaim Barlas, head of the Jewish Agency's Vaad Hahatzalah in Istanbul, transmitted in his usual Hebrew code, which read in part, "Received today the despairing letter from Krausz of June 19. . . . Until today Tawelef [400,000] deported to Birkenau, the vast majority to their death. . . . Next week is the turn of Budapest Jewry. Krausz notes that the sole means of rescue is through Palestine Certificates."[40] Within a day, on June 24, Barlas responded to Posner's cable: "[R]eceived the tragic news which he [Posner] dispatched to both friends in Istanbul as well as Chaim [Weizmann], Moshe [Czertok, in London] and Nahum [Goldmann, in New York]. Aktion is on the way."[41] Two days later, June 25, Posner elaborated on the situation in a second cable to Barlas, in which he referred to the Auschwitz Report and the Hungarian Report: "Re the cable of June 23, the Krausz material details the concentration camps and the deportations. . . . Krausz's address is the Swiss consulate."[42]

Also on June 25, Posner dispatched a similar cable to Yitzchok Grünbaum, head of the Jewish Agency's Vaad Hahatzalah in Jerusalem. Grünbaum in turn cabled Moshe Shertok in Cairo, Beryl Locker in London, and Nahum Goldmann in New York: "Received info from Istanbul confirming deportations [of] 400,000 Hungarian Jews to Poland . . . [deportations of the] remaining 350,000 . . . in Budapest . . . begins this week."[43]

Richard Lichtheim, the Jewish Agency's representative in Switzerland, also received copies of the Mantello material from both Mantello and Posner. He sent a detailed dispatch to Grünbaum in Jerusalem on the twenty-sixth, which read in part, "Meanwhile we have received most distressing reports about the situation in Hungary. . . . There is no longer any hope. . . . In fact they are saying good-bye to us . . . 12,000 are daily deported to the death-camps. . . . I have informed our offices in London and New York . . . but there is very little hope."[44]

On the same day, Grünbaum, who had also received the Mantello information through Schwalb, cabled Rabbi Stephen S. Wise as follows:

According cable from Hechalutz [Schwalb] Geneva which partly corroborated Polish reports over 450,000 Hungarian Jews mostly youth deported Silesia Galicia remainder expecting same fate stop feel convinced nothing but unprecedentedly [*sic*] drastic measures can halt wholesale slaughter Hungarian Jewry stop please do utmost publicize above facts and organize effective steps by community stop view recent announcement American government they prepared set-up large refugee camps North Africa would suggest Protecting Power [*sic*] be required instruct its representative Hungary issue large numbers of permits to Hungarian Jews.[45]

Developments in Sweden

In Sweden, soon after the German occupation of Hungary, three men undertook several initiatives to help the Jews: Norbert Masur and Koloman Lauer, both members of the World Jewish Congress, and Ivor Olson, representative of the War Refugee Board. Early in June, Freudiger of the Budapest Jewish Council had sent a copy of the Auschwitz Report to Moshe Krausz, who had forwarded it to Swedish minister Carl Ivan Danielsson.[46] At about the same time, Dr. Valdemar Langlet, Swedish lecturer at the University of Budapest, received a copy of the Auschwitz Report from the Jewish Council (most likely from Freudiger or from a man named Peto, to whom Freudiger had shown it), and he too forwarded that information to Danielsson. Danielsson in turn informed Masur, Lauer, and Olson of the contents of the Auschwitz Report.[47] These men then enlisted Prof. Hugo Valentin, and all of them sought out the influential Swedish chief rabbi, Marcus Ehrenpreis, asking him to use his influence to send a Swede with diplomatic immunity to Budapest to assist the Jews.[48] They also discussed providing temporary passports for Hungarian Jews who might be even remotely related to Swedes or connected with Sweden somehow. Some practical steps were taken to implement these ideas, and passports were made out for several hundred people. On June 23, Raoul Wallenberg was designated by the Swedish government as the delegate to Budapest.[49]

Meanwhile, the Swedish legation in Budapest sought to save thousands of women, children, and older people by arranging for temporary refuge in Palestine or Sweden, or, at the least, by having them protected by the IRC. Because the expenses for their upkeep were expected to come from Jewish sources, the Joint appealed to the Jewish Agency to arrange for a million Swiss francs to be deposited with the Swedish legation in Ankara.[50] However, as historian Leni Yahil has pointed out, despite Sweden's efforts, its narrow and legalistic stance changed only after June 30, when the king dispatched a cable to Horthy (see below). Despite much pressure from Swedish activists to force the government to send someone to Budapest to help the Jews, Wallenberg did not leave until July 6. He arrived on July 9, two days after Horthy had already halted deportations from Budapest.[51] The seeming impotence of both the Swedes and the Swiss would shortly be disproved publicly as the Swiss press and church campaigns began achieving results (see chapter 8).

Then, on June 26, Rabbi Zvi Taubes sent an urgent cable to Chief Rabbi Marcus Ehrenpreis of Sweden, informing him of the "reliable" reports of mass deportations of Hungarian Jewry and demanding that he intervene immediately with the Swedish king.[52] Before receiving a reply, Taubes sent a second cable, requesting again that Ehrenpreis urge the king to send a delegate from Sweden to help the Jews in Budapest.[53] The next day, June 27, Posner sent a similar cable to Ehrenpreis with the same plea; a third cable was sent by Yitzchok Grünbaum, head of the Jewish Agency's Rescue Committee in Jerusalem. Grünbaum had received the Auschwitz Report indirectly from Mantello through Lichtheim, who in turn had based his cable on the copy Mantello had given Posner; he sent his cable upon Posner's request. The Swedish chief rabbi, who had previously done little on behalf of persecuted Jewry, was finally moved to act, convinced that the information hailed from "absolutely reliable sources" and that the Germans had indeed ordered the deportation of all Hungarian Jews.[54] Ehrenpreis immediately handed Taubes's cable—and most likely those of Posner and Grünbaum as well—to the Swedish foreign minister, Christian Günther. On the twenty-eighth, Günther obtained approval from the Council of Ministers to appeal to the king to send the message to Horthy; they did so, and the king sent his message on June 30. Thus, as a result of the publicity and Ehrenpreis's entreaty, the Swedish government changed from a passive to an activist role, and began arrangements to send a personal envoy to Budapest to facilitate rescue. This man, as mentioned, was Raoul Wallenberg, who turned out to be a major hero of the Holocaust.

The Protestant Church Gets Involved

At this point, it is important to return to Switzerland, as Mantello acted to enlist the aid of the Protestant Church in publicizing the Auschwitz atrocities. He began by making a bold and surprising move. On Saturday morning, June 24, Rabbi Zvi Taubes was presiding over services in the synagogue of the Israelitische Kultusgemeinde[55] in Zurich when Mantello suddenly stormed in. Following an ancient Jewish custom of interrupting services for vital communal and even personal matters, Mantello banged on the rostrum and demanded that Rabbi Taubes leave the services with him. He dragged the incredulous rabbi out of the synagogue and into a taxi on the Sabbath, telling him that he was taking him to see Vogt. Taubes was on good terms with the pastor; he had introduced him to Mantello, who supported Vogt's volunteer relief agencies.[56]

Vogt was no stranger to the plight of refugees in Switzerland, both Jewish and non-Jewish, and he frequently spoke out on their behalf. The most famous preacher in Switzerland and head of a Protestant refugee organization called Flüchtlingshilfe, Vogt was known for his outspoken support of refugees from Nazism. As early as October 1942, after news about deportations of Jews to the East and their death had appeared in the Swiss press, Paul Vogt had declared October 1 a day of prayer on their behalf. In his appeal, Switzerland's most popular preacher placed special emphasis on "what we in Switzerland were in a position to know, and ought to know, of the fate of the Jews of France." The October issue of *Die Reformierten Flugblättern,* published by Vogt's Evangeli-

Pastor Dr. Paul Vogt. Switzerland's most popular preacher, known
as the Refugee Pastor for his concern for all refugees coming into
Switzerland. He enlisted the important Swiss clergy to support Mantello's rescue efforts, including the initiation of the church campaign
whereby all the churches heard sermons based on the atrocity reports
and the need to help Hungarian Jews. He published the first book
containing these and other atrocity reports, entitled *Soll ich meines
Bruders Hüter sein?* (Am I my brother's keeper?) in July 1944, only weeks
after the arrival of Mantello's reports. A second printing
appeared a month later. Courtesy of Ringier Pressehaus.

cal relief organization for refugees, stated: "A vast pall of death has settled over God's people, the Jewish people. Europe is ablaze with rattles. Europe is filled with the scream of the dying as they are shot and gassed."[57] As Alfred A. Haesler noted in his classic *The Boat Is Full*, it is important to realize that besides Paul Vogt, even before the press campaign, there were numerous Swiss people whose voices were heard in Parliament and in the church and press. These included Dr. Arthur Frey, the Reverend Walter Luthi, supreme court judge Dr. Max Wolff, Dr. Gertrude Kurtz (known as the "Mother of Refugees"), and Dr. Regina Kaegi-Fuchsmann, among others. This was so despite ten years of Nazi anti-Semitic propaganda aimed at Switzerland and a generally strong German influence in the country. However, even these outspoken leaders who banded together in the Jews' defense were unable to counter the negative influence of Rothmund or von Steiger, and others of their ilk, who viewed the Jews as a danger to Switzerland. It was only the upheaval wrought by the press and church campaigns, instigated by Mantello and taken up by the entire Swiss people, that initiated major changes in Swiss policy. Later, in 1943, Vogt had publicized photos of Nazi atrocities and preached the doctrine of Christian love for all oppressed people, including Jews. His motto was, "A church that offers no haven for the suffering can never be a church of Jesus Christ." He was a fearless spokesman for these victims of government authorities' persecution; in the words of one Swiss author, Vogt "recognized and accepted the duty of being the voice of the silent and the emissary of the hunted."[58]

Typical of Vogt's courage and concern for Hitler's Jewish victims was a sermon that he delivered on August 29, 1943. Inveighing against the racist Swiss policy of "refoulement," whereby border guards shunted illegal Jewish refugees back into German hands and to certain death, Vogt thundered, "We shudder at the death of the Jewish people. But we shudder equally at so much coldness and cruelty and stubbornness among Christians, chilled to the freezing point."[59] An important element in Vogt's influence was the fact that the stringent Swiss censorship did not apply to the Church, thus enabling him to publicize crucial information without hindrance.

Vogt had attended the very first meeting called by Mantello, on the morning of Saturday, June 21. Now, under prodding from Taubes and Mantello at this extraordinary meeting, he became fully immersed in the rescue campaign. That same day, he called a meeting attended by his assistant, Pastor Hans Schaffert, and Prof. Alphons Koechlin, president of the Evangelical Church

Council, along with Mantello, Taubes, Taubes's son Dr. Jacob Taubes, and Rabbi Armin Kornfein.[60] The first practical result of this meeting was Professor Koechlin's important appeal on June 26 to Bishop Dr. László Ravasz, his Hungarian counterpart, which included the following:

> We in the Swiss Evangelical Church have been deeply shaken by the fate of Hungarian Jewry. . . . The guilt that Hungary bears for the extermination of its Jews is most painful to bear. It will affect the relationship of Hungary with other countries for many years. It will also damage the trust between [international branches of the church] if the [Hungarian] church does not do everything to stop the action of the present government. My dear bishop, you will surely understand my request that you raise your voice and bring to bear all possible influence to halt these atrocities during these last hours. . . . At any rate, one cannot permit silence by the Evangelical Church without the enormous guilt of complicity . . .[61]

At that meeting, Vogt asked Mantello to guarantee the Auschwitz and Hungary Reports personally, which he immediately did. From then on, because he trusted Mantello, Vogt came to the forefront of the campaign within the influential Swiss Protestant Church to awaken not only the Swiss people but the free world to the plight of the Jews.[62]

The following day was Sunday, June 25. Mantello and Taubes met again with Vogt and Koechlin (Swiss member of the Provisional World Council of Churches), who spoke together to members of the Federal Council in Bern. The two men then turned to the IRC with a request that it provide protection for the Jews in Budapest.[63] That same day, Dr. Visser't Hooft, the Dutch head of the Provisional World Council of Churches, and Dr. D. A. Freudenberg, executive secretary of the Ecumenical Council, cabled the following message to Dr. William Temple, the archbishop of Canterbury, and Dr. Samuel Cavert, secretary of the American Protestant Union: "TRUSTWORTHY REPORTS STATE TWELFETHOUSAND [sic] HUNGARIAN JEWS DEPORTED DAILY TO AUSCHWITZ UPPERSILESIA STOP TOTAL ESTIMATED ALREADY FOURHUNDREDFIFTY THOUSAND STOP. . . . MANY DEAD ON ARRIVAL STOP [SO] FAR NO PUBLIC REACTION HUNGARIAN CHURCHES STOP SUGGEST NEW RADIO APPEAL AND WARNING TO WHOLE HUNGARIAN NATION STOP OECUMENICAL [sic] REFUGEE COMMITTEE ALSO ISSUES APPEAL T'HOOFT, FREUDENBERG."[64]

Switzerland's Protestant leadership played a magnificent role in fomenting the protest against the German murder of the Jews and against Hungary's complicity in this extermination. Vogt approached the annihilation of the Jewish people with sympathy and alacrity. He not only produced and distributed reports within several days, but he also delivered extraordinarily empathic sermons on this tragic subject in various churches. On June 27, in the important Leonhardkirche in Basel, Vogt delivered the first of his numerous sermons. It began with a citation from the Old Testament:

> The Lord spoke to Cain: "Where is your brother Abel?" He answered: "I do not know. Am I my brother's keeper?" The Lord answered: "What have you done? Behold, thy brother's blood cries out to me from the earth." [Gen. 4:8–10]
>
> Today, God's scrutinizing and inquiring eyes are focused upon us Christians . . . and He demands of us, "Where, where, where! Where is your brother, the homeless Jew? . . . Thou protective and nursing Christian mother who loves your children, where are the homeless Jewish children today? . . . Where are the widows, the orphaned, the hungry, the thirsty and the strangers?" . . . God's inquiry always concerns the brother. . . . Today and here the question focuses very clearly on the brothers of the people of Abraham. Where are they all? You Christians, tell me, where?
>
> Cain gave the classic response of those shirking their responsibility: "I don't know!" From his response, one can glean a thinly veiled allusion of rebellion: "Oh God, of what concern is it to You where my brother is? And what does where my brother is have to do with me?" . . . Today, Christians respond in the same classic fashion of irresponsibility: "I do not know where the Jew is! Nor does it concern me in the least."
>
> Oh Holy God, it is with profound shame and deep fear that we come before Thee today. Thou hast inquired of us regarding our brother the Jew. . . . We are not worthy of standing before Thee, because we Christians loved so little and had so little faith. . . . In the midst of our Christendom, godlessness seeks to exterminate the entire Jewish people, and we can no longer prevent it. . . . Oh Father, have mercy, have mercy, forgive us our enormous sin. ' . . . Oh help, so that Your earthly church truly repents in sackcloth and ashes for ignoring Your words and will, and for its contempt of Your promise. . . . Tear us out of our indifference, all our Cain-like thoughts and perspectives. . . . Help Your earthly flock truly become the protector of the disenfranchised, the worthless, homeless, and helpless. Have mercy upon the persecuted Jews. Have mercy upon the sorrow-laden Jews![65]

This and other such sermons by Vogt and his colleagues soon resounded in churches throughout the country for Vogt not only aroused his own congregants, but also inspired other pastors to deliver similar talks. In a report to the pastors of the Canton Basel, Dr. Erny echoed Vogt's message:

> The events are so gruesome that the church dare not remain silent. As soon as I heard about it, I immediately wrote to the Bundesrat and the International Red Cross to do everything possible to rescue any living Jews. *However, I am convinced that this is insufficient. I want to suggest that you arouse your congregations to public prayer on behalf of Hungarian Jews. I also want you to wake up our sister Evangelical churches of Hungary that they be worthy of the strength and words which they need so badly at this moment, as they bear such terrible guilt.*" (emphasis added)
>
> These events follow each other so rapidly that it is possible that all Hungarian Jews will soon be annihilated. Therefore, I beseech you to act as quickly as possible, before it is too late. You can expect to hear more from me soon. The administration of the Church Council will meet Thursday, July 6th, to discuss further steps to be taken.[66]

Dr. Alphons Koechlin was a theologian who, as we have seen, had previously been contacted by Taubes. He had already followed this up with two letters to major political figures, and he now contacted the church leadership. On June 28, he wrote a report in which he requested that the pastors of the Reformed Church publicize the Jewish plight. It read in part:

> For seven years from China[67] and four from Europe, the dreadful war-related news has penetrated into our quiet country almost imperceptibly. And we are deeply shaken by the suffering of all peoples. However, we gather here today in the cathedral for a very special cause. That which has happened to the Jewish people for over ten years, and that which has been inflicted upon the remnant of God's people in German-occupied Europe during these recent months, weeks, and days, is, in its satanic fashion, something extraordinary and totally unrelated to the war. The revelations that have appeared in all the newspapers derive from absolutely reliable sources. Half of the 800,000 Hungarian Jews are no longer alive, and day after day thousands are sent to their deaths. In our human helplessness and despair, we turn to God. On behalf of the Jews of Hungary, we pray and beseech God to order a halt and rescue what is left to be saved.[68]

Dr. Koechlin concluded with the announcement that "the Board of Directors will meet on July 6th to discuss further steps to be taken."[69] That same day, June 26, Koechlin also sent a letter with copies of the two reports to Max

Huber, president of the IRC. In his plea, Koechlin described the anguish of the Christian churches upon the receipt of the horrific news and urged the IRC to take action that would help end these events. He offered the practical suggestion that the IRC, in conjunction with a neutral power, place a number of areas under its protection. These areas would serve as safe havens for the persecuted Jews until the end of the war.[70]

In the meantime, Vogt was not satisfied merely with inspiring sermons on this sensitive issue; he felt it equally important for the public, and especially officialdom, to read the reports in print, for they were hardly likely to act on the basis of sermons alone. His optimistic view of the possibility of going into print was based on the fact that the growing number of news articles seemed to have weathered the threat of censorship. Vogt made sure that his moving message reached not only church audiences, but also the organs of the church and other newspapers through the Evangelic News Agency.[71]

In addition, in a little more than a week's time, Vogt's refugee organization produced and distributed several thousand copies of the Auschwitz Report in a seventy-five-hundred-word version that included the Mantello material plus some additional information on the fate of Hungarian Jewry. Vogt's brief introduction to this report, which later served as the preface to the first book edition, included a powerful indictment of Swiss religious society. Vogt wrote:

> It is your disgrace and shame that such a monstrosity could develop in our Christian world. Christ is being crucified with every trampled human being. . . . Through these factual accounts, the Christian community is being called to total repentance. We have to be cleansed of every trace of anti-Semitism, because it is at the same time the spirit and force of antichrist. In view of the millions of murdered Jews, any further anti-Semitic thought and any mean word is criminal madness. . . . This is our Christian atonement for the Christian sin of hate for the Jewish brothers, which has brought about a bloody end.[72]

However moving Vogt's introduction, the report's veracity was not accepted by all who read it. One skeptic was U.S. ambassador Lelland Harrison, who, like his colleague McClelland, had long been the recipient of numerous versions of the Auschwitz and Hungarian Reports. As late as July 4, when the Mantello material had been distributed with the full endorsement of four outstanding Swiss theologians, Harrison expressed his skepticism to Klahr Huddle as to whether the German term *Entjuden* really meant mass murder or merely removal or deportation.[73]

Vogt's report fell into the hands of *New York Times* reporter Daniel Brigham, who wrote the paper's first two articles on the Auschwitz mass murder on the third and sixth of July. Only after these appeared did other reporters take the matter seriously.[74] A few weeks later, Vogt enlarged and published his report as part of a small, powerfully moving German-language book entitled *Soll ich meines* [sic] *Bruder's Hüter sein?* (Am I my brother's keeper?), published in Zurich by the Evangelical Church. The book, more than a hundred pages long, was first published in an edition of nine thousand copies in July, only weeks after the Mantello reports made their appearance. Within a month, it was completely sold out or distributed, and a second printing (without the preface) appeared in August. The book included the text of Mantello's version of the Auschwitz and Hungarian Reports, the Krausz letter, a number of sermons Vogt had delivered, and other documents depicting Nazi and Hungarian atrocities against Jews.[75]

The significance of this book is severalfold. To begin with, it represented the first widespread distribution of the two reports in book form. Moreover, the national reputation of Pastor Vogt and the Evangelical Church added great weight to its veracity and moral imperative, making it acceptable in political circles and to deeply religious, church-oriented Swiss people of every ideological stripe. In the eyes of the Swiss, the sanction of these major Protestant theologians had authority virtually equal to the pope's encyclicals.[76]

The pressure began to mount. On June 27, with an uncommon sense of urgency, Pastor Visser't Hooft and Dr. Freudenberg again cabled Temple and Cavert in London, demanding that they immediately use various means, including radio broadcasts, to inform the people of Hungary about the monstrous crimes that were being committed by their leaders.[77] Two days after a sermon he delivered in the Leonhard Church, Vogt sent an invitation to all Jews to attend a special service on Saturday, July 1, at the imposing Wasserkirche (water church) in Zurich on behalf of the persecuted Jews. His invitation to the Jews began thus:

My Dear Mourning Jews,

This satanic persecution and horrible suffering which have recently appeared concerning Hungarian Jewry have also filled many Christians with deep pain. We have done everything within our power to publicize the atrocities, to visit responsible authorities to undertake any action humanly possible that will save the remnants of Hungarian Jewry.[78]

Vogt's sermon made a deep impression on his listeners in the church, as is evident from the many Swiss papers that reprinted the entire sermon. One noted in addition:

> Vogt first read from the shattering reports, which had just been brought into Switzerland, describing the situation in Hungary and the extermination camp in Upper Silesia. 450,000 Jews were concentrated and deported to Upper Silesia. In that place, only death rules, with no hope of saving one's life. Gassed and then burned—this is the fate of Hungarian Jewry. And at the same time, we live here, neither too disturbed nor too affected.[79]

To further arouse the Swiss public and its leadership, Mantello asked Vogt to compose and sign a letter of support to accompany additional distribution of the Auschwitz Reports. Vogt responded, "While I may be well-known in this country, my name means very little to Americans and the British. However, I will speak to some prominent and highly respected figures such as Karl Barth, Emil Brunner, and Visser't Hooft, whose international reputations will serve your cause far better." With the help of Rabbi Zvi Taubes, Vogt soon obtained the support of these renowned personalities and their written endorsement on July 4.[80] His letter, containing all four signatures, read:

> We are sending two reports from Hungary with an accompanying letter of June 19, 1944, which came via diplomatic channels to Switzerland from a highly reliable source. *These reports have profoundly shaken us. Due to our deep sense of responsibility, we feel obligated to make you aware of these two reports.* We have no doubt that you will make the effort to read these reports and *spread them among your circles.* The proper authorities have already been fully apprised of them. (emphasis added)

> Signed :
> Carl Barth, Emil Brunner, W. A. Visser't Hooft, Paul Vogt[81]

There are three elements in this important document that set it apart sharply from most other rescue reports: the expression of sympathy by men recognized as great humanitarians, their absolute certainty of the reports, and the desire and even responsibility to inform as many people as possible. Moreover, because this letter carried the authority and moral support of these outstanding Protestant theologians, it became the primary vehicle for breaking down the strict Swiss censorship, thus penetrating the silence of the world regarding the monstrosity of Auschwitz and the complicity of the Hungarians.[82] This letter also provided the moral leadership necessary to overcome the hesitancy of government officials and the International Red Cross, both of which had refrained until then from having anything to do with the rescue of Jews. The Auschwitz and Hungarian Reports that accompanied the letter transformed the attitudes of many petty bureaucrats whose attitude toward the fate of the Jews had been indifferent, if not negative.

Fully aware of the implications of the four theologians' letter, Mantello immediately sent a note of gratitude to Vogt. In his usual humble manner, Vogt responded, "My heartfelt thanks for your dear letter. We would like to apply all our strength to fight these dreadful things, in order to awaken the [world's] conscience to save those still under death's threat. During these fearful times, I feel intimately close to you and your people, and can only hope that the Almighty helps and gives one the strength to help."[83]

So effective were these first stages of Mantello's campaign to publicize Auschwitz that they elicited almost immediate responses from the West. The next chapter will focus on the press campaign; still, it is relevant here to touch upon the very first articles that were published.

The early articles were based primarily on Garrett's press release with its Ankara dispatch, as well as the Mantello material distributed in various forms by different groups, especially Vogt's Ecumenical Council. These articles presented, for the first time, the facts about Auschwitz and the deportations of Hungarian Jews. A typical example is entitled "The Fate of Hungarian Jews," which appeared simultaneously in the *Thurgauer Arbeiterzeitung, Die Tat,* and *Die Arbeiterzeitung* of Basel on June 28, 1944. It read in part:

> In all, 335,000 Jews from Hungary and from the annexed territories were deported during the four weeks from May 15 till June 10. . . . According to authentic information, the majority of these Jews were sent to Auschwitz (Oswiecim) concentration camp in Upper Silesia. What fate awaited them there is without doubt, according to the former and latest reports regarding this camp. . . . There were installations for diabolical tortures, a gas room, and a torture room furnished with instruments that surpassed the tools of the Middle Ages for inventive torture.[84]

These articles were profoundly shocking and caused a great upheaval in the thinking of the Swiss public. The first reaction to Mantello's activities came two days later, on June 25, 1944, in the form of an open letter from Pope Pius

XII to Hungary's Regent Horthy, "*Supplications have been addressed to us from different sources* to exert all our influence to shorten and mitigate the sufferings . . . of this noble and chivalrous nation . . . [and that you] do everything in your power to save many unfortunate people from further pain and sorrow" (emphasis added).[85]

The pope's early response indicated that he was fully aware of the tragic Jewish situation in Hungary and elsewhere, even though the highly selective *Vatican Documents* on the Holocaust show that the Vatican received the Auschwitz Report only in October.[86] There is little doubt in my mind that many versions of the Auschwitz Report and other atrocity reports reached the Holy See during April through July. During this time, many people, both Jewish and non-Jewish, petitioned the Vatican on behalf of Hitler's victims, including the May 22 petitions of Palestine's two chief rabbis, Isaac Herzog and Ben-Zion Meir Uziel. (The chief rabbis' urgent message was transmitted through the apostolic delegate's office in Cairo. However, their attempts to arrange a personal meeting with the pontiff were unsuccessful.) In addition, the War Refugee Board pressured the apostolic delegate in Washington to influence the pope.[87] Some of these messages must have been received by the Vatican.

Besides information on the Jewish plight received through requests, the Holy See had the most effective intelligence network in every Nazi-occupied country, not only through its official diplomatic presence in every country, but also through its thousands of priests on all levels of the Catholic hierarchy. For instance, Tiso, president of Slovakia, where the first deportations to Auschwitz took place in March 1942, was an ordained priest in the Catholic Church. In addition, virtually all Jewish representatives dispatched copies of the Auschwitz Report and other atrocity reports to the Vatican and its emissaries.[88]

Horthy's reply to the Holy See came on July 1. It read as follows:

> I have received the telegraphic message of Your Holiness with deepest understanding and gratitude. I beg Your Holiness to rest assured that I shall do everything in my power to enforce the claims of Christian and humane principles. May I beg that Your Holiness not withdraw his blessing from the Hungarian people in its hours of deepest affliction.
>
> Nicholas Horthy, Regent of Hungary[89]

Meanwhile, on June 26, President Roosevelt sent the first of two strongly worded warnings to Admiral Horthy, demanding that he stop the deportations immediately. The warnings were sent through Secretary of State Hull, who in turn communicated through the Swiss legation in Budapest. Roosevelt concluded, "I rely not only on humanity, but also upon the force of weapons. . . . Hungary's fate will not be like that of any other civilized nation . . . unless the deportations are stopped."[90] On July 2, Budapest was subjected to a heavy American air raid, which Horthy saw as a sign of American displeasure.[91]

Pressure on Horthy began to build, particularly because of the public response to the cables of Garrett, West, and Dulles. The added combination of the pope's letter and Roosevelt's warning, which were not only delivered personally but also reported on prominently in the Swiss papers, prompted his first reaction on June 26, when he called an urgent meeting of his Crown Council. At that meeting he gave the first indication of his change in attitude and policy regarding the Jews. He declared,"I shall not tolerate this any further! I shall not permit the deportations to bring further shame on the Hungarians! Let the Government take measures for the removal of László Baky and László Endre! The deportations of the Jews in Budapest must cease! The Government must take the necessary steps!"[92]

On June 27, at a follow-up meeting, Horthy responded to the pope's cable and the American note of the previous day, which had been personally presented to him by Maxim Jäger, the Swiss minister in Budapest. The Crown Council also discussed the earlier Swiss and Swedish proposals to permit about 7,000 Hungarian Jews, especially children, to immigrate to Palestine. Resolutions on both the immigration and the halt of deportations were discussed and, despite opposition, accepted by the council.[93] However, Horthy was still insufficiently motivated to defy the German might completely, even though the Russians were already close to Hungary's borders. Much more internal pressure, as well as external pressure from the West, would have to be applied before he would take the next major step.

On June 26, Barcza, Hungarian ambassador to the Holy See, joined a group of nine former Hungarian ambassadors residing in Switzerland in issuing a joint declaration protesting Hungarian complicity in the deportations. This declaration was broadcast on the *Voice of America,* on July 17.[94] It prompted Sztojay, Horthy's prime minister, to deny the reports in the neutral press about Hungary's role in a secret message of June 27 to Hungarian embassies in eleven nations. He declared, "News has been published in neutral and hostile press that Hungarian Jews are being deported to Germany. This is untrue."[95]

In the meantime, across the Atlantic, on June 28, 1944, Archbishop Spellman reacted to the two reports he had received from Allen Dulles by addressing Regent Horthy and the Hungarian nation in an impassioned radio plea: "This news has shocked all men and women who have a sense of justice and possess human sympathy. . . . The action of the [Hungarian] government is in flagrant contradiction to the Catholic faith possessed by the great majority of the Hungarian people. It represents a negation of the most glorious pages of the Hungarian history and cultural traditions of the country."[96]

That day, under the prodding of the War Refugee Board, the Committee for Foreign Affairs of the House of Representatives, headed by Congressman Sol Bloom, reached the following decision: "The House of Representatives hereby expresses its deep concern over the plight of the threatened millions in Nazi-dominated territories. . . . It expresses its determination to assure that . . . the criminals who are guilty of this inhuman conduct shall be brought to justice. . . . This is particularly directed at Hungary, where the lives of a million Jews hang in the balance."[97]

Particularly amazed and worried by the emerging publicity about the deportations, as well as by the changing mood of the regent, was Veesenmayer, the arrogant German ambassador. He had been utterly confident that the deportations would not even be noticed by the West, and he awoke suddenly to the realization that his plans were going awry. He cabled his government that "suddenly more and more steps are being taken by foreign organizations with the purpose of improving the situation of the Jews." He also stressed the fact that the Hungarian government was taking a benign attitude to these initiatives, especially those of Sweden and America.[98] Its favorable inclination toward Swedish requests, he explained, was because Sweden and the Swedish Red Cross had represented Hungarian interests in the belligerent states during the First World War, and continued to do so at present. In regard to Hungary's concern for American opinion, Veesenmayer cited the fact that many wealthy and influential Hungarians were living in America.[99]

Sympathetic to the Germans but under the pressure of a wavering Horthy, Sztojay requested a clarification of the German attitude concerning the intervention of the Swedes, Swiss, and the Americans.[100] In a third cable that same day, Veesenmayer informed the German foreign office that he had to postpone the "Aktion" (i.e., deportations) for ten days because of Horthy's objections. He was no doubt still certain of his ability to control the regent.[101]

Meanwhile, the Catholic Church in Hungary, at long last, took some action. On June 29, after having received entreaties from Switzerland and the nuncio in Budapest, Cardinal Jusztinián Serédi sent out a pastoral letter condemning the deportations. Though he did not succeed in having it widely distributed, it did make an impact on Hungary's ruling circles.[102]

On June 30, prodded by the sensational news and the pleas of Rabbi Taubes and other figures in Switzerland, Sweden's eighty-five-year-old King Gustav V transformed his country's previously sympathetic but essentially passive stance into an activist rescue role. The first step he took was to write a letter, which was handed to Regent Horthy by the Swedish ambassador on the thirtieth. It read in part, "I have been informed of those . . . measures which your government employs against the Jewish population in Hungary. . . . In the name of humanity, I may ask you to intervene for the benefit of those unfortunates who could still be saved. . . . [It is] my sincere wish that Hungary may preserve her good name before the nations of the world."[103]

A few days later, Horthy responded, "I received the telegraphic appeal of your Majesty, which I accept with the greatest understanding. I ask your Majesty to believe that I shall do whatever is possible in my present position so that the principles of humanity and consideration may prevail. I am touched by the kind feelings which your Majesty exhibits towards my country, and ask you to retain this feeling for the Hungarian people in these difficult days of grave trials."[104]

The next step the king took was to approve Wallenberg's mission to Budapest on that same day.[105]

These incredible efforts initiated by Vogt were only the beginning of what was to become a shining hour for the Protestant Church during these sorrowful times.[106] The leadership of the Swiss Catholic Church, on the other hand, did not join so readily in the campaign to halt the Nazi genocide in Hungary. Only one exception to the Catholics' guarded silence deserves mention: Dr. Johannes Duft, a lawyer and influential member of the Swiss Catholic Party and the Nationalrat (Swiss lower house), who had worked closely with Josef Mandl and Rabbi Taubes in obtaining support for rescue among other members of the Nationalrat. After a discussion of the Jews' situation with the sympathetic Bishop Josephus Meile of St. Gallen, Mandl and Taubes asked Dr. Duft to write an appeal to Bishop Dr. Victor Bieler, dean of the Bishops of Switzerland. Dr. Duft obliged by writing a two-page letter on June 30, which read in part:

Surely you and all Swiss bishops have been made aware of the gruesome fact that the persecution of the Jews of Hungary has reached an extent far beyond anything that normal human beings can comprehend. According to authentic reports, 450,000 Jews were deported between May 15 and June 7 of this year. . . . More than ninety percent of the deported came to Auschwitz-Birkenau . . . where 6,000 human beings were murdered daily by gas and burned in four crematoria. . . . The number killed from April 1942 to April 1944 was 1,715,000. . . . These beastly mass murders force the entire civilized world and particularly all Christians to scream and protest. I express the feelings of a wide circle of Swiss Catholics when I ask you, as the dean of the Swiss bishops, to please support a demonstration of Swiss Episcopates against these barbaric persecutions and mass murder, which is unique in the history of mankind. The protest of the Swiss bishops will undoubtedly make a deep impression upon the Catholics of Hungary and will help stem the flood of inhuman treatment throughout Europe. Speed is of the essence!

> Signed,
>
> Dr. Johannes Duft[107]

The response to this appeal was continued silence. No conclave of bishops ever took place.

The impact of the Protestant sermons and the press campaign manifested itself in many ways. For example, On July 8, an article particularly critical of Hungary was clandestinely circulated in Budapest, and made a strong impact on Horthy.[108] Another result was that the Federation of Swiss Women's Organizations sent a forceful letter to Horthy's wife. This group raised its voice "in the name of countless Swiss women to express our shock and pain at the inconceivable suffering that has befallen the Jews threatened by extermination in Hungary." On the next day, Madame Horthy replied that she would "do everything in her power [to] obtain recognition for the principles of humanity."[109]

The Swiss public, long known for its staid imperturbability, was strongly aroused by all the publicity. There were actually mass demonstrations in Basel and Schaffhausen, and memorial services in Basel and Zurich. Letters of protest, many of them addressed to Horthy, were published by churches, city councils, labor unions, and organizations of all kinds.[110]

Amid the frenzy of the first few days of Mantello's press campaignn, efforts were made by his nemesis, Rothmund, to have the Department of Foreign Affairs declare Mantello persona non grata.[111]

While Mantello's campaign was gaining momentum, the situation of the Jews in Budapest was growing more ominous. On Sunday, June 24, several days after Manoliu had returned from Budapest with the Auschwitz Reports, thousands of Hungarian gendarmes arrived in the capital, ready to carry out the Final Solution. László Endre, Horthy's pro-Nazi minister, spoke on the radio about the threat to Hungary posed by the Jews.

As we will see, Mantello's press campaign would soon grow and achieve dramatic results, making a profound impact in Switzerland, Hungary, and the West, and affecting the fate of the surviving Jews of Budapest. The following chapter will examine this campaign in its full glory, demonstrating how it inspired the great humanitarian spirit of the Swiss people as a whole.

8

The Press Campaign in Full Swing

During the week after June 23, Mantello and his collaborators took the first concrete steps to inform Switzerland and the rest of the world about Auschwitz and the Hungarian deportations. Their efforts were soon to accelerate, snowballing into an incredible press and church campaigns whose effects radically transformed the prevailing Swiss climate of opinion against Auschwitz, the Germans, and their Hungarian accomplices. In fact, contrary to the assertions of historians who advocate the "powerlessness" theory, it is not an overstatement to say that the dual campaigns substantially altered the outcome of the Holocaust.

Let us examine Mantello's campaigns and observe the slow but steady influence it had not only in Switzerland, but also in the free world, and above all on Horthy and Hungary. In fact, Hungary was so affected that for the first time since the German occupation, the regent reasserted his authority and defied the Nazis by halting the deportations. All this, of course, did not happen at once. Rather, it was a slow, fluctuating process whose practical effects took several weeks to become apparent.

Pastor Vogt was equally effective in using to the maximum the influence of the Swiss Protestant Church and its vast resources. As we have noted, he persuaded a number of important Protestant Church bodies to follow his lead and inspired numerous pastors to deliver his message to their flocks throughout Switzerland. Moreover, he used the Church's varied media, including newspapers and publication facilities, to carry Mantello's Auschwitz reports to thousands of influential government and church circles. Finally, he was the very first to publish a book incorporating the reports, as well as additional material on the Jewish tragedy.

The publication of the first newspaper article on June 24 served as a catalyst for the press campaign, which began to escalate in geometric proportions. The publicity achieved a series of practical results, pushing Hungary to halt deportations on July 7 and to pronounce an official halt of deportations on July 18. The impact abroad was felt in all political theaters, affecting the Allies, especially the United States and Britain; the Axis, particularly Hungary and Germany; the neutrals, including countries such as Switzerland, Sweden, Spain, and Portugal; and such neutral bodies as the Vatican and the International Red Cross.

The statistics alone are impressive. From June 24, when the first article appeared in the *Neue Zürcher Zeitung,* through June 30, twenty-one articles came out; from July 1 through 7, when Horthy first halted deportations, there were an additional thirty-two. Within the next ten days, when the deportation halt became public, more than two hundred additional articles appeared. In fact, Horthy's act, rather than reducing the intensity of the campaign, increased it. On July 14 and 15, the numbers reached their apogee, with thirty-eight and thirty-five articles appearing respectively on each day. This, of course, was besides the numerous articles the campaign inspired in the rest of the free world. According to one estimate, the press campaign produced 470 articles in 182 newspapers, totaling what would amount in print to a book of about eight hundred pages. The campaign declined in August and petered out in September.[1]

As we have seen, during the first week alone, Mantello and his colleagues had already achieved an impressive array of accomplishments within Switzerland itself. These included the distribution of Walter Garrett's news release to all Swiss and foreign papers, and to all foreign legations in Switzerland, including the German and Hungarian. Allied intelligence had informed London and Washington, while Mantello's reports were disseminated to representatives of all Jewish organizations in Switzerland. A few of these, such as Posner and Lichtheim, dispatched their own follow-up cables to the key Zionist offices in London, Istanbul, Jerusalem, and New York.

The press campaign mushroomed to thirty-one articles by the end of the first week. Many of these were front-page articles, which for the very first time revealed the gruesome facts of Auschwitz, the role of the Germans, and the complicity of the Hungarians. The fact that the appearance of the first series of articles with the Ankara dispatch had no negative repercussions inspired other newspapers to follow suit, and by July 12, the campaign had reached such credibility that the Ankara dispatch was dispensed with altogether. By then, the formerly solid wall of Swiss censorship had been broken down. After their early triumphs, Mantello, Garrett, and Vogt remained active catalysts, fueling the tempo and intensity of the press and church campaigns throughout its two-month duration. As more and more protests poured in from Western leaders, Mantello and Garrett fed this new information to all the local and foreign newspapers in Switzerland, as well as to the diplomatic circles, including the Hungarian and German legations.

Despite this effective first wave of activities, it would take another week or two before the Swiss government and the International Red Cross would begin to change their abysmally indifferent, if not negative, attitude toward the Jewish tragedy. In the meantime, the combination of the Protestant sermons, the distribution of thousands of copies of the reports, and numerous newspaper editorials created an uproar in the country. Mass demonstrations were held in Basel and Schaffhausen, as well as memorial services in Basel and Zurich. Letters of protest, many of them addressed personally to Horthy, were published by churches, city councils, labor unions, and women's organizations (see chapter 10).[2]

There were several reasons for the early success of Mantello's extraordinary campaign. First was the single-minded drive of the man himself. Distraught over the murder of his parents and his extended family of more than two hundred souls, he disregarded all logical boundaries in his pursuit of rescue and threw himself ferociously into the orchestration of every step of this complicated campaign. Second, the personal involvement of Garrett of the British Exchange Telegraph, with the encouragement of the Allied intelligence heads, helped spearhead the first breakthrough into the strictly censored Swiss press. Moreover, as spelled out in one of Garrett's cables, the fact that the Auschwitz Reports had been obtained and sanctioned by a neutral diplomatic observer and a noted Catholic personality lent support to their authenticity. Mantello was also fortunate to have the support of his two most influential collaborators: Garrett himself, who kept everyone informed of the latest results of the press campaign throughout the world, and Pastor Vogt, whose singular and multifaceted personal campaign used all the facilities of the Swiss Protestant Church.

Within three weeks, there was no longer any faction of the Swiss press that exhibited the slightest hesitancy to say whatever it desired about the Auschwitz atrocities. By July 12, there erupted a veritable explosion of articles that fearlessly attacked all the former Swiss sacred cows, including neutrality, the government, the Church, and the International Red Cross. The results were remarkable, with immediate, ongoing, and long-range ramifications, both national and international.[3] Let us review some of the early results of this unprecedented campaign.

The first stage began June 23 and ended July 7. This two-week period involved the distribution of Mantello's reports to key people, all Jewish organizations, the Swiss government, and all foreign legations. It also saw the entry of the four theologians into the fray and the first public protests of world leaders. To still the avalanche of Western protests, Regent Horthy offered to permit the unconditional exit of more than 10,000 Jewish children from Hungary if the West provided them a safe haven, a move which came to be known as the "Horthy offer." The period concluded with the regent's complete, albeit unofficial, halt of deportations (see chapter 10).

The second stage, from July 8 to 12, elicited additional international repercussions, accompanied by a greater national awareness of the burgeoning power of the press. Steered by the moral leadership of the four theologians, the Swiss censorship guidelines were completely eradicated, permitting full expression of Switzerland's underlying humanitarian impulses.[4]

To comprehend the press campaign's enormous, worldwide impact, it is useful to look more closely at the articles themselves. A number of them appeared in a wide range of papers, and the headlines were frequently duplicated in still other papers. Everyone had ready access to the articles, including the Jewish organizations, most of whom referred to the press campaign in their publications. Some organizations and individuals even made their own collections of articles. One of the best of these collections was made by Roswell McClelland and his staff at the War Refugee Board.[5]

Headlines

A good perspective of the new climate developing in the Swiss public opinion can be gleaned just by reviewing a small portion of the scores of headlines that appeared in the Swiss press in July 1944. Here is the sampling: "The True Face of the Hungarian Regime,"[6] "Protests and Warnings,"[7] "We Cannot Remain Silent,"[8] "Jewish Deportations in Hungary,"[9] "Appeal and Sermon by Archbishop Spellman,"[10] "The Persecuted Jews,"[11] "The Extermination of Jews, Europe Will Pay for this Crime,"[12] "Barbarity,"[13] "Cordell Hull Holds Hungarian Nation Responsible,"[14] "Great Jewish Tragedy,"[15] "The Tragedy of Hungarian Jewry,"[16] "A Journal of Terror,"[17] "This Death Camp of Auschwitz,"[18] "A Storm of Indignation Has Arisen in the Hearts of All People"[19] "Shocking News from Hungary . . . Regretably No Similar Protest among Cathlic Officials in Hungary,"[20] "'For the Sake of Humanity;' Clara Neff,

Women's Society, Sends Cable toMrs. Horthy,"[21] "The Protest of the Swiss People,"[22] "Easing the Plight of Hungarian Jews: Concession to Swiss Intervention,"[23] "Mass Murder of the Innocent"[24] "The Diary of Atrocities: The Fate of Jews in Hungary, Barbaric Extermination"[25] "We Are All Guilty in the Unheard of Crime Toward the Jews,"[26] "Qui s'excuse, S'accuse! Barbaric Chivalry,"[27] "Le Martyr Juif,"[28] "The Camp for Slaughter by Gas in Auschwitz,"[29] "We Cannot Remain Silent,"[30] "Our Federal Government Is Silent: Our Censors Tried to Control Information but the Press Ignored Them,"[31] "The Church Broke the Silence,"[32] "The Earth Has Not Yet Seen Such Things,"[33] "The Voice of Humanity"[34] "Horror and Disgust of the Whole World,"[35] "Frightful Abomination,"[36] "FDR Protests, Hull Condemns Again,"[37] "Where Is the Swiss Government?,"[38] "Impossible to Believe."[39] The next day the Swiss government responded, as the following headlines declared: "The Federal Government Breaks Its Silence,"[40] "The Co-Responsibility of the German Nation,"[41] "We Swiss and the Grief of the World,"[42] "Open Letter to the President of Federal Council,"[43] "Protests by Students of Zurich,"[44] "Mankind, How Low Have You Sunk?,"[45] "What Did the World Do to Prevent the Murder?"[46] "Protesate Contro Odiose Persecuzioni,"[47] "We Are All Guilty,"[48] "Collective Guilt in a Rascist Mass Murder"[49] "The Great Terror,"[50] "The Hungarian Persecution of Jews and the Swiss Press Censorship,"[51] "Finally" [the IRC acted],[52] "The Success of the Federal Government and the IRC,"[53] "The Butchery of Men,"[54] "Factories to Murder Human Beings,"[55] "Reason for Satisfaction" [Federal Government and the IRC],[56] "The Hungarian Outrage,"[57] "Proud of the Swiss Press,"[58] "Vis-a-vis Such Crimes There Is No Neutrality," Q[59] "Hungary Ends Deportations,"[60] "Response to the Success of World Outcry: The Horthy Offer."[61]

Although the headlines of the articles provide an indication of the changing Swiss attitude and some reflection of its impact abroad, a careful look at their content will reveal the tremendous moral fervor of the campaign. Switzerland, in its ethical stance, soared far above and beyond every other country in the free world during this tragic period. Within about two months, the campaign also virtually eliminated the dark ten-year chapter of the Swiss government and the IRC's previous official indifferent policy toward Jewish refugees, one which did not reflect well on their humanitarian instincts. It also silenced, if not eliminated, the many pro-Nazi Swiss groups and brought out the best within the Swiss people. Since the end of the war, the Swiss have displayed several instances of breastbeatings over this negative policy in reports, books, and films, but they have never taken justifiable pride in their subsequent moral activism, which went far beyond anything exhibited by other neutral countries or even by the Allies.[62] The articles that appeared during the Swiss press campaign would never have been published in an American or British newspaper at that time. Let us look at some excerpts.

On July 6, an article entitled "We Cannot Remain Silent" cited the view of Vogt's evangelic circles: "The war that is being waged today as a total war, even on women and children, is a crime. The shooting of hostages is a crime. . . . But the greatest crime of all is that an entire race . . . is being exterminated by fire and sword."[63]

On July 7, Switzerland's largest daily, the *Neue Zürcher Zeitung*, carried the headline "Jews Deported in Hungary." The story read: "Ninety percent of the Jews deported from Hungary have been brought to the Auschwitz camp, in Northern Silesia, labeled as an extermination camp. . . . The inmates . . . are delivered to death by gas in groups, later to be burned to ashes in crematoria. . . . Qualified voices which are above suspicion . . . have raised their voices against this shocking crime, confirming with certainty the reports about the 'extermination camp' in Auschwitz."[64]

Garrett continually provided the Swiss press with new information relating to the persecution of the Jews and the world's outcry at the German barbarities. For example, on that same day, July 7, he released to the Swiss papers the text of the earlier-mentioned sermon by New York's Archbishop Spellman, which strongly condemned the persecution of the Jews in Hungary. The sermon read in part:

> Anyone who possesses human sensibility and a sense of justice must be filled with horror hearing about the persecution of the Jews in Hungary. What is happening there now is contrary to the doctrines of the Catholic faith, to which the great majority of Hungarian people belong. The Hungarian nation is about to betray the most noble pages of its history and to forget its cultural tradition. It seems unbelievable that the nation which has defended Christianity through many troubled periods is now turning to the most abominable ways, swayed by tyrants and false ideologies of blood and race. . . . Anti-Semitism is irreconcilable with the Holy Principles of the Catholic Church and should be disdained by real Christians. . . . We still refuse to understand that the Hungarian nation, with its glorious past . . . is participating in the mania of hatred perpetrated by the National Socialists. . . . The one who hates his neighbor cannot be a true Christian.[65]

The following excerpt of July 12 perhaps typifies the almost universal response of the Swiss press and the Swiss public, an essentially religious people, to the revelations of the Nazi atrocities:

> The entire Swiss people was shaken by deep shock resulting from information, about whose accuracy there can be no doubt, which gave us an insight into the dreadful destiny that has befallen Hungarian Jewry. . . . There are things which awaken the most insensitive spectator of this drama from his peaceful comfort and compel him to stand up as a human being against such barbarities. . . . When we hear that a population of nearly one million souls was chased from their homes . . . herded together in ghettos like cattle, deported in freight cars . . . and murdered in a sophisticated manner in a few months, when we realize that this is happening in our days, in the heart of Europe, in a country whose culture we praise so much, and which is so justly proud of its Christianity and chivalry, *then we are no longer able to continue with our neutral reserve,* which does not pretend to make any judgment as to the admissibility or utility of war behavior. . . . It is our duty not only as men and Christians, but also as Swiss, to raise our voices. . . . We are shocked to see hundreds of thousands of defenseless people sent to their deaths because they have been stripped of status on biological grounds. . . . *There exists no neutrality in regard to such behavior.* (emphasis added)[66]

The next day, July 13, Karl Zimmerman of the *Neue Zürcher Zeitung* authored a similarly emotional article, entitled "A Word Regarding the Persecution of the Jews," which read more like a sermon:

> There are events which force us, the Swiss, to express our opinion, for we would commit treason against our Swiss heritage by remaining silent. We are bound to humanity in the name of the Cross . . . like [the great educator, Johann H.] Pestalozzi, who aspires to be "a man, a Christian, and a citizen." This is the outcry of a Swiss man before the terrible atrocities committed against Jews of Hungary, of which we have learned from irreproachable witnesses. . . . When we watch hundreds of thousands of men and women, infants and the aged . . . loaded onto cattle cars and sent to the extermination camps, all because they belong to the same religious community . . . then we have to speak up, for even the stones cry out.
>
> Who can imagine the suffering of hundreds of thousands of people? That is known only to God alone, the Father of all, to whom the persecuted are holy. It is to Him that the blood of the innocent cries out from the earth. . . . We, the Swiss Christians, can think only of the absolute shame that there are

Christians, or at least former "Christians," who, in carrying out these crimes, are hurting the name "Christian" and exposing the Christian faith to scorn. . . . We Swiss love Hungary. . . . It is impossible to understand . . . how it disregards the sign of the Cross . . . and allows such barbarities to take place. . . . We are deeply agitated by these terrible events. . . . If we Swiss people have a mission, it can only be to side . . . most passionately and energetically with the persecuted, whether he be Swiss or a foreigner, a Christian or a Jew.[67]

By July 12 the campaign reached such a pitch that it broke through the last traces of resistance shown by some reluctant Swiss papers, which were either still skeptical or less than enthusiastic in their defense of the Jews. The censorship bureau could now do no more than protest—unsuccessfully—the unauthorized publication of all these articles, declaring, "This dispatch contains a deliberate collection of carefully selected quotations on the persecution of the Jews, which has a propagandistic character that we cannot countenance."[68]

For weeks afterward, virtually no paper would appear without undisguised protest against the Nazis' mass murder and deportation of the Jews. Some of the headlines are of a patently critical tenor, such as "The Destiny of Hungarian Jews,"[69] "Gassed and Burned,"[70] "Protest These Atrocity Crimes!,"[71] and "The Persecution of the Jews."[72] "Murdered by Gas, Then Burned"[73]—"The persecution of Jews and the extermination facilities in Auschwitz and other places have changed Europe into a spiritual and moral desert."[74]

Another particularly poignant article pointed out the following:

The first news about the terrible mass slaughter of Jews in Hungary was at the outset not believed by a part of the population. It seemed *impossible,* impossible even in this world full of blood and terror. It is now three weeks since the publication of the reports. Neither the Germans nor the Hungarians have denied the facts. There has been no attempt to contest the affirmed facts or to weaken the impact of their terror. . . . There were several hundred thousand innocent children, women, and men, elderly, sane, and ill, systematically murdered in the "extermination camps." . . . The entire world displayed great indignation at such crimes; there are no words in German adequate to describe them fully. . . . *The Swiss protest against this barbarity, which is unheard of in human history.* . . . It is a farce to compare [the perpetrators] to animals. There is no animal in this world which would behave in such an abominable way with other creatures. The extermination camps could only be conceived in the fantasy of men so base that they are far beneath animals. *Soon we shall be ashamed of being men in front of a dog.* (emphasis added)[75]

Speaking of dogs, another paper, the *Berner Tagwacht,* condemned a reprehensible appeal from the Budapest Animal Humane Society: "The society has invited the public to bring in the ownerless cats and dogs whose [Jewish] masters had been deported . . . so that they can rescue the 'poor' creatures. The [society] takes upon itself the obligation to take care of the homeless dogs and cats. . . . The Budapest Animal Humane Society is concerned about dogs and cats. That is what we call humanity in the twentieth century!"[76]

A number of the articles that follow focused specifically on the horrors of Auschwitz, whose name was virtually unknown to the world until Mantello and his many helpers made it a household word. For instance, after describing in detail the mass murder of 1,715,000 Jews in the unique death factory of Auschwitz, another article, entitled "Despicable Crimes," added: "Now it is the turn of Hungarian Jews [to suffer]. Mankind, painfully tested by war and hunger, cannot remain silent in the face of such terrible crimes. The men-become-beasts who invent, order, and execute such horrors have lost all rights to compassion and indulgence."[77]

Another article was simply titled "Auschwitz." It made the following observation:

> We have already heard and read about Dachau, Oranienburg, and Buchenwald, and it is known that people were poorly treated there and even tortured to death. But it is far worse in Auschwitz! There are the death chambers, where people are subjected to agonizing death by gas in a systematic way. [This has been going on] for months, and maybe even years. In Hungary alone, it is estimated that between 300–400,000 people were "liquidated"—what a monstrous, dreadful word. There is talk about two million who were murdered by gas in Auschwitz and then burned to ashes.
>
> The only crime of these people is the fact that they are sons of Israel! The National Socialists have avowed a deadly hatred of Jews, and there is no precedent in world history for such expression of hatred. The [Germans'] bombing of cities by unguided planes without pilots [i.e., V-1 and V-2 rockets], against young and old alike, does not seem to us equal to the profound brutality of the death chambers in Auschwitz. . . . We have to ask ourselves, Lord in Heaven, is this possible ? Is this really possible . . . a crematorium with two million human beings murdered by gas?[78]

One front-page headline captured the widespead incredulity at the existence of an Auschwitz in Europe's midst: "Mankind, How Low Have You Fallen?"[79]

A cry of distress reaches our ears these days. It is so shrill that it is louder than the uproar of the battles, so desperate that it breaks through the soundproof walls of modern times; the censorship of the mail and press cannot silence it. It is so violent that it agitates our hearts, which have been dulled by the horrors of present times. . . . A long line of railway wagons, full of children without parents, relatives, or attendants, was deported to a slave camp and then to death by gas. . . . Do you have children? Do you like children? Two, three, four years old, pathetic in their helplessness and harmlessness, [they were] packed [into] railway wagons on a single day, deported in cold blood to foreign death camps! Happy are those who died on the way! . . . Up to now there were some 400,000 Hungarian Jews [deported] . . . mostly to Auschwitz. . . . [Evidently] the English and American protests, as well as the reprimands of the King of Sweden and the voice of the Swiss public, all remain futile. . . .[80] We have become accustomed to the most atrocious tragedies. . . . We learn to accept anything and we do not protest. The horrible news is here to shake us up; it must wake us up from our complacency [and stir us] to a real human participation.[81]

While most of the Swiss press concentrated on the immediate consequences of Nazism and Auschwitz, one article, authored by a highly respected journalist, is arguably the very first to point out the long-range impact of the creation of such a death factory:

We received the attached reports from a quarter which leaves no doubt as to their veracity. . . . Yet, regardless of the indisputable proofs, something within us still refuses to believe them. We are stung by the annihilation of European Jewry, we are stung by the destruction of and renunciation of humanity . . . this method of dealing with a conflict by the most ghastly, inhuman, and disgusting means. These are things we somehow cannot accept as true, inasmuch as the consequences for the future of civilization will be immeasurable and eternal. . . . Here are complexes of guilt and horror, with consequences beyond imagination. . . . Europe is sicker than we would like to admit.[82]

Because almost all the newspapers reflected a deep religious outlook, they described the creation of Auschwitz, designed by the world's most cultured nation, in terms of their own Christianity. One such article, which exemplified the general outcry, was entitled "Unbelievable and Incomprehensible."

For the past week we have been reading information about the persecution of Jews in Hungary, reports which have reached unbelievable and incomprehensible [proportions], and which have yet to be refuted by any reliable or trustworthy source. A storm of indignation has arisen in the hearts of all people to whom humanity is the most important thing in life. . . . The persecution of Jews, both before and during this war, has never reached such a degree of horror as in recent days. Hungary has the "honor" to be at the forefront of the persecution of the Jews. . . . What happens today to the unfortunate Jews who are being deported from Hungary by the hundreds of thousands? They are tortured to death, killed by gas, and then burned to ashes. They are being taken to the so-called "extermination camps." The hand is reluctant to write down these atrocities. . . . There can be no more silence. It would be cowardice. . . . Let us raise our voices in the name of Christianity: We cry out in the name of humanity. We appeal to all other countries where there are Christians. From the depths of our souls, we cry out for help for the Jews.[83]

The Protestant Church, under Vogt's leadership, not only led the efforts to break through the silence about Auschwitz, but it also was responsible for encouraging the Swiss people to demonstrate openly. Proud of its part in making Auschwitz a public issue, it demanded that the Swiss government follow suit, in an article entitled "The Earth Has Not Yet Seen Such Things":

Since it has been inhabited by man, our planet has seen much mischief and crime . . . but everything fades in light of what has been happening in Hungary in recent weeks. . . . It was left to the National Socialists to achieve the crowning glory of all horrors by its systematic extermination of Hungarian Jews. . . . The terrible news . . . has upset the Swiss public, which until now was hardly aware of the extermination of the Jews under the heel of Nazism.

Led by "refugee pastor"[84] Paul Vogt, the Swiss Evangelical Church inspired special church services and public protests concerning the deportations of Hungarian Jewry and the extermination camps:

Some of these protests took place on July 9 in some cantons, where the Council clarified its stand . . . which was important in view of the earlier [censorship] that forbade the open discussion of certain subjects. . . .[85]

These open protests destroyed the false picture of reality created by indifference . . . and silence . . . [which was] due in part to the frightened behavior of the press censor. . . . [Such] denunciation will surely meet with the sincere approval of all Swiss citizens with a sense of justice. . . . [Presently] a wave of indignation and abhorrence pervades the entire civilized world . . . [furthered by] the King of Sweden's intervention with Horthy. . . . Will our government take similar steps?[86]

The fact that the moral campaign to raise the public's conscience was a virtual Protestant monopoly aroused much criticism of the Swiss Catholics. Particular blame was directed at official Catholic circles for failing to join in the protests of the Swiss people. An article entitled "The People's Expectations" gave vent to such feelings:

> The shocking news from Hungary about the measures undertaken by the present government for the total extermination of Hungarian Jews has created in Switzerland an atmosphere of indignation and protest. . . . It is especially regrettable that no official Catholic circles have made protest against the barbarities in Hungary. . . . How can the Church claim higher ethical and religious postulates of the people when it disavows the Man Himself, and with Him the natural foundation of Christianity?[87]

It is most important, however, to realize that while condemnation of Catholic officialdom was justified, the public voice of its adherents was no less critical of the Nazi horrors than that of their Protestant brothers and sisters. This was manifested in almost all Catholic newspapers, which were part of the press campaign. An example of the Catholic press's protest against the persecution of the Jews was an article in the Catholic *Basler Volksblatt* of July 15, entitled "The Horror and Disgust of the Entire World":

> Millions of victims . . . fell into self-dug graves, killed by machine guns or suffocated in locked freight trains. [Others] met their sad end in the gas chambers, later to disappear in an anonymous heap of ashes . . . men, women, frail children, and weak old people. . . . The knowledge of [these atrocities] has been declared openly more than once in the troubled proclamations of the Holy Father and the national church princes. They call for justice with the anxious concern that retaliation and counter-retaliation may in the end loosen all the bonds of human society. . . . Our contemporaries . . . had for a long while resisted belief in the veracity of these horrors. . . . Declarations by Allied politicians about "war criminals" and their punishment were taken as war propaganda catch-words. . . . *All this has changed with one stroke, as numerous, well-documented reports from Hungary leave no more doubts that the persecution of Jews is in fact a systematic, cold-minded mass murder of the innocent. The outcry against such terror can now be heard all over the world.* (emphasis added)[88]

Gradually, the newspaper articles began openly to attack their own government's silence and the censor's heavy hand in the face of the Jewish tragedy. For example, *Der Aufbau,* featured an article entitled "The Assassination of Jews."

Everything we knew about the dark Middle Ages seems pale in the face of these atrocities. The news has deeply moved a large segment of our population. Our federal government is silent. . . . Our censors were in a hurry to control the worst information, but the papers, as one can see, have ignored such attempts to suppress the outcry of conscience. This has shown once again that *the censors are the worst enemy of the world's conscience.* (emphasis added)[89]

One of the first major results of the press campaign came in 1944 from its relentless pressure against the tragic policy of *refoulement,* which had resulted in the return of many thousands of "illegal" Jewish refugees across the Swiss border where they fell into German hands. The campaign succeeded when the Swiss government finally rescinded this racist regulation on July 12, 1944. Dr. Heinrich Rothmund, the powerful and dreaded head of the Swiss Alien Police with the full complicity of Federal Councilor Eduard von Steiger was responsible for the implementation of these regulations. They had been put into force in October 1938,[90] and became even more stringent on December 29, 1942, when a new law declared that Jewish refugees who crossed into Switzerland were not even permitted to contact their relatives.[91]

In her correspondence with McClelland, at about this time, Recha Sternbuch requested that McClelland use his powerful office to influence the Swiss to rescind the harsh laws of *refoulement,* pointing to the example of Sweden, another neutral country afraid of Germany. Yet, Sweden not only permitted the entry of Jewish refugees—including the 7,000 Danish Jews rescued in September 1943—they also permitted the refugees to work. Recha added, "It was six years ago [1938] that I learned to appreciate the refugee problem—as a result of a St. Gallen jail experience, after we brought hundreds of people across the borders from the Nazi territories."[92]

In his response, the unsympathetic McClelland wondered "why she chose to live in Switzerland when Sweden was far more friendly to refugees." Undaunted by the powerful official, the mother and housewife replied, "I do not believe that I should have to leave my mother country of the past thirty-five years and move to Sweden just because I disagree with some things, such as the laws of refoulement. I believe that much more should be done for these unfortunate ones. . . . I consider it my duty to remain here, where I can contribute to an improvement, however modest."

Responding to McClelland's attempt to besmirch her Swiss loyalty, she gave the haughty American a lecture on patriotism:

One is not a better Swiss or American merely by totally agreeing with every action or law carried out by one's country. Nor, by the same token, is one a worse citizen for being dissatisfied with any of these. Good Swiss tenets of patriotism are based upon free and open criticism, as long as it remains within its constitutional limits and is pursued by legal means. . . . I can only assure you that my views coincide with those of Switzerland's greatest personalities whose voices we frequently heard in the National Assembly and recently from private and highly respected sources as well. I have much greater respect for the [true] Swiss mentality than do those people who keep silent or demand . . . *refoulement.*

An article in *The Nation* of July 13 added fuel to the fire of indignation at the inertia of the Swiss government. The writer declared prophetically: "We are convinced that the Federation [of Swiss Cantons] must evolve stronger initiatives than have been in place until now. We cannot remain satisfied with the results. We must raise our voices, which may become the [unified] voice of a great moral power, for the benefit of all the persecuted and tortured. There are at this very moment hundreds of thousands of Jews being deported from Hungary to Polish extermination camps."[93]

A unanimous, 91-0, declaration by the Council of the Swiss Canton of Zurich added further to the pressure on the federal government. The declaration was but one of many similar resolutions by other cantons, and provided grisly details of the mass murders in Auschwitz:

Shocking information about the persecution of Jews in Hungary has reached us recently. According to reliable reports, there are one million people of Jewish origin threatened by death in Hungary . . . men, women, and children. . . . It is high time that this dreadful murder is stopped by a vast wave of worldwide protest. The Council of the Canton of Zurich expresses herewith the horror of the people of Zurich at these unimaginable brutalities, and appeals to all thinking men to join in protest against the continuation of this hideous crime.

There is no question about who is behind these bestial deeds, which scorn any concept of humanity. . . . The world did not believe it . . . yet we believe that there is a Judge above all nations Who guides history. . . . No misdeeds remain without their penalty, even when His mills work slowly. Maybe the expiation is even nearer than we believe.[94]

On July 12, the *National-Zeitung* also attacked the Swiss government in the sharpest terms:

The voices against the crimes in Hungary are getting louder. In Monday's edition of our evening paper we published the protest of the Council of the Canton of Zurich against the daily slaughter of men, women and children, expressing the horror of the Zurich population over the unbelievable barbarity. The Federation of Swiss Churches [i.e., Koechlin] got in touch with the Federal Council and the IRC with the request to do everything in order to save the Jews of Hungary. *And the Federal Council remains silent!* Why does the Federal Council have to be requested and urged, *why does it not utter a word?* Why does it not support the Swedish King in his efforts? (emphasis added)[95]

Two days later, on July 14, the Federal Council came under further pressure. First, an urgent request was sent by Pastor Vogt to both the president of the Federal Council and the Federal Council in general to consider a practical plan for implementing the rescue efforts on the agenda. His letter of July 14, which again displayed his great humanity, began, "My conscience won't let me rest," and concluded with a practical suggestion for the Federal Council to consider sending fifty Swiss citizens to Budapest to facilitate rescue. The same day, the Federal Council called an emergency meeting on the issue of rescue.[96]

Unaware of the action taken by the Federal Council, the Zurich-based *Schweizer Wochen-Zeitung,* in its July 15 issue, continued admonishing the foremost Swiss political body, using the same headline: "And the Federal Council Remains Silent." Finally, on July 16, a jubilant *National-Zeitung* announced a breakthrough with the headline "The Federal Council Breaks Its Silence." It informed its readers of the following:

In a communique, Pilet-Golaz informed his committee of the steps that had been taken to help the persecuted Jews of Hungary. . . . *We know how much the Federal Council had to be pressured by public opinion.* . . . After having expressed our surprise at the silence of the Federal Council . . . [w]e have to point out with satisfaction that in the "Tour d'Ivoire" a window has been opened, and *the Federal Council has broken its silence.* In the meantime, our readers confirmed many times over how deeply and painfully the Swiss nation was affected by the official reserve. You can be certain that this is also the opinion of the majority of our people. . . . The people are already disgusted by the inevitable eloquence of the Federal Council's sanctimonious defense which they are certain will follow. . . . It is a capital error of the Federal government and other authorities, as well as the newspapers and cultural organizations of our country, not even to have protested against such scandalous treatment of human beings. (emphasis added)[97]

What is of particular interest is the fact that Pilet-Golaz was not only the influential minister of foreign affairs, but also was part of the same Federal Council, along with Eduard von Steiger, which, on December 29, 1942, approved the racist regulations of *refoulement.* Von Steiger was in charge of the strict censorship that sought to prevent news of the Holocaust from reaching the Swiss public. Thus, under the twin pressures of the church leaders and the press, Pilet-Golaz was moved from a very reluctant and even unsympathetic stance to an active pursuit of rescue efforts on behalf of Hungarian Jewry. Moreover, von Steiger had to knuckle under the same twin Swiss pressures.

Not only church leaders voiced their strong protest to their government against the German-Hungarian inhumanity toward the Jews. On July 13, a protest was targeted at the Swiss Federal Council (Bundesrat) by the Federation of Swiss Women's Organizations, headed by Mrs. Clara Nef. She wrote an article called "We Women," which read in part:

> Protests are a platonic gesture. Yet there are events against which one must protest, because if humanity is silent, then the stones must cry out! . . . For five years we have had news of mass deaths, bombardments, persecutions, deportations. We hear it, but somehow it doesn't enter our conscience. . . . We cannot turn away from what has been happening to the Jewish people, who are also our brothers and are like all others before God. We women as well want to raise our voices in an emotional, passionate protest . . . [against] the events which are far worse than [those of] the darkest Middle Ages.[98]

Unsatisfied with a mere protest to the Swiss government, Mrs. Nef cabled a message directly to Mrs. Horthy on July 23, in language that was very explicit. The cable read,

> Deeply shocked by the atrocious destiny of Jews in Hungary, we implore Your Excellency, in the name of Swiss women and mothers, to use your great influence to save these people, who are also our brothers before God.
>
> Signed,
>
> The Union of Swiss Women's Societies
> The Swiss League for Women's Suffrage
> The Swiss Voluntary Social Work Women's Society[99]

Mrs. Horthy responded the very next day in a cable saying she would do everything in her power "to obtain recognition of the principles of humanity." The cable was publicized in the *Neue Zürcher Zeitung* of July 25.[100]

University students also joined in the protests. At the University of Zurich, the student body and the Life Savers' Society, representing more than half a million Swiss students, along with members of sports and athletic clubs, sought to pressure the Swiss government into protesting to the Germans. They addressed an open letter to the federal president, which read:

> [We have noted] the terrible mass execution of 1,700,000 of our neighbors from various European countries. . . . In the name of Christianity and humanity, we plead with you to protest immediately and solemnly to the German government against these shocking events and to entreat it to rescue those surviving Jews from this terrible fate. . . . Most revered Mr. Federal President, the Swiss youth extend their minds and hearts, imploring you to listen to their free and fearless voice! Pray accept, Mr. Federal President, the expression of our highest esteem.[101]

Pointing to the success of the ongoing pressure on the federal government and the International Red Cross, a reporter of the *Volksrecht* remarked, "As we gather from yesterday's report of the Proxy Commission debate, the Federal Council, as well as the IRC, have decided to undertake possible steps to rescue those who can still be saved."[102]

Ironically, the press campaign was not stilled even by the International Red Cross's public announcement on July 18 that Hungarian policy had become more favorable toward its Jews, and that Regent Horthy had offered to permit the exit of more than 10,000 Jewish children. On the contrary, the campaign continued unabated, only now with greater emphasis on self-criticism. There was a general realization that so much more could have been accomplished had the same pressure been applied earlier to the Swiss government and the IRC, both formerly revered symbols of Swiss nationality. Many articles lashed out particularly against the IRC's late entry into the fray, especially because it proved so powerful once it decided to act.

Das Volk of July 19 admonished the Swiss with a story entitled "The Guilt of Silence." The editor pointed out the tragic error of many of his countrymen, and of the free world in general:

> It may be true that for *a small neutral country, under certain circumstances, "silence" is tantamount to diplomatic prudence. But it must be described as a guilty cultural cowardice in today's situation, when the unheard-of crime of the mass extermination of Hungarian Jews by gas cries out to the heavens.* But it did not start in Hungary. . . . Reliable reports indicate that . . . this is but the end

of a process which began eleven years ago. . . . Today, when over four million Jews . . . equivalent to the entire Swiss population, have already been exterminated in a criminal manner, we must seek to answer the question: *What did the [free] world, which witnessed this violent drama, do to prevent it?* . . . There is a great tragedy behind what has happened between 1933 and the present . . . not the least of which is the failure . . . to make more than superficial protests against the unheard-of attacks against justice and humanity. . . . The intellectual elite of Europe and America preferred . . . to remain silent. . . . History will not forget that . . . *what happens today is not the beginning but the logical end of a development about which the large majority kept silent until it was too late.* (emphasis added)[103]

In the same vein, there was a major article entitled "We Helped Hitler by Our Silence," in which the writer remarked that it was not only Switzerland that was guilty of silence in the matter of the extermination of Jews, but also the so-called cultured world. In a sarcastic vein, the article also noted the well-known case of the shooting of fifty British air force officers in Germany, an event that had aroused great indignation:

The civilized world raised its voice against the destruction of artistic and historic monuments, which happened in the course of routine military undertakings. Special committees were formed to make appeals to the public [about these monuments]. But they did not speak out when hundreds of thousands of children and women were murdered with wild ferocity.[104] The four million Jews who were murdered by the same Germans in the last two years did not manage to shake this "conscience." Only about the fifty corpses did the British press speak out. . . . When one considers that the [recent] protest of the so-called world-conscience against the murder of Hungarian Jewry was enough to save at least some of these unfortunate people from the worst, then it is possible to imagine how many Jews could have been spared from Auschwitz and Sobibor. And finally, if . . . Great Britain, the United States, and the Soviet Union would have opened their frontiers at the beginning of the conflict, how many millions of Jews would still be alive. . . . And we all helped in this by our silence.[105]

Another outstanding example of the self-criticism that erupted in the Swiss press, even after the halt of deportations, was published in *The Nation* of July 20, under the rubric "A Tragic Error":

If we could only cease to talk about the terrible mass murder of Jews. What are the Jews? They are people! Men like you and me. Women like our women.

Children like our children. Whether they are Jews, Negroes, or Chinese, they are men, equal before the Supreme Judge, equal in joy and sorrow, through thick or thin. . . . Even the horrors of the Inquisition or witch burnings, the enormous capital crimes of the Church, seem nothing in comparison with the crimes of our days. No, it is not "just Jews," it is the case of all men, of mankind. Can we still speak about war. . . . Is not the entire policy of dividing the European nations into the [two] races of masters and slaves one great error?[106]

One of the amazing results of the Swiss press campaign was the fact that it attracted even those xenophobic, anti-Semitic Swiss who were on a par with Lorenzo and Rothmund. So powerful was its impact on the Swiss public that soon after it began, virtually no Swiss paper, even those not particularly sympathetic to Jews, could afford to ignore the newly created humanitarian climate. Virtually every paper joined in the condemnation of Auschwitz and of the German and Hungarian crimes against the Jews. As Saly Mayer's confidant, Marcus Weiler, noted to his friend in his report of early August on the press campaign, "Even such a non-philo-Semitic newspaper as the earlier-mentioned *Aufgebot,* in its July 20th edition, readily accepted the accusations as true. Moreover, in an editorial in its August 1st edition entitled 'Jews and Hostages,' it talked about mass murder. Likewise, the *Silent Observer* published a remarkable, popular article on the 'indescribable massacres of entire trains of Jewish children, who were gassed, 300,000 to 400,000 human beings murdered in cold blood.'"[107]

A similar article on July 23 in the *Burgdorfer Tagblatt,* entitled "The Butchery of Men," noted: "There is no lack of anti-Semitism, even in our country. Even in these days, one courageous journalist was rebuked by such [anti-Semitic] individuals for describing the truth of the mass murder of the Jews."[108] Still another article in the July 16 edition of the *Neue Zürcher Zeitung,* a paper with an unfavorable attitude toward Jews, noted: "One can have his own opinion regarding the very complex problem of Jewry, but no Swiss can deny that the systematic slaughter of hundreds of thousands of men, women, and children is in no way a solution to this complicated question."[109]

As far as the Swiss Jewish press itself was concerned, it first dared to react publicly to the press campaign only in mid-July, after it was already in full swing. For example, on July 22, an article by Rabbi Dr. L. Rothschild appeared in the *Ostschweizerisches Tagblatt,* describing the Auschwitz Reports and the destruction of Hungarian Jewry.[110]

The Swiss people were so moved by the press campaign that they began to organize public protests in the streets and in the town square. Among the groups who demonstrated were representatives of labor, women, and university students, who displayed an unexpected affinity for the Jewish victims of the Holocaust, despite the fact that Switzerland (and the rest of the world) were totally unaccustomed to public protest.

The publicity these street protests were given in the press widened their impact, and the fact that a large Christian contingent participated in them lent them a high moral character. This was not true in the case of the anti-Nazi demonstrations made by American Jewry in New York's Madison Square Garden, which were attended almost solely by Jewish audiences and were directed at the British to open the doors of Palestine. Moreover, other than the march by four hundred Orthodox rabbis in front of the White House in October 1943, there was not a single public demonstration in the United States to protest the American government's indifference to the fate of European Jewry, and hardly a word from the great liberal and humanitarian leader, President Franklin D. Roosevelt.[111]

One Swiss protest, which was held on Thursday, July 27, at the Cathedral Square in Münsterplatz in Basel, was organized by the Worker's Union and several other labor parties. It was attended by about three thousand men and women, and was addressed by four members of the Swiss Parliament. At this demonstration, the first speaker noted:

> We came here to protest the barbarities we have witnessed, which have no equal in world history. Our rally should point out to those responsible that the sense of humanity is not dead and that people will not tolerate the presentation of crimes as if they were heroic acts. At the same time, we want to show our sympathy to the victims of these atrocities. . . . We can do little here in Switzerland for the persecuted in Hungary, Poland, France, and other countries, but we cannot remain silent and be guilty of indifference.[112]

Attacking the censorship that had previously prevented the publication of atrocity reports, the speaker demanded that, at very minimum, "we must search for justice at home."

The following speaker voiced dissatisfaction even with the "improved" Alien Police regulations of *refoulement,* of July 12 and the indifference of the Federal Council:

The new regulations of July [12,] 1944, promulgated by the Federal Council concerning the admittance of refugees, are [still] inadequate and untenable. This belief was demonstrated by the brave inhabitants of Neuenkirch, who acted spontaneously and took under their protection the workers from the East, who had been ordered to return across the border, and therefore prevented them from being sent back. . . . It is not true that we have too many refugees. We can and we will take all who are in danger and who come to us.

Quoting the author Romain Rolland, the speaker concluded, "Let us create a brotherhood of all who suffer." The next speaker declared:

We witness with deep shame the terrible crimes. Respect for humanity is being dragged through the mud. We were dulled by the many horrible deeds we live with, but now we have reached the . . . stage where we have to make clear: *Neutrality has no place when confronting such a crime!* To this point and no further! . . . We have to put a stop to the mass murder . . . and ask the Federal Council to raise its voice . . . to protest the crimes committed against the Jews and other people!

The demonstration concluded with a resolution that read in part: "The Assembly raises an ardent protest against the terrible murders of several hundred thousand Jews in Hungary. . . . The Assembly asks the Federal Council to undertake all necessary steps to save the lives of those still threatened by extermination. We expect [them] to permit entry and provide asylum to all who search for a safe haven in Switzerland."[113]

The gathering was reported in the *National Zeitung* of Basel on August 4, in an article entitled "Neutrality Does Not Apply When Confronting Such a Crime." Among other things, the reporter commented on the major changes the protests had effected on the racist Swiss policy of *refoulement*. A mass demonstration with a similar theme was called by another labor union for Friday evening, August 8, and was reported in the *Arbeiterzeitung* on the following day.

No less sharp were the words of the Labor Party in Geneva, which passed an urgent motion attacking the Federal Council, reading in part:

Our entire nation was shocked by the fate of the Jews who are doomed . . . [and] are murdered by gas in the hundreds of thousands. . . . [The Labor Party] sees its duty to express the feelings and . . . [to] inform the Federal Council that they must do everything possible to put an end to these inhuman tortures.

. . . They [must] approach the Federal Council in the name of the population of the Basel Canton, which is completely united on this question and whicn is deeply affected by these terrible facts.[114]

The press campaign and the resulting protests and demonstrations had achieved more dramatic results than anyone had anticipated. Homes, hearts, and consciences were awakened in Switzerland; it now remained to be seen what effect the publicity would have on the perpetrators.

9

The Response by the Hungarians, the Germans, and IRC

Mantello's initiatives in Switzerland, which quickly blossomed into the extraordinary response of the Swiss press, church, and people, had enormous repercussions abroad. We have already discussed the immediate response of Western leaders during the first week of the campaign, including the protests of the pope, Hull, Eden, the king of Sweden, and the archbishops of Canterbury and New York. These brought about Horthy's first declaration to halt the deportations; however, his outburst of June 26 was more a cry of frustration at this unexpected turn of events than a desire to repent his role as accomplice in the mass deportation and murder of almost half a million Hungarian Jews. After all, Eichmann's contingent of 160 or so SS officers in Hungary was hardly capable of accomplishing this monstrous deed without the full cooperation of the Hungarian gendarmerie. Although there is no doubt that Horthy's initiatives must be viewed within the context of Germany's deteriorating military situation, it was far from the primary factor in the fate of Budapest Jewry; the press campaign played the strongest role in pressuring world leaders to respond to the cry for help.

Hungary's response to world opinion was a slow, tortuous process, beginning June 26, when Horthy regained full control of his government and halted deportations on July 7, until he begged the International Red Cross to inform the West of his changed policy on July 18. His transformation progressed in incremental steps, each of which required the steadily increasing pressure of the press and church campaigns, under the constant prodding of Mantello and his heroic Swiss collaborators. Their efforts were aided and abetted by the two Allied air raids on Budapest on July 2 and 14, and by the entry, under the steady pressure of the Swiss theologians and press on the Federal Council and the IRC, into the rescue arena. Soon afterward, other neutral states such as Sweden, Spain, and Portugal, as well as the papal nuncio in Budapest, followed suit.

At many points on this slow road to the public declaration of a new Hungarian policy toward the Jews, there were counterpressures from the Germans. Regardless of the Russians' encroachment on Hungarian borders, Eichmann, Veesenmayer, and their Hungarian accomplices sought at all costs, even at the expense of Germany's war efforts, to complete the Final Solution, and they tried in every way possible to subvert Horthy's attempts to put a stop to the deportations.

For the first three months of the German occupation of Hungary, Horthy had abdicated much of his power, creating a vacuum readily occupied by László Baky, László Endre, and Andor Jaross, his pro-Nazi ministers. Unimpeded by their weakening regent, they carried out Eichmann's plans for the liquidation of Hungarian Jewry at an extraordinary speed. By late June, through the Department of the Interior, they controlled all the instruments of coercion, such as the police, the civil service, and the gendarmerie. They were able to progress with their plans until Horthy's change of heart, which began to manifest itself during the two crown meetings of June 26 and 27. Here he expressed for the first time his apprehension about the public response of Western leaders to the deportation of Hungarian Jewry, and he set into motion steps to defuse such protests.

In an urgent cable of June 29 to the German foreign office, Veesenmayer openly expressed his concern and dismay at Horthy's apparent change in attitude. He pointed out that, although the mechanism to complete the Final Solution of Hungarian Jewry was already in place, suddenly "more and more steps were taken by foreign organizations with the purpose of improving the situation of the Jews." He then identified the governments behind these steps on behalf of the Jews.[1] The next day he regretfully informed Ribbentrop that Horthy had decided to postpone the deportations of Budapest Jewry for at least ten days, to July 10.[2] At the same time, more internal pressure was exerted on Horthy by two of his confidants, Count Moric Esterhazy and his friend Count Istvan Bethlen, who was in hiding at the time. Bethlen suggested that Horthy replace the Sztojay government, "[to] put an end to the inhuman, stupid, and cruel persecution of the Jews . . . which has besmirched the Hungarian name before the eyes of the world. . . . These barbarous actions must be put to an end, because otherwise, Hungarian Christian society itself will become incurably infected."[3]

At that stage, Veesenmayer did not fully comprehend the impact the press and church campaigns was having on Horthy, and he was still sufficiently confident that "the complete liquidation of the Hungarian Jews is an accomplished fact."[4] To the German ambassador's dismay, however, that confidence soon proved unwarranted. On that same day, June 30, upon the plea of King Gustav of Sweden and the public protests of the archbishops of New York and Canterbury, Horthy quietly resolved to reassert his power. He indicated as much in his response to the pope's plea on July 1, and in a talk he had with the Swedish ambassador as a follow-up of the king's cable.[5]

Horthy's sudden turnabout explains the desperate efforts of Baky, Endre, and Jaross, under Eichmann and Veesenmayer's inspiration, to remove him from the scene entirely and to replace him with Szalasi and those Hungarian figures closely identified with the National Socialists. The major goal of the two men was the completion of Eichmann's Final Solution through the deportation of the last Jewish enclave in Budapest.

During the first few months after the German occupation, Budapest Jews were not placed in a ghetto, and when they were moved, it was into a collection of twenty-six hundred buildings, containing approximately thirty-three thousand apartments, scattered throughout the city. Each house was marked with a yellow star of David.[6]

Then, during the first few days of July, the conspirators imported from the provinces 1,600 "plumed" gendarmes armed with bayonets, and placed them on the streets of Budapest. The official explanation was that they had been brought in to supervise the relocation of Budapest's Jews into the designated yellow-star houses.[7] In addition, details had been worked out for the deportation of the remaining Jews in and around the capital. Endre had even prepared three detention centers to hold the Jews before their deportation: the great market square, the pig market, and the sports grounds near the Vaci-Road.[8] The sudden appearance of these gendarmes, combined with the regent's own intelligence reports about the impending coup, jolted him into taking the first steps to reassert his authority. His effort to thwart the Baky-Endre plan to depose him was reenforced by the very heavy Allied air raid on Budapest on July 2.

Horthy began his stand by calling off the ceremonies that were to have been the signal for the Baky-Endre coup, on the pretense of the danger posed by the bombing. He then ordered the gendarmerie to return to their bases in the provinces.[9] With the help of two trusted officers—one of whom was Gen. Geza Lakatos, whom he was soon to name premier—he brought in an armored and an infantry regiment to parade in Budapest. The next day, under cover of a long "air-raid" alarm, Horthy's men replaced the gendarmerie's pro-Baky officers.[10]

The regent's removal of the gendarmerie from the capital meant not only that he eliminated the immediate threat of a coup by the Eichmann-Baky-Endre clique; it also aborted their deportation of Budapest Jewry, which they could not have accomplished without the active help of the gendarmerie. To add insult to injury, Horthy told Veesenmayer on July 4 of his plan to get the SS out of Hungary, because he intended to "reassert his authority in his own country." Although pledging his devotion to the anti-Bolshevik cause against Russia, Horthy complained bitterly about "the recent deluge of cables and protests from Switzerland, Sweden, and the IRC" against the deportation of the Jews.[11]

At the Crown Council of Ministers on July 5, Horthy and several ministers continued to focus on the Anglo-Saxon countries' negative reaction to the deportations, which were being equated with the daily extermination and gassing of six thousand Jews. He had just obtained intelligence reports on cables from Jewish organizations in Bern, which had been intercepted on their way to Washington and London, and which were obviously based on the Mantello material. There is no doubt that among these cabled appeals were those sent by Dulles and West on the twenty-third, containing the details of the Auschwitz Protocols; also among them were cables sent by McClelland on the twenty-fourth, which included Weissmandl's request to bomb the rail lines to Auschwitz and Mantello's figure for the number murdered in Auschwitz, rounded out to 1.5 million. The Weissmandl-inspired cable, which had been given to McClelland by Czech ambassador Kopecky, also included a brief description of the fate of the deported Jews and suggested retaliatory measures such as the pinpoint bombing of Budapest. In addition, one of the intercepted cables contained a list of the names and addresses of seventy key Hungarian pro-Nazi figures.[12]

By this time, Horthy had come to realize that the Allied warnings clearly placed him in the category of "war criminal," a designation he ardently attempted to avoid.[13] Despite Sztojay's dismissal of Allied threats to bomb Budapest as irrelevant, Horthy was still under the pressure of the cables, which had left its imprint not only on the regent but on some of his ministers as well.[14] He intimated to his chief of staff at the Crown Council meeting that he intended to carry out his declaration of June 26 to prevent further removal of Jews from Budapest.[15]

The following day, July 6, after talking with Sztojay, an agitated Veesenmayer informed Ribbentrop of Horthy's halt of the deportations, indicating that the regent had been affected by the worldwide propaganda and "the flood of both domestic and international appeals to rescue the Jews."[16] At the same time, Gen. E. Wagner, a German officer, suggested to Ribbentrop that they ignore the Allied and Swiss requests for the release of Jews and inform the Hungarian government of this decision. Wagner felt that by the time the Allies actively intervened, the "action" (i.e., deportations) would already have been completed.[17]

On July 7, the regent finally made public the intention he had declared at the June 26 Crown Council meeting to "order a halt in the transfer of Jews to Germany."[18] He also publicly declared his new policy toward the Jews. Horthy personally called Veesenmayer to inform him that, because of the impending coup by Baky and the gendarmerie, he had mobilized his loyal troops and ordered the withdrawal of the gendarmerie from Budapest. Veesenmayer readily confirmed this news in a cable to the foreign office on July 8, in which he complained that the "action planned for that day was stopped, and the gendarmerie, which was responsible for carrying it out, has been returned to their base."[19] Thus, for the time being, both the coup and the Jews' fear of deportation were put to rest.

Horthy, however, still equivocated. Although he asked that the Jews be treated more humanely, he also said that he would soon approve a resumption of deportations. In the meantime, Veesenmayer was willing to make some concessions to the demands of the Swiss, Swedes, and Americans on June 29, among which was an exit quota of about 7,000 Jews.[20] This number would soon reappear as part of the "Horthy offer" (see chapter 10).

The same day, a worried Otto Winkelman, head of the SS in Budapest, wired Himmler about the change in Horthy's policy toward the Jews. He reported that "due to the mounting domestic and international pressure, Horthy was compelled to intervene on behalf of the Jews." Winkelman felt that Veesenmayer was no longer able to handle the matter and requested firm new instructions from Hitler.[21]

The Hungarian legation in Switzerland played a key role in pressuring Horthy to reassert his authority and challenge Hitler's Final Solution in Hungary. Two anti-Nazi Hungarian diplomats were primarily involved: Imre Tahy, the acting chargé d'affaires, and Bela Sarrossy. Sarrossy acted as the conduit for presenting the products of the press campaign to Budapest in a way that could not have been achieved by an outsider. The two men not only provided a graphic description of the impact of the press campaign on the Swiss public, but they also conveyed the ensuing world contempt for Hungary.[22]

As early as June 16, the Hungarian chargé d'affaires in Bern, Imre Tahy, sent copies of the Exchange Telegraph cables containing the first news of the atrocity reports to the Hungarian Foreign Ministry. In addition, a cable to Regent Horthy in which he described the horrors of the deportations as detailed in the Swiss press, adding:

> These reports have caused a great sensation and great scandal within the [Protestant] relief organizations in Switzerland. According to press reports, the Hungarian authorities are responsible for the atrocities committed. It is feared that anti-Hungarian feelings will develop in neutral countries. . . . The best impression would be made if an official denial of the reports that the Jews were being deported were issued and if guarantees were given that they are only being removed and not murdered.[23]

Three days later, on June 29, the Swiss Foreign Political Department (FPD), or better, Department of Foreign Affairs, already confirmed the impact of the nascent press campaign on the negative Swiss attitude toward Hungary, and quite presciently, prognosticated its future course. In a memo to Eduard de Haller, Dr. Carl Stucki, director of the Department of Foreign Affairs, described his conversation with Imre Tahy, writing in part:

> When I used the occasion to explain to him that this policy has resulted in a great uproar in Switzerland, he was very moved. . . . The Protestant Church circles had just begun to get involved by sending a request [for action on this matter] to the Federal Council. So far, the press has been relatively mild and only cited reports emanating from a news agency in [Ankara] Turkey. But I am very much afraid that the press will continue with its usual reserve. In that case, it will be difficult for us, if not impossible, to restrain it. What effects this will have on Swiss-Hungarian relations is clear, and needs no further commentary. . . . Tahy showed complete understanding and [felt that] these [reports of anti-Jewish] events are responsible for very negative [anti-Hungarian] propaganda, for which Hungary will one day have to account. . . . In Budapest, he [Tahy] did not remain silent and made quite clear [to the Hungarian authorities] the extent to which [news of the deportations] inspired negative reactions in a neutral country like Switzerland. In the meantime, he hoped that the IRC would succeed in doing something useful in this regard. . . . The two reports about the persecution of Hungarian Jewry and the con-

dition in the [death] camps of Auschwitz and Birkenau were first brought to our attention by Pastor [Alphonse] Koechlin, and a few days later by Refugee Pastor Paul Vogt.[24]

In a communiqué to Horthy of July 4, for example, Tahy informed the regent of the "hatred of Hungary and Hungarians engendered by the protests in Switzerland." One of the cables begged, "It would be nice if you could deny the mass murder."[25] Another cable was sent on July 6 by the Swiss Department of Foreign Affairs to the Swiss legation in Budapest, spelling out the general impact of the press campaign in Switzerland; it described the rising wave of indignation and disgust inspired among Swiss citizens by the news of Auschwitz and the Hungarian deportations of Jews. The cable revealed the fact that *for the first time, demonstrations had been organized in religious and political circles.* Above all, it pointed out how public opinion had pressured the Swiss government into ending its silence and initiating vigorous rescue efforts, and concluded by stating that the Swiss public was unable to comprehend the Hungarian people's participation in such atrocities. Such incredulity by the Swiss was certain to affect relations between the two nations adversely. The writer requested that this cable be brought to the attention of the Hungarian authorities and said that the Swiss government was awaiting a response.[26]

On July 12, when the press campaign had produced more than 130 articles, the Swiss Department of Foreign Affairs sent another cable to its legation in Budapest, reiterating that the news from Hungary had shaken up Swiss public opinion and produced a rising wave of condemnation and disgust. It noted that political and religious circles had organized demonstrations, which were all reported in the press, and that numerous emphatic appeals had been made to the Swiss government to put an end to its silence. Perhaps most important, the FPD admitted in this cable that it was incapable of stopping the publication of such reports now that Swiss censorship had broken down. The cable evinced the same note of incredulity found in many news accounts, saying that the FPD found it difficult to believe "the deeds perpetrated in Hungary, which ran counter to what was considered the chivalrous Christian tradition of the Hungarian people." The cable concluded with a strong warning that these deeds "were liable to influence the current and future relations between the two countries negatively."[27]

The shock of the press campaign was felt not only among the Swiss, but also within the German legation in Switzerland itself. On July 2, Swiss intelligence recorded a revealing phone conversation between two high-ranking German diplomats, Isserland and Ullmann. Isserland had invited his colleague to go for a walk, but Ullmann responded that he was too depressed by recent events. He said that he was not referring to the German military defeats, but to the recent murder of 400,000 Hungarian Jews; all the Swiss papers were full of such reports, and the most recent one had so depressed him that he had lost all interest in his work. When Isserland denied the accuracy of these atrocity reports, Ullmann responded that he had confirmed the information with Pastor Freudenberg, a trustworthy contact, who had seen the official reports. Ullmann added that he considered the reports true, and that the Germans would all have to pay the price someday.[28]

In his postwar testimony, Swiss consul Charles Lutz recalled the consternation caused by the Swiss press campaign in Hungarian government and German embassy circles:

> I myself have seen the red-lined articles from the Swiss press in the German embassy. The Germans said that they would . . . see to it that these "horror" stories would no longer be circulated. As a matter of fact, *under the pressure of this campaign, the deportations were really stopped.* Roosevelt's note [i.e., warning to Horthy] was also inspired by this press campaign. It was a combination of the Swiss press campaign and Roosevelt's note that caused things to change in Budapest. (emphasis added)[29]

Meanwhile, Horthy was unaware that, despite his halt of deportations, Jews in communities around Budapest were still being deported behind his back. By July 11, more than 55,000 Jews were deported, making a total of 437,000.[30] A few days later, Veesenmayer again pointed out to the foreign office Horthy's change of policy regarding the Jews, which he attributed to the overwhelming influence of letters from world leaders, including the king of Englan [*sic*], adding that Horthy intended to write a personal letter about his decisions to Hitler.[31] Although Horthy never sent the letter, its contents were revealed to Veesenmayer, who brought the führer's angry response to the regent. Although Hitler approved the emigration of a few Hungarian Jews, he threatened Horthy directly should he depose the ministers who supported the deportations.[32]

Veesenmayer was unaware, however, that the immediate cause of Horthy's anxiety was a top-secret report of July 10 that he had received from Bela Sar-

rossy at the Hungarian legation in Bern.[33] This report detailed Hungary's policy toward minorities since 1919 and its image as a proud, chivalrous Christian
country that defended the rights of all its minorities. However, because of its
oppressive treatment of the Jews since the German occupation in March 1944,
Hungary's reputation had been radically altered. This was the outcome of the
Swiss press campaign, as a result of which world opinion of Hungary had now
become not only negative, but also hateful. Sarrossy noted that the Church,
led by Pastor Vogt, had been most vocal in its criticism. Vogt had been responsible for introducing prayer services on behalf of Hungarian Jews in every
church in Zurich and in Basel. Most surprising, Sarrossy remarked, was the
fact that such vehement censure should come from *the Swiss, who were known
for their reserve.* The report also pointed to the active role of the world-famous
theologians Carl Barth and Emil Brunner, who had distributed the atrocity
reports to thousands in the academic circles.

Alluding to the role played by Manoliu, Sarrossy pointed to the "protocol,"
which was distributed to all embassies, referring to the Hungarian Report, and
added the following:

> Thus, our enemies [i.e., Romanians], our land-thirsty neighbors, obtained in
> the most critical moment of our history a trump card in their hands. . . . The
> Romanians have begun a violent campaign against us. They base their argu-
> ments about these atrocities against Jews upon incontrovertible documents
> and photos, whose negatives were supplied personally by trustworthy people.
>
> Even the moderate press, which publishes only from absolutely reliable
> sources, is clearly against us. . . . For months they accused Hungary and its
> people, and they are supported by the Church, as well as by the Swiss gov-
> ernment. . . . Everything points to the consequences with which we shall have
> to deal. . . . Moreover, we have reliable information that the whole world is
> preparing additional attacks on our nation, our people, and even our race. . . .
> We stand alone. . . . The main point of the accusations consists of the depor-
> tation of Hungarian Jews to places where there can no longer be any doubt
> about their extermination. . . . There is only one possibility of avoiding per-
> manent damage to the reputation of the Hungarian nation: it must show the
> world that it has remained the same gallant, humane, morally eminent peo-
> ple that it has been for a thousand years. This can only be accomplished when
> Hungary takes under its protection those defenseless . . . [whom it has] pro-
> vided with asylum until now.

Dr. Carl Barth. Basel. The world-renowned theologian
whose prestige and active efforts were crucial in persuading
the Swiss government and the International Red Cross to
enter the rescue mode. Courtesy of Corbis Images.

Prof. Emil Brunner, one of the four signers of Vogt's letter
of July 4, 1944. Courtesy of Ringier Pressehaus.

To counter all the terrible accusations and public protests, Sarrossy proposed
that the Jews be placed in a specific territory under the care and supervision
of the International Red Cross and other relief organizations, and that they
be evacuated at a convenient time to a neutral country. Attached to this report
were the following enclosures:

1. A public statement by the Swiss Protestant Church.
2. Copies of the four original British Exchange Telegraph cables.
3. A selection of articles from the Swiss press.
4. A press release of June 30 by the British Exchange Telegraph, with
   details about the deportations from the Hungarian provinces.

What is interesting is that all this material was supplied to Sarrossy by Mantello. Sarrossy's report was confirmed two weeks later in another report by Imre Tahy, which shed additional light on the press campaign's impact in Switzerland and in Hungary.[34]

While Horthy was regaining his power and getting ready to change Hungary's "Jewish policy," the opposing faction, led by Eichmann, Veesenmayer, Baky, and Endre, worked feverishly to thwart him every step of the way. During the three days before Horthy's pronouncement, July 4 to 6, by which time deportations had unofficially ceased, they were able to quietly deport almost 30,000 Jews from locales surrounding Budapest.[35] The tug-of-war did not abate even after Horthy's official pronouncement on the seventh. In fact, as we shall see below, by October 15, the pro-Nazi faction succeeded in their coup attempt.

The IRC Responds

Another important catalyst in the rescue of Budapest Jewry was soon to come on the scene as a direct result of the Swiss press and church campaigns: the International Red Cross, the single most influential international body during the war, which had virtually ignored the pleas of numerous Jewish organizations to alleviate the plight of the Jews. Until now, for example, the IRC would not recognize the Jewish inmates of concentration camps as civilian detainees, although they had accorded such status to many Allied civilians, to whom they regularly distributed food and other packages. Interestingly, the sole exception to the general indifference of the IRC was the Spanish Red Cross; with the approval of General Franco, it not only facilitated the distribution of thousands of food packages from Tangier to Auschwitz and other camps, it even provided free postage, using printed labels officially declaring the Jewish inmates "Prisoners of War."[36]

As the press campaign heated up, the Swiss people began to single out both the IRC and the Swiss government for their lack of interest in the Jewish tragedy. Let us look a little more closely at the slow-moving but critical path taken by these two bodies in the rescue efforts, keeping in mind that the IRC was in reality merely an arm of the Swiss government.

The involvement of the IRC had begun with the active role of Dr. Koechlin of the Ecumenical Council in the press campaign. On June 26, Koechlin informed his counterparts in Hungary of the Jewish situation, as we have seen, and he also informed Max Huber, president of the IRC. Conveying the anguish of the Christian churches, he implored Max Huber to do everything in his power to stop the killing.[37] Further, he suggested that the IRC provide "safe areas" in Hungary until the end of the war, under the protection of the IRC and a neutral power such as Switzerland or Sweden. Koechlin beseeched Huber to take this idea seriously, which he eventually did.[38] Besides the IRC, Dr. Koechlin urged Federal Councilor Marcel Pilet-Golaz to convey the same plea to the Swiss government before it was too late.[39]

That same day, June 26, Jean Schwartzenberg, an IRC delegate in Geneva who was involved in aid to the Jews, received a copy of the Auschwitz Report from Friedrich Born in Budapest. There is little doubt that Schwartzenberg, as well as the rest of the IRC officials in Geneva, had already obtained copies of these reports from Mantello and from Visser't Hooft of the World Council of Churches. How difficult it was to alter the IRC's negative perspective can be seen from the following two incidents. In the first, Schwartzenberg sent a copy of Mantello's report to Nicholas Burkhardt, the IRC delegate in London, with specific instructions "*not* to pass on this report to Jewish organizations" (emphasis added).[40]

The second incident involved Max Huber. Although he received Koechlin's appeal on the twenty-sixth, he did not call an emergency meeting for the next day, but instead waited a week for the normally scheduled weekly meeting of July 3. At that meeting, Huber admitted to having received copies of the reports from "several sources," which, he remarked, "*if verified,* indeed belong to the most terrible manifestations of this war." He did add that he would send a message directly to Horthy, "in view of the many reports reaching the IRC" about the great outcry throughout Switzerland.[41] Evidently, these reports did not have the same effect on Huber as the earlier-mentioned letter from the head of the World Council of Churches.[42] At the meeting, however, he provided the usual rationale for the IRC's inactivity in regard to the Jews: "[The IRC's] first duty was to provide the aid that it was able to provide effectively, and not to jeopardize this by attempting tasks which seemed condemned to failure at the outset. . . . Asking the impossible of the IRC was a way of using up its credit . . . and any decision to act would entail a departure from its customary line of conduct."[43]

By this time, however, pressure from various sources had mounted furiously. The press campaign had now amounted to more than thirty news articles. Public responses had also come from the pope, the archbishop of Canterbury, the

Max Huber (*center*), president of the International Red Cross.
Accompanying him are Captain Draudt (*left*) of the German Red
Cross and the president of the German Red Cross, Supreme Court
Justice von Winterfeld (*right*). Courtesy of Corbis Images.

king of Sweden, and the Allies. Moreover, Vogt's campaign at home to spread the reports to all the churches was highly successful, and it clearly had an impact on Huber. This is reflected in Huber's response to Eduard de Haller in an interview of July 4. De Haller had spoken to Huber on behalf of Pilet-Golaz, in response to Koechlin's letter of June 26. In this interview, Huber pointed out to de Haller that "pressure put on the IRC has been so great that it is obliged to intervene just for the purpose of appearing to save its honor."[44] After meeting with de Haller, Huber wrote a confidential letter to Koechlin, in which he pointed out that "in view of the nature of the rumours [*sic*] currently circulating, the International Committee of the Red Cross has decided to take up the matter with the Hungarian Regent personally, and to send a special delegate to discuss it with the Hungarian government. I would be grateful if you would treat this information as strictly confidential."[45]

The following day, July 5, at the next IRC meeting, Huber informed the delegates of his plan to send a personal messenger to Horthy in Budapest. An additional factor in Huber's rationale must have been the fact that, on the previous day, further distribution of the reports was accompanied by the crucial, supportive letter of the four renowned theologians. This letter, whose moral authority would be the major factor in breaking the back of Swiss censorship, surely influenced the indifferent Huber as well. To save the honor of Hungary in the eyes of its citizens, his letter to Horthy was written in the same delicate and laudatory manner as the cables of the Holy See and the king of Sweden, but his demands of the regent were quite explicit:

> From all parts of the world, queries, items of information, and protests reach the International Committee of the Red Cross every day regarding the severe measures *allegedly* taken against Jews of Hungarian nationality. . . . *[The IRC] does not have any verifiable information.* Details brought to our attention seem so entirely contrary to the chivalrous traditions of the great Hungarian nation that we find it almost impossible to give credence to even the slightest part of that information. (emphasis added)
>
> [We ask you to] issue instructions which will enable us to refute these rumors and allegations. . . . We beseech the Royal Hungarian Government to prevent the occurrence of the slightest act that might give rise to such monstrous reports.[46]

However delicate, this letter signaled the end of the long silence about the mistreatment of the Hungarian Jews—or, more correctly, the end of the public's and the government's ability to avoid taking a stand on the issue.[47]

The bureau of the IRC decided to send Huber's letter to Horthy through a special envoy, Dr. Robert Schirmer, deputy head of the IRC's delegation in Berlin. The following day, July 6, Schirmer left Berlin on his mission to Budapest, although, for inexplicable reasons, it would take him another two weeks to reach his destination. As it turned out, however, events would not depend on his arrival.

That same day, quite independent of any action by the IRC, there were rapid developments. The number of Hungarian Jews deported until then had risen to 410,000, and Budapest had already been prepared for deportations. Veesenmayer was ready to complete his objective when Prime Minister Sztojay told him that Horthy was ready to halt deportations. Sztojay cited especially the "flood of appeals, both internal and international, to rescue the Jews and . . . the intercepted telegrams sent to England and the U.S.A. by Jewish representatives in Bern, Switzerland."[48]

The next day, July 7, Horthy met with Veesenmayer and informed him of his change of heart and of his intent to halt the deportations, because of "mounting domestic and international pressure." At the same time, Winkelman, the Higher SS and police leader in Hungary, informed Himmler that, apparently, "Veesenmayer is no longer able to handle the matter."[49]

On July 9, two days after Horthy halted the deportations, Raoul Wallenberg arrived in Budapest to begin his mission to help the Jews, backed by the newly awakened Swedish government and the assistance of the Swedish consulate (see chapter 10).[50] The fact that the Swiss press campaign echoed in Sweden reenforced Wallenberg and his cause; the Swedish press had mirrored its king's concern about the fate of Hungarian Jewry, a fact that the German embassy in Stockholm duly reported to its foreign office.[51] Although the Swedish delegation in Budapest per se was no great catalyst for rescue, as evidenced by its meek response before the Swiss press campaign, it was impelled to action by the dynamic example of Wallenberg—a courageous man who brooked no bureaucratic legalism in his rescue efforts.[52]

On July 7, the same day that Horthy halted deportations, Claude Pillaud, head of the IRC's Delegations Commission, requested that the Swiss Department of Foreign Affairs transmit a confidential message to Born in Budapest. The message was like the one Schirmer carried to Horthy, and in fact, Pillaud asked Born to assist Schirmer. Most likely the message was intended to pacify Born, who may have been piqued by the fact that a higher-ranking delegate from Berlin had been sent to Budapest, even though Born himself had been fully aware of the German atrocities and had already tried to warn the Swiss.[53]

The Swiss government's chagrin in the face of the ongoing press campaign arose partly from the fact that the IRC was under its auspices. On July 14, the indefatigable Pastor Vogt tried to press the IRC into action when he submitted the earlier-mentioned practical rescue plan to the president and the members of the Federal Council. He suggested that this highest Swiss political body cooperate with the IRC and the United States to send a contingent of fifty Swiss citizens to Budapest to help carry out the rescue plan, which entailed the Swiss absorption of 10,000 Hungarian Jews. The plan would be supported by American money, and the refugees would be guaranteed postwar emigration elsewhere. Vogt's plea pierced the smugness of more than one member of the Federal Council. His message was "gentle" but authoritative and quite specific, and was disseminated through various publications:

> My conscience does not allow me any rest. I must convey to you several ideas whose implementation would have practical rescue effects. Hopefully, you will give these ideas your serious attention, and [they will] inspire you to rescue this endangered people. . . . I urgently plead with the Federal Council to decide whether it will permit the realization of this plan.[54]
>
> I realize that the plan is immense and difficult. However, the distress of those marked for death is equally immense and dreadful. The duty of the Swiss people is to help as much as we can. My conscience would be burdened if I did not submit this plan to you. I beg of you—in the name of the Jewish people who knock on my door, in the name of our master Jesus, who through the humblest of his [Jewish] brethren knocks mightily on the doors of our Swiss houses, which fortunately have been spared, and who knocks on the doors of our hearts—to do everything that will transform the will of the Swiss people into active assistance.
>
> Why were we Swiss, in our dear homeland, spared through God's wonder? Surely not to live each day without a thought [of the matter]. *Certainly not for the purpose of celebrating endless parties and smugly praising our virtues.* And most assuredly not, with a sense of self-righteousness, to criticize and judge other nations. . . . If this is the purpose of our having being spared, then we will appear before history and future generations as petty, ugly, and mean. (emphasis in original)[55]

Undoubtedly this emotional plea by Switzerland's most eloquent preacher, in what was then a deeply religious country, added to the pressure placed on the Swiss government.

On July 17, the Swiss government finally took its first concrete step. Maximilian Jäger, the formerly hesitant Swiss minister in Budapest, now warned Sztojay that the Swiss public had been greatly angered by Hungary's policy toward its Jews. He added ominously that Switzerland was toying with the idea of breaking off relations with Hungary.[56] Jäger's only weapon to force Horthy to comply was his threat to resign and thereby create chaos in a country almost solidly behind him; the resignation of such an important minister could have only negative repercussions on the regime, something Horthy would want to avoid at all costs.

On that same day, however, under the ever-increasing international pressure, Horthy stood up to Hitler. In his talk with Veesenmayer, he responded to the führer's threats by pointing to the former government's brutal and inhuman treatment of the Jews, oppression that had "been applied by no other nation, and [which] has produced the disapproving criticism of even the German authorities in the country."[57]

On July 12, five days after Horthy halted the deportations, Eichmann, with the aid of Endre and Baky, sought to negate this important move by spiriting out about 1,500 Jews from Kistarcsa behind the regent's back. Eichmann's effort was foiled because Horthy and the now-vigilant neutral observers were tipped off by Sandor Brody, a representative of the Jewish Welfare Bureau. Brody quickly informed the Jewish Council, which in turn informed Jusztinian Cardinal Seredi, the primate of Hungary, Vilmos Apor, bishop of Gyor, and the diplomats of the neutral countries. Now all of these officials approached Horthy, who acted immediately to bring the Jews back. A week later, however, a furious and determined Eichmann succeeded in his nefarious objective by putting the entire Jewish Council under house arrest while he renewed this deportation.[58]

This incident is symptomatic of two crucial factors that had come into play since the successful impact of the Swiss press and church campaigns. The first was the fact that many previously "passive" neutral observers, including Wallenberg, Lutz, the papal nuncio Angelo Rotta, and the Catholic leaders of Hungary, began to take a vigorous stand on behalf of the surviving Jews of Budapest. Second, it indicates the constant struggle that Horthy and the neutral observers had to maintain with both the Nazis and their Hungarian cohorts, who had never given up their primary objective of deporting the Jews.

Veesenmayer continued to experience frustration in his efforts to influence the regent to maintain Nazi policy toward the Jews. On July 13, one day after

Eichmann's failure to send out the Jews from Kistarcsa, Veesenmayer tried to explain Horthy's actions to the foreign office, claiming that the regent was in a deep depression and that he was overwhelmed by letters from abroad, including the pleas of the pope, King Gustav of Sweden, and the king of England.

For his part, Horthy informed Veesenmayer that he would address a letter to Hitler on this public outcry.[59] No doubt adding to the regent's determination to take control was the second heavy Allied air raid on Budapest on July 14. On the following day, Horthy began to display an even stronger backbone, informing Veesenmayer of his intention to appoint Gen. Geza Lakatos as prime minister. The German ambassador then assessed the implication of Horthy's new stand, not only for deportations but for the broader German war economy, and he decided that at all costs, Horthy would have to go.[60]

In the meantime, Horthy continued to try to alter Hungary's policy toward the Jews radically by dismissing László Baky and László Endre, the main anti-Semitic ministers. Naturally, this enraged Hitler. Two days later, the führer voiced his protest of these moves, demanding the immediate deportation of Budapest's Jews and the reinstatement of the deposed ministers.[61]

At this point, Horthy was unaware that the Germans had produced a propaganda film for Swiss and foreign journalists in Bern as a means of countering the worldwide agitation of the press. When he found out about it, he was particularly irked by the fact that the film attempted to shift the blame for the cruelty of the deportations onto the Hungarians; it accomplished this by splicing in segments of real films depicting the cruelty with which the Hungarian Arrow Cross forces treated the Jews during the deportation process. These segments were played up in contrast to the second part of the film, which showed sympathetic German nurses removing and treating the Jews, by then more dead than alive, who arrived in cattle cars at the Auschwitz station. Naturally, the film did not show what the "merciful" Germans did after their "gentle" removal of the Jews from the trains. Clever as it was, the film could not erase the memory of the hundreds of articles in the Swiss press, nor did it convince skeptical Swiss and foreign journalists of its authenticity. After the Hungarians found out about the film, they were highly incensed and demanded angrily that it be removed from circulation.[62]

After the failure of the film, Veesenmayer tried other methods to counter the impact of the Swiss press campaign. He issued statements against "enemy propaganda concerning atrocity stories about the alleged treatment of Hungarian Jews. . . . These rumors are a fictitious part of the imagination. In organizing and executing the transports, humanitarian concerns were taken into account [and] members of families were not separated."⁶³ He also used the propaganda value of the American bombing of Budapest by contrasting the "inhumanity" of the Allies to German "humanitarianism." He pointed out that, although Budapest's Jewish population of 200,000 was not subjected to foreign labor, they did suffer considerable losses from the Anglo-American air attacks of July 2. Veesenmayer, trapped by the intensity of the press campaign, was anxious to transmit the German denial of the rumors to all Hungarian legations, "since the atrocity propaganda is running at high speed against Hungary."⁶⁴ These efforts at placation were transmitted to other diplomats, but they were insufficient to allay public concern; an open, public denial of the atrocities was needed.⁶⁵

On July 18, the day after Ambassador Jaeger's threat to break off relations with Hungary, the regent sent Tahy to meet with Carl Burkhardt in Geneva to present the IRC with a detailed response to its inquiry and an outline of the Hungarians' concessions. Horthy virtually begged the IRC to use its prestige to broadcast his own good intentions to the world, thereby reducing the growing anti-Hungarian sentiment engendered by the press campaign. As Tahy noted in the preface to his report, "The orders of Your Excellency in this respect . . . [are] something of a salvation, because foreign opinion regarding the Jewish question was already causing great apprehension in the case of Hungary, as I have already described in my previous dispatches."

The first and most important point Tahy made on behalf of the regent was the fact that Hungary had stopped the deportations. Horthy hoped that the IRC would use its great international status to inform the West of Hungary's new policy. For his part, Tahy tried to play down the atrocities involved in the deportations and the death camps, at the same time denying any Hungarian complicity:

> The massacres and brutalities mentioned in the press campaign, the accuracy of which we cannot check, must have happened outside Hungarian borders, so that their denial is the responsibility of the Germans. . . . We stopped the departure [deportation] of the Jews *as soon as we heard the foreign voices which had drawn attention to these alleged atrocities, made credible by the foreign press.* . . . It is unjust that now, evidently due to the changed course of the war, the same Hungary which used to give asylum to the Jews . . . should be branded as inhuman and uncivilized. (emphasis added)

The immediate basis for the regent's desperate plea to the IRC was surely the fear of further American bombing of Budapest, especially in the light of the second air raid of July 14. Tahy reported on his meeting with Burkhardt: "I beseeched Mr. Burkhardt to use his weight as representative of the International Red Cross, as well as his personal influence with the competent places [the West], to ask for the ending of the American terrorist air raids [on Budapest]. . . . [Horthy feared that] all that has been built through our goodwill could be wrecked by the counterpropaganda."

In the same report, Tahy described his meeting with a number of diplomats, including the papal nuncio and the ambassadors of Germany, Finland, and Bulgaria, all of whom approved of the halt in the deportations. He added that although the Romanian ambassador was also present, he did not discuss the issue with him, for he was fully aware that "all the information reached Switzerland from Hungary via a Romanian [*sic*] courier." Tahy also noted that Mr. Stucki, head of Switzerland's Foreign Political Department, was very pleased to hear of Hungary's new policy concerning the Jews.

In his reply to Tahy's presentation of Horthy's defense, Burkhart noted the following:

> *The mass [press] campaign has reached unlimited, worldwide proportions. . . .* [Yet,] despite some exaggeration, there is incontestable information which is not without a real basis. [However], Horthy has hopes for [the IRC's] success in appeasing world opinion. . . . [And the IRC] will not fail to inform the competent places [the West] . . . to end the so-called terrorist air raids against Hungary. The Red Cross will publish a press release with the aim of reassuring public opinion . . . [and] preventing any further defamatory attacks by the press . . . (emphasis added)[66]

When Tahy told the German ambassador in Switzerland about the IRC's press release, which had Hungary's approval, the ambassador replied that he also hoped that "this terrible campaign might soon cease." He added that he had approached Federal Councilor Pilet-Golaz about "the question of the press campaign," and that Pilet-Golaz had responded, "The voice of the press cannot be suppressed without running the danger that it will find still more dangerous means of expression." Tahy then told the ambassador that Hungary had taken steps to halt the attacks of the press, and that the Germans should also provide a denial of the rumors about the Auschwitz and Birkenau camps.[67]

In response to Roosevelt's earlier warning and oral inquiry of June 26, the

Hungarian foreign office sent a long letter to the American government via the Swiss legation in Budapest. Most of it consisted of a rationale for the mistreatment of the Jews and concluded with a declaration that "the Jewish situation has recently changed for the better." It added that "as a result of the efforts of the IRC and the War Refugee Board, the Hungarian government would permit material assistance to the Jews in Hungary and facilitate the emigration of Jews to Palestine or neutral countries."[68]

On the same day, July 18, the IRC released its communiqué, whose headline read "Hungary Stops the Deportations." This release was immediately distributed to all the Swiss and foreign newspapers, as well as to the British ambassador in Bern. It pointed out that, with the full approval of the Hungarian government and with assumed German consent, the IRC was authorized to carry out the following conditions:

1. Distribute packages to the interned Jews in the camps and ghettos.
2. Help in the emigration of all children younger than ten, whose admittance to various countries was assured.
3. All Jews with Palestine certificates were permitted to leave to go to that country.
4. All Jews who had parents in Sweden or who had business relations with Swedish citizens were permitted to emigrate either to Sweden or to Palestine.[69]

The assumption was that police passports would serve as travel documents. Arrangements for the implementation of this plan were to be made by the Swiss legation in Budapest, with the special assistance of Carl Lutz, working in conjunction with Moshe Krausz at the Palamt, who was still under Lutz's protection in the Swiss compound.[70]

Despite the IRC's success in obtaining major concessions from Horthy, an angry Swiss public still remained skeptical as to whether the Hungarian government would carry out its promises concerning the Jews. This doubt is evident from a conversation between a Swiss reporter and de Haller of the Department of Foreign Affairs. The reporter pointed out that "in view of the storm aroused by the persecution of the Jews in Hungary . . . it would be useful to bring to public knowledge . . . details of the action taken by the federal government and the results achieved."[71]

The steady and successful pressure on the IRC to get involved in rescue was matched by the transformation of politically important figures, especially Pilet-

Golaz, minister of foreign affairs and a member of the Federal Council. As we have seen, he had been pressured by Alphons Koechlin, head of the Swiss Protestant Churches, and by Carl Barth's crucial letter to the president of the Federal Council. These, in addition, to the public letter of July 4, signed by the four Protestant theologians, urged all political and religious leaders to get involved. All of this activity was inspired largely by the ever-growing Swiss press campaign that initiated the introspective period of internal criticism of the Swiss government and the IRC for their silence.[72]

Thus, although Pilet-Golaz first responded only on July 21 to Koechlin's appeal of June 26, it did not mean that the minister had done little or nothing to help Hungarian Jewry. On the contrary, he had now become the most active Swiss political figure to press the government into action. He noted this in his official response of July 21:

> As the reading of recent communiqués on the work of Parliamentary commissions of special war powers will have confirmed to you, that this grave problem [of Hungarian Jewry] has occupied the entire attention of the Federal Council, which has done what was in its power to contribute to its resolution. . . . I am happy to inform you that, according to the latest news from Budapest, the situation in Hungary is improving in the domain in which we are actively working. . . . Moreover, I am patting myself on the back because the communiqué of July 18, from the IRC, announcing assurances of the Hungarian government, has brought some relief to all those who, like your Federation [of Swiss Protestant Churches], were moved by the events in Hungary.[73]

The slow but steady impact of the press and church campaign on Swiss opinion, and on some previously indifferent officials, can be seen from Rothmund's memo of July 11 to someone in the Department of Foreign Affairs. This memo also manifests various fears and concerns by the Swiss about certain policies affecting the changing Swiss-Hungarian Jewish situation. Also evident in this memoir is concern for the impression that any action—or inaction— regarding Hungarian Jewry would make on the Swiss public and on the United States.

One issue involved the desire of the WRB to approve the transfer of $1.5 million to Saly Mayer. This money was for Mayer's potential negotiations with Becher for the continuation of the Brand offer to rescue thousands from deportation. Rothmund was concerned that this money represented the larger sum of 6,000,000 Swiss francs, although he admitted that much of it would be spent in Switzerland for medicine and food. Still, he had a real fear that most of it would be used for "bribery," which was absolutely anathema to this super-legalist. Rothmund's concern about the money and about public opinion is reflected in his memo: "Considering the fact that we have to be much more reserved concerning the persecution of Hungarian Jews than local [Swiss] and foreign circles would like, we should seriously explore the question of whether, with relatively minor effort, we have a real opportunity to help, for which we would have to get credit. Also, in view of of our good relations with the U.S., a compromise would be justified."[74]

For their part, the Germans openly acquiesced to Horthy's agreement, passed onto them through the IRC, although they never decreased their strong efforts to frustrate his plans behind the scenes. Veesenmayer informed Ribbentrop that, despite his pressure on Sztojay to continue the deportations, the Swiss and the Swedes were busy preparing to facilitate the emigration of thousands of Jews to Palestine.[75]

The Germans readily appreciated Horthy's suggestion that they deny the atrocities; this was apparent from their immediate presentation of the film. Undoubtedly, however, they were aware of the failure of both the film and Veesenmayer's earlier denial to the diplomats. On July 20, they arranged for a conference for the foreign press to be conducted by Helmut Sündermann, the Reich's press director and assistant to minister of propaganda Joseph Goebbels. Sündermann's statement was reported in the pro-Nazi *Pester-Lloyd* of July 21. The headline read, "The World Will Enjoy Peace Only after the Establishment of an International Quarantine for All Jewry." Speaking openly before the representatives of the foreign press, Sündermann characterized the outcry in the Swiss press as "international agitation and instigation, especially statements disseminated by the enemy about the allegedly serious grievances in dealing with the Jewish residents in Europe. . . . They [the Jews] are instigating newspapers and other organizations to spread false information throughout the world about alleged mistreatments and grievances."[76] He further sought to create the impression that "the deported Jews were merely being quarantined for the benefit of mankind."

Different facets of Budapest Jewry's changed situation at this time can be seen from perspectives in two letters from Budapest to Switzerland. The first was from Peretz (Szigály) to Natan (Schwalb), written about July 20, two days after the IRC announced the cessation of deportations. It read in part: "The general situation is a complete mystery. After the first stormy and bloody week, the atmosphere is so calm and so totally unexpected. Imagine, today the radio officially told us that all protective papers and passports of the neutral consulates, as well as their institutions, if the holders also have an immigration permit, they will be treated as extraterritorials under the protection of the IRC. . . . We work with all authorities, primarily through [Friedrich Born], the IRC delegate, [Carl] Lutz of the Swiss Embassy, and Secretary of the Swiss Embassy."[77]

About this time, on July 20, Carl Lutz sent a letter of acknowledgment to Mantello. Although he had already become familiar with Mantello because of the constant dispatching of Salvadoran papers to his department in Budapest, the Swiss consul had been unaware of Mantello's involvement in the press campaign and in the halt of deportations. In his letter, Lutz described his discovery:

Dear Mr. Mantello,

As I have learned recently, you stand out as the "spiritus rectus" behind the press campaign in Switzerland, which has brought to the public at large information concerning . . . [the] distress of the Jewish population of Budapest. . . . Even now I am receiving copies of Swiss papers with detailed reports about the atrocities committed upon the Jewish population. Responsible circles are naturally very agitated by the fact that this information infiltrated into neutral [countries], and from there into enemy countries. . . . The reactions, as expected, were very strong. . . . Every government official asked himself whether he would be held responsible one day. Everyone denies any responsibility beforehand. . . . No one wants to be identified with these atrocities. . . . There are many who are aware of the consequences of their anti-Semitic activities. The immediate effect has been the suspension of the deportations. I observed this readily especially after I had delivered the American State Department's note, which contained the threat of punishment as a war criminal for anyone participating directly or indirectly in the deportations. . . . It can be said that thanks to your campaign, the imminent catastrophe was greatly reduced.[78]

Goebbels corroborated the pressure induced by the press and the neutral countries in an analysis entitled "Difficulties Concerning the Deportation of Jews from Budapest," which appeared in the August 23, 1944, edition of *Die Lage,* the Nazi information journal: "The last phase of the measures against the Jews should have involved the deportation of the appproximately 260,000 Jews of Budapest. In the meantime, however, *the pressure from the foreign enemy and from neutral sources (Hull, King of Sweden, Switzerland, and the Pope) became so strong* that the philo-Semitic circles in Hungary tried to influence the Hungarian Government to prevent any further German measures against Jews" (emphasis added).[79]

When the IRC finally entered the rescue arena on behalf of the Hungarian Jews, it was stung by the constant pressure in the press, for even after it got involved, the criticism did not abate. On the contrary, as we have seen, the press campaign began to reflect introspectively on Swiss silence, in the process indicting the Swiss people, its government, and the IRC, the paradigm of Swiss humanitarian efforts. Between July 12 and the end of the month, more than 220 articles enlarged the scope of the press campaign. Among the headlines were "Where Is the Swiss Government?,"[80] "Impossible to Believe!,"[81] "The Federal Government Breaks Its Silence,"[82] "We Swiss and the Grief of the World,"[83] "Open Letter to the President of the Federal Council,"[84] and "We Are All Guilty."[85] The day after the IRC released its communiqué, one short but sharp headline expressed relief: "Finally!"[86]

On August 1, an irritated IRC spokesman aired the organization's annoyance at the public's constant pressure. In an article in the *Volksrecht,* which had previously published many such protest articles, the IRC spokesman voiced his complaints: "Many newspapers continuously publish reports about Jewish persecutions which cannot stand up to a precise examination of the facts. Such 'sensational' information will certainly not make the work of the IRC any easier. Rather, it will hinder it. The persecuted Jews will not be helped by 'certain protests.' On the contrary, it is those who cannot remain silent who harm the work of the IRC."[87]

A response to the IRC's "defense" and its policy toward the Jews appeared in the same paper about two weeks later and listed dozens of Swiss and international personalities who raised their voices on behalf of the Jews. The author asked:

Is it not to the contrary? Is not the one who remains silent in the face of such misleading opinion the one who harms the work of the International Red Cross? Was it not precisely the public and passionate protest by the whole world, and especially in Switzerland, under the motto "We cannot remain silent about the extermination of the Jews of Hungary," which awoke the conscience of mankind?

Did all these personalities and organizations really harm the efforts of the International Red Cross by not maintaining silence? Is it not rather the case that when world public opinion arose in powerful protest, the International Red Cross achieved one of its best, if not the very best, result?[88] . . . It is proper to congratulate the Committee of the IRC for its intervention on behalf of the Hungarian Jews. Nonetheless, it is with a feeling of despair that one has to take notice of public opinion in high places at this very late hour, when the fate of hundreds of thousands, maybe millions, of Jews of all nationalities has been sealed, without the intervention of anyone. The success of the IRC confirms that with more energy and with some more will, one would have been able to obtain suspension of the measures of deportation and extermination, if one had really wanted to act. . . . It is up to the International Red Cross that the [Hungarian] promises become reality. . . . The fate of Hungarian Jews . . . is in the hands of the IRC.[89]

Noting that, with this "official" change in policy the tide of public opinion would subside, with no guarantee that the promises would be carried out, the IRC's declaration to the Department of Foreign Affairs continued:

In publishing its communiqué, the IRC has undertaken a heavy responsibility. As a result of this communiqué, the ardent public opinion and protest that has been heard from all sides will no longer have a reason to exist, and the press, which has echoed the indignation felt by everyone concerning the Jews, will not speak of it any longer. The responsibility of the Red Cross is therefore even greater. . . . It is up to the International Red Cross to keep a constant survey of the situation in Hungary to assure the fulfillment of the promises. The fate of Hungarian Jews . . . is not only in the hands of Hungarian Nazi authorities. It is in the hands of the IRC. . . . World opinion has greeted the communiqué of the IRC with great relief. But enlightened world opinion will not be fooled by simple promises. . . . It will judge the IRC according to its deeds and its accomplishments.[90]

On July 21, three days after Tahy presented Burkhardt with Horthy's new policy regarding the Jews, Schirmer finally arrived in Budapest. He met first with Sztojay and later with Horthy, to present Max Huber's letter and position. Among other things, Huber asked Sztojay to end the deportations, and he also requested permission to visit some of the yellow-star houses, several detention camps, and some Jews concentrated in ghettos such as Theresienstadt.

Two days later, Sztojay provided Schirmer with the Hungarian government's response to the IRC's requests. After noting the official halt of deportations, he suggested that an IRC delegation visit the Kistarcsa and Savar internment camps, as well as a few carefully selected yellow-star houses that had been established at the end of June. Schirmer conducted this visitation only a short while after Eichmann had managed to sneak out 1,300 from Kistarcsa and 1,500 from Savar, which left the camps relatively uncrowded. He reported that conditions were acceptable. Such visits, however, were inadequate to reveal the real horror in the many brickyards and entrainment camps, let alone the ultimate fate of the deported Jews.[91]

Schirmer also asked Veesenmayer for permission to send packages to the deportees and to visit a concentration camp. In his response of August 2, Veesenmayer approved the first two requests "after adequate preparation" (i.e., cover-up), though he rejected a request to accompany the deportation train to Kassa on the grounds that "it would violate the secrecy related to the travel route and destination."[92] Despite the limited success of their requests, Schirmer's trip was not in vain. The IRC, in conjunction with the Swiss legation, was soon to play a crucial part in the protection of the surviving Jews of Budapest, especially the children (see chapter 10).

One newspaper article, written right after the IRC communiqué declaring the halt of deportations, expressed the satisfaction of much of the Swiss public at the government's and the IRC's decision to participate in rescue. It was headlined "A Reason for Satisfaction: The Success of the Federal Council's Efforts Regarding Hungarian Jews." The article read in part:

> The terrible persecution of Jews in Hungary produced a wave of deep indignation all over our country. The IRC came in the meantime with a message to the public which was received with a sigh of relief. The Hungarian government gave guarantees that further deportations of Jews were stopped . . . and that the IRC would give assistance to the interned Jews and cooperate in the evacuation of [Hungarian] Jewish children to safe havens. . . . Switzerland has also made known its readiness to accept the Hungarian children. . . . The efforts of the Federal Council, and especially those of the Department of Foreign Affairs, in close cooperation with the IRC, have brought a marked improvement in the situation of the badly persecuted Jews.[93]

The victory over the IRC in its obstinate and tardy response to pleas for rescue is echoed privately in a July 24 letter from Dr. Hans Schaffert, Vogt's able assistant, to Mantello. Among other things, Schaffert pointed out, "As far as the atrocities in Hungary were concerned, one simply had to do everything possible to publicize the [two] reports and thereby produce a groundswell of protest by the people, which first led to the intervention of the IRC. . . . Thank God our efforts were not futile."[94]

The press now realized the very important role it played in changing Hungary's policy toward the Jews. It gave voice to its pride in its influence in an article published about a week after the IRC's communiqué, entitled "Destructive Forces in Hungary":

> The great storm of protest by the Swiss press and several Swiss institutions against the treatment of Jews in Hungary was not without success. Even before the IRC intervened in this matter, one could see the effect of Swiss public opinion on the thinking of those responsible in Hungary [for the mistreatment of Jews]. The power of the free world was strong enough to be able to save the lives of hundreds of thousands of people. . . . The result of the Swiss intervention in Hungary is proof that one can bring human beings to reason without bombs and cannons. . . . If voices had been raised after the first atrocities, hundreds of thousands of people in other countries could have been saved, [but] the world kept silent.
>
> The Swiss press can be satisfied with the fine mission which was fulfilled during the past weeks. It carried the banner of freedom and humanity, and underlined the fact that if its hands are not bound and [it] listens only to its conscience, *the press is a superpower.* (emphasis added)[95]

The press campaign was immense; before it was over, it involved more than 180 Swiss newspapers, from the large, urbane Zurich- and Geneva-based publications to small, parochial journals emanating from rural areas. It also spanned the full political ideological spectrum, from the Socialist Left to the ultraconservative, usually Catholic Right. In more than 470 articles, amounting in words to a book approximately eight hundred pages long, the courageous Swiss press attacked the Third Reich, its brutal policies toward Jews, the monstrosities of Auschwitz, and the complicity of the Hungarians. Amazingly enough, all this had begun only eight days after a special exhortation by the Swiss Ministry of the Interior to all editors of Swiss newspapers to avoid disseminating any atrocity tales: "This was particularly important in view of the fact that the war was rapidly approaching our border . . . and that *it is more important that we keep our neutrality*" (emphasis added).[96]

The Impact of the Swiss Press Campaign in Other Countries

The Swiss press campaign was felt not only in Budapest and Berlin, but also in other capitals such as Stockholm, London, and the United States. Newspapers in Stockholm, for example, reflected concern about the fate of Hungarian Jewry and even printed editorials critical of the Germans and Hungarians. A dispatch from the Swiss embassy in Stockholm to Bern noted that an editorial of the *Svenska Dagbladet* of July 2 or 3, entitled "In the Name of Humanity," fully supports the stand taken by the king.[97]

> By this act Sweden follows the tradition which it upheld in favor of the Danish Jews and the Norwegian Academic youth. At the time Sweden contacted Berlin. As far as the Jews were concerned, the results were continued, quiet persecution, while in regard to the students there was a furious protest to [the German Foreign Minister] Joachim von Ribbentrop. Following the coup [German occupation of Hungary] . . . [so] many reports have now come to light about conditions in Hungary that the whole world is aware of the various facts and suspect even worse.

This editorial was followed by a presentation of additional facts from the *Neue Zürcher Zeitung* [i.e., the Auschwitz Report), which:

> is based on higly reliable sources. Following this, an even darker chapter involves the treatment of 800,000 Hungarian Jews in Hungary, the sole large reservoir of surviving Jews who [until then] had defied Hitler's threats of annihilation. In order to avoid a repetition of earlier atrocities. King Gustav has now contacted Admiral Horthy, who is still considered the Head of State. . . . In the face of calculated mistreatment planned against innocent and helpless human beings [the press] considers it an honor for Sweden and its king to speak out on behalf of humanity.[98]

Another report from the Swiss embassy in Stockholm to Bern cited a report by Bert Wyler, Bern correspondent for the Swedish paper *Aftenbladet,* of July 17, 1944. He noted that "the Swiss people are deeply in shock over Hungary's treatment of its Jews. All over Switzerland there were mourning services conducted and protest resolutions were implemented against such persecution. The Swiss people are equally in shock over the shameless behavior by Hungary and its agreement with Germany. It is a virtual slap at human freedom. . . . [Bert Wyler added that] Federal Councilor Pilet-Golaz report to the Nationalrat about the steps taken by official federal commission to help the persecuted Jews."[99]

In Britain, the influence of the Swiss press campaign is spelled out in the notes of Philip Paneth, the foreign editor of the *Daily Express*. He pointed out that it was the dispatches of Walter Garrett of the Exchange Telegraph in Bern, which provided the first, and in many ways the most consistent, information on the situation of Hungarian Jewry. Before his reports, much of the information had been publicized (in Britain) by Chief Rabbi (Joseph H.) Hertz, but it was sparse and frequently unreliable; and the information held in official hands generally remained classified.[100] The dispatches originating at the Exchange Telegraph in Switzerland were the first to reveal the news of Auschwitz and the tragedy of Hungarian Jewry.

The indignation of the British press, which had never been sympathetic to Jewry, was very great, and it headlined this news for ten days. As foreign editor of the *Daily Express,* one of the world's largest papers, Paneth asked the Swiss representative for further details of the Jewish tragedy; the reports from Switzerland were accepted by the British as factual, in contrast to the skepticism with which they had greeted earlier Polish reports of the mass murder of Jews.

In Britain, it was the evening press that was the first to reveal the substance of the Auschwitz and Hungarian Reports, soon followed by the daily papers, which all had front-page articles on the plight of Hungarian Jewry. Within a few days, members of Parliament and even the House of Lords were debating the matter. Mr. Sidney Silverman, a Labor MP and a member of the World Jewish Congress, had received copies of all reports. Soon afterward the British government officially condemned the persecution of the Jews. It was the first time in history that the House of Commons rose for a moment of silence in tribute to the millions of Jewish victims.[101]

The impact of the press campaign in the United Sates was even more pronounced than in Britain, although the results in either were as successful as in Switzerland. Several newspapers, including the *New York Times,* had already published articles devoted to the horrors of Auschwitz and the deportations of Hungarian Jewry. Inspired by Vogt's original seventy-five-hundred-word report, most of the American articles based on information derived from the Swiss press campaign were printed during the first ten days of July 1944. On July 6, the *New York Times* published a second, more extensive article on Auschwitz, which provided statistics and names of countries from which Jews had been deported.

Still, as Deborah E. Lipstadt pointed out in her excellent survey and analysis of the American press during the Holocaust, this news "was treated with equanimity if not disinterest."[102] American articles surely did not evince the deeply religious and humanitarian emotions displayed by the Swiss press. Apparently, the news itself did not shock the press sufficiently, nor were there outstanding religious leaders who pressed for action and for the publicity of this horrific information throughout the nation. McClelland, the WRB representative, sent the complete Auschwitz Report at least five months late, so that it arrived in the United States on November 1 and first made it to the front page of the *New York Times* on November 26, 1944; and only then was there a public stir.

John Pehle, head of the WRB, had to overcome the opposition of Elmer Davis, head of the Office of War Information, whom he described as "a recognized liberal." Davis was angry at Pehle for wanting to publicize the Auschwitz Report, "because," he claimed, "Americans would think it was propaganda." As Lipstadt pointed out, Pehle refused to heed Davis's warning and the information was not dismissed as propaganda.[103] In my opinion, the real basis for Davis's objection to publicizing the Auschwitz atrocities was his worship of Roosevelt as the author of the New Deal and as the "messiah" of the secular humanists' hopes. Liberals, therefore, did not want to place any pressure on the president, however crucial other priorities might be.[104]

The publication of the Auschwitz Report in the *New York Times* marked the first occasion since the pogrom of Crystal Night in November 1938 that a Jewish tragedy related to the Holocaust made its front page.

The government-supported "authenticity" of the report was reflected in several newspapers' headlines, such as the *Times*'s "U.S. Board Atrocity Details Told by Witnesses at Polish Camps"; the *New York Tribune*'s "U.S. Charges Nazis Tortured Millions to Death in Europe"; the *Louisville Courier Journal*'s "The Inside Story of Mass Murdering by Nazis: Escapees Give Detailed Accounts of the Gassing and Cremating of 1,765,000 Jews at Birkenau, From an Official Publication of the War Refugee Board"; the *Philadelphia Inquirer*'s "1,786,000 Jews Killed with Gas"; and the *Washington Post*'s "Two Million Executed in Nazi Camps."[105]

Although most of the Anglo-Jewish newspapers could not afford reporters in Europe, all made use of the *New York Times,* quoting its articles, especially this one on the Auschwitz Report, on many of their own front pages.[106] The publication of these news articles in the United States, especially in New York

City, became the inspiration for demonstrations by various Jewish groups. The largest took place on July 31, 1944, at Madison Square Garden, which drew a crowd of between 50,000 and 100,000 (20,000 inside; the rest outside). For various reasons, especially the ideological worship of Roosevelt, this gathering did not use its great potential political power and did not ask the president to bomb Auschwitz. This was a rather minor request for a president in the heat of his crucial fourth-term election campaign. Therefore, little activity of practical value came out of this enthusiastic forum. The fact remains that only the Swiss people made a major difference in the fate of Hungarian Jewry. Galvanized by Mantello and inspired by outstanding church leaders, they sought to use the press and church to effect changes made in the events in Hungary, and they succeeded beyond anyone's expectation.

Romania

The news about the press campaign reached Romania through the same Manoliu who had originally obtained the two atrocity reports from Moshe Krausz in Budapest on June 19. Manoliu continued cooperating with Mantello and his brother Josef Mandl on behalf of rescue in other ways as well. While Mantello worked primarily via the Bányai Committee to reach certain circles, Josef used the Swiss-Romanian Committee and especially his friend Manoliu to communicate with important Jewish and governmental circles in Bucharest. Like the Bányai Committee, the Romanian counterpart consisted primarily of Swiss Jews of Romanian origin, especially from the Siebenbergen area in Transylvania, intent on the rescue of as many of their coreligionists as possible.

On August 1, 1944, Josef asked Manoliu, on behalf of the committee, to go on a special mission to Bucharest, to report to Jewish and non-Jewish circles on the important results of the Swiss press campaign. Josef sent a long letter to Mr. Wilhelm Filderman, president of the Jewish community, which outlined the ongoing work of the the Swiss Romanian Committee and the impact of the press campaign. Josef introduced "the bearer of the letter [i.e., Florian Manoliu], as a gentleman from the Romanian Legation in Bern who, through his participation in our interests has earned the gratitude of the entire Jewish community." To visually impress the head of Romanian Jewry with the echoes of the press campaign in Switzerland and abroad, Josef sent along a collection of news clippings. He said that "thanks to the success of the press campaign, due primarily to the bearer of the letter that the world first learned of the tragedy of Hungarian Jewry." It was not long after that the press campaign had an impact on Romania itself, as evidenced by the fact that several days earlier a cable from Bucharest declared that henceforth "the refugees from the neighboring country [i.e., Hungary] would be accepted."

Josef also detailed to Filderman some of the activities of the Swiss-Romanian Committee. Like his brother George, Josef complained about the Jewish establishment organizations' dislike of anyone "meddling" in their affairs, even if it involved the rescue of thousands of their fellow Jews. This hostility toward the "outsiders" went on even though the representatives of the Jewish organizations in Switzerland had few contacts and little knowledge of the situation in Romania. Nor did they know how to deal with this government particularly vulnerable to outside pressure and readily susceptible to bribery.

The committee (especially Josef, through his friend Manoliu) also used its contacts with the influential Grigore Gafencu (the liberal former Romanian foreign minister now in Bern) to send several petitions to Bucharest on behalf of the incarcerated and ill-fed Jews in Transnistra. Quick responses by Romanian officials point to the success of this intervention, which helped to improve the shortage of food and medicine. Josef also pointed to the existence of a recently formed (Romanian) rabbinic organization, headed by Rabbi Joel Teitelbaum, the newly released Hassidic admor, who cooperated closely with the committee. Finally, Josef suggested the Jewish leadership took this trustworthy bearer (Manoliu) into their confidence, because he and his connections could greatly facilitate their rescue efforts. Despite the paucity of documentation, we know of at least a few positive accomplishments.[107]

Although Mantello's inspired Swiss press campaign achieved his primary goal of halting the deportations, its influence both in Switzerland and abroad had further ramifications. The next chapter will focus on some of its far-reaching consequences.

10

Horthy Takes Charge

New Circumstances

Although the Western world, including the Allies, the neutral countries, the Vatican, and the IRC had been fully aware since at least December 17, 1942, of the German atrocities against the Jews, they rarely raised a voice on their behalf, let alone actively intervene; they couched their indifference in legalistic or even moral tones, and spoke of military necessity. Yet strangely, by the end of June and early July 1944, all contemporary Jewish representatives and historians admit that the entire picture in Hungary changed radically. However, they ignore the Swiss press and church campaigns and attribute this change to the apparently victorious Allied march, especially the advance of the Russian armies on the eastern front.

What they ignore is the basic fact that there were many others besides Hitler in the German high command, as well as in the Hungarian upper echelons, who maintained their early stance and fought to the very end for the implementation of the Final Solution, and who surely would have succeeded if not for the press and church campaigns. In fact, Veesenmayer noted after his talk with Hungarian prime minister Sztojay, in which Sztojay had commented on Ambassador Jaeger's threat to break off relations between Switzerland and Hungary, "In case we are victorious, the threat [to try the Hungarians as war criminals] will be meaningless, whereas in the opposite case his [Sztojay's] life will at any rate be forfeit."[1] Veesenmayer made it clear that he was unintimidated by any outside threats. If the Germans won, Sztojay would be off the hook, and if they lost, the Americans would hang him as a war criminal. Veesenmayer had no personal concern for his cohorts; his only concern was to annihilate the

Jews, and he planned to do so despite Allied resistance and despite the press and church campaigns—whose powers he did not comprehend.

There is no doubt that the change in the stance and activities of the neutrals and the Allies was a direct result of this incredible Swiss press and church campaigns. The publicity not only stirred up the Swiss people on behalf of the Jews in an unprecedented manner, but it also had a great impact on the rest of the free world and especially on the Hungarian regent. We have already seen how Horthy was pressured into halting deportations on July 7. Further, his publicizing of the halt through the IRC on the eighteenth, and the IRC's official communiqué to this effect on the twenty-first, assured worldwide recognition of this major change in his policy. Horthy not only redirected his country's policy toward the Jews, but he also went much further than even the IRC had requested.

Concomitant with the halt in deportations was a major transformation in the perspective of all the neutral observers in Budapest. From timid, well-meaning, but helpless bystanders, these observers turned into courageous activists, and some even put their lives in danger. In fact, courage and daring became infectious, touching many who would never have dreamed of taking the bold initiatives that were necessary to rescue the remaining Jews in Budapest. Strangely enough, these onlookers' rationalizations for their previous silence suddenly disappeared as the neutral countries, the Vatican, and the IRC became active on behalf of the Jews. From now on, these representatives not only kept close tabs on the regent's mercurial changes and the volatile situation of Budapest's Jews, but they also demanded action, put forth suggestions, and frequently acted on their own.

Moreover, as a result of this intensified atmosphere, some of the Jews who had given up entirely, such as Moshe Krausz and members of the Jewish Council, suddenly became bolder and more innovative in promoting rescue schemes during the last half year before liberation.

It is important to remember that as soon as Horthy halted deportations, the Germans and their Hungarian lackeys acted immediately to complete the Final Solution as quickly as possible. It would take all the courage and wits of the new heroes to make the most of a delicate opportunity within desperate and ever-changing circumstances. Especially important were the guidelines for Horthy's new policy toward Budapest Jewry, epitomized by the "Horthy offer," in which he told the Allies that he would allow 10,000 Jewish children to leave the country unconditionally—a public offer that the Allies could not afford to ignore. Although the Jews involved in this offer never made their way to safe havens in either Palestine or the neutral countries, they generally remained unmolested as a result of the neutrals' new protection.

The Horthy Offer

When Horthy first made his offer to allow 10,000 children to exit from Hungary, many different rescue activists scrambled to put names on the list. Many of the people eventually assigned to the list were not children. The project originally began with 7,000 holders of Palestine certificates, plus several hundred people with Swedish entry visas. By June 30, after the first week of the public response to the press and church campaigns, Moshe Krausz of the Palamt was able to persuade the British to declare the certificates as protective papers. He did this with the help of Carl Lutz, the Swiss consul, who represented British interests. Krausz also tried to increase the number of those eligible to leave Hungary by declaring that the certificates represent not only individuals but also entire families. Undoubtedly, he used the Salvadoran papers as his model for both actions, for each Salvadoran paper from the outset had served as protection for an entire family, with virtually no limitations.[2] This "transformation" of certificates into protective papers enabled Krausz to eventually increase the number of those protected from about 7,000 to 40,000.

At first, however, Lutz and Krausz prepared to put the certificate holders under Swiss auspices. As a start, Krausz obtained the help of fifty Jews and had them gather photos of 4,000 people, while Lutz made out four collective passports of one thousand each with a total of 4,000 names. Because he had no authorization from Bern to provide individual protective papers, he issued the "collective passes," which were effective but did not look as official or have quite the same clout. Each person was provided with a Swiss "protective letter" *(Schutzbrief),* without specific names or numbers, which guaranteed the safety of the individual under Swiss auspices until his arrival in Palestine.[3]

The first news concerning the Horthy offer was sent to Chaim Barlas, head of the Jewish Agency's Vaad Hahatzalah in Istanbul, on July 13, in which Krausz included a thousand children; he also added a hundred adults who would be accompanying them, in an attempt to squeeze some extra people into the plan. This number was in addition to the 7,000 holders of Palestine certificates and the hundreds of Swedish exit papers. Tragically, even before Horthy made his proposal public, he checked with the Germans for their approval, a practice he maintained throughout this period. Oddly enough, Hitler himself, at some points, approved the exit of thousands of Hungarian Jews, although he always insisted on two conditions: that they avoid any route toward Palestine, in keeping with his agreement with his close ally, the grand mufti of Jerusalem; and, of far greater import, that Horthy continue deportations for the balance of Hungarian Jewry.[4]

New worries now arose for those who would be receiving the refugees. Although the Jewish Agency sought every means of fostering immigration to Palestine, Great Britain was fearful of a flood of refugees pouring into the country. This is exemplified by the statement of a junior official in the British foreign office in London who exclaimed, "It is clear that the floodgates of Eastern Europe are now going to be opened, and that we shall in a very short time have masses of Eastern European Jews on our hands."[5]

In the meantime, an unrelated effort cast a steady shadow over the so-called Horthy negotiations. This was the Brand mission, involving negotiations by Kastner with the Nazis for a ransom of ten thousand trucks for one million Hungarian Jews, which had been discussed and rejected by the British during July. The Horthy offer, although overshadowed, proved to be a much more serious challenge for the British authorities than the Brand negotiations; there was no doubt about its source, for instance, no demands for a quid pro quo, and it did not involve negotiations with the enemy. The Brand affair not only required direct dealing with the enemy, but it also involved the transfer of important war supplies and the possibility of psychological warfare. As a result, the British readily rejected the Brand project but were somewhat more amenable to the Horthy offer.

Moreover, because of steady pressure from the United States, which was now in the heat of the 1944 presidential election campaign, Britain had to make some sort of positive response to this public rescue offer. However, when the United States set an August 7 deadline for public acceptance of the Horthy offer, the British continued to stall, blaming American Jewish influence for forcing them to get involved in the rescue of the European Jews. They reasoned that in Washington, "the electoral necessities and the War Refugee Board, backed by [the Jew] Morgenthau, must dictate a willingness to play with any scheme, however objectionable, which can be represented as rescuing European Jews."[6]

One British official suggested the placatory measure of setting up refugee camps in the Mediterranean area, preferably far from Palestine. The archbishop of Canterbury, who had been contacted more than a month earlier by both Koechlin and Vogt to publicize the plight of Hungarian Jewry, made a forceful statement by leading a delegation to the British foreign office. He suggested that Horthy be taken at his word, saying, "Let as many of these people as possible go; we can take them all."[7]

On August 8, Horthy wrote an apologetic note to Huber, president of the IRC, in which he deplored the anti-Jewish measures. He repeated his orders for the government to take the fate of the Jews into its own hands, adding that he hoped this would not lead to complications—that is, German interference.[8] In fact, by mid-August, Ambassador Veesenmayer confirmed that the Swiss and Swedish legations in Budapest had been informed about the German consent to the emigration of the 7,000 Palestine certificate holders,[9] but not Krausz's figure of 40,000. This approval was reiterated on August 15, with the German condition that the refugees could go only to Switzerland or Sweden, not Romania, which was a springboard to Palestine.[10]

The United States, through the War Refugee Board, gave its guarantee to Switzerland and the other neutral countries that it would provide subsidies for the support of the refugees, as well as assurance of their postwar emigration.[11] It took the personal intervention of Morgenthau and his assistant Josiah DuBois (who was in London at the time) to persuade Churchill and Eden to approve the joint declaration on August 17.[12] Thus, despite Britain's stalling, the Horthy offer became public on that day. The IRC was not publicly involved in the rescue arena until July 18, but when Schirmer was assigned to present Huber's letter to Horthy on July 5, he simultaneously represented the IRC as the agent to help carry out the Horthy offer. The Allies used the IRC to deliver its message to the Hungarian government. The message was also published the next day in the *New York Times* and read as follows:

> Because of the desperate plight of the Jews in Hungary and the overwhelming humanitarian considerations involved, the two governments [American and Great Britain] are informing the government of Hungary, through the International Red Cross, that despite the heavy difficulties and responsibilities involved, they have accepted the offer of the Hungarian government for the release of the Jews and will make arrangements for the care of such Jews leaving Hungary who reach neutral or United Nations territory, and also that they will find temporary havens of refuge where such people may live in safety. . . .
> The governments of the United Kingdom and the United States emphasize

that in accepting the offer which had been made, they do not in any way condone the action of the Hungarian government in forcing the emigration of Jews as an alternative to persecution and death.[13]

Incidentally, Switzerland had given its own assurance of accepting 8,000 Hungarian Jewish refugees, in addition to 5,000 children, as long as they were provided with an Allied guarantee that they would resettle elsewhere after the war. Moreover, Romania had already permitted the transit of 1,500 Jews from March 30 through May 15, and by the summer many more were permitted entry and transfer to Palestine.[14] Wallenberg's first few weeks of activities, which coincided with the launching of the Horthy offer, made it clear that Sweden was also willing to accept thousands of Jews. Another venture was the American approval of financing for the absorption of children by Portugal; thousands more were expected to enter Spain and other Western countries.[15]

Let us examine both the individual and collective rescue efforts of these neutral observers in Budapest. From the welter of facts, personalities, and events, a few heroes emerge, some unfamiliar, in the final drama of Budapest Jewry, which took place in the turbulent atmosphere of Mantello's press campaign. Among these heroes was Carl Lutz, the Swiss head of the Department of Foreign Interests in Budapest, and Raoul Wallenberg, the newly arrived Swedish diplomat. They and others became involved in the distribution of protective papers for tens of thousands of Jews in Budapest during the final half year of Nazi occupation. Largely through their efforts, these papers were transformed from useless documents into lifesaving devices.

Even before the German occupation, Mantello had provided scores of Salvadoran citizenship papers to individual Jews and Jewish organizations in Switzerland, to be given to friends and relatives in Hungary. Most of these papers went to Polish or Slovakian refugees hiding out in Hungary. The sole genuine Salvadoran passport in Hungary was possessed by Mantello's wife, Iréne, who resided in Budapest with her parents and brothers. As soon as the Germans occupied Hungary, Mantello sent scores of Salvadoran papers into Hungary, even though, other than hints in a few postcards and letters, no response was forthcoming; no one, apparently, had been able to penetrate the iron curtain around Hungary established by the Germans.

We have also seen that part of Manoliu's mission to Budapest was to distribute about a thousand signed Salvadoran papers through Krausz. The supplied signature saved much precious time, for there was no longer a need for the recipient to fill in the information, attach the photos, and send them back to Geneva for Mantello's signature. All the necessary information and photos could now be filled in on the spot, and the papers could be used immediately. Lutz and Krausz were thus able to distribute them very effectively to any Jew they desired. Because each document covered an entire family, they would even "create" families where feasible, to make the most efficient use of them.

Carl Lutz, Swiss consul in Budapest. He was in charge of the Division of Foreign Interests, representing Britain and many of the Latin American countries vis-à-vis the Axis. Courtesy of Ringier Pressehaus.

This new by-product of Mantello's efforts burgeoned into a multifaceted rescue effort. Mantello now began to dispatch an average of two hundred and fifty to three hundred signed Salvadoran papers weekly, via Vatican, Swiss, and Romanian couriers. After the IRC became involved in rescue, they provided Mantello with valuable couriers as well, who carried Salvadoran papers not only to Budapest, but also to other countries, including Poland.[16] Despite early skepticism about the papers' value, they eventually provided the sole protection for almost all recipients and were eventually considered the best protective papers of all (see chapter 11).

Both Lutz and Wallenberg emerged from the Hungarian tragedy as true heroes, although Wallenberg is far better known. Interestingly enough, they shared a number of important experiences in their backgrounds, as well as similar styles of operation. Both used their posts to expand their rescue activities to as many Jews as possible, although Lutz never matched his Swedish colleague's more flamboyant personality and courageous initiatives. However, because Lutz served at his post in Budapest much earlier than Wallenberg and in some ways paved the way for him, we will focus on Lutz first.

Lutz and Krausz

Consul Lutz's role in the broader Swiss rescue efforts in Budapest really commenced after the start of the press campaign, but his earlier diplomatic role had paved the way for it. He was educated in the United States, and in 1935 served in Palestine as head of the Swiss consulate in Tel Aviv. After the outbreak of the Second World War in September 1939, he interceded on behalf of twenty-five hundred German nationals in Palestine who were about to be deported by the British authorities as enemy aliens. This act was to serve him in good stead during his rescue activities on behalf of the Budapest Jews.[17]

On April 6, 1941, when the Germans marched into the Balkans, the Swiss took over the interests of Belgium and Yugoslavia; until Pearl Harbor, the United States had done the same for Britain. By January 2, 1942, however, the Swiss took over Britain's interests as well, including the matter of Palestine certificates.[18] Moshe Krausz, head of the Palamt, worked closely with Lutz in this area. On March 15, a few days after the German occupation of Hungary, the Germans closed the Palamt, and Lutz immediately invited Krausz to take refuge in the Swiss compound. It was at 29 Szabdsag Ter, in the former American embassy building, where Krausz continued to handle the certificates.[19]

During this time, the British and Turks permitted about fifty Jews weekly to make their way to the Yishuv via Romania, the Black Sea, Turkey, and Syria.[20]

Despite continuous work on the certificates, however, as Saly Mayer pointed out, "prior to June 30, the certificates were worthless as protection for their holders."[21] If there were any doubt on that score, one merely had to read Krausz's desperate letter of June 19, describing the despair of Budapest's Jews (see chapter 6). The use of these Salvadoran documents as protective papers served as the model for all the "protective papers" subsequently developed by the neutral diplomats, and provided the impetus for Lutz and Krausz to transform the Palestine certificates from their normal function, as entry visas to Palestine, into protective papers as well. These papers created what, in effect, became extraterritoriality for their holders.[22] After the IRC entered the fray in mid-July, it cooperated closely with Lutz to protect the holders of these papers and certificates, and to aid in the emigration effort.

During the postwar inquiry, when Lutz testified on behalf of Mantello, he recalled how he had first found out about the Salvadoran papers:

> The first [Salvadoran citizenship papers] . . . appeared in Budapest, and the people came to the [Swiss Political Department for the] representation of Foreign Interests to ask for protection. Then we represented fourteen countries. Switzerland and Sweden were the only neutral states, and the people thought that they would find protection with us. We told everybody that we did not yet have the [formal authorization] to represent [El Salvador] because we had not received any communication from the [Swiss] Political Department in Bern to this effect.[23]

By August 25, after Horthy took charge following the protests of the neutral observers, he offered protection for holders of Palestine certificates, as well as holders of papers from any of the Latin American countries, including El Salvador. However, as Lutz pointed out, "there was a problem."[24]

Lutz noted that he had the greatest difficulty with the Nyilas, the Hungarian Arrow Cross (see chapter 11).[25] During these difficult times, both Lutz and Krausz worked tirelessly to persuade both the Hungarian and Swiss governments to recognize the legitimacy of the certificates and to permit their holders to travel to Palestine, a dream that never materialized because of constant German pressure. On the other hand, unbeknownst to Lutz or Krausz, there were several successful behind-the-scenes efforts by some Jewish organizations in America, as well as by Mantello in Geneva, to persuade the American gov ernment to pressure the Swiss government into officially taking over the protection of Salvadoran interests in Hungary (see chapter 11). Thus, while very few of the paper holders ever made it out of Hungary, almost all received protection until the end of the war.[26]

Wallenberg

Wallenberg was perhaps the most recognized of the neutral activists in Budapest at that time. Though he appeared on the scene much later than Lutz, he quickly achieved a reputation as an extraordinary agent of rescue. His fame, unfortunately, had much to do with his tragic, mysterious disappearance; however, primarily his courage, flamboyant personality, and energetic manner set him apart from from his more reserved Swiss colleague, rather than the numbers of people each rescued. Wallenberg was a highly intelligent, sympathetic, and dynamic young man, with Jewish ancestry on his mother's side. He had also lived for half a year in Haifa, Palestine, and had business ties in Budapest. Above all, he was the very antithesis of a bureaucrat, for whom legality and conformity were almighty. He turned out to be the right person in the right place at the right time.[27]

Wallenberg's mission arose out of a series of Swedish entreaties and intercessions on behalf of the Jews. As we have noted, these pleas began nine days after the German occupation of Hungary with the request of Dr. Norbert Masur, an industrialist with interests in Hungary and a representative of the World Jewish Congress. Concerned for his friends in Hungary, he pleaded with the legalist-minded chief rabbi, Dr. Marcus Ehrenpreis, whose previous rescue efforts were nonexistent, to intervene on behalf of Hungarian Jewry. Others who interceded included Mr. Ivor Olson, an American who was to represent the War Refugee Board; Dr. Koloman Lauer, an industrialist with interests in Hungary and a former employer of Wallenberg; Prof. Hugo Valentin; and Mr. Gunnar Josephson, head of the Swedish Jewish Community.[28] Ironically, although Wallenberg had already been selected for his mission at the urging of Dr. Lauer, he failed to impress the chief rabbi, who was shocked at the young man's insistence on using bribery and illegal methods to rescue Jews as a precondition for his project. Two valuable weeks were lost over this disagreement until Lauer was able to persuade Rabbi Ehrenpreis to reconsider and approve Wallenberg's mission.[29]

Though Sweden had already entered the rescue arena by the end of 1942, with the rescue of about 900 Norwegian Jews and, in the fall of 1943, when it took in more than 7,000 Danish Jews, it did not do very much to help subsequently until June 27, the second day of the Hungarian Crown Council meeting. At that meeting, Horthy had responded favorably to Sweden's request for the release of several hundred Hungarian Jews who had Swedish relatives, businesses, or any other connection to Sweden. This took place a day after Taubes's urgent cable to Rabbi Ehrenpreis, which was followed by those of Grünbaum in Jerusalem and Posner in Geneva. These appeals for help resulted in King Gustav's very influential personal message to Horthy to do something to alleviate the plight of the Jews (see chapter 6). Sweden's importance and relevance to Hungary was based on its special relationship with that nation; through the First and Second World Wars, Sweden had represented Hungary's interests, including the exchange of prisoners and care of the wounded. This added great weight to the Swedish king's plea to Horthy on June 30.

About the same time, Taubes sent a second cable to Sweden's chief rabbi, urging him to send a delegate to Budapest to help its Jews. On the following day, July 1, the Hungarian Alien Police, usually referred to by its Hungarian acronym KEOKH, approved the recognition of several hundred Swedish "provisional passports," whose holders were now permitted to remove their yellow stars and to move out of internment.[30] The first approximately 450 passports were issued to Hungarian Jews related to Swedish citizens or having business connections with Sweden. They were issued before the arrival of Wallenberg and were really a kind of "travel document"; under certain circumstances, they could also be given to noncitizens of Sweden.[31]

To provide Wallenberg with diplomatic immunity, he was officially appointed as the third secretary at the Swedish legation in Budapest. He arrived in Hungary on July 9, two days after Horthy's halt of the deportations, and got to work immediately. Besides money and an extraordinary sense of mission, Wallenberg came equipped with a revolver, though he hoped that he would never have occasion to use it.[32] It was a propitious time for his daring approach, with the press campaign in its third week. The first thing Wallenberg did upon his arrival in Budapest was to see Lutz. Lutz himself noted that "[on July 9] he [Wallenberg] visited me. He asked me to inform him about my rescue activities, to show him the text of our *Schutzbriefe*, and to give him copies, so that he could begin a similar *Aktion*. I supplied him with all the desired items and informed him about my negotiations with the Hungarians and the Germans."[33]

In his first phone contact with Stockholm, he described the situation in Budapest to Dr. Lauer, emphasizing, "We have a need for money, money, and more money; without it I cannot proceed." As a result of this talk, Dr. Lauer got in touch with Ivor Olson, the representative of the War Refugee Board in Stockholm, who immediately transferred more than 100,000 Swiss crowns provided by the Joint.[34]

Soon upon his arrival, Wallenberg received a phone call from Mantello, who asked the young Swede to assume the protection of holders of the Salvadoran papers temporarily, because negotiations with the Swiss government had not yet borne fruit. The great humanitarian quickly accepted this additional charge, relinquishing it only after the Swiss finally took over.[35]

Although the Swedish legation in Budapest was fully aware of Wallenberg's rescue mission, his dynamic, unorthodox manner shocked the well-meaning but rather staid veteran diplomats.[36] However, as we will see, his sincerity and magnetism were infectious. He changed attitudes on all diplomatic levels, including that of the very formal and composed Swedish ambassador Danielsson. In fact, it did not take long for him to move to the forefront of the rescue efforts organized by the neutral observers in Budapest.

Wallenberg soon gathered a staff of about forty people, mostly Jews, for whom he obtained special rights, including the removal of their yellow stars. As rescue activities increased, especially after the Szalasi coup in mid-October of 1944, the staff increased to four hundred.[37] After contacting Lutz, Wallenberg went to see some of the Hungarian authorities, including Laszlo Ferency, who provided him with the first three of his "protected houses." On August 4, he met with Horthy and warned him against permitting the rumored deportations, because he was fully aware of the Kistarcsa and Sarvar deportations, which had taken place in July without Horthy's approval. Horthy, already under the pressure of Mantello's second press campaign (described below), now canceled all deportations.[38]

Things appeared to quiet down during August, a fact that Wallenberg conveyed to Stockholm in his second report of July 29. In fact, he even thought that he would soon be able to wind down his mission and return home. Little did he know that his greatest hour and his personal tragedy were yet to come.

No one was more surprised than the Germans, at both the halt of the deportations and the ensuing proliferation of protective papers by the neutral countries. As Veesenmayer noted to the foreign office in Berlin, "There is activity from foreign sources to protect Hungarian Jews by issuing protective passes or giving them citizenship. Particularly surprising in this connection is the attitude of the Swedish Embassy here which in addition to the numbers of 650 persons announced at the time, already 6,000 protective passports have been issued to Hungarian Jews, according to an official report to the Hungarian Foreign Ministry."[39]

Second Press Campaign

We have seen how Eichmann and his Hungarian cohorts made repeated attempts to thwart Horthy and to continue the deportations of the Jews. Deportations from Kistarcsa and Sarvar had taken place on July 18 and 24, causing repercussions in Switzerland. As soon as Lutz informed Mantello about these two deportations, Mantello informed the IRC in Geneva; the IRC, in turn, pressured the Hungarian consulate in Bern, headed by Consul General Baron Karoly Bothmer. In his cable to Prime Minister Sztojay, the Hungarian ambassador declared the following:

> The head of the [International] Red Cross informed me lately that allegedly, the deportations continue once again. . . . With 1,200 men and women from Kistarcsa on [July 19] and 1,500 from Sarvar on the 24th last month. These facts would indicate that the Hungarian government has violated its promises to halt the deportations. . . . *The consequences for the [Hungarian] government and world public opinion would be incalculable.* We therefore ask for the official Hungarian government to respond to the above information. (emphasis added)[40]

The Hungarian Deputy Premier Remenyi-Schneller responded immediately and apologetically: "Please inform the leader of the [International] Red Cross that it is really the Germans who deported the Jews from Kistarcsa and Sarvar, without the knowledge or consent of the Hungarian government. We have made energetic interventions with the German government on this matter. There is no danger of repetition of such incidents . . . since the Jewish question is now handled exclusively by the Hungarian government."[41]

The Hungarian government also gave similar assurances to the neutral diplomats in Budapest, adding, "The Hungarian government has forbidden the deportations, but the Germans carried them out with the help of the Arrow Cross. . . . The government will prevent any further deportations."[42] Horthy's changed attitude, however, did little to crimp the determination of Eichmann and Veesenmayer to destroy the Jews, a desire that far outweighed their concerns for Germany's immediate interests. It therefore comes as no surprise to find that on July 29, Veesenmayer wrote to Ribbentrop that he had ordered the start of new deportations.[43]

Meanwhile, in Switzerland, with the help of Walter Garrett, Mantello pressured the Hungarian government with a renewed press campaign, producing another flurry of articles that condemned the new Hungarian deportations. He also arranged for a novel, two-pronged attack on any further intended Hungarian action. The first involved the production of a special edition of a small, nondescript Hungarian newspaper called *Magyar Nemzet,* which detailed exactly what was happening to the Jews in Budapest and relayed the strong negative reaction of the Swiss papers. It blamed the feudal Hungarian landowners who sold out to the Germans to help them solve the "Jewish Question." Mantello had thousands of copies of this edition stuffed into envelopes and mailed to public and private citizens of Budapest, whose names and addresses he had taken from the telephone directory.[44]

In his second tactic, Mantello mailed a large shipment of additional anti-Nazi propaganda into Budapest: thousands of copies of the thirty-six-page, democratic, German-language Hungarian newspaper entitled *Ungarischen Nationalen Unabhangigkeitsfront* (The Hungarian national independent front). Subtitled "News from Hungary," this paper detailed the horrors of the new deportations. By the time the Germans discovered this trap, it was too late to do anything about it. In fact, SS leader Otto Winkelman reported in consternation on these newspaper reports the next day in a cable to Himmler.[45]

Wallenberg's report of July 29 noted the value of this second wave of the press campaign: "It is well-known that *the foreign press significantly contributes to the alleviation of the situation here;* thus, further publicity would be desirable. My enclosed report about the position of the Jews in Hungary is designed with that in mind" (emphasis added).[46]

Eichmann, however, persisted. When his original ploy to continue large-scale deportations failed, he attempted once again to renew them, unsatisfied by his two small successes at Kistarcsa and Sarvar. However, some members of the Jewish Council had thwarted him during the Kistarcsa debacle by notifying Horthy, and he decided to remove them before continuing the deportations. At the same time, he tried to overpower the reluctant regent with a show of force by parading the SS, with tanks, armored cars, and guns, through the principal thoroughfares of Budapest. As expected, this frightened both the Jewish leaders and the general populace. On August 18, Eichmann had the president and two vice presidents of the Jewish Council arrested, and ordered the deportations to be renewed on the twenty-fifth.[47] Another cause for alarm was the plan to relocate all "protected" Jews into the special yellow-star houses on Pozsony Road, while the "unprotected" Jews would replace them in the vacated apartments.[48]

To obviate this rumored transfer, five vigilant neutral observers, who had been keeping a close eye on the Jewish situation in Budapest, got together and submitted a memorandum. Dated August 21, it was handed to Deputy Prime Minister Remenyi-Schneller by the papal nuncio, who was considered the dean of diplomats, and Swedish ambassador Danielsson. The memorandum, which was surely a product of Mantello's press campaign, included phrases taken from the Swiss press. It read:

> The undersigned accredited representatives of the Neutral Powers in Budapest were informed, to their surprise and dismay, that the deportation of the Hungarian Jews is about to begin. *We know from absolutely reliable sources what deportation means in the majority of cases, even if it is disguised under the term of labor service abroad.* Apart from the fact that restarting the deportations would deal a deathly blow to Hungary's reputation, which is already seriously compromised by the previous deportations, the representatives of the Neutral Embassies, motivated by human solidarity and Christian compassion, feel it is their duty to raise a strong protest against this act, which is unjust and inhumane. It is absolutely impermissible that people should be persecuted and sent to their deaths merely because of their racial origins. It should never have started in the first place, and it is a stain on the human character.
>
> We wish to express our hope that Hungary, according to her oldest traditions, will return to those chivalrous and profound Christian principles and methods which have secured her such a high position amongst the civilized nations of the world. Budapest, August 21, 1944. (emphasis added)
>
> > Signed,
> >
> > Angelo Rotta, Apostolic Nuncio
> > Carl Ivan Danielsson, Swedish Ambassador
> > Carlos de Liz Texaira Branquinho, Portuguese Chargé d'Affaires
> > Angel Sanz-Briz, Spanish Chargé d'Affaires
> > Antoine J. Kilchmann, Swiss Chargé d'Affaires[49]

At this critical hour, while the neutral observers showed courage and initiative under dangerous conditions, American Roswell McClelland of the War Refugee Board was still unwilling to acknowledge the atrocity reports. "Most are exaggerations," he said. He then added, on an ironic note, "Besides, one can't expect any help from neutrals and the Hungarian governments, as long as the Germans are in Hungary." Echoing the official American government's line vis-à-vis rescue, McClelland remarked that the best hopes for any relief were restricted to a speedy end to the war.[50] Fortunately, other activists in Budapest were far more compassionate and courageous than he.

The very next day, Horthy repeated his opposition to the deportations. Besides the added pressure of the neutral observers, he was also affected by several elements in the deterioration of the Axis' military fortunes. These included Gen. Charles DeGaulle's entry into Paris and, of greater import, the defection of Romania from the Axis on August 23 and its declaration of war on its former allies two days later. These developments prompted Horthy to take a much more aggressive stand in his defense of the Jews in Budapest and to take full control of the affairs of his country. Through his deputy minister, Lajos Remenyi-Schneller, he sent a series of demands to the Germans, with a primary focus on taking over the "Jewish Question." Moreover, he considered Eichmann's SS contingent of 160 men "superfluous," and asked that they be removed from Hungary. Finally, he informed all the Hungarian legations of the halt of all deportations.[51] On August 25, four days after the neutrals submitted their memo, Horthy took an even more aggressive stance, further encouraged by Romania's declaration of war on Germany.[52]

Two days earlier, in a top-secret dispatch, propaganda minister Goebbels had noted, "The pressure by the enemy and neutrals [Hull, king of Sweden, Swiss, the pope] became so strong that the circles in Budapest friendly to Jews influenced the government to halt the deportation of the Jews."[53]

On August 26, one day after Himmler cabled the order to halt deportations to Veesenmayer, the Hungarian foreign minister informed Ambassador Jaeger. He, in turn, immediately dispatched this news to Bern. Jaeger added that at the same time, the Hungarians were demanding of the Germans that the SS leave Budapest and permit Hungary to solve the Jewish problem independently. He concluded his cable with the observation that Horthy was displaying a strong hand toward the Germans and was now taking charge.[54]

Besides the interventions and press attacks, which were behind Himmler's decision to halt the deportations, there were geopolitical factors as well. One was the loss of the Romanian oil wells and the fear that this would jeopardize the "now indispensable oil production of Zala District"; another was the danger for German troops in Romania. For all these reasons, Himmler felt that it was not worthwhile to let matters come to a crisis with Horthy and his new government because of the remaining Hungarian Jews. He therefore cabled Budapest at 3 A.M. on August 25, forbidding the continued deportations.[55] At this point, Veesenmayer noted that "obviously, *under the impact of the press attacks inspired by the enemy powers,* as well as the *intervention of several foreign and enemy powers,* the former Reichsweser [Himmler] informed the German government on August [25] of this year, of his decision to prevent any further transports of Hungarian Jews to German territories" (emphasis added).[56]

To prevent any last-minute meddling by Eichmann, Himmler removed him and his associates from Hungary, ostensibly for honoring him with one of Germany's highest medals.[57] At the same time, to take advantage of this weakened German presence in his country, Horthy planned a change of government, and on the twenty-ninth, he replaced Sztojay with Gen. Geza Lakatos. Ironically, this move was to put the Jews in the most perilous situation since mid-June; on the other hand, this period would bring to the fore the true courage of Lutz and Wallenberg, and the miracle of the Salvadoran papers.

IRC

Although the IRC required much pressure to enter into the rescue arena, it proved its great value in Budapest during the last six months of the war, complementing the activities of the neutral observers. One of its immediate and important acts was to change the definition of the Jewish concentration camp inmates from "detainees," which indicated a penal status, to "internees," a civilian category.[58] Jews had not previously been accorded the right to receive the protection and services of the IRC. One crucial example was that packages had been distributed regularly in the camps only to non-Jews; the sole exception had been the Spanish Red Cross, which, under the encouragement of Generalissimo Franco (inspired by Mrs. Reichmann in Tangier), classified the Jewish inmates in the camps as "prisoners of war" (see chapter 11). This protection was now granted officially by the international body of the IRC.[59]

Friedrich Born of the IRC also began to visit the Ministry of Foreign Affairs and other Hungarian and German governmental agencies, in an unsuccessful bid to visit the detention camps. Huber, in Switzerland, likewise discussed this issue with the Hungarian authorities. On July 19, he addressed Imre Tahy, while two days later Schirmer, newly arrived in Budapest, met with Sztojay to discuss several requests.[60] Among them was permission to visit the yellow-star houses, a halt of deportations, and a request that the Jews be concentrated in ghettos such as Theresienstadt; the IRC had recently visited this ghetto but was unaware that they had been presented with a prearranged "Potamkin's Village" facade.[61]

On July 23, Sztojay responded that he essentially concurred with these requests, and suggested that Schirmer visit the Kistarcsa and Sarvar detention camps. Schirmer did survey the two camps on July 27 and 28, but his visit was a repeat of the Theresienstadt deception. He reported conditions in the camps as "acceptable" because they did not seem very crowded, but this was because of the two "surprise" deportations of twenty-eight hundred inmates, engineered by Eichmann, which had taken place only a few days earlier. Schirmer's IRC delegation also visited several yellow-star houses and Jewish institutions, which had also been carefully prepared beforehand and were given "satisfactory" ratings despite overcrowding. Even if they had not been "doctored," however, camps such as Kistarcsa or Sarvar could never provide the slightest inkling of the hellish realities of an Auschwitz or Treblinka. Those conditions were never shown the IRC even in a "Potemkin Village" version.[62]

Another of the IRC's unsuccessful ventures was an attempt to have the representatives of the numerous Jewish national and international organizations coordinate their rescue efforts. As Mantello had discovered to his dismay in 1942, the ideological and personality differences of the leaders were too great an obstacle to overcome, even in the face of the Jewish tragedy. Nevertheless, the IRC did fill an important rescue role during the last months before the liberation of Budapest. It assumed the protection of many Jewish and non-Jewish institutions, such as hospitals, public kitchens, scientific institutes, shops, and homes for the handicapped, the aged, and Jewish children.[63] Each of these buildings was identified by a plate posted at the main entrance, which read Under the Protection of the International Committee of the Red Cross.[64] Moreover, because of its long history of neutrality and protection of the defenseless, the IRC's voice was an important component of the collective rescue activities of the neutral representatives. Now, for the first time, it used the threat of reciprocity as its weapon, virtually the sole weapon to which the Axis had always responded. After all, the IRC still took care of thousands of Axis prisoners, including Hungarians.

Friedrich Born, the IRC's representative in Budapest, was also one of the quiet heroes who did much more than what might have been expected of him. For example, at great personal risk, he not only extended the IRC's protection to its 300 Jewish employees, but he also quietly distributed protective papers to anyone volunteering to assist the organization in its rescue efforts. In the words of a confidential IRC report, these volunteers eventually totaled about 3,000 Jews.[65]

Spain also cooperated with the IRC in a number of rescue projects. This country had been involved in several earlier rescue efforts on behalf of Jews. In 1940–41, it permitted tens of thousands of Jewish refugees from France to transit through Spain on the way to freedom via Portugal or North Africa. In 1943–44, Spain provided protection to 4,000 Sephardic Jews in several German-occupied territories who held Spanish citizenship. About 800 of these were permitted entry into Spain.[66] Moreover, we have seen how the Spanish government and the Spanish Red Cross assisted Mrs. Renee Reichmann and her daughter Eva, under the auspices of their own organization, called "The Tangier Committee for Aid to Refugees," in sending thousands of packages to various concentration camps from 1942 on.[67]

Recha Sternbuch of HIFJEFS, in Montreaux, also took advantage of Spanish clemency. She was aware of the protection provided by foreign papers, especially those from El Salvador, and she attempted to make use of Horthy's offer to permit the exit of 10,000 children by obtaining the names of 500 orphaned children (along with seventy adults to accompany them) from Samuel Frey and Chaim Roth, her contacts in Budapest. She conveyed these names to Mrs. Reichmann in Tangier, her rescue associate on the Vaad Hatzalah, asking her to seek Tangier entry visas on their behalf. With the help of American chargé d'affaires J. Rives Childs, Mrs. Reichmann convinced Gen. Luis Orgaz, the Spanish high commissioner of Tangier, to provide entry visas for the children.

Soon after, she obtained the names of another 700 children in Budapest, and asked Mrs. Reichmann to try once again to obtain protection for them. Despite her daughter Eva's cautionary advice to request no more than another hundred visas, Mrs. Reichmann said, "I'll ask for 700, and he can cut it down to 500." This diminutive but persuasive rescue activist, who in her daughter's recollection "was always one to think big," succeeded in persuading the Spanish high commissioner to approve entry visas for all 700 children, plus the adults who would be accompanying them.[68]

During the Szalasi era, when all the holders of Swiss and Swedish papers and Palestine certificates were placed under the respective protection of the Swedish and Swiss legations, these "Spanish charges" were placed under the protection of the Spanish legation. Spanish chargé d'affaires Angel Sanz-Briz persuaded the IRC to place them in supervised safe houses, and the IRC consented in early August. As Professor Braham has noted, the IRC "thus acquired a legal framework by which to expand its activities to include the protection of 'foreign civilians.'" In fact, this was the beginning of the IRC's large-scale protection of about 5,000 children,[69] including at least 1,200 with Tangier entry visas. As we have mentioned, they also safeguarded the Jewish institutions and children's homes, especially during the dangerous Nyilas era. Friedrich Born, who had made a number of efforts to help the embattled Jews even before the press campaign, was a major player in all these activities.[70]

Throughout the neutral activists' campaign to protect the Jews, pro-Nazi German and Hungarian officials maintained a heavy resistance. Ambassador Veesenmayer continued to complain about Hungary's relaxing its attitude toward Jews by "delaying their deportation from Budapest." He also complained about the neutral diplomats' issuance of protective and citizenship papers. Veesenmayer was particularly surprised by the Swedish legation, which in a short time enlarged its original circle of 650 protected persons to more than 6,000. Hungarian pro-Nazi circles complained about the local Swedish minister (Wallenberg) who was frequently seen mingling with his "protected" Jews, giving them Swedish protective papers and then removing their yellow stars. What shocked him most was the report emanating from a news agency that the El Salvador consul in Zurich, with the approval of the American government, sought "to smuggle in 20,000 pre-dated passports [*sic*] through the good offices of the Swiss government, in order to have these Jews interned under better conditions as foreign citizens. Such camps would be placed under the supervision of the IRC."[71]

Although this specific plan never materialized, Mantello's daily dispatch of hundreds of Salvadoran papers eventually saved between 20,000 and 30,000 Jews in any case.[72] The final three months of the Nyilas era manifested the neutrals' most courageous actions on behalf of the remnant of Budapest Jews, and proved the great success of the protective papers.

11

The Nyilas Era

The Szalasi Coup

Horthy had sought for some time to pull Hungary out of the grip of the Axis, and Romania's defection on August 23 to the Allied camp apparently helped him make up his mind to follow suit. As soon as he appointed Gen. Geza Lakatos as prime minister, the Germans, especially Veesenmayer, plotted to depose him. When Horthy planned an armistice on October 15, the Germans and the Nyilas—or Arrow Cross, their loyal allies—prepared a countercoup, which they carried out with quiet efficiency. All of the conciliatory measures toward the Jews that Horthy had worked to enforce in the face of the press campaign now dissolved completely. The new premier, Ferenc Szalasi, was a Nazi supporter who posed an extreme threat to the surviving Jews of Budapest, for he appeared impervious to the Western pressure that had so affected his predecessor.[1]

Veesenmayer could never reconcile himself to the pro-Jewish policies of Kallay, Horthy's benign premier, which had resulted in the halt of deportations. Along with Eichmann, Veesenmayer never relinquished his treacherous goal of completing the Final Solution in Hungary. This is evident in his complaint to Ribbentrop on October 19, in which he expressed his dissatisfaction with the previous Hungarian regime's lenient policy toward the Jews. The note, while communicating a clear desire to pursue the Final Solution, also included a few concessions for the sake of pacifying international opinion.

> On August [25] of this year, *under the obvious influence of the press attacks, which were initiated by the foreign enemy powers, as well as the intervention of several foreign and enemy powers,* the Reichsverweser [i.e., Himmler] commu-

nicated a *decision* by the German government that *further transport of Hungarian Jews to Germany would not be permitted.*

On the basis of newly started negotiations [under the new Szalasi regime], a final solution to the Jewish Question, including the problem of Budapest, can be expected without delay. Therefore, the German government declares explicitly that *it recognizes the measures and actions of the international organizations in order to avoid attacks by the foreign press,* and is ready to fulfill the assurance in a timely fashion. The German Embassy is therefore empowered to:

1. Provide German transit visas for the 400 Hungarian Jews with Swedish protective papers. The Swedish government will negotiate for the additional 4,000.
2. Provide transit visas for the 7,000 with Palestine Certificates.
3. Provide Portuguese permits for nine people.
4. Provide for the transit of 1,000 children to Palestine.
5. After completion of the above-mentioned measures, *there will remain in Hungary only those Jews with foreign citizenship* [papers] who are either citizens of enemy countries or people, who, despite their protective papers, cannot be recognized as regular citizens. As far as their treatment is concerned, the German government agrees with the Hungarian government that they are subject to Hungarian laws and, like all other Jews, will fall under the measures of the Hungarian government regarding work *within* Hungary [i.e., they will not be deported]. (emphasis added)[2]

Among Szalasi's first accomplishments during the early days of his regime was the establishment of two distinct ghettos, to separate the "protected" Jews from the unprotected. The objective, as noted by Veesenmayer, was to be able to carry out the emigration of the protective-paper holders while continuing the deportations of those in the regular ghetto. Thousands of Jews were expelled without warning to make room for the transfer of the "protected Jews" into the "International Ghetto," which was under the supervision of the neutrals. In all, the protected ghetto comprised a population of about 30,000, not including thousands of "squatters" who managed to get into these protected homes illegally. There were separate houses under the care of each neutral representative, and Lutz managed to obtain twenty-five high-rise houses for his Swiss-protected charges.[3] Eventually, both the number of houses and the population were greatly increased as thousands of additional people obtained Salvadoran and other protective papers. Interestingly, the very successful concept of "protective houses" was a direct outgrowth of Mantello's Salvadoran papers operation, and provided an indispensable avenue of rescue for the neutrals.

The "regular ghetto" for the unprotected Jews eventually housed about 70,000 people. It was supervised by the Judenrat, the Jewish Council, which sought to alleviate its constantly deteriorating conditions. Later, the council had the difficult assignment of transferring into the already crowded ghetto 6,000 children protected by the IRC.[4]

Whereas the Horthy regime had been ready to permit the emigration of 8,000 Jews with certificates to Palestine, as well as forty-five hundred with Swedish papers to Switzerland, Szalasi abruptly halted this process. The Germans now saw an opportunity to resume the deportations, overthrow the benign rule of the Kallay regime, and send Eichmann back to Hungary. Encouraged by Veesenmayer and Winkelman in Budapest, and by Kaltenbrunner in Berlin, Eichmann returned to Budapest on October 17, only two days after Szalasi took power. With the help of the new premier and the Nyilas, he kept up steady pressure to complete the Final Solution of Hungarian Jewry during the final three months before the Russians liberated the city. The new premier was not in the least deterred by an agreement he had made on October 21 with Angelo Rotta, the papal nuncio, and other neutral observers not to deport or to exterminate the Jews.[5]

Because Jews would no longer be permitted to emigrate legally from the country, the neutrals' main battle now was to resist constant attempts by the pro-Nazi elements to isolate, ghettoize, and deport as many Jews as possible— if no longer by trains to Auschwitz, at least by foot to Germany. Leading this battle were Wallenberg and Lutz, supported by the papal nuncio, the representatives of the Spanish and Portuguese legations, and the IRC. These activists worked from a disadvantaged position to thwart the new onslaught, for they did not have the active support of their governments.

These very dangerous final three months of the Nyilas era were to become the neutrals' finest hour. To their credit, they remained in Budapest at a time when most of the regular diplomats had left the capital, including Swiss ambassador Jaeger, who had returned to Bern. Sweden, too, sought to recall its staff, refusing to recognize the Szalasi regime at a time when maintaining some form of diplomatic relations was essential to the rescue effort. Per Anger, the third secretary of the Swedish legation in Budapest, recalled that the Swedish government threw out the Hungarian chargé d'affaires in Stockholm as a protest against the Szalasi coup, to the chagrin of the entire diplomatic staff in Budapest. Ambassador Danielsson was especially perturbed; he correctly felt that for the sake of rescue, it was crucial to retain diplomatic connections.[6] However, under the influence of the charismatic Wallenberg, Danielsson remained in Budapest, braving the political dangers there even to the point of risking his life several times. His presence not only provided a much-needed cover for Wallenberg's activities, but also helped minimize Stockholm's negative move against the Szalasi regime.[7]

The neutrals, with outstanding courage and creativity, were largely successful, eventually rescuing about three-quarters of Budapest's remaining 200,000 Jews. To cite but one instance of their astounding initiative, Wallenberg fooled the Nazis and the Nyilas in regard to the forty-five hundred people whose Swedish *Schutzpaesse* had been approved. He did this by successfully using a separate set of serial numbers, bringing the actual number to more than 8,000.[8]

Among the neutral powers who were extremely helpful to the Jews during these final three months of the German occupation of Hungary was Spain. As we have seen, Spain provided protection for a limited number of Jews, and its high commissioner in Tangier readily acceded to the requests of Recha Sternbuch and Renee Reichmann to provide entry visas for twelve hundred children. Spain's new chargé d'affaires, Angel Sanz-Briz, remained in Budapest after the departure of his predecessor, anti-Nazi Miguel Angel de Muguiro. In November, however, Sanz-Briz also returned to Madrid after protesting the Szalasi coup, but he did not leave without guaranteeing protection for about 3,000 Jews, most of whom were children, and he left word with his successor, Giorgio (Jorge) Perlesca, to maintain this protection.[9] The children were placed under the protection of the Spanish legation, and Sanz-Briz persuaded the IRC in early August to place them in IRC-supervised safe houses. They were among several thousand protected charges of the IRC at the end of the war.[10]

Another country that contributed to the rescue effort was Portugal. Right after the occupation of Hungary, its only involvement with the Jewish plight was a minor agreement with the Germans to permit nine Jews with Portuguese interests to leave the country. During the Szalasi era, however, Portugal was undoubtedly inspired by the actions of the other neutrals to broaden its protective role. Carlos de Liz-Texeira Branquinho, the Portuguese chargé d'affaires, agreed to authorize passports for all Jews who could show that they had relatives in Portugal or Brazil. After he left, he was replaced by Dr. Ferenc Barthe, who headed the special section of the legation, and Gyula Gulden. During the troubling Szalasi era, these two humanitarians acted above and beyond the call of duty. They negotiated with Foreign Minister Kemeny to approve the issuance of five hundred protective papers and exceeded this quota by at least two hundred. The Germans refused to recognize these papers at first, but after Tovar, the Portuguese representative in Berlin, intervened on their behalf, they agreed to accept them. Undoubtedly, this was done with the approval of Portugal's Salazar regime.[11]

The Portuguese legation was in an even more vulnerable position than the others, for it had neither an accredited ambassador nor an accredited consul to the Hungarian government. Nonetheless, its representatives managed to issue these seven hundred authentic passports, as well as protective papers. Moreover, in a ruse to save even more lives, they did not issue separate papers for children under six; these children were added onto their parents' papers and therefore did not take away any places from the seven hundred already on the official list. The Portuguese legation eventually issued another twelve hundred passports to people whose names were not on the list.[12]

The Portuguese did not stop there; they hired forty extra workers to help prepare an additional quantity of protective papers for Jews who were not on any list, and who did not wish to take refuge within the Portuguese protective houses. These added up to another one hundred, bringing the total of those protected by Mr. Gulden to about 2,000. Bearers of these papers were exempted from forced labor, and later on, thanks again to Mr. Gulden's intercession, they were placed in special labor units that were assigned to work on fortifications within Hungary, near the Austrian border. Mr. Gulden was also able to pull out about three hundred and forty people from the Death March later on and place them in protective houses. To finance this undertaking for those without means, the Portuguese delegation turned to wealthy Jews.[13]

All the passports, whether individual or collective, were made out only on a temporary basis. In this manner, they could save lives without the sponsoring countries' fear of a postwar influx of refugees. Amazingly, these passports were eventually recognized by the Szalasi regime.

The Vatican also lent its support to the Hungarian rescue effort. Besides his full participation in the cooperative interventions of the other neutrals, the papal nuncio provided thousands of protective papers, ostensibly for Roman Catholics affected by the anti-Jewish decrees. The original authorization was for only twenty-five hundred papers, primarily for holders of baptismal certificates; however, the nunciature, at the initiative of Roszi Vakay, head of its safe-conduct office, eventually issued as many as 15,000 protective papers, with little regard for the authenticity of the required baptismal papers. Many of the holders of these baptismal papers were hidden in convents, monasteries, and other church institutions.[14]

Recognition of the Salvadoran Papers

At first, there was general skepticism about the efficacy of the Salvadoran papers, because everybody was aware that the holders were not citizens of El Salvador; there was not a single true Salvadoran citizen in Budapest. Lutz therefore cabled Bern to find out whether he could legitimately defend such "citizens." The response he received from Bern was that "President Roosevelt had personally asked for it," a reference to a statement Roosevelt had made upon his creation of the War Refugee Board in January 1944. In his postwar testimony, Lutz noted: "Had we been informed earlier that the State Department was behind Switzerland's protection of the holders of such papers, we could have given these people the same protection [provided for] the other fourteen countries [under Swiss protection]" after the German occupation of Hungary.[15]

Before the Salvadoran papers were to prove their true worth as the best protective paper in Hungary during the Nyilas era, three problems had to be resolved. The first involved the American role in pressuring the Latin American and Swiss governments to provide official recognition; the second concerned the Swiss government's strong and long-standing resistance to serving as the protective power for El Salvador in Budapest; and the third and most volatile problem was the Hungarian government itself. During the favorable period of the Horthy regime, Hungarian cooperation had been smoother, but after the advent of the pro-Nazi Szalasi era on October 15, rescue became an increasingly dangerous gamble. The neutrals did have one important weapon in their meager arsenal: Szalasi's eagerness to obtain the recognition of the neutral countries. This weapon was important but fragile, for the neutral representatives did not have the full cooperation of their own governments, and at times their rescue activities were even at variance with their governments' policies.[16]

The State Department had been partly successful as early as April in influencing the Latin American countries to take initial steps to recognize the validity of their papers (see chapter 3). Despite American assurances to the contrary, however, the department had not been able to eliminate the Latin Americans' lingering suspicion that the Jewish holders of these papers would flood their countries after the war. Obtaining the full approval of the El Salvador government in particular for all of Mantello's earlier documents, as well as those to be issued henceforth, was complex and time-consuming.

An even more difficult task was to persuade the Swiss to assume the protective role of the Latin American countries in Hungary, El Salvador in particular. To begin with, Switzerland did not represent El Salvador in Hungary, Romania, and Slovakia, countries that were considered "independent" despite German domination. The Swiss also objected to the fact that thousands of what they considered illegal papers had been issued earlier by Mantello, before their approval, and the notion of granting them retroactive authorization went against their legalistic grain.[17] In addition, the recognition of the papers would require more workers and more money.

Switzerland's official recognition of the Salvadoran papers was a long-drawn-out affair because of its precarious balance between two strong forces: its strong distaste for the illegality represented by Mantello and his semilegal papers on one hand, and the pressure of the press campaign and the American government on the other hand. Rothmund and McClelland's vehement dislike of Mantello and his operation complicated matters even more. The result was a see-sawing of policy that veered from recognition of the papers to complete denial of their validity.

The complications did not end there. The Swiss detained Mantello in May on charges of profiting from the "sale" of these papers, a suspicion that lingered on through the early postwar years (see chapter 12). Moreover, only several weeks later, amid the press campaign, Rothmund sought to have Mantello removed from his diplomatic post,[18] and he continued to search for other methods of obstruction even after the official Swiss recognition of the Salvadoran papers. To make matters worse, the new Szalasi regime, under constant pressure from its Arrow Cross cohorts and the Germans, was characterized by mercurial policy changes, and official pronouncements of the papers' protective value were made and withdrawn more than once. These bureaucratic entanglements, coupled with Swiss procrastination and McClelland's negative views, resulted in the loss of much valuable time, undoubtedly resulting in the needless deaths of many additional victims.

Despite these problems, the Salvadoran papers eventually did attain full protective status. As early as August 9, Banyai of the Swiss Hungarian Committee reported to McClelland that Switzerland had taken over the interests of Salvadoran paper holders. Mantello reiterated this position three days later in his correspondence with Moshe Krausz. However, by August 16, Lutz still had not received official word from the Swiss authorities on this issue, and he could give no concrete answer to the numerous Jews inquiring about their status. He pointed out that regardless of assurances at home that recognition of the papers would become official, until such word arrived in Budapest he could not provide protection. He noted that "under the present difficult circumstances, such recognition would provide a real, humanitarian rescue action," and that he "would personally do everything possible to obtain recognition [by all parties] for such papers."[19]

On August 28, Dr. Johannes Duft reported to Krausz that he had received a cable two days earlier from Lutz, to the effect that Salvadoran citizens were now considered enemy aliens who could not leave Hungary. This meant that they could not be deported, in contrast to holders of Palestine certificates and other papers, who retained their Hungarian citizenship; in effect, the retention of Hungarian citizenship permitted the victims' deportation.[20] This was further confirmed in a report by the IRC, which stated explicitly: "Those who held Palestine certificates retained their Hungarian nationality, which meant that the Swiss could provide them with only limited protection. Those with Salvadoran papers, however, were considered 'foreigners,' to whom the Swiss could now extend their full protection."[21]

Once the American requests were forcefully presented to Switzerland, Lutz received an official memo stating that Switzerland now represented the Salvadoran papers. It then became far easier for him to go to the Hungarian government and ask them to take these papers seriously. His next steps were to affix notices to the protected houses and to provide the holders with special Swiss certificates of protection, which they were to present to the authorities. (Protection extended to the holders' property as well.)

By September 25, a few days after Lutz found out about Mantello's role in the press campaign, he was finally able to report to Mantello that the Swiss had formally approved recognition of the Salvadoran papers. Nevertheless, he cautioned that he must still make sure that the Hungarian Alien Police (KEOKH) were made aware of this development and would give their approval.[22] Moreover, this "formal approval," as we shall detail, turned out not to be the final word; true recognition would not be forthcoming for more than two months. Even as late as December 21, after all the arrangements had officially been made, Riegner, based on Krausz's report, was still requesting that Lutz put more pressure on Bern to save additional lives.[23]

Ironically, Lutz's initial good news about the authorization of the papers was short-lived, aborted by the Szalasi coup on October 15. Lutz and Krausz were forced to engage in a new round of negotiations with the Szalasi regime, as well as with various Hungarian agencies, before there was a breakthrough. On October 24, Krausz was able to report optimistically to Mantello about Swiss recognition of the papers, adding that he was amid sending him photos so that Mantello could affix them to the papers and return them immediately. A week later, Krausz reported that he and Lutz were still busy "informing all the authorities that holders of Salvadoran papers are exempt from the restrictions imposed on the others."[24]

Even when the Swiss finally took over protection of the Salvadoran papers, they were still expressing concern over technicalities. As late as November 3, the Swiss government was still going through the motions of inquiring of Consul General Castellanos about the legitimacy of Mantello's role as a distributor of the papers. Castellanos responded, "The Consulate General of El Salvador in Geneva hereby certifies that Mr. Georges Mandel-Mantello, First Secretary of the Consulate General in Geneva, has served as Director of the Consulate General of El Salvador in Bucharest from 1939 to 1942, and that following that date, he was transferred as First Secretary at the Consulate General of El Salvador in Geneva."[25]

Still not satisfied, the Swiss inquired whether Mantello was paid a salary in his official position. Castellanos replied again on November 4, "I wish to let you know that Mr. George Mantello, the First Secretary of the Consulate of El Salvador in Geneva, who has taken a particular interest in Jewish affairs at my consulate, has waived all payments."[26]

In a letter that Lutz wrote to Mantello on October 28, almost two weeks after the Szalasi coup, he explained the advantages as well as the pitfalls of the official Swiss recognition of the Salvadoran papers.

Dear Mr. Mantello,

In the matter of representation of the interests of San [sic] Salvador, I would like to report the following. The operation is already in full swing. Hundreds of people occupy the office at Szabadsag, so that we have had to increase the number of police on the street. The requests to our department exceed our forces, so we have had to add additional personnel, who have been very difficult to find. At the suggestion of [Swiss] Minister Jaeger, I have temporarily appointed Mr. C[arl] Hofer to the San [*sic*] Salvador matter, under my supervision.[27] It would be important for me to meet with you to discuss personally the matter of San [*sic*] Salvador citizenship. However, I am very busy and cannot get away even for a short trip to Switzerland. It is a question of whether San [*sic*] Salvador certificates can be used for immigration to San [*sic*] Salvador and whether [the holders] could receive passports for this purpose. For the time being it is important that they have protection against attacks and deportation.

Recently an order was issued, according to which *people in possession of foreign passports cannot be transferred* [i.e., deported] *to work in Germany or to German-occupied territories like Poland.* Naturally, under the present chaotic conditions, attacks do occur, but it must be said that the San [*sic*] Salvador certificates have already saved thousands of lives. With our control in the Jewish camp in the [Obuda] tile factory, where people were brought in before the [death] march to Germany, we always came across S[an] [*sic*] S[alvador] certificate holders, for whom we were able to obtain freedom because of these papers.

As far as the protection of the holders of these San [*sic*] Salvador papers is concerned, it was possible for me to achieve success at the [Hungarian] Foreign Ministry, as well by providing preprinted certificates which state that "the resident of this particular apartment, house, or room" is under the protection of the Swiss Embassy" [quotation marks in original]. With few exceptions, these certificates were recognized, and we hope that they will be recognized as well by the Russian military authorities. Russian-language certificates are already being prepared. (emphasis added)

Lutz continued with a bold declaration in response to the few Swiss legalists in the government (such as Rothmund), who, even at this stage, eschewed tampering with any bureaucratic rule regardless of the countless lives at stake. He also declared his intent to pursue his mission despite the growing discomfort and personal danger:

> *The fact that the American State Department demands the representation of San* [sic] *Salvadoran interests gives us the necessary support not only in regard to the Hungarian [authorities] but also the German authorities.* If enemies of the Jews [tell me that they are] appalled that the [Swiss] Embassy is involved in an illegal activity, I respond to this calumny with a clear conscience, [saying] that Switzerland can retort that they are saving thousands of [people] from a terrible death.
>
> Since the conclusion of the war is drawing near, the situation is getting

worse for me and for all of us, and people are becoming more furious, unafraid of revenge. Recently, in the process of checking the papers of residents of Swiss-protected houses, [my wife and I] were threatened with a revolver by [members of the] Arrow Cross. I was able to summon aid immediately from the [Hungarian] Foreign Ministry, and they arrested three of the Arrow Cross, who were condemned to death for having punched [Zoltan] Bagossy, the third highest member of the party, in the head. [Despite this,] we are quite optimistic about our expectation of survival. *I hope, eventually, to report to you personally on this period of Sturm und Drang that we are undergoing.*

Nevertheless, you can take satisfaction in the fact that . . . it was your management of the San [sic] Salvadoran interests which has enabled us to create a humanitarian work that will bring you the thanks of thousands of rescued people. It must be clearly established that San [sic] Salvador is the only state to overcome any hesitancy and to undertake an active rescue operation. (emphasis added)

We have to take into consideration the fact that at any moment we can expect to be encircled [by the Russian army], and [we can then] no longer expect to carry on any communications with Switzerland via mail or cable. For my part, I wish to assure you that I intend to remain at my post as long as is feasible, [working] to the best of my ability to represent the interests of San [*sic*] Salvador, as commissioned by your government and President Roosevelt.

Signed with an expression of my highest esteem,

[Carl Lutz][28]

By October 30, Krausz was pleased to report to Mantello that he and Lutz were "busy informing all the relevant [Hungarian] authorities . . . that such holders of Salvador papers are exempt from the restrictions imposed on the others."[29] After the issue of the Salvadoran papers was fully resolved, the IRC became directly involved in distributing them, as is noted in its memo to Mantello of December 15:

We transmitted these [Salvadoran] documents to Budapest on November 28, and we know that they have actually reached our delegate there. We are making sure that these certificates reach the persons they were destined for as rapidly as possible. Our delegate has also been instructed to deliver the appropriate documents to Mr. M[oshe] Krausz, the director of the Palestine Office in Budapest. We will keep you up to date on the final distribution. Please accept our assurance of highest esteem. S. Ferriere.

Once the Swiss finally recognized the Salvadoran papers, they became the most-sought-after protective documents available, and even Swiss citizens in Budapest who were married to Jews requested them. For example, on November 24, Lutz requested that Mantello "provide our legation in Budapest with [Salvadoran] certificates for two Jews [married to Swiss citizens] as soon as possible, since they are in constant danger of their lives. Photographs are included."[30]

Let us look at the experience of one family in its search for shelter through Salvadoran papers. The following is taken from the postwar testimony of a Miss Neufeld (see chapter 12). She was originally from Vienna but had moved to Budapest with her mother; her father was in St. Gallen, Switzerland.

When Hungary was occupied by the Germans in March 1944, we turned to father for help, cabling him on an almost daily basis. He informed us that he would send Salvador papers to provide [us with] protection. The fact that my father provided photos was of great help, since there were many who did not have them. Still, the Swiss consulate provided us with a letter for the Hungarian Alien Police. The Swiss papers were the first to be recognized. Without the validation [of KEOKH], the documents would have been useless.

About the time that the authorities began to set up special houses and we changed our address, we received the papers by mail. We looked for guidance and made our way from one consulate to another, but none were able to help us. We finally went to the Swiss Consulate when we heard that it had taken over El Salvador's interests. The consulate gave us a letter of protection with which we could go to the Hungarian Alien Police. The letter stated that Switzerland had taken charge of the representation of Salvadoran interests. It also confirmed the fact that we were citizens of El Salvador and were exempt from all laws relating to Hungarian Jews.

I was the first to receive such a letter, but at that time we were afraid to present ourselves to the alien police, because people were being deported from there without due process. There were even many with Swedish protective papers who went to the alien police and were simply deported. In fact, the Swiss consul told us that we were going there at our own risk. But we gambled and went to the alien police. As it turned out, our papers were better than the Palestine certificates, because father had originally sent those to us, and they proved to be of no use.

The Swiss consulate was our salvation. Whenever we needed another letter, they sent it to us. Once we were scheduled to go into the Labor Service, and the consulate confirmed that we were exempt. We received a certificate from the alien police to the effect that we were considered foreigners, and were thereby exempt from wearing the yellow star and other restrictions applying to Hungarian Jews. [After receiving this certificate,] we went to live in a Christian home, but we constantly had to present ourselves to the Hungarian police, [who were] always looking for new confirmations that we were allowed to live in a Christian house. From about the middle of 1944 we were left alone, until the Russians came on January 18, 1945.

We know that father didn't pay for the documents, because he had no money. As far as I understand, the people who gave them out did so as charity.[31]

The great irony of the success of the Salvadoran papers is that even the Nazis sought them. In February 1945, more than three months before the conclusion of the war, many Nazis, including those in the higher echelons, began to seek false Swiss, Swedish, or Latin American passports "in preparation for fleeing into neutral countries or for alleged legalization [in Germany] in case of Russian occupation."[32]

Besides the Salvadoran papers, there were other protective papers that were used by the Jews of Budapest at this time, including Swedish Schutzpaesse and Palestine certificates. Although all were protective, their conditions and relative value varied.

Although the Hungarian racial laws did not exempt holders of Palestine certificates from punitive measures, because they were still considered Hungarian nationals, it did exempt foreign nationals. Thus, holders of the Swedish Schutzpaesse were considered Swedish subjects and were thereby exempt from such persecutory measures as the wearing of the yellow star. As a result, KEOKH made them resign their Hungarian citizenship.[33] Thus, these papers became more like the Salvadoran citizenship papers, whose holders were always considered foreigners. In addition, the Swedish papers were considered superior in their rescue value to the Palestine certificates because they did not have many of the markings of a true passport: they had neither a stamp nor a signature, while the Swedish papers had a serial number, a photo of the holder, and the personal signature of Ambassador Danielsson.[34]

Because the neutral representatives made collective appeals, protective rights granted by the Hungarians to one neutral embassy were equally applicable to the others. This was especially true in the case of the Swiss and Swedes, who were in constant contact with each other and collaborated fully.[35]

Swedish protection, however, held a special attraction. It is important to realize that, despite the protracted negotiations, the holders of Salvadoran papers were protected by Sweden through Wallenberg from the time of his arrival in Budapest. Moreover, even after the Swiss took over complete protection of the Salvadoran paper holders, there were hundreds who preferred to retain their Swedish protection.

For example, the Jews with Salvadoran citizenship who were in the required age-group for forced labor were exempt from the most taxing and dangerous assignments. They were especially grateful to be exempt from digging the anti-tank ditches, for which the Germans enlisted many thousands from the labor battalions or the ghetto. Rather, these men were placed in special "foreign" labor battalions. After the Swiss took over the protection of the Salvadoran paper holders, these "foreign laborers" preferred to remain under Swedish protection, thinking it more valuable. However, when Wallenberg conducted some of his most courageous acts, plucking Jews from trains or death marches on November 28, he made no distinctions between those protected by Sweden and Switzerland, and they all remained in Budapest.[36]

About this time, December 1, 1944, the IRC followed the model of the Spanish Red Cross by recognizing incarcerated Jews as "prisoners of war," with all the advantages that accrued holders of this designation.[37]

When it became apparent to the Jews in Budapest that protective papers could possibly save their lives, thousands of Jews fled to the Swiss and Swedish legations, as well as to other neutral legations, in an effort to obtain these valuable pieces of paper. Once Lutz was armed with official Swiss approval in September to take over the interests of El Salvador in Hungary, he and Moshe Krausz began to negotiate with the Horthy regime. After the Szalasi coup on October 15, he and other neutral representatives continued to negotiate with the new regime and its various agencies, making numerous entreaties especially to Foreign Minister Baron Gabor Kemeny. As a result, by October 30, the new government recognized all the protective papers issued by the Vatican and other neutrals, as well as the extraterritoriality they provided the holders.[38] Occasionally, Lutz noted, some minor official refused to recognize a specific paper, or simply disregarded them no matter how authentic they were.[39]

On November 8, Lutz was able to report to Mantello that he had succeeded in having the Salvadoran papers recognized by the Hungarian government. So well were things going in this respect that Lutz even asked Mantello to provide papers for several Jews married to Swiss citizens.[40] Word of the official recognition of the Salvadoran papers' special protection against deportation spread rapidly. In his first postwar report, on July 1, 1945, Lutz described the situation following the coup:

> Suddenly, the letters of our protection division, in which we confirmed that the holder had been noted for emigration and had been entered in the Swiss collective passport, now had the value of life-saving certificates. Naturally, this occurred only when I succeeded in getting the recognition of these confirmations at the Hungarian Foreign Ministry. [The certificates] saved the owners from the fate of being taken to Germany or to the East.
>
> Virtually the entire Jewish population came to our offices, so that I was forced to rent two more buildings [i.e., the "Glass House"] in which to prepare the emigration of a few trains [loads] from Switzerland. Often we needed mounted police in order to push back a multitude numbering in the thousands. A mass of people also stood in front of our offices all day long because they felt more safe there than in their apartments. Whoever succeeded in gaining entry into our offices stayed there, and we were unable to remove them in the evening. When the situation became more and more threatening, I did not have the heart to send these people, who feared death, into the street, and I let them stay. . . . In the three offices of the Protection Department, 3,000 human beings sought refuge, in particular the volunteer employees of the Emigration Bureau, formerly [Krausz's] Palestine Office, and their nearest relatives. New groups were always pushing into our office, into the cellar, into the garage, etc. Sanitary problems and support problems were a major concern.

Lutz wrote that because of the fighting in the Balkans at this time, it was impossible to carry out the original mission of sending the certificate holders to Palestine via Romania and Turkey. He had therefore negotiated with the Hungarian government to provide the people at his doorstep with "temporary refuge" until they could be sent to their destinations. Finally, he noted:

> I received the agreement to concentrate those people with protective letters in several houses which were given to us especially for this purpose. This was accomplished within twenty-four hours by 200 policemen. When this became known, the masses immediately [sought shelter] in these houses, which had been provided with Swiss plaques of identification. There were thirty modern apartment houses, which were filled to capacity with about 18 to 20,000 people. The soul of this enterprise was Miklósz [Moshe] Krausz, the director of the Palestine Office.

The Glass House

In anticipation of a greater demand for papers, Lutz rented additional quarters. The largest of these was a former mirror factory with a glass front; it had been dubbed the "Glass House" by the owner, Mr. Arthur Weiss, who remained in his apartment within the building. Lutz set up this facility as a separate department for Salvadoran papers. Because of the official government recognition of the papers, he was overrun by people holding them. No matter how quickly Mantello could dispatch papers to him through his couriers, it was not fast enough, nor were there enough papers to satisfy the needs of the crowds that filled the street in front of the Glass House. Things became so hectic that Lutz had to enlist the aid of Hungarian police to maintain order. The police also had to make sure that the crowd dispersed before the 8 P.M. curfew.[41]

Lutz recalled how his legation's activities sometimes made tremendous demands on its employees and the entire administrative apparatus:

> Every new government proclamation brought new assemblies of people in front of our office. Events happened so quickly that we were barely able to control the situation because at this time, air raids became more frequent and the first artillery shells began to fall in the city. During the day the thunder of heavy artillery could be heard, and at night one could see the lightning of the firings and rocket signals in all their colors on the horizon. Many of the employees had problems overcoming their nervousness, but it was not possible to ask Switzerland for new personnel. Some of our employees, mostly volunteers, worked day and night, and lived in bitter poverty.
>
> In addition to a larger staff, we also needed foreign exchange in the form of bank notes and gold . . . in order to intervene in individual cases, to secure protection, to make houses and districts safe against violations, and to keep the extreme enemy elements in check, because they too suffered from hunger and deprivation. Also, larger programs could have been carried through in order to save people. Feeding the many thousands in the protected houses, the hospitalization of the sick and infirm, and the care of children took large sums of money. The greatest portion of the funds was raised by the Jewish community itself, and additional means in pengos were provided by the representatives of the Joint.
>
> It was therefore a great misfortune that we were not notified about the existence of a fund for saving people. If we had had such a fund at our disposal,

we could have obtained several cars in order to bring people who were in the border villages and who had protective letters back to Budapest. They considered those of us who stayed in the [Swiss compound] as people risen from the dead because every day they saw with their binoculars the low airplane attacks over our roof and the [artillery] fire.

Those who were unable to obtain papers from Lutz were quickly able to get them from numerous private and organizational forgers, who reproduced such papers by the thousands. Because of this proliferation of false Salvadoran documents, the Nyilas threatened at one point to revoke the protective validity of all the papers unless Lutz weeded out the counterfeit holders. Lutz described this task as one of his saddest moments:

> A major portion of my time was spent in constant negotiations with government officers about the many violations. . . . We had a number of headaches because of thousands of protective letters which were falsified wholesale and sold by irresponsible elements to these unhappy people, after our legal quota of about 8,000 people was filled. Naturally, everyone tried to obtain [one of these] life-saving certificates.
>
> [T]o separate the genuine letters from the falsified ones, all the houses had to be combed through, with the help of a strong police force. Finally, all the inhabitants were ordered to the street or to the park and were examined. Hundreds of owners of these so-called protective letters had already been brought into the brick factory, where they had to wait for [orders to] march to the German border. There also, thousands of letters had to be examined, which was a most painful task for us.
>
> Along with my wife, I once stood for four hours in snow in this notorious brick factory in Obuda, forced to do the sad work of separating the protective letters. Heart-rending scenes took place [there]. Five thousand of these unhappy people stood there, freezing, trembling, hungry, loaded with little bundles, and showed us their letters. Never will I forget those frightened faces. Many times the police had to intervene because the people almost tore my suit off my body when they made their requests. It was the last display of their will to live before their resignation, which ended so often in death. It was psychological torture for us to separate [the papers]. Even today I have to ask myself how many people were sent to their doom, outside of those we could save. On these occasions, horrible scenes took place where human beings [holding forged papers] were beaten with whips [by Hungarian gendarmes] and then laid on the floor with bloody faces. We were threatened with guns when we

tried to intervene. Often I went with my car to the place where people were marching to the brick factory to encourage them, until an armed unit stopped me on the way.

Among those most active in the production of forged Salvadoran papers was a Zionist youth group, composed of members of various Zionist factions, ranging from Hapoel Hatzair on the left to the Orthodox Mizrachi on the right. This youth coalition, whose rescue efforts were dubbed "Operation Hatzalah" (Hebrew for rescue), performed its most useful activities during the era of the Salvadoran papers.

Lutz's "Glass House" turned out to be far more than a shelter for 4,500 Jews.[42] Under the careful supervision of various committees, it became an educational and cultural station for a people who looked to the future. The former glass factory was outfitted with a makeshift kitchen, headed by a Mr. Stern, the evicted former owner of a kosher restaurant. Some of the *halutzim,* trained in farming, planted gardens to grow potatoes and other vegetables, but often additional food had to be procured through "illegal" commando operations to feed the large population. Despite the crowded conditions and lack of amenities, individuals organized an amazing array of educational, cultural, and even religious activities for young and old. For example, professors in different fields provided lectures in the Hebrew language and Jewish history, while others made preparations for a better life in Eretz Israel. Choirs rehearsed Hebrew songs, and each of the Zionist factions focused on its particular ideological themes: the more left-wing groups envisioned a future Jewish state built on socialism, while the Orthodox studied biblical and talmudic texts, dreaming of a Torah-imbued environment in Eretz Israel. Yet, when it came to rescue efforts, these valiant youth, no matter what their affiliation, were close comrades at arms who risked their lives for other Jews and for one another.[43]

The Zionist group mass-produced various protective papers, especially Salvadoran papers, and managed to provide them to Jews who were incarcerated in prison, detention camps, and even Nyilas headquarters. To accomplish their legendary feats, they dressed up in Nyilas or SS uniforms, armed with the proper weapons, linguistic skills, and official papers, at times even driving diplomatic cars flying the Swiss flag. They acted with such great courage and audacity that they frequently fooled the Arrow Cross, SS guards, and even Hungarian officials. Pinchas Rosenbaum (of Mizrachi), one of the heads of the "commandos," specialized in portraying SS officers or high-ranking Nazi officials, bringing Salvadoran papers to secure the release of inmates of labor camps and other restricted areas.[44] The group's weapons and supplies were kept in a special, well-stocked bunker in a deserted house at 31 Vadasz Street, directly across from the Glass House and connected to it by an underground tunnel.

The Zionists were often forced into daring rescue feats when a colleague was captured—and they did not always succeed. Torture and death dogged them constantly, and as time and conditions worsened, their numbers dwindled; but the Glass House became a symbol of hope and refuge for many a desperate Jew. One victim of Nyilas cruelty, who was thrown into the Danube but survived, recalled, "I was only wounded, but doubtless I would have let myself die if, at the last moment, the idea hadn't crossed my mind that in this world of hatred and death, in this pitiless city, a shelter still existed for Jews—the House of Glass. Almost without thinking, I began to swim through the hail of bullets toward Elisabeth Bridge. . . . I waited a moment and then jumped onto the dock. The darkness saved me. Soon after, two partisans on a rescue mission picked me up. I knew where they were taking me."[45]

On November 14, word came to the Glass House that many unprotected Jews in the Obuda brickworks were being deported on foot, for the railroads had been made useless through constant bombing. The Zionist commandos immediately went into action. Lacking even the meager shield of immunity available to a neutral official such as Lutz or Wallenberg, they managed to free numerous marchers through their bold rescue operations.[46]

McClelland—A Silent Antagonist

Throughout this tragic period, as Lutz and his cohorts struggled to save lives, Roswell McClelland, the American representative of the War Refugee Board, rested coolly and apathetically at the opposite end of the continuum. This was a time that was ripe for rescue; America's strength was at its military and political apogee, Switzerland no longer feared possible invasion by the Germans, and Mantello's press campaign had made a strong impact on all of the Western world. McClelland, however, remained stubbornly aloof, maintaining his legalistic stance concerning the use of the Latin American papers. He never used his energy and potential in representing American power, and in fact took an even harsher stand than the State Department, which was not especially known for its sympathy toward the Jewish plight. Ironically, in his distaste for anything even remotely illegal and in his constant stalling, he displayed the same proclivities as the Swiss government; the one prominent difference was that he had been sent by the War Refugee Board specifically to facilitate rescue, while the Swiss, at least, had some legitimate fears. Let us briefly examine his negative role in the recognition of the protective papers.

When Maitre Muller sought McClelland's help in this matter, he met with little but frustration. From May 1 through May 16, Muller made four urgent but fruitless calls to McClelland, requesting an audience to discuss the need to pressure the Swiss into accepting the role of protective power for the Salvadoran papers. When Czech ambassador Jaromir Kopecky took up Muller's cause on May 21, McClelland finally agreed to meet with him, but even the intervention of this sympathetic diplomat proved futile. McClelland noted to Kopecky:

> Since I saw no less than five separate persons last week in connection with this same matter [i.e., Latin American papers], I frankly do not see the use of talking to Muller. . . . I personally doubt that the present Hungarian government would accept Switzerland's role as protective power, should the Swiss agree to undertake it at the request of the Salvadoran government. . . . The large increase of *such illegal Latin American documents* . . . may quite possibly jeopardize the precarious safety of those persons already in German internment camps. (emphasis added)[47]

When McClelland was informed on August 2, 1944, that the Swiss had indeed agreed to represent the interests of the Salvadoran paper holders in Budapest, he was not particularly pleased. He declared, "It is difficult to see what value these papers would have, since *they do not entitle their holders to emigrate to El Salvador.* At best, as I have always told you, I feel that *these false documents offer only very slight protection,* and that increasing the number of them only weakens the precarious position of the many other people already holding them at present" (emphasis added).[48]

As we mentioned earlier, the very fact that the holders of Salvadoran papers were not entitled to emigrate was a major advantage, for *it meant that they could not be deported from Hungary.* They were to be treated as citizens of a protected foreign country and were not required to relocate to the ghetto or to wear the yellow star.[49] McClelland paid no heed to this important fact. Moreover, he was ill disposed toward an idea approved by the Swiss that Mantello send two Swiss members of the Salvadoran consulate, at his own expense, to assist its Budapest embassy in dealing with the Salvadoran paper holders.[50] His response was, "I can only say that I remain somewhat skeptical." Naturally, his skepticism translated into inaction. Tragically, as Lutz himself testified after the war, if he had had an additional thirty Swiss workers to help him, he could have provided protection for thousands of additional Budapest Jews.[51]

In September 1944, McClelland still referred to the Salvadoran papers as "documents fraudulently issued" by the Geneva consul general (George Mantello), as though it were a crime to issue false papers to save lives.[52] He maintained his position even though the Salvadoran papers, unlike other Latin American papers, were issued with the full knowledge of the Geneva consul general, and involved no profits. He did not change his stance even after September 12, 1944, when the Salvadoran government granted full approval to this project. Its explicit sanction is evident from a memo of that date sent to McClelland by the State Department, which stated, "The Government of El Salvador recognizes and will recognize the validity of the documents of Salvadoran nationality. . . . I request that your Excellency's Government transmit the foregoing [approval] to the Department of Foreign Relations of Switzerland."[53]

Several days later, McClelland found reason once again to question the validity of the Salvadoran papers, this time on a technicality.[54] However, the State Department sent him the following telegram at the WRB: "Your attention is drawn again to the general Salvadoran declaration which was reported in [the American] Legation's [cable no.] 3671 of June 17, 1944. . . . The confirmation by the Salvadoran government of documents of specific persons whose names were submitted to it does not (repeat, not) imply either the need or desirability of forwarding to that government further specific names. You are therefore requested to proceed along the lines of . . . previous communications."[55]

The State Department had been chafing under pressure from the New York–based Vaad Hatzalah since April to push for authorization of the Latin American papers. In as diplomatic a way as possible, the secretary of state tried to persuade McClelland to facilitate, not obstruct, rescue.

The same consideration should also guide you in dealing with documents of other American republics which have notified the Swiss government that *persons in enemy territory who are subject to persecution, to whom documents have been issued in their names, must receive treatment as nationals of such republics* from the enemy. In this connection, your attention is drawn to Department No. 2490, July 21, sixth paragraph, in which there is set forth *the desirability of placing the most liberal possible construction on any communication from any American republic with respect to the protection of persons from cruelty and persecution,* and in which it is stated that *slowness in action arising from unwavering attachment to technicalities,* which would be proper enough under ordinary circumstances, merely *results, in these abnormal times, in ruthless killing of further numbers of innocent people.* Even though this passage was intended primarily as a suggestion for Swiss officials, *it is suggested that the attitude you adopt be governed by it.* (emphasis added)[56]

On January 11, 1945, Sternbuch again requested that McClelland pressure the Swiss into taking a stronger stand on the Salvadoran papers, pointing out that as early as June 1944, Agudath Israel of the United States had cabled him that Salvador had recognized the holders of its papers;[57] but McClelland remained just as cool and unresponsive. He claimed that Salvador had not provided the proper recognition necessary in this instance, and that the United States was *not* represented by the Swiss for the "papers issued by Mr. Mantello of the Consulate of El Salvador at Geneva."

In December 1944, a key member of the State Department, exasperated and tired of the constant red tape emanating from the American legation in Bern, issued the following memo: "[There is] doubt whether McClelland [and the American legation], isolated from the U.S. and very much overworked as they are, have a sufficient grasp of the problem, and [Benjamin Akzin] asked whether it would not be advisable for the [War] Refugee Board to send [James] Mann [WRB representative in London] on a brief mission to Bern in order to acquaint the Legation and McClelland with the situation, as well as to have a talk with appropriate officials at the Swiss Foreign Office."[58]

During this stalemate, the need for papers in Budapest grew more urgent. On December 4, Krausz pleaded with Mantello to send more Salvadoran papers, adding, "I'm sending my mail both to Posner and to you, so that you get a detailed picture of the situation."[59] Riegner, too, realized the true value of the Salvadoran papers, and tried to convey as much to McClelland in a letter of December 21. He emphasized the desperation of Budapest's Jews, as described in the report Krausz had written:

If there is a chance left to save at least a certain number of those still in Budapest, then it can be done only by extending the protection accorded by the IRC and various foreign legations, who have already issued protecting [*sic*] documents or passports to a considerable number of people.

I understand that Swedish [protective] passports, a few Portuguese passports and a *large number of El Salvador* [sic] *certificates of nationality have been
issued,* and that the Swiss legation has accorded a document of protection to
those in possession of Palestine Immigration Certificates. It appears from the
reports received that the number of such documents could be increased, especially in the case of El Salvador [sic] documents and Palestine certificates, in
order to protect larger groups of people still in Budapest.

[We urge you] to submit to the American Minister [L. Harrison] a proposal to impress again on the Swiss government the urgent necessity to instruct
their legation in Budapest to be helpful in this matter and in the general matter of protecting [sic] documents, and to facilitate the transmission of such
documents (El Salvador [sic] nationality papers and others) from Switzerland
to Budapest.[60]

Mantello-Trumpy Plans

Besides Mantello's successes in rescue efforts, he and his brother were involved
in three other rescue efforts that failed because of circumances beyond their
control. Still, these attempts are a further manifestation of the enormous number of creative efforts and ideas tried by the two brothers during the crucial
period after the occupation of Hungary.

Mantello's primary contact with the Germans was Curt Trumpy, the Swiss
representative of Messerschmidt, the German plane manufacturer, who had
good connections to German higher-officials. At times, Trumpy worked with
Max Otto Boden, a German merchant, and Otto Bindlinger, a German representative of Messerschmidt. At virtually every step, however, Nationalrat
Duft, Mantello's lawyer, participated in each facet of the negotiations.[61]

In late June 1944, Mantello and Josef had made Trumpy aware of the enor-
mity of the Nazi extermination of the Jews, by showing him the two reports.
Within two weeks the brothers had finalized the first of the rescue efforts,
though it would drag on for months. September 15, 1944, Veesenmayer
reported on this plan to his foreign office, stating that:

there is news that the San [sic] Salvador consul in Zurich, [sic] in agreement
with the USA government, wants to smuggle in pre-dated San [sic] Salvador
passports [sic] for 20,000 Hungarian Jews, through the good offices of the
Swiss government. [This], in order to succeed in having these Jews interned

as foreign citizens under better conditions than the Hungarian internment camps, which the Hungarian government also wants to put under the supervision of the International Red Cross.[62]

Though the plan didn't succeed, the number of Jews in Budapest eventually rescued through Salvadoran papers and protected by Lutz did not differ much from those projected in this plan.

Mantello's second plan involving Trumpy concerned the efforts to release approximately seventeen hundred Jews on the so-called Kastner Train, to Switzerland or some other neutral country, which was only finalized on August 1. The train, an early fruit of Kastner's negotiations with the Germans, had left Budapest on the evening of June 30, and, after an unexpected three-day stop in Bratislava, wound up in Bergen Belsen on July 8.

This plan called for sending Trumpy to Germany to negotiate for the release of the entire Bergen Belsen train. The Germans were willing to deal with him, in the hope that would unify the many Jewish groups who sought to obtain the release of their friends or ideological colleagues. For example, six hundred Zionists were divided by party, in the original group, who were the interest of the particular party representatives in Switzerland. Another group was headed by Leo (Leibish) Rubinfeld, a Hasid and former member of HIJEFS who had a particular interest in Rabbi Joel Teitelbaum, the admor of Satmar, and several other rabbinic leaders on the train.[63] Mantello himself was also very much involved with Rabbi Teitelbaum (see chapter 12). In fact, on August 10, 1944 (see below), Mantello sent a letter with Trumpy, in which he informs the venerable rabbi that the bearer is bringing medicine and other (unknown) items intended for him.[64] For this objective, he deposited 100,000 SF for Trumpy, conditional upon the release of his "clients." Similarly, other groups arranged for the liberation of their own friends and ideological adherents. However, for the Germans, the key to the release of the train was not so much money as the availability of tractors, so vital for the fall harvest.

This idea had its origin in the fecund mind of Rabbi Michael Ber Weissmandl, as did most of the "ransom plans." Ever since early June, when Joel Brand had not returned from his mission to Turkey (see chapter 3), negotiations between Kastner and the Germans were about to break down, the arrangement for the train in Budapest had hardly begun, Weissmandl had tried to present an idea that became the linchpin for this and almost all future negotiations. He informed the Germans through his fictitious character "Ferdinand Roth," the alleged representative of world Jewry in Switzerland, that several hundred trucks (later switched to tractors) were available for the Germans in Switzerland.[65] "Roth's message" was conveyed to the Germans "from Switzerland," via the Freudiger-Link connection in Budapest. In turn, they informed Sternbuch of the need to provide forty tractors to get the train going.[66] As Mayer himself informed Eduard de Haller of the Swiss foreign office, the Germans made clear that "without tractors, no Jews would be released regardless of which country they [the Bergen Belsen inmates] would be sent to."

To obtain the release of the entire train, both Mantello and Sternbuch sought to borrow the necessary 750,000 SF from Saly Mayer and the Joint. At first, Mayer seemed interested in the Mantello-Trumpy negotiations. Trumpy managed to reach Bergen Belsen, where he delivered the earlier-mentioned letter and medicine to Rabbi Teitelbaum, and attempted to negotiate for the release of the various groups. However, as soon as Mayer heard about the tractors, he not only withdrew any offer of money, but also immediately informed his fellow legalist McClelland, who absolutely forbade any such "dirty business," of the plan to ransom the passengers using war material (tractors) for the Germans. Mayer now refused to extend this money to either Sternbuch or Mantello. For some unknown reason, Sternbuch's attempt to obtain the money and work together with Mantello to obtain the release of the train did not succeed.[67]

What made the Germans release the first convoy of 318 from Bergen Belsen into Switzerland was Sternbuch's production of a letter of credit for 150,000 SF, intended as a down payment.[68] Had they come up with the entire 750,000 SF, the entire group would most likely have been routed to Switzerland at the outset. Even this step required tremendous pressure from the Vaad Hatzalah in New York and Washington on both Morgenthau, the WRB, as well as the Joint, to obtain this sum. The Joint eventually pressured Saly Mayer into paying out the balance of the 750,000 SF.

Moses A. Leavitt of the Joint in New York cabled to Joseph Schwartz in Lisbon: "The Orthodox groups [Vaad Hatzalah] here [are] deeply disturbed [by Mayer's refusal to fund the release of the train] . . . and [are] exerting great pressure on us. . . . We are just as interested in rescuing these elements, and we hope every effort is being made to save them." This also explains why Mayer did not even tell McClelland about these later payments.[69]

Little information is available on Mantello's most ambitious rescue effort through Trumpy. Sometime in October, he tried to negotiate with the Germans, along lines like the Kastner-Mayer-Becher deal, for the release of more than 700,000 Jewish inmates of the concentration camps, to be placed under the care of the IRC.[70] This was one of four rescue plans that Mayer mulled over for months. He finally chose his connections with Kastner and Becher. This was primarily a ploy for time, for neither he nor McClelland was interested in paying out the Germans. This plan was finally replaced by a frustrated Himmler with the Sternbuch-Musy-Schellenberg negotiations (see below) during December–February 1945. Until it was eventually sabotaged, this new negotiation resulted in the release of a trainload of 1,210 inmates from Theresienstadt into Switzerland and the prevention of the destruction of several concentration camps during the last days of the war.[71]

New Dangers

Less than one week after the confirmation of Mantello's official role in the Salvadoran consulate, Eichmann had made an agreement with Gabor Vajna, the ministerial commissioner in charge of concentration of the Jews, to accomplish his ongoing goal of liquidating the Jews. Vajna's record of brutality toward the Jews in the Obuda brickworks prepared him well for his new job; he was to round up thousands of Jews and send them to Germany as laborers, ostensibly to build a last line of defense at the Austrian-Hungarian border. For Eichmann, this was to be the first of several new deportations, through which he intended to empty Hungary of its last Jews.[72]

By October 23, Eichmann succeeded in having the first 25,000 of the remaining Jews sent to Germany for forced labor. The rest made the trip on foot from the brick factory at Obuda to Vienna, a distance of 150 miles, between November 10 and 22. Eventually, between 50,000 and 60,000 people were forced to make this horrific journey, soon to be dubbed the "Death March."

The columns of marchers organized at Obuda consisted primarily of women, children, and older men, because most men of military age were already in labor battalions. The marchers, who had been beaten at Obuda and who had not received any food for almost three days before the trip, were forced to cover fifteen to twenty miles per day, an ordeal that could only be described as sheer torture. The hungry, tired, and sick dropped out quickly and were usually shot by the Nyilas guards. An estimated 10,000 souls eventually disappeared along the way.

Conditions were so bad that Dr. Nandor Batizfalvy, the surprisingly sympathetic superintendent of the Hungarian Alien Police, informed Wallenberg of the situation and offered his services. On November 22, Wallenberg arranged for a meeting of representatives of the neutral embassies. Interestingly enough, Lutz, who had been unable to attend, sent Moshe Krausz as his Swiss representative. Dr. Batizfalvy gave a confidential report concerning the Jews' march and offered to help in any way he could.[73]

The neutrals proved their mettle once again during the march. Wallenberg, Lutz, the papal nuncio, and others rushed to the Obuda brickworks, distributing hundreds of presigned, blank protective papers. The recipients quickly filled in their names and were pulled out of the brick factory. Later, the neutrals were able to rescue people directly from the Death March in the same fashion. The nuncio proved his moral leadership when he sent his representative, Sandor Gyorgy Ujvary, to distribute scores of obviously illegal, presigned certificates to the marchers—including allegedly pregnant women. Before sending him on his mission, the nuncio reassured Ujvary by saying, "What you are doing, my son, is pleasing to God and to Jesus, because you are saving innocent people. I give you absolution in advance."[74]

During the hectic period near the end of December, some of the Nyilas thugs, who neither cared about nor were involved in any diplomatic negotiations, totally disregarded official government pronouncements and paid no heed to any identity papers. They became reckless and anarchic, kidnapping and torturing Jews regardless of their papers; they grabbed hundreds of persons from the ghetto, even from Swiss or Swedish protected houses, shot them, and threw them into the Danube. Even the Swedish legation itself was no longer safe. On Christmas Day, Nyilas armed guards entered the Swedish legation and seized sixteen of its employees, including Asta Nilson, a cousin of the king of Sweden, and Margaret Bauer, two women who frequently represented Jewish interests. With great difficulty, Friedrich Born of the IRC was finally able to rescue these people.[75] During this time, the neutrals, especially Wallenberg and Lutz, displayed the depths of their courage. Wallenberg rarely slept in the same place for more than one night at a time, because he was literally in physical danger, and Lutz's legation took direct hits during the incessant air raids and bouts of shelling. Lutz was personally threatened as well, as we have seen, but neither he nor the other neutrals left their posts.

On December 22, Wallenberg sent his last warning to the Nyilas' foreign ministry, capitalizing on their fear of the approaching Red Army:

the Royal Swedish Embassy represents the interests of the Soviet Union in Hungary, and Hungarian interests in the Soviet Union, so that if Budapest were to be occupied, the Embassy could be in a position, if it had the opportunity, to continue its humanitarian operations. . . . It might be able to point out to the occupiers that the present-day government had recognized its activity and had supported it. . . . If the conditions of the ghetto do not improve, and if the [Swedish] Legation does not achieve its purpose . . . then this negative attitude of the Hungarian authorities would be regarded in Sweden as an indication that the Hungarian circles would not be willing to maintain the cordial and friendly relations which have existed thus far between our two countries.[76]

On the following day, December 23, despite Wallenberg's best efforts, the Nyilas transferred 6,000 Jewish children into the general (unprotected) ghetto, despite earlier promises to the contrary.

During the very trying days of January 1945, not long before the liberation, Wallenberg arguably accomplished his most heroic and successful feats. He found out, for example, that the Nyilas thugs had decided to murder the 70,000 Jews in the unprotected ghetto. Instead of appealing to the Nyilas government, however, he went straight to the German commander, General Schmidthuber, and demanded that he prevent the killing; if not, Wallenberg warned the general, "You will not be tried as a soldier, but will swing on the gallows as a murderer." Shaken by these words, Schmidthuber stopped the planned operation, thereby saving 70,000 Jews who were not under any protective power.[77]

Lutz, through his presence alone, was responsible for a different but equally effective rescue effort, which saved as many as 60,000 Jews in the "protected" ghetto. A German diplomat informed him after the war that German authorities had given orders to the Nyilas not to harm the Jews under Lutz's care as long as he remained in Budapest. This gesture was a token of gratitude to Lutz for having looked after the interests of several thousand German nationals in Palestine during 1939 and 1940, whom the British had wanted to expel.[78]

The Russians entered the city and brought the fighting to a halt on January 17 and 18 in Pest, where both ghettos were located, and on February 13 in Buda, where numerous Jews still struggled to survive. When Lutz finally closed down his consulate, it was upon the orders of the Russians, who in early April 1945, ordered all foreign consulates and embassies to close down within twenty-four hours. And after a trip through Bucharest, Istanbul, Lisbon, and Barcelona, he arrived in Geneva.[79]

Upon his return home to Switzerland, he was able to resume his distinguished diplomatic career; for Wallenberg, his courageous colleague, the future was not so bright. The conclusion of this tragic era was to spell his doom as he was "swallowed" by the Russians, never to be heard from again.

One of the interesting sidelights to the press campaign was its influence on other negotiations carried on by representatives of Jewish organizations with the Germans for the release of Jews under their control. One of the more fascinating ones, which has received only scant attention from historians, involved the Sternbuch-Musy-Himmler negotiations.[80] This began sometime in September of 1944, when Recha Sternbuch found out that Dr. Jean-Marie Musy, a former president of Switzerland, a known Fascist publisher of an anti-Semitic paper, and a friend of Himmler, had taken money to obtain a Jewish couple's release from incarceration.

In her search for the inmates of Vittel who were deported in April 1944, Recha began to deal with Dr. Musy. She asked him to use his friendship with Himmler to press for the release of all the inmates of the camps in exchange for money and goods. Unlike Saly Mayer and McClelland, the Sternbuchs, with the full support of Vaad Hatzalah in New York, had no hesitation in using bribery or ransom to effect the release of Jews from the Nazi terror. They promised Musy money for himself as well as for Himmler. The negotiations went well, and agreement was made to release 300,000 Jews from the camps for (U.S.) $5 million (later reduced to $1 million). Himmler, however, added a rather puzzling demand: he wanted a "good press." Himmler explained to Musy that because the Jews "controlled" the press, especially in the United States, they should portray the Jewish inmates as having received good treatment from "civil" Germans after being released from Theresienstadt. Interestingly enough, the Sternbuchs were able to interest several newspapers in Switzerland and in the United States to publish a spate of articles favorable to Germany. However, the Socialist press in Switzerland condemned the negotiations for dealing in ransom for human beings. The negotiations were eventually halted by the few examples of "bad" press that were shown to General Kaltenbrunner, who, in turn, showed them to Hitler. For our purpose, however, it is important to realize that, after the tremendous impact of Mantello's press campaign during the summer in Switzerland and in the free world, Himmler was merely trying to mitigate its catastrophic, negative effect on

Germany's image, at least to some degree. This demand by Himmler for a "good press" was clearly visible in a number of his other negotiations and the memoirs of those involved in them.

The numbers of those saved in Budapest are at best only good estimates, and different figures are given in different sources; yet, the statistics are impressive. At the time of the Szalasi coup in October 1944, the IRC estimated that there were between 200,000 and 225,000 Jews in Budapest. Mantello put about ten thousand Salvadoran papers into circulation,[81] and, according to Lutz, his department used them to protect between 20,000 and 30,000 people.[82] This figure is supported by an IRC report of December 15, 1944, entitled "The Jewish Situation in Hungary," which pointed out that the Swiss legation in Budapest had taken under its protection the greatest number of Jews. In the beginning, they had had a limited allocation of seventy-four hundred people who possessed immigration certificates for Palestine, in addition to holders of Swedish travel passes, but the number of people protected by the legation rose to 30,000. Citing one example of Lutz's courageous rescue efforts, the report notes that 180 Jews scheduled for forced labor in Germany were provided with Swiss entry visas at the last minute, enabling them to remain in Budapest. In this manner, "the Swiss legation managed to withdraw 15,000 people from forced labor contingents."[83] According to one reliable estimate, the Swiss compound eventually protected about 60,000 people in all.[84]

Mantello's Salvadoran papers were behind the rescue of these people, but statistics alone do not tell the full story of his role in the survival of approximately 140,000 Budapest Jews. All the heroic work of the neutrals would not even have been necessary if the most significant event of the Holocaust had not taken place: the halting of the trains from Budapest to Auschwitz by Mantello and his Swiss colleagues and the Swiss people. The final chapter will show that the end of the war in Europe did not spell the conclusion of Mantello's rescue efforts.

12

Postwar

Mantello's press campaign and Salvadoran paper operation were his two most outstanding wartime achievements, but certainly not his only ones. Amid his superhuman rescue activities during the last half year of the Jewish tragedy in Hungary, he somehow managed to find the time to address the concerns of persons who appealed to him—rabbis, scholars, and average people who sought his help. Let us pause for a moment to look at some minor relief and rescue efforts in which he was involved during the final few months of the war and in the years that followed.

Mantello and his brother Josef were actively involved in the successful attempt to secure the release of a number of people from Bergen Belsen into Switzerland.[1] Among the larger group of thirteen hundred or so, released in December 1944, was Rabbi Joel Teitelbaum, the admor of Satmar. He was among the most prominent Hungarian rabbis and a major anti-Zionist leader; coincidentally, his father had been a student of Mantello's grandfather. Although Mantello was no longer Orthodox, he never lost his family's respect for the rabbi and for other Jewish religious leaders he had revered as a youngster. Even before Rabbi Teitelbaum arrived in Switzerland, Mantello had made arrangements to rent a villa for him in Geneva. Chaim (Edmund) Stern, a respected communal leader in Budapest and fellow passenger on the train, noted to Mantello in later years, "I was witness to and know all about what you have accomplished for the Satmar Rebbe. You [rented] a villa for him in Geneva, the likes of which he surely never saw in his life, with a gardener, etc.; a veritable palace, for which you alone absorbed all the costs."[2]

After Rabbi Teitelbaum's release from the Caux refugee camp in Switzerland, Mantello spread the word that this distinguished rabbi had arrived in the country. As a result, the president of the Bundesrat invited the rabbi to a special assembly, where he was publicly honored. When the minister of religion saw the venerable sage, he remarked, "He looks just like Jesus."[3]

Another renowned Hungarian talmudic authority who was liberated in December from the Bergen-Belsen train was Rabbi Jonasan Steif, formerly head of the rabbinical court in Budapest. His stature was recognized by the Union of Swiss Rabbis, who resolved to enable him to achieve financial independence. They obtained commitments from various sources, including Mantello, to support this illustrious scholar, and they agreed to provide the rabbi with fifty francs monthly.[4]

At that time, the Swiss government required guarantees from sponsors who would agree to assume full responsibility for the support of refugee camp inmates before releasing them. Refugees and noncitizens were not permitted to seek employment in Switzerland as a source of livelihood, making a sponsor necessary—and providing Mantello with another philanthropic outlet. One person for whom he provided a guarantee was Dr. Elie Munk, an Orthodox rabbi from Paris who managed to escape across the French-Swiss border with his wife and six children in the midst of the war. After a brief stay in a civilian refugee camp, Mantello arranged his release. It was undoubtedly Maitre Muller, who knew Rabbi Munk from Paris, who interceded with Mantello on his friend's behalf.

After his release, Rabbi Munk arrived in Geneva, where he tried to eke out a livelihood by giving lectures on Jewish topics. However, with a large family to support, he could not even afford a weekly chicken, the basic staple for the Sabbath meal. Mantello immediately saw to it that a chicken was delivered to his home every Friday and on the eve of the holidays, to enhance his Sabbath and festival meals. Mantello maintained this tradition until the rabbi could return to Paris after the liberation of France.[5]

Another case involved Chaim Stern, an earlier-mentioned Orthodox communal leader who had been active in Budapest during the war years. He had used his position as manager of Freudiger's mills to help support hundreds of Jewish scholars who could never have obtained ration cards without "proper employment." By mid-1944, he, like most Budapest Jews, was impoverished, and he was barely able to pay his way to get on the Bergen Belsen train. Upon arrival in Switzerland, he was placed in the Caux refugee camp, along with most of the other passengers. As a result of Rabbi Teitelbaum's recommendation, Mantello sponsored Stern, enabling him to leave the camp. Mr. Stern testified during Mantello's postwar inquiry that he and more than a hundred others were able to leave the refugee camp only through Mantello's largesse:[6]

> I wanted to be freed from the [Caux] camp, so Rabbi Teitelbaum told me that he would present my case to Mr. Mantello, who had accomplished so much. Later, I had a chance to speak to him personally. He told me that he was ready to guarantee for many of us. In eight days I was out of the camp. [Moreover,] Mantello loaned me a substantial sum of money, because at that point I had no other means. There was never even any mention of returning the money with interest. [Although] I have given back most of this money, Mantello didn't want to take it at first, saying that I might need it and that I could be a "baal chov" [a debtor] as long I wanted to.[7]

Mantello also provided guarantees for Mr. Theodore Fischer, president of the Romanian Zionist Federation and a former member of the Romanian Parliament, and his wife, as well as several of their relatives. When this prominent couple left the refugee camp, he provided them with a room in his house and took care of all their needs.[8]

Mantello was also helpful to a group of twenty-nine young members of Betar[9] who were also passengers on the Bergen-Belsen train. Their leader, Elisha Katz, mentioned to Mantello that every other Zionist group on that train, except for his own, received financial support from its Zionist organization, either in Switzerland, the United States, or Palestine. Eventually, when the Betar youth were permitted to leave the internment camp at Caux to go to North Africa, they owned nothing except the shirts on their backs, and these were certainly not in good condition. Mr. Katz appealed to Mantello to help provide them with clothing and equipment.

Soon after this appeal, Katz wrote to Mantello a second time, thanking him for "the shipment of clothing for the *chaverim* [masculine in Hebrew for members] and *chaverot* [feminine] of the Betar group in Caux, sent through the firm Adler in Geneva, which has just arrived." It had taken no more than five days for Mantello to fill this request.[10] In all, he was responsible for guaranteeing the release of about one hundred inmates from the Caux refugee camp.[11]

Another area of endeavor concerned Jews who sought to leave Romania after the war, especially following the Communist takeover in 1948. Rabbi Zusia Portugal, the admor of Skulen and one of the great rescue activists in

Romania, specialized in the care of children in Transnistria and elsewhere, and he was in dire need of money to help get them out of the country. One of his colleagues, Mr. Mendel Brach, formerly of Romania, reported that when he presented a list of Rabbi Portugal's needs, Mantello immediately offered $15,000.[12]

Interestingly enough, the usefulness of the Salvadoran papers did not dissipate after the war's end. On a small scale, there were a number of individual requests for intervention that Mantello readily fulfilled. A few of these were made by people who had already received Salvadoran papers from him at some point. They had no interest in going to El Salvador, but wanted instead to go to the Netherlands for a few months, and then to the United States. As former German nationals, however, they were afraid that the Dutch would not be willing to provide them with visas. They therefore requested that Mantello forward confirmation of their Salvadoran nationality to the Dutch authorities.[13]

Though Jews were the major recipients of Mantello's papers, he did not restrict his rescue efforts to his coreligionists. Whenever he was made aware of endangered non-Jews who sought the protection of Salvadoran papers, he quickly accommodated them, assisting in a number of cases involving French Maquis (resistance fighters), as well as others. One episode involved a leader of the French Maquis who was technically a member of the police, but who in reality worked for the underground. He and his wife were caught by the Nazis and were in extreme danger. Swiss intermediaries requested that Mantello provide the couple with Salvadoran papers, and he readily complied.[14] Another instance of Mantello's aid to non-Jews involved a Christian couple who were harassed by the Nyilas; they too requested and received Salvadoran papers.[15]

On a grander scale, someone else found a good use for about a thousand copies of the Salvadoran papers that had remained in Mantello's possession after he left the consulate at the end of the war. This final rescue effort was the brainchild of Dr. Jacob Griffel, a member of both the Moetza of the Jewish Agency's Vaad Hahatzalah and the New York–based Orthodox Vaad Hatzalah. Dr. Griffel was stationed in Istanbul, Turkey, during the war years and continued his rescue efforts for many years afterward. His major postwar objective was to help several hundred thousand survivors from the concentration camps in Europe, those exiled in 1941 to Siberia and central Russia, enter the Western zones.[16] He was especially active on behalf of those who were caught in Communist-dominated Poland, enabling them to find their way either to Eretz Israel or to a safe haven in the West.[17]

In western Europe, safety meant a Displaced Persons (DP) camp in the western zone of Germany or in France, which was very liberal in accepting Jewish survivors. The key gathering place for most of these survivors was Prague, a centrally located city in a hospitable country, which served as a major hub for the rerouting of refugees to various Western countries. To leave Poland, for example, one had to have a visa to another country, also called an end-visa. Dr. Griffel was able to get thousands of Italian visas, which the Jews used to get to Eretz Israel with the help of the Bricha. This was an organization of Jewish Palestinian veterans of the British army stationed in Italy, especially from the "Jewish brigade," who spirited thousands of Jews from the DP camps and other European locations to Eretz Israel through Aliya Bet, an "illegal immigration" route that used boats to sneak the Jewish survivors into the country.

Griffel traveled to Switzerland to meet with Mantello on Salvadoran visas. He found out that Mantello had kept hundreds of duplicates of the Salvadoran citizenship papers he had sent out to Nazi-occupied countries. Griffel suggested that they could change the photos and use these "duplicate" Salvadoran papers for Jews who needed end-visas to leave Poland. Moreover, Czechoslovakia was permitting Jews who had such citizenship papers to come to Prague. Mantello gave Griffel a large satchel containing about a thousand papers, virtually all he had left. Each paper could be used for an entire family, amounting to approximately five or six thousand people.

Griffel brought these "used" Salvadoran papers to Prague, where Rabbi Victor Vorhand tapped his excellent connections in the Czech government to help bring thousands of Jewish survivors to Prague. From there he helped them immigrate to Western countries, or to Eretz Israel via Italy. What was particularly valuable about the Salvadoran papers was the fact that the British were not concerned that their holders would try to go to Eretz Israel illegally, a problem that concerned them in regard to the Italian visas, for Italy was usually the stepping-stone to Eretz Israel. El Salvador seemed rather innocuous in this regard.[18]

What was probably Mantello's last act of rescue took place in Austria and in Switzerland a few years after the war and involved a non-Jewish Hungarian political figure, Monsignor Bela Varga. Varga was the last legitimate president of the Hungarian Parliament before the Communist takeover. He had been a parish priest in the town of Balaton (on the shores of Lake Balaton), and later a member of Parliament as head of the Small Landowner Party. During the war, he had been particularly active in helping Polish refugees by providing them with foreign identity cards. Among the recipients were several Jews who equally benefited from his help, and for such aid to the "enemy," he was persecuted by the pro-Nazi Nyilas authorities. It was because of his rescue activities that Mantello came to know of him. As Varga put it, "Mantello was more aware of what was happening in Hungary than most Hungarians."[19]

After the national elections in 1945, Monsignor Varga became president of the Hungarian Parliament, a position he held until the Communists began to arrest anti-Communist politicians in 1947 and 1948.[20] He, too, was arrested. In prison he met Wallenberg, whom he had helped during the war by acting as a translator because Wallenberg did not know Hungarian. Varga believes the Russians executed Wallenberg there in prison.

Despite the Communist efforts to delegitimize him by depriving him of his citizenship, Varga never officially resigned his post and never lost his status as president of the Hungarian Parliament. Most non-Communist parties continued to recognize him in his leadership role.[21] Varga was soon able to escape to Austria, though he was still pursued by the Communist agents, who were particularly dangerous because they controlled the Russian-occupied zone in Austria.

Mantello's job was to spirit Varga from the Russian zone into Vienna, and from there to the Swiss border. He was able to convince a number of important Swiss officials of Varga's importance and succeeded in having the border sealed to all for a short period, except for Varga and himself. Mantello's car had a five-number license plate from St. Gallen, Switzerland, but to avoid detection, he had the plates changed again. Eventually, he had to change them five times, and even so, the Communists remained on Varga's heel.[22]

In a resort near Vienna, Mantello personally rescued Varga from a Communist assassination attempt. Varga was staying there under the alias "Wagner." As he recalled, they were sitting in the lobby of a hotel when a strange character burst in through the front door, shouting, "Where is Varga, where is Varga?" Mantello was immediately suspicious, for no one addressed Varga by his last name alone; he was called either Monsignor Varga or Father Varga. He also noticed that the man kept his right hand in his pocket. Mantello jumped up, ran over to the man, and grabbed his hand, discovering that he indeed held a gun. He wrested the weapon away and then lifted the man bodily and threw him out the door. Realizing that the Communists were rapidly closing in on Varga, Mantello enlisted the aid of the American OSS and Swiss intelligence to smuggle him into Switzerland quickly.

Varga remained in Switzerland for several months, with Mantello supporting and protecting him. To remain out of reach of the Communists, the exiled politician was forced to move from one monastery to another. Finally, he came to the United States, where he remained until after the first free Hungarian election in 1990. He was reinstated as president of the Hungarian Parliament in 1991, and died a few years later in his homeland.

Varga was not the only anti-Communist Hungarian refugee whom Mantello helped. He himself noted that Mantello used all his connections to help dozens of others, especially Hungarian Social Democrats, to escape into Switzerland.[23]

Although Mantello certainly did not receive the recognition due him for his efforts, some more sensitive individuals and Jewish organizations did express their appreciation for his help. One letter, dated October 16, 1945, came from the Jewish community of Geneva, which had absorbed a number of refugees:

> Now that all of the refugees who had been in our country are going back to their own homelands, we are eager to express in this letter our deep appreciation of the great kindness and the spirit of humanity that you have shown to thousands of human beings who, during these recent terrible years, had seen their days on earth threatened.
>
> Indeed, our unfortunate coreligionists who owe their lives to you number in the thousands. Appeals came to you from every country—France, Belgium, Holland, Czechoslovakia, Poland, and Hungary; and to each and every one you responded by sending Salvadoran citizenship papers, using the Jewish organizations and the Swiss Federal Political Department as intermediaries. Thanks to these citizenship papers, thousands of men, women, and children— Jews and non-Jews—of all nationalities escaped a horrible death in the Nazi extermination camps.
>
> It is impossible for us to adequately express our gratitude to you for the tremendous, altruistic work you have done, sparing neither your time nor your financial resources to come to the aid of the wretched victims of the Nazis. We can, however, bear witness to the fact that your help was entirely without personal motive. Not only have you declined to accept any reimbursement for the innumerable papers you sent to us, but, in your life-saving mission, you have also spent considerable sums of your own money.
>
> We are particularly grateful that you were willing to expose yourself to dangerous publicity in your mission to bring the tragic fate of the Hungarian Jews to the attention of the world. Your actions contributed to the enlightenment

of the public. It is now absolutely certain that it was worldwide public opinion, alerted by your cries, which pressured the Hungarian government into changing its policies.

Moreover, in 1944, when Hungarian refugees coming from camps in Germany arrived in Switzerland, you immediately intervened on their behalf. Due to your efforts, numerous refugees were able to live in freedom outside of the camps. Thanks also to the financial guarantees that you made them and the means which you placed at their disposal, you permitted them to spend their time in Switzerland in more favorable conditions.

We are sending with the same messenger a letter to the Consul General of the Republic of El Salvador, thanking him and his government for the humanitarian efforts of their Consul General in Geneva.

On behalf of the Jewish Community of Geneva,

Signed,

M. C. Levy-Walich and Germaine Grumsinger[24]

The second letter is particularly instructive because it was written by Andre Biss, an engineer who was a member of the Vaada, the rescue committee in Budapest headed by Rudolph Kastner. Biss was especially close to Kastner and took his place as leader of the Vaada from January to May of 1945. He was active in rescue efforts in Budapest not only during the war, but also worked with the Hungarian Red Cross afterward. He eventually wrote a book about his wartime experience, entitled *A Million Jews to Save.*[25]

What is important about Biss's letter is that he had firsthand knowledge of the press campaign. The fact that he wrote this unsolicited letter on March 5, 1945, only a few weeks after the liberation of all of Budapest and two months before the conclusion of the war, is proof of its veracity.

Now, after the awful suffering and loss of countless lives, the population of Budapest is finally liberated, and each day we have an opportunity to ascertain that there are many thousands of persecuted people who have been saved through the El Salvador citizenship papers, or through the worldwide press campaign that you orchestrated in June 1944 for the purpose of saving Hungarian Jewry.

This press campaign awakened people's opinion in the whole world, and it is thanks to this that the Swiss and Swedish protective papers have been issued, following [the example of] El Salvador.

Most of the people who were saved know that this was thanks to you and your consul general, as well as the generosity of the Christian Swiss clergy. They are full of deep gratitude to you and to the government of El Salvador, and they have asked me to convey this to you.

We are writing to you today on their behalf to convey to you their heart-felt feelings of obligation for having saved their lives through the Salvador citizenship papers.

We further request kindly that you transmit . . . the letter of gratitude that we have addressed to the Salvadoran government. The Hungarian democracy shall never forget the great service that you have rendered to the persecuted and the abandoned.

Please accept the expression of our highest esteem.

Signed,

Ing. [engineer] Biss Andor[26]

Sadly, when Biss eventually wrote his book in 1966, he not only changed or distorted numerous facts and events, but also completely omitted any mention of Mantello and the Salvadoran papers. The press campaign was dismissed with the brief statement, "Articles appeared in the Western press about Hungary."[27] His colleague, Rudolph Kastner, who was even more closely involved with Mantello's efforts, managed to mention the efficacy of the press campaign in his postwar *Bericht,* although he ignored Mantello completely: "Only once was there an energetic Western response [to the Hungarian catastrophe], and this was sufficient to convince Horthy to halt the deportations. It was the result of a cooperative effort of the King of Sweden, the Pope, the IRC, the Hungarian churches, and especially President Roosevelt."[28]

A Bitter Ending

Sadly, Biss's letter, along with those from several Jewish organizations, were the exceptions rather than the rule. Countering the good feelings engendered by such complimentary letters were malicious rumors against Mantello, some sent by informers to the Swiss government, alleging that he had dealt on the black market and profited from the "sale" of Salvadoran papers—an accusation that particularly pained him. In addition, many Jewish representatives, and later historians, refused to admit his role or to give him any credit for his rescue efforts. Mr. Arye (Leon) Kubowitzki of the World Jewish Congress wrote, "I met Mr. Mantello in Geneva in February 1945 and had several conversations with him. At that time his reputation was under attack in many respects. I should add that the rivalry and jealousy of the various rescue bodies was such that it was quite difficult to get an unbiased report on any social worker or social organization."[29]

While Riegner attempted in the earlier letter to downplay Mantello's rescue efforts, he admitted the following to Kubowitzki: "There is no doubt that he [Mantello] has sent several thousand [Salvadoran] nationality papers and that he has saved many Jews in doing so. . . . It also seems to be a fact that Mantello sacrificed much money of his own for this purpose." Moreover, while Riegner noted that "the British seemed to trust Mantello," he quickly qualified this statement by quoting McClelland, who had told him that "they do not trust him, but they make him believe so."[30] This is rather strange in view of the full cooperation and help that British intelligence and the British Exchange Telegraph had provided Mantello throughout the press campaign during the crucial summer of 1944. What is even more inexplicable is why the British should feign helping him, if there were no real basis for it.

Another example of the denial of Mantello's activities is found in a letter written by Abraham B. Hyman, executive secretary of the Joint, in response to a request by Mr. Carlos Bernhard of the Organización Sionista de El Salvador for verification of Mantello's claim concerning the distribution of Salvadoran papers. Mr. Hyman noted:

I regret that it was not possible to answer your letter of February . . . because it has taken some time to make a search of our rescue files. . . . This search has now been completed, and it does not seem to support the contention of the El Salvador consul [Mantello]. We do find a record of a very small number of El Salvador visas issued to inmates of concentration camps in Germany, but this record does not link these few visas with the El Salvador consul, and certainly does not warrant the claim that the El Salvador consul participated in the mass rescue of Hungarian Jews. Of course, while our files do not confirm the claim, they do not positively repudiate the contentions. All we can say is that our files are devoid of information which supports the contention.[31]

The frustration Mantello suffered in his attempts to combat both the wartime allegations and the postwar rumors is evident from a letter he wrote to Maitre Muller, who was on his way to a conference of World Agudath Israel in London in December of 1945. Because Mantello had been denied a visa to England, where he wanted to present his case, he requested that Muller convey to the Agudath Israel the extent of his rescue work and the problems with which he and his team had contended:

> In particular, I'd like you to point out the great struggles and difficulties we encountered in our attempt to accomplish our goals. . . . The obstacles that were placed in our way did not come so much from official sources as from Jewish personalities in Switzerland, who themselves were supported from abroad. . . . In our work, [however,] we had not the slightest financial support from any Jewish organization. We paid virtually all expenses from our own pockets and devoted ourselves to the cause in seriousness and honesty. It is obvious that with the [limited] funds at our disposal we could save only a small fraction of those of our brothers who were sentenced to death.
>
> We also had to defend ourselves against the other Jewish authorities, which caused us great difficulties. . . . Why did these organizations fight against us? They saw in us a dangerous competitor. We were in a position to give something for nothing to thousands of people, something that, up to this time, had cost several thousand francs per person; and we dispensed it without any "protektzia," intervention by higher authorities, [and without making] the slightest distinctions among the recipients. They were afraid that [we would] end their monopoly.
>
> [From the outset] we made efforts to unite all the [Jewish] committees for common efforts, but unfortunately to no avail. You can judge how much more could have been accomplished had we cooperated with each other. While we distributed thousands of Salvador papers and made sure that they reached the endangered people, we also made sure that the proper authorities took over their protection. All the other organizations were fully aware of our activities, but they acted as if they didn't notice a thing. . . . Instead of helping us, they hindered. . . . [All this time] the gas chambers were busy functioning at full speed and snuffing out the lives of our unfortunate brothers.
>
> Unfortunately, when the tragedy of Hungarian Jewry first started, we were only able to obtain reports [of the atrocities] by June 21, through our courier; other organizations had already received them in May, but they treated them as a state secret. With the help of several personalities, the Hungarian Committee, rabbis and Protestant clergy of Zurich, journalists, the British embassy, and the Exchange Telegraph, we succeeded in developing a major Swiss press campaign to inform the world about the catastrophe of Auschwitz and Birkenau. [The press campaign] was picked up by the press of the entire free world. Through this press campaign we were able to mobilize the diplomacy of the entire free world, and [we] were even finally able to convince the International

Red Cross to intervene in Jewish matters. . . . Mr. [Philip] Freudiger's report to us from Budapest confirmed the fact that the deportations from Budapest were stopped as a direct consequence of the press campaign and indignant public opinion in the neutral and Allied countries. This was at a time when everyone, God forbid, considered the Jews of Budapest to be lost.

We were sabotaged and even undermined by informers. . . . And don't think that this campaign [against us] has stopped. To some degree they want to claim credit for our work, while others simply continue their informing, thereby making it impossible for me to obtain a visa [to England]. . . . I hope you will shake up the Jewish public and let them know that a quick, effective cooperative effort on behalf of the surviving European Jews is necessary, if we don't want to lose them as well. Please convey my greetings to the [Agudah] Conference, [along with the] hope that the next one will take place in a "free Eretz Israel."[32]

Mantello indicated in this letter that after all his efforts, he had been denied an entry visa to England as well as to France. Astonishment at such an ironic turn of events is expressed by a reporter for the British *Daily Express,* who had made a tour of the Balkans after the war. He wrote to Maitre Muller:

During this trip I met hundreds of people whose lives were saved thanks to Mr. Mantello. These persons were rescued from Nazi terror by means of the El Salvador citizenship certificates signed by Mantello.

Through my own investigation I found out that Mr. Mantello always acted in the most selfless manner, and that he often dipped into his own pocket to pay for the delivery of these papers via special couriers, [a service] which was very expensive during the war. In all of the Balkan states, as well as in Hungary, the name of Mr. Mantello is venerated. One of those involved with [the Salvadoran] papers is a Mr. Antel, the present Hungarian Minister of Reconstruction, who was head of the resistance during the Nazi era; he spoke to me of Mr. Mantello in the most laudatory terms. He told me, in these exact words, that hundreds of thousands of human lives could have been saved had there been among the Allies several men like Mr. Mantello.

I was dumbfounded to learn that this courageous benefactor was denied an entry visa to France! I am convinced that this must be either a misunderstanding or else a case of personal vengeance.[33]

The denial of visas was only one aspect of the harassment that Mantello endured at the hands of the Swiss. Without any real awareness of what was going on in the Swiss bureacracy, this reporter had struck at the heart of the matter when he mentioned "personal vengeance." It was just such a vendetta which evidently motivated Rothmund, the anti-Semitic head of the Swiss Alien Police, to continue to harrass Mantello for several more years—to the point where Switzerland was even ready to deprive him of his right of residence and to expel him from the country.

Johannes Duft, a member of the Swiss parliament who was one of Mantello's lawyers as well as a good friend, found Switzerland's actions puzzling, to say the least. He wrote to Mantello on October 31, 1946:

> According to reports [of the Swiss Alien Police], you are supposed to leave Switzerland in the next few days as an undesirable foreigner, mainly [on the charge] that, as Secretary of the El Salvador consulate in Geneva, you issued citizenship papers for people who were not citizens of that state.
>
> This attitude of the Swiss police is very surprising, especially since I am fully aware that the issuance of Salvador papers in 1944 was carried out with the full approval of Colonel Castellanos. I am also aware of the fact that the United States of America had specifically approved the issuance of these Salvador citizenship papers. . . . Furthermore, the Swiss Political Department is equally aware of your activities. In fact, Dr. Stucki, then representative of the Department of Foreign Affairs, and now Swiss Ambassador in Athens, told me that the Department of Foreign Affairs recognized that you issued the papers on a purely humanitarian basis to save endangered lives, and that they provided you with neither personal advantage nor profit.
>
> In fact, I can personally testify that on my initiative, you issued two Salvador papers for a Christian couple who had been captured by the Nyilas, and for which you did not ask compensation. It is my belief that your unselfish humanitarian activities should receive proper recognition from the Swiss authorities. Under no circumstances should you lose your resident's permit.[34]

Besides Duft, Mantello had other Swiss allies in his struggle to clear his name. One of these was Jules Peney, president of Geneva's City Council, who served as a character witness for Mantello on January 9, 1947. He wrote to Adrien Lachenal, another prominent lawyer, on Mantello's behalf:

> I am recommending to you Mr. G. Mantello, who was the First Secretary of the Salvador Consulate in Geneva. In that capacity he provided Salvador citizenship papers to non-Salvadorans. In doing so he saved the lives of numerous people, for which he should be praised rather than criticized.

In fact, [during the Nyilas era] the Federal Political Department itself appealed to the Consul General of El Salvador on behalf of [Swiss] people whose lives were in danger. (See the letter dated Nov. 24, 1944, in the [F.P.D.] file.)

I don't doubt for a moment that you have studied the material in that file and that you will succeed in convincing Bern to rescind the order of deportation issued against G. Mantello.

This gentleman is extremely honorable and really deserves the title of "benefactor."

Signed,

Jules Peney[35]

The contradictory behavior of the Swiss Department of Foreign Affairs during the last few months of the siege of Budapest, as well as the persistent postwar harassment of Mantello, made it clear that several factions within the Swiss government sought to disenfranchise him. It appears that Rothmund, Mantello's old nemesis, who had been behind his arrest in May 1944, was the primary culprit. Rothmund, head of the Swiss Alien Police, disliked foreigners in general and Jewish foreigners in particular. He and Federal Councilor von Streeiger had been the major catalysts behind the German policy of stamping the *J* on all German-Jewish passports to prevent a mass flight across the German-Swiss border, Rothmund also enforced the racial laws of *refoulement* on "Jewish" "racial" refugees in contrast to the more acceptable "political" refugees. Moreover, as we saw earlier, Mantello never hesitated to respond to Rothmund without fear or even respect, a fact that surely exacerbated the police chief's animosity.[36]

Rothmund's attitude eventually softened, but it took three years after the war and a changed climate of opinion in Switzerland, which finally welcomed foreigners and even permitted them to work for a livelihood. On February 14, 1948, Rothmund came to the pragmatic conclusion that he could no longer maintain his hostile policy toward Mantello's "illegal" rescue efforts. He revealed the basis for his change of heart in the following note:

In no case should Mantello be accused of distributing San Salvador [*sic*] papers to Jews in German[-occupied territories]. According to everything I heard about this matter, the distribution of such passports by several Latin American states was the only means of saving a few thousand Jews from being sent to the extermination camp Auschwitz. Germany had formed a special camp for these people. They were treated as enemy aliens and somehow evaluated against the good treatment of Germans in Latin American countries. Because our strict enforcement [of the laws of *refoulement*] left many Jewish refugees at the mercy of the Germans, we should not act upon [charges of] illegality against those who succeeded in saving a few thousand from death.

In my opinion, we should bring the last of the wartime [charges] to a close. The Mantello case could be concluded by sending him away and closing the border to him; if this could be justified, it could actually be done. But I have the uncertain feeling that despite its justification, it wouldn't be very smart.[37]

Only a few months later, after reading Lutz's report of his rescue efforts in Budapest during 1944, Rothmund finally admitted to Lutz, "We really could have taken in several hundred thousand [Jewish] refugees."[38]

Nine months later, on October 15, 1948, Mr. Claude Gautier, a government attorney, informed Mantello through his lawyer, Mr. Jean Brunschvig, of the following good news: "I confirm that, according to the documents you have shown me, the illegal restraint imposed upon Mr. Mantello on February 7, 1947, was lifted a few days later. [Moreover,] the suit opened against Mr. Mantello by the War Economy Board [which had accused Mantello of dealing in the black market during the war] *was closed*" (emphasis added).[39]

Postwar Inquiry

Mantello was enormously frustrated by the negative reaction to him personally and to his rescue efforts. Besides the rumors and general harassment, he was formally accused of three "crimes" by the Swiss. The first involved his conducting business in Switzerland, which was not permitted for noncitizens, refugees, tourists, or visitors. He was also accused of distributing "fraudulent" Salvadoran papers to Jews who were not really Salvadoran citizens, despite the full approval of the Salvadoran consul general, a former Salvadoran president residing in Switzerland, and the government in San Salvador itself. Lastly, he was accused of bringing his son Enrico illegally from Budapest into Switzerland, without a Swiss entry visa.

To clear his name permanently, Mantello finally requested an official inquiry into these charges and into his wartime conduct in general. With this inquiry, he also sought to set an example for all Jewish rescue activists, encouraging them to open their books to public scrutiny, especially because they had raised money from the broader American Jewish community and therefore had an obligation to reveal their books. On September 25, 1945, five months after the end of the war, Mantello sent a letter to the Federation of Swiss Jewish Communities (SIG) requesting a panel of judges to oversee a public inquiry, to which they would be free to invite anyone to testify.

SIG complied and appointed three highly qualified Swiss Jewish personalities to serve on the panel. The first was Dr. Paul Guggenheim, head of the Swiss branch of the World Jewish Congress and a judge at the International Court at the Hague in the Netherlands, as well as a professor at the University of Geneva. The second, Dr. Max Gurny, was a judge on the Swiss supreme court in Zurich; the third was Dr. George Brunschvig, president of SIG and a military magistrate in Bern. The committee elected Dr. Brunschvig its chairman. Some witnesses testified personally; others sent in affidavits, none of which were made public.[40]

Among the first to testify was Wilhelm Fischer, head of the World Jewish Congress in Romania and a leading rescue activist in that country for many years. He described his own rescue efforts during the final few months of the Nyilas era:

> I continually cabled to Mantello the names and addresses of my Budapest acquaintances and friends, so that they could save themselves with Salvador papers. We had [also] published appeals in the Bucharest Jewish papers, [asking] Romanian Jews to provide the names and addresses of their relatives and friends. In this manner, we collected several thousand names and spent more than three million lei [approximately $20,000 U.S.] on the cables [frequently fifty pages long]. Naturally, we didn't have to pay anything for the papers.[41]

Dr. Abraham Silberschein, head of RELICO and member of the World Jewish Congress, who had used protective papers of all kinds in his rescue efforts, also testified:

> I first came in contact with Mantello in 1941. My brother was then in danger in Yugoslavia, and all my attempts to rescue him were futile. Then Mantello came to our assistance. In 1943, when it was necessary to pay two to three thousand Swiss francs to the Polish embassy for one [Paraguayan] passport, Mantello used to issue the [Salvadoran] citizenship papers entirely free of charge. Others had been making enormous profits by selling protective papers in Switzerland, but Mantello put an end to this. Naturally, those whose interests were jeopardized by Mantello tried to put obstacles in his way, even to the point of denouncing him to the police. I know for sure that Mantello covered all the expenses from his own means, never asking or taking any money from any organization.

The Salvador papers were recognized even by the UNRRA [United Nations Relief and Rehabilitation Administration] after the war. [During the war] even the Gestapo used to sell these papers [for profit], taken from deceased recipients, and the [new holders] were then sent to Bergen Belsen and Vittel instead of Auschwitz. . . . We even sent large numbers of Salvador papers to the concentration camps Vittel, Bierbach, Westerbork, etc.

Some Jewish organizations were reluctant to get involved in [Mantello's paper distribution], which they considered illegal. Others looked upon this enterprise with envy, for it surpassed their own rescue activities. In his effort to assist refugees, Mantello paid substantial sums out of his own pocket.[42]

Dr. Hans Klee, head of Schweitzerischen Fluechtlings-Hifskomitee, the Swiss Refugee Relief Committee, reenforced this view in his own testimony:

I have to mention a delicate question concerning the activities of all the Jewish organizations who were engaged in rescue efforts. All were of the opinion that any efforts they were not involved in were not valid. . . . *They saw little grace when an outsider intruded into their territory and achieved good results.* These organizations continually stressed that [Mantello's] papers had no utility, even after everyone knew how helpful they were. We therefore kept on sending them regardless of such warnings. *It was simply a matter of the interested parties' jealousy* of those who dared to help—and what is more, did so with great success. (emphasis added)[43]

Maitre Muller, who was in charge of the Salvadoran papers office in Geneva, testified next, providing many details about the entire Salvadoran paper operation: "We had the feeling that the Germans needed such 'foreign nationals' in order to exchange them for Germans in [Latin] America; [without the 'foreigners,'] there were only a few [Latin] Americans in Europe [for them to exchange]. The price for such Latin American papers rose to several thousand Swiss francs apiece, until Mantello put an end to this abuse. Mantello covered all expenses from his own pocket."[44]

Rabbi Zvi Taubes, the chief rabbi of Zurich, who had worked closely with Mantello even before the occupation of Hungary, provided a personal portrait of the man:

Mantello always used to come to me with new plans for the rescue of European Jews. . . . Since he provided his Salvador papers free of charge, it was a great relief no longer to have to pay for the foreign passports and to be able to obtain as many as necessary. Since the outset, *I had the feeling that Mantello had thrown himself into this guerrilla activity with heart and soul, like a man who had escaped from the Gestapo hell himself.* Here I witnessed his singular and, to many, his barely comprehensible behavior. I admit that under normal circumstances here in Switzerland, no one has any appreciation for such guerrilla activities, which may be the basis for much of the misunderstanding [of Mantello]. In Switzerland such a person is known as a hothead. . . .

We had twelve meetings to discuss the circumstances of the train [expected] from Bergen Belsen. While others saw the ceiling for expenses in this venture at a maximum of 5,000 Swiss francs, Mantello asked for 300,000 Swiss francs. I had to ask myself, "Is this man normal?" I had the impression that after all he had gone through, he had lost all sense of the value of money. . . . In him lived the spirit of a Serb partisan or French Maquis [resistance fighter], something beyond our comprehension, but which we could only respect. [emphasis in original)[45]

The final person to testify was Walter Garrett, head of the British Exchange Telegraph, who had been the first to cooperate with Mantello on the press campaign. He began by telling the judges, "It is my duty and honor, though unasked, to present myself to you as a witness."

We [of the British Exchange Telegraph] learned about the [Salvadoran] certificates in question in 1943. During the following months we ascertained that these documents, despite some problems from a strictly legal point of view, resulted in great benefits for the larger number of recipients.

Because we were aware of the fact that certain Latin American circles had set up a flourishing business with passports and certificates (people paid from two to three thousand Swiss francs for such dubious documents), we were determined to find out whether there was any financial arrangement behind the Salvador papers. After careful scrutiny, we established beyond the shadow of a doubt that *Mr. Mantello, whom we came to know on this occasion, had set up a relief organization which was not only absolutely untainted by any selfish or financial interests, but was amazingly successful and effective.* (emphasis in original)

Only after we had convinced ourselves in an incontestable manner that Mr. Mantello and his local collaborators worked selflessly did we give his venture our total support. It was obvious to me that the documents were of dubious legality. At the same time, they were frequently the sole opportunity to deprive Hitler's murderous maniacs of their victims. . . . Our steady contact with Budapest kept us aware of the efficacy of these Salvador papers.

In [June] 1944, Mantello passed on to us the first reports on Auschwitz obtained through intermediaries in Budapest. We immediately gave [them] to the world press. These were the direct cause for President Roosevelt's now-historical appeal, which we dispatched directly to Budapest. . . . Mantello also provided an account of the Hungarian deportations. This was soon followed by an extraordinary [Swiss] press campaign, which resulted in [large-scale] reactions toward this barbarism.[46]

One refugee who was saved by Salvadoran papers concluded his testimony by declaring, "I am convinced that Mantello deserves a monument in Palestine."[47]

The panel concluded its hearings on June 27, 1946. It not only cleared Mantello completely of even the slightest wrongdoing, but also provided a highly complimentary portrait of this much-maligned rescue activist, even going so far as to imply that the accusations of various groups against Mantello were based primarily on envy. The closing statement read in part:

Mr. Mantello was the First Secretary of the Salvador Consulate in Geneva, a post he assumed on August 25, 1942. Already in Bucharest, where he was a textile manufacturer, he had been assigned to the Salvador Consulate [as honorary consul]. Upon his arrival in Switzerland, Mr. Mantello attempted to found a trust company with the help of Jewish organizations such as SIG, the Jewish Agency, the World Jewish Congress, the Joint, and others, which would assist Jews in Nazi-occupied territories. [This plan] never got off the ground due to irreconcilable differences between the Joint and the World Jewish Congress.

During the second half of 1942, he found out that Jews in German-occupied [territories] who had Latin American passports enjoyed special treatment. For these passports one had to pay anywhere from 500 to 3,000 Swiss francs each. This inspired [Mantello] to seek a solution which would provide Jews with such papers for nothing. He successfully persuaded [Col. José A. Castellanos,] the Consul General of the El Salvador Consulate [in Geneva], to approve his issuance of Salvador citizenship papers as a rescue tool. While the Consul General's original agreement limited the number of such papers, they quickly dropped this limitation as the requests began to mushroom. Such requests came from individuals as well as from Jewish organizations, who sent [papers] to Holland, Belgium, France, Poland, and Czechoslovakia, and even to some [incarcerated] in Germany. . . . At first they averaged about fifty a month, which rapidly increased to hundreds, and eventually even more.

During the summer of 1944, a very large number of such papers were sent to Hungary via mail or couriers. After a while, the Swiss representative in Hungary [Consul Lutz] provided Swiss [protective] papers which confirmed that these holders were Salvadoran citizens and that they were under the protection of the Swiss Embassy. At first, the Swiss Federal Political Department remained cautious in regard to these papers, leaving it to the discretion of the local Swiss representatives. By August 1944, the local Swiss representative [Lutz] was instructed to give protection to 5,000 holders of these papers. Given the large number of additional requests and his limited staff, he was unable to give protection to all.

It is certain that Mr. Mantello initiated the operation for the issuance of Salvador papers, as well as involving himself in their delivery to the applicants. . . . While these documents were not equally effective in all countries and the owners were sometimes subject to arbitrary treatment . . . the majority were sent to Hungary, where a vast number were rescued, thanks to these citizenship papers.

There is no reason to suppose that Mr. Mantello and his close collaborators would have organized the issuance of Salvadoran papers with the intention of gaining profits from them, nor that the operation per se would have been on a for-profit commercial basis. The Commission is of the contrary opinion: that *Mr. Mantello organized the entire operation solely for the purpose of assisting his endangered coreligionists in a totally selfless manner.* (emphasis in original)[48]

Confirming the commission's conclusions was a statement by José Gustavo Guerrero, the esteemed president of the International Court at the Hague and former president of El Salvador. He had carefully observed and supported Mantello and his Salvadoran paper operation from the very outset, and he stated proudly, *"Through the actions of George M. Mantello, the Republic of El Salvador has contributed substantially toward the rescue of Nazi victims"* (emphasis in original).[49]

Another confirmation of Mantello's work was sent by Max Cahn, a refugee in Switzerland who worked as an assistant to Maitre Muller from February 1944 to February 1945. Unable to testify in person, he wrote:

I was particularly active in the production and distribution of the Salvador papers. I made out thousands of Salvador citizenship papers, which were then signed by Mr. Mantello. Whether day or night, there was no time too early or too late for Mr. Mantello to involve himself personally [in the project]. I placed thousands of papers before him to be signed, and never did he receive even one penny [literally, *rappen*] for this. I have the greatest admiration for this man. Mr. Mantello, with the greatest of pleasure, always made these papers available to anyone who asked for them, since he was certain that they were either Jews or other persecuted people.[50]

As the inquiry came to a conclusion, Mantello left the Salvadoran consulate and set his sights elsewhere. One of the first places he sought to visit was Eretz Israel. Two decades had passed since his first trip to the Holy Land as a youth; now he was eager not only to see the country again, but also to follow up on the fate of numerous survivors who were now streaming to their homeland both legally and illegally.

The British, in the light of Mantello's open Zionist sympathies, would not give him a visa, but with the help of the Salvadoran consulate, he was able to get there on his own. Once he arrived, he sent a postcard to the British consul in Switzerland, who had refused him the visa, letting him know that he had accomplished the feat independently. When he returned to Switzerland, the British consul called him up and told him, "The next time you want to go, we'll give you a visa. Don't go illegally." Mantello went to the consul in person and said to him, "I'm a proud man. You didn't give it to me before, and I don't need it now. I'll get the first visa that Israel issues." Mantello did obtain the third visa issued by the provisional Israeli government and showed it to the dumbfounded British consul, who replied, "You're amazing!"[51]

Mantello returned to Israel in 1947 and again in 1948. On these visits, he discovered a new venue for his philanthropic instincts; this time the Israeli government itself benefited from his largesse. The Israelis needed arms and ammunition quickly. In 1948, Mantello spoke to Ben-Gurion's military attaché and discovered that the Israelis had been "shopping" for arms in Switzerland. The problem was that they did not have immediate cash and would have to purchase on credit. Ben-Gurion gave Mantello his "wish list." Immediately upon his return to Switzerland, Mantello contacted one of his Swiss friends, an arms manufacturer named Mr. Burla, and arranged credit for the Israelis through him.

Of German origin, Burla had been a German army officer before Hitler's rise and had developed a large arms industry. Later, he had fled to Switzerland. Because he had once traded with the Germans, he was indebted to Mantello for helping him get off the British blacklist. As usual, Mantello never accepted any of the personal rewards Burla offered him, preferring instead to use his connections on behalf of his beloved Israel. Burla was glad to help with the financing of Israeli arms, making them available on credit at a time when every bullet had to be paid for in cash. In all, the Israelis purchased about $800,000 (U.S.) worth of weaponry at the extraordinarily low rate of 2 percent, when the going rate was about 30 percent.[52] Mantello also suggested to the Israelis that they could get much more credit at the low rate of 3 percent by establishing a bank in Switzerland, and he went into partnership with the government in establishing the Swiss-Israel Bank in 1950.

Dr. Norman Lamm, president of Yeshiva University, awarding
honorary doctorate to George Mantello in 1989. Courtesy
of Yeshiva University Photo Department.

Postscript

Although the case against him had been closed, Mantello left Switzerland in 1956 to make his permanent residence in Rome. Throughout the balance of his long life, he maintained close relationships with numerous friends and relatives in Israel, traveling there at least twice a year. His love for Israel prevented him from testifying against Kastner at his trial in 1956. Although he had some criticism of Kastner's actions in Budapest, Kastner represented the Jewish Agency, which was the voice of the Mapai Labor Party of Israel, and Mantello felt that speaking against him would reflect poorly on the government. He therefore chose to abstain, not wanting to damage the success of the Jewish Agency in building the fledgling state.[53]

During his lifetime, Mantello received no recognition for his valiant efforts either from historians or from the State of Israel itself; only during his last few years was he the recipient of a few honors in the United States. He passed away in Rome in 1992 and is buried in his beloved Israel, outside Jerusalem.

Afterword

> There are those who achieve immortality in a mere moment.
>
> Talmud

Before the war, George Mantello had been a successful businessman and financier, content in his personal life and secure in his place in society, with no thought of making a broader imprint on the world. This was true even during the two years that he served as honorary consul for El Salvador, from 1939 to 1941. When he miraculously eluded Nazi clutches and escaped to Switzerland, he thought only of respite, hoping to sit out the war in his beautiful, adopted homeland. However, the deep commitment to his fellow Jews, and to Zionist and democratic ideals, which had been nurtured by his family and his traditional roots, made him particularly sensitive to the suffering of others and did not permit him this luxury. Instead, this nonestablishment Jew was inspired to achieve the impossible: to inform the world of the nightmare of Auschwitz and to halt the trains that were headed there from Budapest.

Mantello brought to his mission a keen business acumen and diplomatic expertise, as well as enormous energy and drive; but he could not have achieved his great feats all on his own. His rescue efforts required the full cooperation of a host of collaborators, most of whom were non-Jews. Part of Mantello's genius was to be able to bring out the very finest instincts in this select group of individuals, which included, as we have seen, diplomats, clergymen, newsmen, intelligence officials, underground workers, and concentration camp escapees—an elite and frequently unacknowledged assembly of exceptional humanitarians.

Backing the efforts of these heroic people, shining in its accomplishments during the tragic period of mid-1944, lay Switzerland itself. Not its perfidious banks, which dealt in and retained the gold taken from Jewish victims; not its government or the IRC, both of which had achieved well-deserved notoriety for their failure to act on behalf of the Jews. Rather, the prize goes to the Swiss people as a whole. Their moral support enabled Mantello and a group of courageous editors and publishers to create the extraordinary press and church campaigns that defied an indifferent, if not hostile, government to spread the news of the monstrosity of Auschwitz to virtually every corner of Switzerland. These editors and theologians rose up to attack the German and Hungarian atrocities, and even challenged their own government and its political arm, the International Red Cross, for their disinterest in the fate of Hitler's victims. They roused every segment of Swiss society to indignation: Protestants and Catholics, men and women, young and old, students and professors, conservatives and radicals. With their strong pens and moral courage, they were able to reverse the placidity of their compatriots and promote them into the vanguard of rescue in what was truly Switzerland's finest hour.

Barely 1 percent of the articles in this press campaign ever appeared in the media of the Allied or neutral countries, and the ones that were published did not have the emotional tone and moral fervor found in most of the Swiss articles. This lack of interest is best illustrated by the fact that only one article about the Auschwitz Report ever made the front page of the *New York Times*.[1] One can only speculate about the results that could have been achieved had the United States followed Switzerland's lead, had people poured into the streets to demonstrate against America's indifference to the deportation of Hungarian Jews, had they raised their voices at the time of their greatest power to defend their fellow human beings across the ocean. Given President Roosevelt's extreme sensitivity to political pressure, especially during the heated 1944 election campaign, it is difficult to imagine how he could have refused to carry out Weissmandl's relatively minor request to bomb the rail lines to Auschwitz. It is painfully difficult to understand how those who had the power and authority to halt the murder of so many innocent people remained silent.

An additional significance of the Swiss press campaign is seen from the evaluation of the news stories about Auschwitz that appeared in July 1944. Lipstadt noted:

> One cannot attribute the paucity of press coverage on Hungarian Jews to skepticism. It may have been that by the summer of 1944 most journalists had simply tired of this story even though they had never really paid it much attention.

It was a familiar tale, and its very familiarity rendered it unworthy of page one or even page ten. *It is possible that if the press had raised a major outcry, noth-ing would have happened.* The Allies were as intent on adhering to a policy of rescue through victory as the Nazis were intent on destroying the remnants of European Jewry before their defeat. . . . But the press does not decide how it will treat a story on the basis of whether attention to a topic will effect a change in policy. The press pays attention to those stories it considers significant. Even at this late date, for much of the American press this news was still a minor sidelight. (emphasis added)[2]

Lipstadt was unaware, as are most historians of the Holocaust, of the extraor-dinary Swiss press and church campaigns, and especially of the activist roles played by Mantello, the great theologians, and a very willing Swiss people, in rescuing the Jews. She could not fathom that a nation's press, let alone the entire nation itself, should want to affect events far away, and that it should succeed in doing so. In this light, one can better appreciate the outstanding optimism displayed by Mantello in the face of apparently insurmountable obstacles, and the incredible drive that he had to inform the world of the horrors of Auschwitz and to halt the deportations of Hungarian Jewry. It is remarkable as well that the great theologians and, above all, the Swiss people themselves, were inspired to make a real difference in the policies of the Allies, the neutral countries, Hungary, and even Germany itself.

Besides the Swiss people and their moral leadership, one must add the extremely valuable support for all of Mantello's rescue efforts by the Salvadoran government and its officials; the Salvadoran consulate in Geneva, especially Consul Colonel I. H. Castellanos, former president of El Salvador José Gus-tavo Guerrero, and finally the government in San Salvador, headed by Presi-dent General Castenendu Castro. Without their early wholehearted support of Mantello's rescue efforts, he could not have issued a single Salvadoran citi-zenship paper and surely not his broader rescue efforts.

The successful rescue efforts of Mantello, the Swiss people, and the Sal-vadoran government are the perfect refutation of William D. Rubinstein's fatal-istic thesis in his book *The Myth of Rescue: Why the Democracies Could Not Have Saved More Jews from the Nazis.*

George Mantello was able to live out the balance of his life unburdened by his conscience. At a time when he was needed, he did not hesitate to do every-thing in his power to assure the survival of the Jews of Budapest. He was the driving force behind the incredible transformation of the Swiss people, who carried on their newly found tolerance for refugees long into the postwar era; he was the catalyst behind the protective papers operation that saved countless lives. Although the Holocaust surely showed the depths to which humanity could sink, he, his colleagues, the Swiss people, and Salvadoran officials were proof of the lofty heights to which it could rise. He was like a meteor that streaks through the sky to illuminate the horizon for a brief moment, and then disappears into oblivion. For a short, blazing moment, Mantello lit up the darkness of the Holocaust, reaching the apex of rescue—and then faded into the recesses of history.

Abbreviations

Notes

Bibliography

Index

Abbreviations

Notes

Introduction: Switzerland's Finest Hour

1. Although not subject to the draft, young Jewish men were taken into the labor battalions, and many thousands died during their dangerous work on the eastern front.

2. The War Refugee Board, established by President Roosevelt in January of 1944, was a governmental agency dedicated to the rescue of European Jews.

3. Although more recent estimates of the number of victims give a figure as low as 1.1 million, the reports at the time use the number of 1.765 million.

4. Although smaller deportations had already taken place in Hungary during April 1944, the mass deportations of ten to twelve thousand per day began on May 15.

5. Although the International Red Cross had obtained information earlier they never made it available to the Jewish organizations.

6. Mandl was Mantello's original family name.

7. *Yad Vashem Studies* 1:125–52.

8. While his older brother Josef retained the original family name of "Mandl," George changed it to "Mandel," while as a diplomat in Switzerland he changed his name to Mantello. After the war, and for the rest of his life, he and his children retained the combination of "Mandel-Mantello."

9. San Salvador is the capital of El Salvador and is frequently (mistakenly) used interchangeably in this text, as well as in cited documents.

10. *Yad Vashem Studies* 1:125.

11. Winant to State, March 2, 1944. Papers of War Refugee Board [WRB]. Franklin Delano Roosevelt Library (FDRL), Hyde Park, N.Y.

12. See esp. Richard D. Rubinstein, *Myths of Rescue: Why the Democracies Could Not Have Saved More Jews from the Nazis* (London: Routledge, 1997).

1. Background

1. Copy of letter in Mantello papers [MP], part of my archives.

2. Mantello interview. This, and virtually all subsequent interviews with Mantello, were conducted on tape. In my possession.

3. Mantello displayed similar courage in his old age. One night, when he was more than eighty years old, four armed robbers broke into his house in Rome. They repeatedly demanded the key to the strongbox, but Mantello had forgotten where he had put it. At one point, one of them hit Mantello's younger son on the head with a gun and threatened to shoot him if Mantello did not produce the key. Mantello struck the robber in the face and yelled at him, "Don't you dare hurt my son!" One of the robbers struck Mantello on the head, inflicting a wound that required five or six stitches.

4. Veesenmayer had entered the German diplomatic service in 1932 and was active in the Balkans. He was attached to the German legation at Zagreb in the beginning of 1941. *Encyclopedia of the Holocaust,* ed. by Israel Guttman (New York, 1990) [*EH*], 4:1562.

5. Mantello interv. Cf. also Jen Levai, *Abscheu und Grauen: vor dem Genocid in aller Welt* [Levai, *Abscheu*] (New York: Diplomatic Press, 1968) 10–12.

6. It was this act that prevented the Joint from sending in money to support starving Jews in Shanghai or German-occupied countries until the end of 1943, when the State Department changed the rules under certain circumstances.

7. Mantello interview. See also Levai, *Abscheu,* 12–14.

8. Mantello interview. See also Levai, *Abscheu,* 14.

9. Mantello interview.

10. As Mantello explained it, couriers from such countries as Portugal (which actively cooperated with the British and other Allied powers) and Salvador carried the instruments in their diplomatic pouches to Lisbon and from there to Bermuda, traveling for six days by ship. Although the British and American intelligence documents have not been made available, we can surmise as much from the close relationship Mantello maintained with Allen Dulles and Commodore Freddie West, who provided indispensable assistance to Mantello in his rescue efforts. Other evidence includes the postwar testimony given on Mantello's behalf by Walter Garrett, head of the British Exchange Telegraph, which was closely connected to the British intelligence.

Dulles was head of the Swiss section of the Office of Strategic Services (OSS), the predecessor of the CIA. The head of the OSS was "Wild Bill" Donovan, appointed by President Roosevelt in 1941. Commodore West was a major British intelligence officer in Switzerland.

Although Mantello recalled the route for the chronographs to get to Britain via Bermuda, I have found evidence only from Swiss documents that accuse Mantello of making large purchases of Swiss chronographs and shipping them to New York. It is possible that he used both the New York and the Bermuda connections.

11. After the war, the couple was divorced, and Mantello remarried and had two other children, a son, Andrea, and a daughter, Suzannah.

12. Mantello retained this courage in his later years. In the 1950s, he and his elder son, Enrico, went to examine a large estate near Geneva whose gate had been left open for them. As they were walking across the grounds, two German shepherds leaped from a copse and raced toward them, barking furiously. Mantello maintained his calm, appearing annoyed that he had been interrupted in the middle of speaking. When the dogs came

close, he screamed at them in Hungarian, and the dogs stopped dead in their tracks. He walked over to them and patted their heads. Then he briskly turned around and continued his conversation with his son as the subdued animals yawned and lay down on the grass.

2. Switzerland as an Information Center

1. For a very brief survey of Switzerland as an island of refuge, see Leni Yahil, *The Holocaust: The Fate of European Jewry* [Yahil, *Holocaust*] (New York: Oxford Univ. Press, 1990), 595–99. Another article by Yahil, which clarifies the issue of rescue and rescue potential in both Switzerland and Sweden, is "The Historiography of the Refugee Problem and of Rescue Efforts in the Neutral Countries," in *The Historiography of the Holocaust Period,* ed. Israel Gutman and Gideon Grell (Jerusalem: Yad Vashem, 1998), 513–34. For a good survey of the role of the representatives of major Jewish organizations in Switzerland, see Walter Laqueur, *The Terrible Secret* [Laqueur, *Secret*] (Boston: Little, Brown, 1980), esp. chaps. 2, 6.

2. During the crucial summer of 1944, Dr. Posner temporarily ran the Palamt as Dr. Scheps completed his term as a reservist in the Swiss army. Most historians have based their views of Dr. Posner's rescue efforts on interviews with him, ignoring the primary role played by Dr. Scheps. (During the 1960s and 1970s, Dr. Posner served on the Board of Yad Vashem.)

For Dr. Scheps, see correspondence of Dr. Scheps to me, Sept. 3, 1990. Included are his comments on Posner's rescue claims, made in the 1980s to the historians Martin Gilbert, Walter Laqueur, Anita Shapira, and Yehuda Bauer, as well as Dr. Chaim Posner and his son Avi (who changed the spelling of his last name to Pazner). This correspondence is in my possession, courtesy of Dr. Scheps.

For an example of a historian's error in regard to Posner, see Randolph L. Braham, *Politics of Genocide: The Holocaust in Hungary* [Braham, *Genocide*] (New York, 1981), 697, 712. There, Braham labels Posner "co-director" of Palamt.

3. See Bronia Klibanski, *Archives of Dr. A. Silberschein (Record Group M-20),* Yad Vashem Central Archives [YVA] (Jerusalem, 1984), esp. 2–5. See also Bronia Klibanski, "RELICO: Relief Committee for the War-Stricken Population," in *EH,* 3, 1254–55; "Rescue Efforts with the Assistance of International Organizations: Documents from the Archives of Dr. A. Silberschein," *Yad Vashem Studies* [*YVS*] 7, (Jerusalem: Yad Vashem, 1970), 69–79.

4. This strategy of the use of Latin American papers was initiated by the Sternbuchs. See chap. 3.

5. For Lichtheim, see Laqueur, *Secret,* et passim. His voluminous papers are found in the Central Zionist Archives [CZA], Jerusalem.

6. See my taped interview with Mr. Natan Schwalb. Because, as head of Hehalutz in Switzerland, Schwalb gave Saly Mayer a copy of virtually everything he received, hundreds of copies of Schwalb's papers can be found in the papers of Saly Mayer, in the Joint

archives [JDCA] in New York. Schwalb's own immense collection of papers is in the archives of the Lavon Institute for Labour Research [AML] in Tel Aviv.

7. For a thorough analysis of Stephen Wise's role during this period, see David Kranzler, "Stephen S. Wise and the Holocaust," in *Reverence, Righteousness, and Rahamanut: Essays in Memory of Rabbi Dr. Leo Jung,* ed. Jacob J. Schacter (Northvale, N.J.: Jason Aronson, 1992), 155–92. See p. 156 for a list of other perspectives on Wise. For information on these and other representatives, see Laqueur, *Secret,* esp. chap. 6.

8. For a detailed and highly sympathetic portrait of Saly Mayer, see Yehuda Bauer, *American Jewry and the Holocaust: The American Jewish Joint Distribution Committee, 1939–1945* (Detroit: Wayne State Univ. Press, 1981), esp. chap. 18. Bauer was the "official" historian of the Joint, which closed all its papers for years until he completed his official history. The Saly Mayer papers remained closed to all scholars for years after the rest of the Joint papers were opened. Access to the official minutes of the Joint are still not open to other historians, though copies of individual meetings are found among other papers. For a different perspective on Saly Mayer, see David Kranzler, *Heroine* and *Thy Brother's Blood.*

9. This is evident in the papers of most Jewish organizations.

10. See Kranzler, "The Role in Relief and Rescue During the Holocaust by the Jewish Labor Committee," in *American Jewry During the Holocaust,* ed. Seymour Maxwell Finger [Kranzler, "JLC"] (New York: American Jewish Commission on the Holocaust, 1984), Appendix 4-2. See also the Robert F. Wagner Labor Archives, New York Univ., *The Papers of the Jewish Labor Committee,* ed. Arieh Lebowitz and Gail Malmgreen; *Archives of the Holocaust: An International Collection of Selected Documents,* 14 (New York: Garland, 1993).

11. Kranzler, "JLC," 11.

12. The JLC also helped the Vaad Hatzalah, the Orthodox Rabbis' Rescue Committee, arrange for the Soviet Union's approval of the shipment of food packages to friends and relatives in Siberia, Tashkent, and Samarkand. Kranzler, "JLC," 19. For the Vaad Hatzalah, see n. 13.

13. For the establishment of the Vaad Hatzalah by Rabbi Eliezer Silver, who served on the presidium of the Union of Orthodox Rabbis of the United States and Canada, see the good but journalistic account in *Churban und Rettun* (New York: Vaad Hatzalah Book Committee, 1957), sec. 2, chap. 2. Rabbi Silver was joined in 1940 by Rabbi Abraham Kalmanowitz and in 1941 by Rabbi Aaron Kotler, forming the presidium of the Vaad Hatzalah.

Unless noted otherwise, the term Agudath Israel in this work refers to the three combined parts of the organization: (1) World Agudath Israel, the international parent organization, (2) national branches, and (3) Agudah Youth, most of whose members were in their twenties. Agudah Youth was particularly active in the United States.

14. For the early rescue activities by Recha Sternbuch and her Swiss accomplices, see Kranzler, *Heroine,* esp. chaps. 3–4.

15. See Kranzler, *Heroine,* chap. 5. After 1941, Recha's husband, Isaac, who ran the fam-

ily's small business, became involved in rescue affairs, helping with paperwork and eventually playing a role in post-1943 rescue efforts. See also Kranzler, *Thy Brother's Blood,* et passim. For the conflict between Rabbi Kalmanowitz and the Joint concerning his willingness to transfer funds illegally in order to save Jewish lives in Shanghai and Europe, see David Kranzler, *Japanese, Nazis, and Jews: The Jewish Refugee Community of Shanghai, 1938–1945* [Kranzler, *JNJ*] (New York: Yeshiva Univ. Press, 1976); *Thy Brother's Blood,* 54–57.

16. See Nathan Eck, "The Rescue of Jews with the Aid of Passports and Citizenship Papers of Latin American States," *YVS* 1 [Eck, "LA Papers"] (Jerusalem: Yad Vashem, 1957), 125–52. Interview with Eli Sternbuch. He started his Latin American paper venture with Paraguayan passports, which at first entailed only nominal expenses. After a few months, when this venture was taken over by the Polish legation, the price skyrocketed.

17. Dr. Kuhl came to Switzerland from Poland as a young man and wrote his dissertation on Polish-Swiss commerce not long before the war. He was assisted by the Polish legation, which gave him entrée to its facilities, including its diplomatic code and pouch. He developed a friendship with Polish ambassador Lados, who provided him with much information. See Kranzler, *Thy Brother's Blood,* 200–2.

18. Ibid. See also Kranzler, *Heroine,* et passim. See also Laqueur, *Secret,* 178–79. See Carl Ludwig, *Die Fluchtlingspolitik der Schweiz Seit 1933 bis Zur Gegenwart (1957)* (Bern, 1957), 234–35.

19. Oral interview with Julius Kuhl and Eli Sternbuch. See also Laqueur, *Secret,* 178–79. Kuhl's papers are part of my archives. Courtesy of Dr. Kuhl.

20. See esp. Kranzler, *Heroine,* chap. 9. I was unable to find out Mr. Huegly's first name.

21. Kranzler, *TBB,* 191–93.

22. See *Fifth Agudah Reports,* 3–4.

23. Mantello interview.

24. Interviews with George Mantello and Maitre Muller.

25. See *Fifth Agudah Report,* 3–4. Muller interview. See also correspondence between Goodman and Mantello in the Mantello papers [MP].

26. Laqueur, *Secret,* 136–37. For the complete text of the Bund Report, see Yehuda Bauer, "When Did They Know?," *Midstream* (Apr. 1968), 57–63.

27. Laqueur, *Secret,* 115.

28. Ibid.

29. For the text, see Arthur Morse, *While Six Million Died: A Chronicle of American Apathy* (New York: Random House, 1967), 8.

30. Monty Noam Penkower, *The Jews Were Expendable: Free World Diplomacy and the Holocaust* (Chicago: Univ. of Illinois Press, 1983), 60–62. Like a number of other Jewish representatives, Riegner tended to focus on his own role. Thus, he refused to reveal the name of his source, the German hero Eduard Schulte, even after Schulte's death, when the excuse of endangering Schulte's safety no longer existed. Based on his interview with

Dr. Chaim Posner, Penkower claims that Posner obtained this information secondhand from Prof. Edgar Salin, and in turn passed it on to Sagalowitz, head of the Swiss-Jewish news agency in Zurich, who gave it to Riegner.

31. See Morse, *While Six Million Died,* chaps. 1–2. See also David S. Wyman, *The Abandonment of the Jews: America and the Holocaust,* 1941–1945 (New York: Pantheon, 1985), chap. 3; Penkower, *Expendable,* chap. 3.

32. See Kranzler, "Wise," 177–79. See also Kranzler, *Heroine,* chap. 8.

33. The Orthodox were the only Jews to take up the offer by the Polish government-in-exile to make use of this marvelous but illegal means of worldwide communications between the United States, Switzerland, and Turkey. This rescue tool was shunned by all the other Jewish organizations. See Kranzler, *Thy Brother's Blood,* et passim, esp. 203–4. See *Morgenthau Diaries* [MD], Feb. 28, 1945, 2. In New York, Dr. Isaac Lewin, a representative of both Agudath Israel and Vaad Hatzalah, was the intermediary between the Polish government-in-exile and its Polish embassy in Washington, which transmitted the secret cables to Dr. Lewin at the Agudath Israel office in New York.

See Isaac Lewin, "Attempts at Rescuing European Jews with the Help of Polish Diplomatic Missions During World War II, Part I," *Polish Review,* 22:4 (1977), 3–7.

34. Laqueur, *Secret,* 177–79. Kuhl interview; Landau interview.

35. Laqueur, *Secret,* 82, 117.

36. For the cable's impact on the Nuremberg trials, see John Fox, "The Jewish Factor in British War Crimes Policy in 1942," *English Historical Review* 92, no. 1 (Jan. 1977), 82–106.

37. Lewin, "Polish Rescue," 1:5–7.

38. Ibid.

39. Isaac Lewin, ed., *Comfort, Comfort My People: A Collection of Essays and Speeches by Moreinu Jacob Rosenheim* (New York: Research Institute of Religious Jewry, 1984), 251–55.

40. Ibid., 252; Wyman, *Abandonment,* 45–46.

41. See Kranzler, "Wise," 177–79. See also Kranzler, *Thy Brother's Blood,* 91–93; Wyman, *Abandonment,* 47.

42. Laqueur, *Secret,* 115, 104–5, 131–32.

43. See Kranzler, "Wise," 178–79.

44. All historians have misread a number of the code words in the Sternbuch letters. For example, "Eisenzweig" does not refer to "ironworkers" but to Guta Eisenzweig, the first recipient of a Paraguayan passport, who later married Eli Sternbuch in 1944; and "Mrs. Gefen" is her grandmother. Nor does Riegner identify the Sternbuchs as the source of the crucial letters. They are simply referred to as "friends in St. Gallen." Morse, *Six Million,* 15–16.

45. See. Kranzler, *Thy Brother's Blood,* esp. 98–99. Although the committee was resuscitated in March 1943 under the name of "The Joint Emergency Committee to Save European Jewry," it lasted only until December of 1943, when Wise, using illegal political maneuvering, succeeded in permanently dissolving it.

46. When Weissmandl sent his pleas for money to effect his rescue plans, he used much harsher language with his fellow Orthodox contacts than with the non-Orthodox,

demanding, rather than requesting or begging, for help. For example, see Michael Ber Weissmandl, *Min Hametzar* (Heb.) (New York: n.p., n.d.), his classic, albeit unfinished, work on the Holocaust, 56, 73.

47. See esp. Robert Rozett, "Slovakia," in the *EH,* 1364–70.

48. See also Fuchs, *Unheeded Cry* (New York, 1984); Livia Rothkirchen, *The Destruction of Slovak Jewry: A Documentary History* (Jerusalem: Yad Vashem, 1961), 7–51. Although Rothkirchen is technically correct in describing Fleischmann as the head of the Working Group, Weissmandl devised virtually all the rescue ideas and imparted the sense of urgency so frequently cited.

In fact, Weissmandl designated Fleischmann head of the Working Group. His objective was twofold. First, he reasoned that because Fleischmann was a representative of both the Joint and WIZO (Women's International Zionist Organization, the women's division of the Joint in Slovakia), the representatives in Switzerland would be more amenable to her entreaties. Second, he assumed that, as a woman, she would not arouse a sense of competition and jealousy. See Weissmandl, *Min Hametzar,* 49, 53, 77. See also my taped interviews with Andre Steiner.

49. For Weissmandl's communications with Griffel, see Griffel's unpublished *Memoir,* 27. Copy in my archives, courtesy of the late Mrs. Dora Griffel. On Fleischmann's direct access to Switzerland, see Fuchs, *Unheeded Cry,* 70.

50. Saly Mayer papers. JDCA.

51. Copies of such reports were given me by Mr. Schwalb. See below, chap. 5.

52. See Roswell McClelland, "List of Expenditures, 5/1–10/31/44," 7. Sent on Nov. 27, 1944. On May 11, 1944, McClelland wrote: "Schwalb's organization is doing very credible work in rescuing people and I should accordingly recommend that we send this wire for him. I think it would be worthwhile for the WRB to foot the bill, as the Hehalutz group, the left-wing of the Zionists, is none too well off." WRB. See also McClelland to General O'Dwyer (Pehle's successor as head of the WRB), May 30, 1975, sec. 4, which lists two expenditures of $60,000 on Dec. 2, 1944, and $50,000 on Feb. 1, 1945, for Hehalutz.

53. McClelland's voluminous papers (WRB) are replete with such reports sent by representatives of all Jewish organizations.

54. Gerhart Riegner to me, May 15, 1990. Riegner also did not send copies of his reports to Jerusalem. Ibid. See also Yahil, "Historiography," 519.

55. Lichtheim to Dobkin, July 3, 1944. Although Dobkin, cohead of the Jewish Agency's Immigration Department, was normally stationed in Jerusalem, he was then on a mission in Lisbon. RG-L-22/135, Richard Lichtheim papers [LP], Central Zionist Archives [CZA] Jerusalem. See also Lichtheim to L. Lauterbach, May 5, 1944. LP. RG-L22/149. CZA. For Weissmandl's perspective on the disunity in Switzerland, as contrasted with the prewar European situation, when a greater measure of unity existed, see Weissmandl, *Min Hametzar,* 87–89.

56. Kubowitzki to Dr. Irving Dwork, Jan. 18, 1945, WJCongress Papers, RG H-318 [WJCP], American Jewish Archives [AJA], Cincinnati, Ohio.

57. Mantello interview. Herman Landau interview. Mr. Landau was the secretary of HIJEFS.

3. Early Salvadoran Papers

1. Eck, "LA Papers," 125–52. See also Kranzler, *Thy Brother's Blood*, 102–4; Mantello's Post War Inquiry [PW Inq.] Jan. 20, 1946, p. 3. This important rescue tool has not been given proper attention by historians.

2. Interview. Eli and Guta Sternbuch and Dr. Hillel Seidman. See also letters to Sternbuch from Warsaw, which served as major evidence regarding the mass deportation from the Warsaw Ghetto in Aug. 1942. See chap. 2.

3. Lichtheim to Jewish Agency, May 5, 1944. Papers of the World Jewish Congress. RG H-105. AJA.

4. See Bronia Klibanski, "Relief Committee for the War-Stricken Jewish Population" (RELICO), *EH*, 3, 1254–55.

5. Eck, "LA Passports," 126–27.

6. Ibid.

7. John Winant to State Department, March 2, 1944; *Morgenthau Diaries* [MD] 705:281.

8. Mantello to George Brunschvig, president of SIG. He was a judge in Mantello's Postwar Inquiry Nov. 20, 1945. See below, chap. 13.

9. Mantello interview. See also PW Inq., Jan. 1, 1946, p. 1.

10. Mantello, PW Inq., Nov. 20, 1945.

11. Mantello interview. See also Levai, *Abscheu*, 436; PW Inq., Nov. 20, 1945.

12. Mantello interview.

13. See chap. 11.

14. Mantello interview. See also Lutz testimony, PW Inq.

15. Muller to Mantello, Oct. 10, 1945.

16. Mantello interview. See copies in MP.

17. Muller to Saly Mayer, Administrative File #5, June 7, 1944, JDCA. See also Mantello interview.

18. Copies of these instructions are in the MP.

19. Mantello interview. Copies of both originals as well as photostatic copies are in the MP.

20. Joel Brand was a member of the Zionist Vaada. See his book, *Desperate Mission: Joel Brand's Story* (New York: Criterion Books, 1958), chap. 5. For the Vaada's rescue activities, see chap. 4. See also p. 43. A common error, even in some documents, is the confusion of the capital, *San* Salvador, with the country, *El* Salvador.

21. Mantello interview; Muller interview. See also Mantello to Brunschvig, PW Inq., Nov. 20, 1945. See also Muller to Mantello, Oct. 1, 1945. For Eis's death, see (Jacob Rosenheim) *Fifth Agudah Report*, 3.

22. PW Inq., Jan. 20, 1946. The notary was usually a man named Jeandin, whose fee ranged from seven to ten Swiss francs, while the translation into French was carried out by a Mr. Bolle. Ibid., 33.

23. PW Inq., Jan. 20, 1946, p. 3.

24. Lutz testimony, PW Inq.

25. Mantello at PW Inq., Nov. 20, 1945. See also chap. 5.

26. John Winant to State Department, Mar. 2, 1944, *MD* 705:281.

27. Lewenstein to Mantello, Feb. 2, 1944. MP. Incidentally, this same rabbi served as the liaison between the Dutch Queen Wilhelmina and Mantello, in Mantello's efforts to obtain recognition for the Salvadoran Papers. Mantello interview.

28. Kornfein to Mantello, Feb. 13, 1944. MP.

29. Taubes to Mantello, Dec. 16, 1943, MP. Rabbi Taubes was eventually to work closely with Mantello in his press campaign to publicize the Auschwitz Report. See chaps. 6–7.

30. See copy in the MP.

31. Abraham Shulman, *The Case of Hotel Polski* (New York: Holocaust Library, 1982), 32.

32. Ibid., 25–28. Also interviews with Guta (Eisenzweig) Sternbuch and Dr. Hillel Seidman.

33. Shulman, *Hotel Polsky,* 27.

34. Guta Sternbuch interview. Guta was among three survivors of the 238 inmates in Vittel, who were sent to Auschwitz in April and May of 1944. Guta, her mother, Sarah Eisenzweig, and Dr. Seidman hid out during the deportation and survived the war. She married Eli Sternbuch, who had sent her the Paraguayan passports originally.

35. State Department cable to the American embassy in Asunción, Paraguay, Apr. 24, 1944. *MD,* 718:86. See also *MD,* Apr. 6. 1944, 718:93. Only Paraguay and Bolivia were represented by Spain as a protective power. The rest of the Latin American countries and Great Britain were represented by Switzerland for the use of Palestine certificates. See J. Klahr Huddle (counselor to the American legation), to Richard Lichtheim, Apr. 22, 1944, RG 55, WRB.

According to historian Bronia Klibanski, in July of 1943—at about the time that the Jews in Pawiak Prison were to be sent to Vittel—a United States diplomat in Bern named Madone announced that the protective papers were illegal because they had been issued without the knowledge of the foreign offices of the countries involved. In consequence of Madone's statement, the South American governments declared these passports invalid.

Madone was director of the United States consular division and representative of the Pan-American Alliance in Switzerland, and part of the American legation in Bern. Klibanski, "RELICO," *EH* 3:1255. Mantello considered him an anti-Semite. Mantello interview. Although Madone may have made the above statement, I disagree on the basis for Germany's rescinding its recognition of the Latin American papers; rather, I attribute the German policy change to Paraguay's refusal to accept Jews with Paraguayan passports in exchange for Germans in Paraguay. See below.

36. See Sternbuch's cable to Rosenheim, Dec. 15, 1955. SP. Copies of all the papers in my archives. See also undated document [ca. Dec. 11, 1943] SMP. RG-25. JDCA.

37. See Sternbuch cable to Rosenheim, Dec. 15, 1955. SP. Copies of the Sternbuch papers in my archives.

38. For the entire episode, see Kranzler, *Thy Brother's Blood*, 7–11.

39. Following Torah law, when lives were at stake, these Orthodox rabbis and laymen traveled on the Sabbath and the Jewish holidays, even on Yom Kippur, the holiest day of the year. State Department officials themselves realized the severity of the situation when they saw the rabbis travel on these days, which under normal circumstances is a serious violation of Jewish law.

The three rabbis at this meeting with Morgenthau were Abraham Kalmanowitz, Shabse Frankel, and Baruch Korff. Korff, at twenty-six, was the youngest, an American-educated and highly sophisticated individual with an uncanny sense of public relations. He was a speechwriter since 1937 for Speaker of the House John McCormack, of Massachusetts, and was also very close to Sen. John Mead of New York. These two powerful American political figures, sympathetic to the cause of the Jewish plight in Europe and supportive of Korff, provided him with the clout necessary to deal with both Morgenthau and Secretary of State Cordell Hull, which he used fully in his campaign to help save the Jews in Nazi-dominated Europe. One must remember that during those days, one could not get to see members of Congress, let alone a member of the cabinet. Moreover, no one, except Rabbi Stephen S. Wise, ever got to see the president, and, for his own rationale, explained below, Wise would not press Roosevelt for this and other Holocaust-related catastrophes. See Kranzler, "Wise." For the above meeting, see Kranzler, *Thy Brother's Blood*, 10–11, and Baruch Korff's *Flight from Fear* (New York: Elmar Publisher, 1953).

40. MD, Apr. 7, 1944, 718:221.

41. State Department to America's embassy in Asunción, Paraguay, Apr. 24, 1944. This detailed cable refers to the earlier, briefer requests, which had not spelled out the issuing countries' lack of responsibilities. RG 46, WRB.

42. Ibid., 2–4.

43. See below, chap. 11.

44. Ibid. See also a foreign office memo of June 13, 1944, which reiterated America's interest in using the Latin American papers for rescue objects. Swiss Federal Police files. RG E 2001 (D)/3:484. Bundesarchiv, Bern [BB].

45. See chap. 2.

46. Interviews with Mantello and his son, Enrico. Dr. Rothmund was the primary bureaucratic figure behind Switzerland's successful request to affix a *J* to every Jew's passport. His principal political supporter was Federal Councilor Dr. Eduard von Steiger. This "racial" act was implemented in 1938 so that Switzerland could distinguish between the "good" Germans entering the open border between Germany and Switzerland, and "racial" refugees, that is, Jews. This resulted in a policy known by its French term, *refoulement*, whereby Swiss border guards sent thousands of Jewish refugees fleeing from Aus-

tria, Germany, and, later, occupied France back across the border into German hands, where they met with certain death. See David Kranzler (with Joseph Friedenson), *Heroine of Rescue* (New York: Mesorah Press, 1984), esp. chaps. 1–4. See index in Kranzler, *Thy Brother's Blood,* Switzerland, refugee policy.

For a thorough Swiss analysis of its refugee policy, see (Carl Ludwig,) *Die Fluechtlingspolitik der Schweiz Seit 1933 Bis Zur Gegenwart: Bericht an den Bundesrat* ([Bern:] n.p., [1955]). A more popular perspective is found in Alfred A. Häsler, *The Lifeboat Is Full: Switzerland and the Refugees, 1933–1945* (New York: Funk and Wagnalls, 1969). See also RG E 2001 (D) 3/262. Also E 4264-1988/2/59. BB.

47. For the Swiss perspective on Enrico's illegal entry into Switzerand, see the files of the Swiss Federal Police RG E 2001 (D) 3/262. Also E 4264-1988/2/59. BB.

48. This ambassador was a brother-in-law of Count Ciano, who was a son-in-law of Mussolini.

49. For Rothmund's complaint to Castellanos about Mantello's "unauthorized procedure" to bring in his son, Enrico, see Rothmund to Castellanos, Mar. 10, 1944. E 2001 (D) 1968/74. Bd. 14. Also box 4264/1988/2/59, file P 54015. BB.

4. Jewish Rescue Efforts in Hungary

1. Joel Brand's attempt (in May–July 1944) to carry out Weissmandl's original request to negotiate for the ransoming of Hungarian Jewry trade for $2 million, now transformed into "goods for blood," or ten thousand trucks for 1 million Hungarian Jews. For details, see Brand, *Mission.*

2. For example, the Istanbul branch of the Jewish Agency's Vaad Hahatzalah received pleas from Bratislava for the Allies to bomb Auschwitz, and passed these on to Jerusalem. See Menachem Bader's testimony at the so-called Kastner trial. Sholom Rosenfeld, *Tik Plili 124* [Rosenfeld, *Tik Plili*] (Jerusalem: Karni Publishers, 1955), 50.

3. For example, after Schwalb received his two versions of the Auschwitz Report on May 16, the day after deportations had begun, he went together with Saly Mayer, Gerhart Riegner, and Richard Lichtheim to Monsignor Bernadini, and asked him to intercede with the Holy See. Schwalb interview. See copy of the Auschwitz Report dated May 17 and Schwalb's letter of May 19 to the Jewish Agency, presented to me by Mr. Schwalb. See copy in Schwalb papers, RG IV, 103/104. MLA. Another copy of this version of the Auschwitz Report is found in the SMP, JDCA; also McClelland papers, RG 60, WRB.

4. In the Trianon treaty of 1920, the Allies had split up the Austro-Hungarian empire, resulting in the loss of one-third of its territory and three-fifths of its population. To induce Hungary to join the Axis, the Germans forcibly returned many of these territories to Hungary.

5. Braham, *Politics,* chap. 6, esp. 193–214.

6. Ibid., 199–206. For more details on the massacre in Kamenets-Podolsk, see Braham, "The Kamenets Podolsk and Délvidék Massacres: Prelude to the Holocaust in Hungary," *YVS* 9, (1973):133–56. For the halt in the massacre, see 141–42.

These Jews were forcibly deported in a manner like the deportation of the Jews, who, having crossed the border into Switzerland during the years 1938 to 1944, were returned into German hands. For the Swiss practice of *refoulement,* or returning refugees across the border, see Kranzler, *Heroine,* chaps. 2–3; Kranzler, *TTB,* index Switzerland: refuge policy, esp. 118 ff. For the broader Swiss refugee policy during the Second World War, see *Ludwig Report,* esp. secs. 1–2. Interestingly enough, the Hungarians adopted the Swiss system of alien laws. Braham, "Kamenets," 135.

7. The Hungarian Joint representative was Josef Blum. Livia Rothkirchen, "Hungary— An Asylum for the Refugees," *YVS* 7 (1968):135. See also Braham, *Politics,* 103–10, esp. 109.

8. See Braham, *Politics,* 106–10, esp. 108. For Stern's legalistic attitude and its consequence for the ransom negotiations, see Weissmandl, *Min Hametzar,* 59–60; Brand, *Mission,* 59. For similar legalistic perspectives of the Joint and how they affected relief and rescue efforts, see Kranzler, *Japanese, Nazis, and Jews,* 461–63, 558–59; Kranzler, *Thy Brother's Blood,* 50–51, 54–55.

9. Braham, *Politics.* Braham acknowledges that the Orthodox were willing to use extralegal means to help the refugees. See Zehava Schwartz, *The Orthodox Jewish Community in Hungary,* 1939–1945 [Schwartz, *Orthodox Community*] (unpublished Ph.D. dissertation, Ramat Gan: Bar Ilan Univ., 1989); Rudolf Kastner, *Der Kastner Bericht: Über Eichmann's Menschenhandel in Ungarn* (Munich: Kindler Verlag, 1961), 35, 39; "Report on Hungary: March 19–August 9, 1944," by Philip Freudiger et al., in Braham, *Hungarian-Jewish Studies lll* (New York, 1973).

This "Hungarian Report" was authored collectively by three Orthodox leaders: Philip Freudiger, head of the Budapest Orthodox community; Alexander Diamant, deputy chairman of the Budapest Orthodox community; and Gyula Link, a leading member of the Orthodox rescue committee. Link was very helpful in responding to Weissmandl's desperate request for money to ransom the remainder of Slovakian Jewry. See also Weissmandl, *Min Hametzar,* 112. The Hungarian Report was written at the request of Dr. Wilhelm Filderman, head of the Romanian Jewish community. "Hungarian Report," 75. See also Philip Freudiger, "Five Months," in *The Tragedy of Hungarian Jewry: Essays, Documents, Depositions,* ed. Randolph L. Braham (New York: Institute for Holocaust Studies of the City Univ. of New York, 1986), 237–88; Rothkirchen, "Hungary," 135.

10. Brand, *Mission,* chap. 2. The transliteration is that used in *Mission,* 18–91. I prefer the transliteration of *V* (Vaada) rather than *W* (Waada) for the *vav.* See also Randolph L. Braham, "Relief and Rescue Committee of Budapest," *EH,* 1250–54.

11. For the role of the three-man presidium, see Brand, *Mission,* chap. 2. See also Asher Cohen, "Li-Demutah shel Va'adat Ha-Ezrah ve-Hatzalah be-Budapest Bereshit Darkah," *Yalkut Moreshet* (1980), 143–57. See *EH,* 1250, regarding the hiding of weapons for eventual self-defense. See also Brand, *Mission,* 38.

12. Brand, *Mission,* 19–20, 33–34. See also my interview with Sámuel Springman, Jan. 23, 1980.

13. Braham, "Relief," 1250. See also Kastner affidavit on behalf of Kurt Becher in Bra-

ham, *Destruction of Hungarian Jewry: A Documentary Account* (New York: Federation of Hungarian Jewry, 1963), 907–8. For the Jewish Agency's Vaad Hahatzalah in Istanbul, see Dalia Ofer, "The Activities of the Jewish Agency in Istanbul in 1943," in *Rescue Attempts During the Holocaust* (Jerusalem: Yad Vashem, 1977), 435–50.

14. See chap. 4, 55.

15. For examples, see Weissmandl, *Min Hametzar,* 117; Braham, "Rescue Committee," 1251. See also the papers of Saly Mayer, JDCA; Natan Schwalb, MLA; and Roswell McClelland, WRB.

16. The Abwehr was headed by Adm. Wilhelm Canaris. Canaris was aware early on that Hitler's war was a lost cause, and he made contacts with the West to conduct eventual negotiations. He was involved in the unsuccessful generals' plot to assassinate Hitler on July 20, 1944, and was executed only a month before the end of the war. See the entry on Admiral Canaris in the *Encyclopedia of World War II,* ed. Thomas Parrish (New York: Simon and Schuster, 1978), 162. For the Vaada's relations with the Abwehr, see, among other sources, Brand, *Mission,* chap. 4.

17. The failed 1943 Europa Plan was intended to ransom the Jews of Nazi-occupied Europe, except for Poland, for $2 million. Weissmandl, *Min Hametzar,* 102–3, 202. Unlike the Vaada, Weissmandl, Schwalb, and Mantello realized that Abwehr couriers were untrustworthy. Nevertheless, they sometimes had no choice but to use them. Taped interview with Mantello and Natan Schwalb (Dror) (Hebrew name).

18. For the interrogation of the refugees, see Brand, *Mission,* 22–23.

19. See chap. 3. See also Brand, *Mission,* 43.

20. So influential was Krausz that his first name, Miklós, became the code word for Hungary in the correspondence of the Zionist underground. See the correspondence of the various Zionist underground movements among the papers of Saly Mayer and Natan Schwalb, as well as the Vaad Hahatzalah–Jewish Agency in Istanbul. See also my taped interview with Moshe Krausz.

21. This restrictive policy was tightly enforced by Britain during Jewry's most tragic era, just as the doors of most countries closed even more tightly.

22. See Noah Lucas, *History of Modern Israel* [Lucas, *Israel*] (New York, 1971), esp. chap. 9. For the white paper, see Wasserstein, *Britain and the Jews of Europe, 1939–1945* (London, 1979), 17–25, et passim. See Abraham J. Edelheit, *The Yishuv in the Shadow of the Holocaust* (Boulder, Colo., 1996), esp. chap. 10. For Krausz's role and his conflict with Kastner, see Brand, *Mission,* 51–52;, "Hungarian Report," 131–35. See also my interview with Moshe Krausz, who noted with pride that he once gave a certificate to a non-Zionist *melamed* (Hebrew teacher) and his family because they spoke a flawless Hebrew.

Interestingly, Brand wrote about a British demand that the Vaada reserve this monthly allotment of certificates for downed British airmen, whom the Vaada was expected to find and spirit out of German hands. Though the British were inflexible in their monopolistic demand for these life-giving papers, the Vaada was somehow able to continue using them for Zionist refugees. Brand, *Mission,* 47–51.

23. "Hungarian Report," 75. See n. 11. Braham omits Kahan-Frankel, who was one of

the three Orthodox leaders contacted by Weissmandl during his desperate search (in 1942) for the $25,000 necessary to ransom Slovakian Jewry. Weissmandl knew Kahan-Frankel long before he got to know Freudiger. See also interview with Moshe Kahan-Frankel, son of Samuel Kahan-Frankel. Moshe was already an adult during this period. Weissmandl also gave special praise to Link. See Weissmandl, *Min Hametzar,* 112. Of the three, Freudiger conducted the most frequent communications with both Weissmandl and Sternbuch in Switzerland. See Kranzler, *Thy Brother's Blood,* et passim. See also SP, Agudah Archives, New York. Copies in my possession.

24. Interview with Chaim Roth. Mr. Roth provided me with the original collection of documents, including lists of thousands of Jewish refugees whom his organization provided with papers. See also Braham, *Politics,* 108–9. Braham seems to be unaware of Roth's extensive rescue work.

25. Interviews with Chaim Roth, Samuel Frey, and Rabbi Jacob Bein, the chaplain at the detention house, and Rabbi Joseph Ashkenazi, who was the assistant to Rabbi Joel Teitelbaum, admor of Satmar. Among the incarcerated after the Nazi occupation were Rabbi Yekusiel Teitelbaum, known as the admor of Klausenburg (Hasidic leader of Cluj), and his wife and ten children, who were thus spared for several months. Rabbi Yekusiel Teitelbaum and his family were later deported to Auschwitz. He survived the camp but his family was murdered.

26. See, for example, Schwartz, *Orthodox Community,* 10–11. See also Bela Vago, "The Destruction of Hungarian Jewry as Reflected in the Palestine Press," Braham, *HJS-3,* p. 308; Braham, "The Uniqueness of the Holocaust in Hungary," in *The Holocaust in Hungary: Forty Years Later,* ed. Randolph L. Braham and Bela Vago (New York: Institute for Holocaust Studies of the City University of New York, 1985), 183–84.

27. Jeno Levai, *Eichmann in Hungary: Documents* (Budapest: Penonia Press, 1961), 58–61. See also Braham, *Docs,* 1, pp. 229–42; Braham, *Politics,* chap. 7, esp. 246–47; Braham, "Uniqueness," 185; Gyorgi Ranki, "Hungary," in *EH* 2, pp. 693–98. For the rumor that warned "if a ghetto were established for the Jews, the Allies would not bomb it, but would devastate the rest of Budapest," see Samuel (Samu) Stern, "A Race Against Time," in *HJS-III,* 23. See the effects of this fear, chap. 7.

28. Schwartz, *Orthodox Community,* 13, 114. Schwartz notes that Freudiger received the Auschwitz Report from Weissmandl by late May. Freudiger himself, though, claims that he received it no earlier than June 5 or 10. Braham, "What Did They Know About and When?," in *The Holocaust as Historical Experience: Essays and a Discussion,* ed. Yehuda Bauer and Nathan Rotenstreich (New York: Holmes and Meier, 1981), 119. See also Braham, "Uniqueness," 183–84. Given Weissmandl's constant contact with Freudiger even before Hungary's occupation, and his early attempts to warn Hungarian Jewry (Weissmandl, *Min Hametzar,* 112–15), it is hardly likely that Freudiger did not receive his copy at least at the same time that the Sternbuchs or Natan Schwalb did—that is, by May 17. Moreover, he must have gotten Weissmandl's version of May 22, which eventually found its way to Czech ambassador Kopecky and from him to Riegner by June 10, and who

then made it available two weeks later to McClelland (see below). Freudiger first provided this information to the other Jewish leaders by early June. Still, he was the only Hungarian Jewish leader to show the Auschwitz Report to the other Jewish leaders in Budapest.

In contrast, Kastner, who by several accounts received a copy of the Auschwitz Report virtually as soon as it was produced (the end of April), never showed it to any of the other leaders. See Braham, "When?," 119. In his postwar memoirs, Kastner admits that because of "dubious political reasons the Jewish leaders remained silent." Kastner, Bericht, 125, 345.

29. Braham, *Politics,* 922.

30. For a full background on this crucial era of Hungarian history, see Mario D. Fenyo, *Hitler, Horthy, and Hungary* (New Haven: Yale Univ. Press, 1972), esp. chaps. 4–8; Braham, *Politics,* chap. 11. For a brief summary of this period, see Braham, "Uniqueness," 182–90.

31. See Braham, *Politics,* 12–16. Braham omits the relevant fact that Kun was Jewish, as were the leaders of several other failed Communist regimes in central Europe during 1917–20. This was surely an important factor in the intensification of anti-Semitism in Hungary and other European countries. See Jerry Z. Miller, "Communism, Anti-Semitism, and the Jews," *Commentary* 86 (Aug. 1988), 28–39.

32. For the Kallay era and Kallay's search for peace with the West, see Braham, *Politics,* esp. 247; Fenyo, *Horthy,* chaps. 7–8.

33. "Hungarian Report," 76–77. Horthy himself, in a postinvasion visit to Hitler from May 16 to 18, declined to exterminate or deport Hungary's Jews to concentration camps. In his memoirs, Horthy claims that he told Hitler that such drastic measures would prove too harmful to the Hungarian economy. However, these policies were carried out by the Sztojay pro-Nazi government formed after the German invasion.

34. Braham, *Politics,* 240–42.

35. Levai, *Eichmann,* 64.

36. Braham, *Politics,* 369–70.

37. Braham, "Uniqueness," 186–87.

38. Braham, *Politics,* 374, 926–28.

39. The Jews of biblical Persia, who were saved from an annihilation plot by Haman, King Ahasverus's vizir. The day after Purim is a semiholiday called Shushan Purim, or the Purim that was celebrated in Shushan, then the capital of Persia.

40. Weissmandl, *Min Hametzar,* 117, 122. Weissmandl had devised various ransom plans, beginning in Slovakia in 1942. In May 1944, he was the first to point out the connection between the gruesome facts cited in the Auschwitz Report and the imminent fate of Hungarian Jewry. See esp. chap. 5. One of Weissmandl's students had volunteered to sacrifice his life by blowing up a locomotive under the key tunnel whose tracks led to Auschwitz. However, objections by other members of the Working Group stopped this idea (118–19).

To varying degrees, Weissmandl himself or his plans were involved in virtually every major rescue effort of the war. Tragically, he and Mantello, who were kindred souls in their approach to rescue, were unaware of each other's existence until they met in Switzerland toward the end of the war.

41. Weissmandl, *Min Hametzar,* 116–17. At that point, in Mar. 1944, Weissmandl had to create his own letters detailing the Nazi atrocities, for the Auschwitz Report was received only toward the end of April. See chap. 5.

42. Weissmandl, *Min Hametzar,* 116–17.

43. Ibid., 116. Upon reflection after the war, Weissmandl acknowledged that he could not blame anyone for not believing his warnings and leaving their families. After all, they could have readily assumed that the war might end before catastrophe struck (116).

44. Kastner, *Bericht,* 125, 345. See also Braham, *Politics,* 706–7; Yehuda Bauer, *Jews for Sale* (New Haven: Yale Univ. Press, 1994), 160.

45. Brand, *Mission,* 64–65. Brand does not provide the exact date of this meeting, but Kastner does, in his *Bericht,* 53. See also 57; Braham, *Politics,* 706–7.

46. Brand, *Mission,* 63–66. One of the suggestions discussed and then dismissed by Kastner and Brand on practical grounds was an armed defense of Budapest. Still another resolution proposed setting up armed resistance groups (65–66).

47. For a comprehensive picture on the role and dilemma of the Judenrat, see Braham, *Politics,* chap. 14. For the perspective of three of the leading members of the Judenrat (called the Jewish Council by Braham), see Samuel (Samu) Stern, "A Race with Time," in *HJS-3,* 1–48; Ernoe (Ernest) Petoe, "Statement," 49–74; Philip Freudiger et al., "Report on Hungary," 75–146.

48. Weissmandl, *Min Hametzar,* 113; Kastner, *Bericht,* 71–72.

49. Weissmandl, *Min Hametzar,* 113, 117. Braham seems unaware of the secret letter to Freudiger; perhaps he is unfamiliar with *Min Hametzar,* which is written in a rabbinic Hebrew that is somewhat difficult for the uninitiated. The fact that Weissmandl passed away before completing and editing his book does not make it any easier to comprehend.

50. Ibid., 115.

51. Rosenfeld, *Tik Plili,* 38.

52. For a very different perspective, see Brand, *Mission,* chap. 4, esp. 77. For example, Brand dismisses the role previously played by Freudiger as "coming to nothing" and claims that he and his family fled to Bucharest by Aug. 1944. Brand ignores the fact that the Vaada was responsible for ousting Freudiger from the negotiations with Wisliceny, evidently persuading the SS that it had better connections than the Orthodox. In his memoirs, Brand also ignores the fact that when he and Kastner began their negotiations with Wisliceny and had to provide a 10 percent down payment of the $2 million, they asked Freudiger and Samuel Stern to obtain the money—which they did. See Weissmandl, *Min Hametzar,* 133; "Hungarian Report," 93–95; Rosenfeld, *Tik Plili,* 36–40.

For the rivalry between Kastner and Krausz, see Brand, *Mission,* 50–52; "Hungarian Report," 131–33.

53. For a reasonably objective view of Kastner and Krausz and their negotiation tac-

tics, see "Hungarian Report," et passim. For the conflict between Kastner and Krausz, see esp. 131.

54. See Bela Vago, "The Intelligence Aspects of the Joel Brand Mission," in *YVS* 10 (1974):111–28, esp. 111–13.

55. Despite several scholarly articles and chapters in books on this highly complicated and fascinating subject, the entire Brand Mission is still clouded by ideological and other factors. Among other sources, see Joel Brand and A. Weissberg, *Desperate Mission: Joel Brand's Story* [Brand, *Mission*] (New York, 1958); Yehuda Bauer, "The Mission of Joel Brand," in his *The Holocaust in Historical Perspective* (Seattle: Univ. of Washington Press, 1978), 94–155; Dina Porat, *The Blue and Yellow Stars of David: The Zionist Leadership in Palestine and the Holocaust, 1939–1945* [Porat, *Blue and Yellow*] (Cambridge, Mass.: Harvard Univ. Press, 1990), 188–211; Braham, *Politics,* 941–51, and his article, "Brand, Joel," in *EH,* 238–40.

Aside from myself, Porat is the only historian to have interviewed Dr. Joseph Klarman, a direct participant, and she takes into account Klarman's, Griffel's, and Brand's own claim that they warned him (Brand) that the British were trying to lure him into a trap. See Porat, *Blue and Yellow,* 194. See also Brand, *Mission,* 157, and Griffel, *Memoir,* 42, where he fully substantiates Brand's account of Griffel's (and Klarmman's) warning. See also *Tik Plili,* 56.

56. I interviewed Lajos Gottesman, who headed the Revisionist Party in Budapest. Gottesman explained the "selection process" by party, confirming an earlier explanation of Krausz's.

57. See Braham, *Politics,* 952–57. Braham only notes that certificate holders and young Zionists were in the group. Originally, the number was 600 certificate holders, but this soon grew to 750. See Kastner, *Bericht,* 77–78, 85–86, 97–98, 106–8, 128–29. See also "Report on Hungary," 118; also interview with Lajos Gottesman, who was a leader of the Revisionists in Budapest and was involved in this selection process. The certificates were given only to bona fide Zionists. Interview with Moshe Krausz. For instance, Rabbi Jacob Bein paid about $8,000 (U.S.) for seats for his wife and two children on the train. Interview.

The Kastner Train left Budapest on Friday evening, June 30, 1944, carrying 1,684 Jews, and went to the Bergen Belsen concentration camp, from which these Jews were eventually ransomed. For a breakdown of the six hundred certificate holders, see Rafi-Perez (in Budapest) to Schwalb, May 19, 1944. Schwalb papers, RG IV, 103/104. MLA.

For the jewels in suitcases, see Kastner, *Bericht,* 116–18. Eventually, the number of passengers reached 1,684, because on the first night of travel, the train stopped at a labor camp, where an additional 484 jumped on. As a result, confusion has reigned within the documents about the numbers; even contemporary historians are confused. Letter from Richard Lichtheim to Grünbaum, Aug. 21, 1944: "Understand, not 1,200 but about 1,650." Lichtheim papers RG L-22/135, CZA. See also chap. 7.

58. See Kastner, *Bericht,* 119–20. For the approximately $2,000 per person required for the other seats, see "Hungarian Report," 119. See Gilbert, *Auschwitz,* 203–5.

Kastner had to pay Eichmann $2 million in cash, jewels, and gold for the train, and he accepted anyone able to pay for their families, as well as for the indigent *chalutzim.* Thus, five hundred additional Jews of all ideological stripes (including my in-laws) came aboard as paying customers. Freudiger paid for the inclusion of eighty Orthodox Jews, including a number of prominent rabbis, such as Rabbi Joel Teitelbaum (the admor of Satmar), Rabbi Jonasan Steif, and Rabbi Solomon Strasser of Debrecen. See minutes of meeting, Apr. 16, 1945 called by Rabbi Joel Teitelbaum, which lists some of the more prominent rabbinic and communal leaders on the train. This increased the original number from seven hundred to twelve hundred. MP.

59. Haskel Lookstein, *Were We Our Brothers' Keepers?: The Public Response of American Jews to the Holocaust* (New York: Hartmore House, 1985), 187.

Even before this prognosis of the dangers for Hungarian Jewry, a report was sent to the International Red Cross in Geneva by Jean de Bavier, its delegate in Budapest, on February 18, 1944, a month before the German occupation of Hungary. In this report, which evidently did not get any publicity, de Bavier noted the following: "There is a risk that a very grave problem will arise here if the country is occupied by the Germans. I am referring to what could happen to the 800,000 Hungarian Jews living in the country. Bearing in mind the events in Germany and the occupied territories, it is a matter of urgency that you should let me know what form of protection might be given to these people in an attempt to shield them from the threat hanging over them. I should be grateful for all instructions for action that can be carried out to avoid letting these people down." Arieh Ben-Tov, *Facing the Holocaust in Budapest: The International Red Cross and the Jews of Hungary,* 1943–1945 (Boston: Henry Dumont Institute, 1988), 102–3.

60. Wyman, *Abandonment,* 256. Wyman noted that Judge Samuel Rosenman was responsible for diluting the War Refugee Board's original language.

61. Lookstein, *Keepers?,* 191–92.

62. Ibid. For the warning of the BBC regarding the bombing of Budapest, see Jeno Levai, *Black Book on the Martyrdom of Hungarian Jewry* [Levai, *Black Book*] (Vienna: Central European Times, 1948), 227.

63. Lookstein, *Keepers?,* 189.

64. David S. Wyman, ed., *America and the Holocaust: A Thirteen-Volume Set Documenting the Editor's Book, The Abandonment of the Jews* (New York: Garland, 1990), 8:13; MD, 717:145, cited by Wyman, *Abandonment,* 236.

65. Wyman, *Abandonment,* 236.

66. Lookstein, *Keepers?,* 189.

67. For the missed opportunity to use Jewish political clout during the summer of 1944, see my "Why Auschwitz Was Really Never Bombed," in *Proceedings of the Tenth World Congress of Jewish Studies,* Div. B, vol. 2:411–17.

68. For the rally, see Lookstein, *Keepers?,* 197–99. For a thorough analysis of Wise and the ideological factors motivating his actions and inaction during the Holocaust, see Kranzler, "Wise."

69. Deborah E. Lipstadt, *Beyond Belief: The American Press and the Coming of the Holocaust,* 1933–1945 (New York: Free Press, 1986), 222–23.

70. See Griffel's *Memoir,* esp. 11, 15, 19.
71. Braham, *Docs* 1, Doc. #169:393.
72. Braham, *Docs* 1, Doc. #172, 397; 78. See also Lookstein, *Keepers?,* 189.

5. Mantello's Early Rescue Efforts

1. For Rabbi Taubes and the Rabbis' Committee, see above, chap. 3. For the Swiss Hungarian Committee [SHC], see esp. the four-page *Minutes of the May 5, 1944, Meeting of the Swiss Hungarian Committee [Min SHC],* which provides a review, intended for the WRB, of the establishment of the SHC. Other copies of these important minutes of the May 5 meeting, which provide some background on the organization, can be found in the papers of the Swiss-Hungarian Committee RG M-20/47-YVA. For the first request to meet with a delegation composed of Riegner, Lichtheim, and Saly Brunschvig, president of SIG, see Bányai to Harrison, April 5, 1944. See also Levai, *Abscheu,* 24–25.
2. Levai, *Abscheu,* 24. Another name was "The Swiss Committee for Aiding Jews in Hungary." For the various names, see the documents in RG 60, WRB. See also papers of the Bányai Committee, RG M-20/47, YV. For Dr. Bányai's role as secretary and Pallai's involvement with McClelland, see collection, Dr. C. Bányai to McClelland, May 16, 1944.
3. Min SHC, 1. The one place where Swiss censorship did not apply was the Church. There, one was permitted to say virtually anything. Hans Schaffert interview. This would prove crucial during the early stages of the press campaign, when news about Auschwitz was publicized in all the churches through the efforts of Pastor Paul Vogt (see chap. 7). For a good, but brief, discussion of Switzerland's policy of "neutrality," see Leni Yahil, "Rescue Efforts in Neutral Countries," in *The Historiography of the Holocaust Period,* ed. Yisrael Gutman and Gideon Grell (Jerusalem: Yad Vashem, 1988), 528–29. Federal Councilor Eduard von Steiger was not only the primary political figure behind Rothmund and the policy of *refoulement,* but also was behind the strict censorship. See, for example, Häsler, *Lifeboat,* 108–16, esp. 110–12.
4. Min SHC, 1. RG 60, WRB.
5. Ibid., 2. Though apparently no record of McClelland's intervention exists, it is known from later documents in the McClelland papers that he was involved with Pallai. Therefore, I assume that McClelland intervened on his behalf. See C. Bányai to McClelland, May 19, 1944, SHC RG M-20-47/YVA.
6. See chap. 12, regarding Taubes's assessment of Mantello's virtually monomaniacal pursuit of rescue. Although Bányai did some very fine work, he lacked Mantello's zealousness and drive, as we shall see below.
7. Levai, *Abscheu,* 25. See also Min SHC, 2. I believe that Dr. Solomon Ehrmann represented the local Swiss Agudah, for he dealt with Mantello in other matters. This was distinct from World Agudah (and Vaad Hatzalah), to which Sternbuch belonged. The two did not get along with each other. OSE was active in France during World War II, hiding children and helping spirit them into Switzerland. I am unaware of the first name of Dr. Rom or the names of the representatives of OSE. For some of the OSE's rescue

work in France, see, for example, Enst Papanek and Edward Linn, *Out of the Fire* (New York: William Morrow, 1976).

8. Jeno Levai, *Zsidosors Europaban* [Levai, *Zsidosors*] (Budapest: Magyar Teka, 1948), 46. Mantello interview. As noted in chap. 3, the information required to complete the papers was brought to Muller's office, where he had them filled out. The last step required Mantello's signature. "Deportations" in Schwalb's correspondence referred to the first small deportation from Kistarcsa to Auschwitz, which was completed the next day. Braham, *Politics*, 483. Evidently, Schwalb received early warning even of this minor transport as soon as movement began.

9. Levai, *Abscheu*, 26.

10. Ibid., 346.

11. Ibid.

12. See Min SHC, 2. See also Levai, *Abscheu*, 348–50.

13. Huddle to Bányai, May 19, 1944; Bányai to Huddle, May 3, 1944. Bányai Papers, RG 60, WRB. The WRB had $1.15 million in "discretionary funds," from which McClelland provided Schwalb with more than $110,000. It is hard to believe that such funds could not have been used for rescue expenses such as cables—particularly because the WRB never used up even half of the originally allocated sum before disbanding in May 1945. It returned the balance to the American government. Beyond the $1.15 million, an additional $1,068,750 was allocated for purchasing and shipping food parcels to the inmates in the camps. See Wyman, *Abandonment*, 213–14, including footnote, and Roswell McClelland to General O'Dwyer, May 30, 1945, "Account of Roswell McClelland," WRB.

14. Min SHC, 3.

15. Ibid., 2. The Saly Mayers papers [SMP] are replete with correspondence, reports, and suggestions of Mantello and the SHC.

16. See *SHC-M-20/47.* YVA.

17. Ibid., Appendix 2, pp. 1–3.

18. Ibid., Appendix 3, pp. 1–2.

19. Ibid., Appendix 9, pp. 1–3.

20. Ibid., Appendix 1, p. 4.

21. Franz Tausky to Paul Vogt, May 10, 1944, RG 60, WRB. Tausky was a member of the SHC.

22. Swiss legation in Budapest to the Hungarian Foreign Ministry, April 25, 1944. For the entire episode, see the correspondence between the Swiss legation and the Hungarian Foreign Ministry for April 19 through 28, Swiss foreign office files RG E 20001 (D) 3/95. BB.

23. RG E 4264-1988/2/59. BB.

24. McClelland to Leland Harrison, June 14, 1944. McClelland papers, box 58. WRB.

25. E 2001 (B)/78 Bd.14.B 24.Sa.11 A-RM/Qe. BB.

26. G. Tait to McClelland, July 5, 1944. McClelland papers, box 58. WRB.

27. Eduard de Haller to Max Huber (president of the IRC), June 6, 1944. Department

of Foreign Affairs to Minister Feldscher, June 6, 1944. Department of Foreign Affairs to Ambassador Jäger, June 6, 1944. RG E 2001 (D) 1968/74 Bd.14. BB.

28. Ben-Tov, *IRC,* 143.

29. Ibid., 144.

30. Ibid., 148.

31. Bányai to Harrison, May 2, 1944, box 60. WRB.

32. See W. A. Visser't Hooft, *Memoirs* (Philadelphia: Westminster Press, 1961), 171. Although he notes that "we issued a communiqué, signed by the World Council's Ecumenical Committee for Refugees, calling attention to the deportation of 400,000 Jews to Auschwitz," this really refers to his signature on Vogt's letter.

33. Levai, *Abscheu,* 27–28.

34. See chap. 5.

35. Josef Mandl, for example, received a card from his sister on May 4, which turned out to be the last contact between the two brothers in Switzerland and any of their relatives in Hungary. His sister hinted that the Jews were cooped up in a brick factory with neither food nor sanitary facilities. She concluded with a desperate plea for help, especially for food packages. Josef immediately appealed to Dr. Silberschein, known for his excellent work under RELICO in sending thousands of packages to Jews in occupied territories, and begged him to use all his facilities to prevent the Hungarian Jews from dying en masse from starvation and disease. Josef Mandl to Dr. Abraham Silberschein, May 12,1944. Papers of Josef Mandl, RG M-20/46, YVA.

36. Ibid.

37. Kastner, *Bericht,* 82. This was already cited in his earlier, much briefer "Report," n.d., received May 10, 1946, 6 WJC, RG. D-108/2, AJA.

38. Erich Kulka, "Escapes of Jewish Prisoners from Auschwitz-Birkenau and Their Attempts to Stop Mass Extermination," in *The Nazi Concentration Camps: Proceedings of the Fourth Yad Vashem International Historical Conference, Jerusalem 1980* (Jerusalem: Yad Vashem, 1984), 409.

39. Ibid. For a detailed account by Vrba of their escape, see Rudolf Vrba and Alan Bestic, *I Cannot Forgive* (New York: Grove Press, 1964). For an interesting chapter on the underground in Auschwitz, see Herman Langbein, "The Auschwitz Underground," in *Anatomy of the Auschwitz Death Camp,* ed. Israel Gutman and Michael Berenbaum (Bloomington, Ind.: U.S. Holocaust Memorial Museum, 1994), 485–502.

40. The escapees' meeting with Steiner is based on Krasznyansky's interview with Gilbert. See Gilbert, *Auschwitz,* 202–3. See also my two taped interviews with Andre Steiner.

41. Most significantly, a plea was appended to various brief versions of the report, asking that Auschwitz and the railway lines leading to it be bombed. Contrary to Krasznyansky's assertion (upon which both Braham and Gilbert rely) that *he* added the plea, it was Weissmandl who did so. To verify this, one need merely look, for example, at the two copies of the Protocols sent by Weissmandl to Schwalb on May 16. The larger, twenty-six-page copy created by Krasznyansy has no plea to bomb Auschwitz attached, but

Weissmandl's five-page summary includes the plea, as do almost all the brief versions he created. In fact, none of the larger versions contain the plea to bomb Auschwitz and the rail lines to this camp, as well as other suggestions to the Allies to halt the carnage. Moreover, Weissmandl cabled hundreds of telegrams after May 16 to *all* Jewish factions, in which this plea was central. Weissmandl, *Min Hametzar,* 122–23. See also Miroslav Karny, "The Vrba and Wetzler Report," in Gutman, *Auschwitz,* esp., 550, 556. See Krasniansky's claim re Weissmandl's distribution in Kulka, "Escapes from Auschwitz-Birkenau," 409.

Likewise, the thirty-three-page version of the Auschwitz Report on Schwalb's stationery, dated May 17, has nothing appended after the central account of Auschwitz and the escape. There is no warning about the fate of the Hungarian Jews, nor a plea to bomb Auschwitz. See both copies in Schwalb papers. RG IV:103–104. MLA.

42. Why Kastner would need a Hungarian-language version for Horthy is unclear, because the regent, like most educated Hungarians, could speak and write a fluent German. See also "Hungarian Report," 108.

43. Kulka, "Escapes," 410–11. See also Karny, "Auschwitz Report," 556–62.

44. Kulka, "Escapes," 410. See also Schwalb taped interview. At this point, I have been unable to trace that version of the Protocols.

45. Though all sources are flawed, for a broad survey of the creation and immediate distribution of the Protocols, see the following: Braham, *Politics,* chap. 25, as well as his "When?," 109–31; Gilbert, *Auschwitz,* chaps. 21–22; Kulka, "Escapes," 401–16; Gilbert, *Auschwitz,* 202–5; Karny, "Auschwitz Report," 553–68. For information on Freudiger's showing his copy of the Protocols to the Judenrat, sometime in early June, see Braham, "When?," 119. According to Freudiger, his "Five Months" report indicated that already in April, several days before ghettoization, Weissmandl warned Freudiger by letters, in Hebrew and in code, via couriers, concerning the danger to the 310,000 Jews of Carpatho-Ruthenia. Moreover, by May 14, he was already informed concerning the agreement with the railroad officials, a fact confirmed via a Jewish former railroad chief. All this was discussed and debated in the council at the time. See *Tik Plili,* chap. 6. Randolph L. Braham Freudiger, "Five Months," in *The Tragedy of Hungarian Jewry* (New York: Institute for Holocaust Studies of the City Univ. of New York, 1986), 252–56. See also "Freudiger's testimony at the Eichmann trial May 25, 1961," cited in *Documents of Destruction: Germany and Jewry, 1933–1945,* ed. Raoul Hilberg (Chicago: Quadrangle, 1971), 191–92; Zahava Schwartz, *The Orthodox Jewish Community in Hungary, 1939–1945* (unpublished master's thesis. Ramat Gan: Bar Ilan Univ., 1989), 114.

46. Copy of a thirty-three-page version of the Auschwitz Report and the letter to Dobkin given me by Mr. Schwalb. See copies in Schwalb papers. RG IV, 103–4. MLA. Also in my possession are copies of Weissmandl's brief versions, which reached Schwalb probably by May 16, a day after the beginning of the mass deportations. Weissmandl's version included his pleas to bomb Auschwitz and other suggestions for the Allies to halt the carnage. By May 17, Schwalb had translated Weissmandl's Hebrew version into German and typed onto his stationery, which he then sent to all his contacts. These reports

reached the Moetza in Istanbul by July 1. See Menachem Bader to London, July 1, 1944. See RG IV, 104–15. MLA.

47. German-language copy in the Schwalb papers, RG IV, 103–4. MLA. Although both Weissmandl and Fleischman signed the plea, Weissmandl penned these and numerous other extraordinary rescue-related documents.

48. For Freudiger, see, for example, his "Five Months," 252–53. Schwalb's papers are replete with Weissmandl's reports and letters. The most crucial of Schwalb's papers dealing with Weissmandl's and Gisi Fleischmann's negotiations with the Nazis, etc., have only recently been made available at the Machon Lavon Archives. Likewise the Sternbuch papers. However, although Bauer, in his official history of the Joint, claims that Saly Mayer carefully respected and placed all of Weissmandl's correspondence together, the archivist at the Joint has been unable to find this important file. However, one can obtain evidence of having received his reports in the correspondence of Schwalb and in letters by Mayer's friend Weiler, e.g., p. 22, in the thirty-page summary of the destruction of Hungarian Jewry in July 1944. It shows clearly that Mayer received the May 22 Auschwitz Report, with his plea to bomb Auschwitz. Dossier 1128. RG 44. SMP.JDCA. Courtesy of Dr. Eric Nooter, archivist.

49. Wyman, *Abandonment,* 290. See also Gilbert, *Auschwitz,* esp. chap. 31.

50. See Wyman, *Abandonment,* 289–90.

51. Ibid., 290.

52. Taped interviews with Mrs. Rivka Paskus and Rabbi Menachem Rubin. See also Lore Shelley, *Secretaries of Death: Accounts by Former Prisoners Who Worked in the Gestapo of Auschwitz* (New York: Shengold, 1986). For the Allied bombing of Auschwitz, see Wyman, *Abandonment,* 299; Danuta Czech, *Auschwitz Chronicle 1939–1945* (New York: Henry Holt, 1990), 692, 708.

53. For American Jewry's worship of FDR, see Kranzler, "Wise." See also Emanuel Pat, *In Gerangel: Yaakov Pat un Zein Dor* (Yid.) (Struggle: Jacob Pat and his generation) (New York: Jacob Pat Family Fund, 1971), 346–47, 360–61. That European Jews thought likewise is evident, for example, from Mantello, "Proposal," Levai, *Abscheu,* 346. See also David Kranzler, "Why Auschwitz Really Wasn't Bombed," in the *Proceedings of the Tenth World Congress of Jewish Studies* (Jerusalem: World Congress of Jewish Studies, 1990), 411–17.

54. Mantello interview. See Schaffert to Rothmund, Sept. 1, 1944, wherein he recounted Mantello's arrest. Swiss Federal Police files. E 4264-1988/2/59. BB.

55. The Swiss files contain a number of anonymous postwar letters accusing Mantello of black-market activities, which even the Swiss police did not take seriously. For the Swiss view, see Swiss interrogation, Sept. 1, 1944, addressed by Messrs. Schaffner and Roe to the Chief of the Section for Fighting Black Market in Bern, Concerning Report #1688 on George Mantello. See also E-2001 (D), 3/278.

56. These letters, from very different but reliable sources, confirmed the catastrophic situation in Budapest that Krausz had described at about the same time, in his letter accompanying the Auschwitz Protocols and the Hungarian Report. They were written

in the weeks before and during the return of Mantello's messenger from Budapest, carrying the two reports that he had received from Krausz. See chap. 6.

57. Ben-Tov, *IRC,* 150.

58. E 2001 (D) 1968/74. Bd. 14. BB. See also Ben-Tov, *IRC,* 150.

59. Ben-Tov, *IRC,* 149–50.

60. Braham, *Docs* 1, Doc. #171, 396.

61. Braham, *Docs* 1, Doc #172, 397.

62. For Kopecky's letter of June 19 and McClelland's notes on it, see box 60, WRB. According to Karny, Kopecky got his first report on or immediately after May 22, and a second, expanded version (with the Polish major's additional information) on or immediately after May 26. The long delay between the time Kopecky received these reports and his dispatch to the various authorities is puzzling. Karny, "Vrba and Wetzler Report," 559.

Virtually all the figures, from Kopecky and others, derive from the same source—Weissmandl, who bribed the Slovakian railroad workers regularly to obtain vital data on deportations. Interview with Shlomo Stern, who worked with Weissmandl and who was responsible for paying off the workers.

63. For Freudiger and Blum's reports, see RG #20. SMP, JDCA. Obviously, both provided Saly Mayer with copies. Very likely, both had the same source of information.

64. Braham, *Docs* 1, Doc. #174, 399.

65. SMP file #47. JDCA.

66. SMP RG #38, 47. JDCA. See also copy in McClelland's papers, box 60, WRB.

67. Schwalb to McClelland, June 20, 1944, box 59, WRB.

68. Kastner to Schwalb, June 10, 1944. SMP file #38. JDCA. A copy of this report was provided to Schwalb, as was virtually every missive from Kastner or other members of the Vaada. See Schwalb papers RG IV/104/103. MLA.

69. Levai, *Eichmann,* 114–15; Levai, *Abscheu,* 201–2.

70. Levai, *Abscheu,* 201–2; Levai, *Eichmann,* 112–16.

71. SMP. RG #20, 45,47. JDCA. See also box 60, WRB.

72. The last name of Kastner's fourth colleague is unknown.

73. Perez et al. to Schwalb, June 24, 1944, SMP RG #38. JDCA.

74. Perez, Zvi, Eli, Yehuda (Kastner's colleagues) to Natan Schwalb, June 24, 1944. WRB.

75. Levai, *Eichmann,* 114–16.

76. Bányai to McClelland, June 18, 1944, box 60, WRB.

77. Lichtheim to Grünbaum, June 26, 1944, RG L-22/135. Central Zionist Archives [CZA].

78. Maher to McClelland, June 21, 1944. McClelland papers, box 58, WRB. My view that the "leader of the Jewish community" refers to Freudiger is based on the following assumptions. Freudiger was not only head of the Orthodox Jewish Community of Budapest and a member of the Jewish Council, but also was the main contact with the Sternbuchs of the Orthodox Vaad Hatzalah in Switzerland. In addition, he had direct

contacts with Weissmandl. He was the only one of the recipients of the Auschwitz Report to pass it on to the Jewish Council. In fact, on May 14 and 15, he and the council already had discussed Weissmandl's warnings concerning upcoming deportations. See Freudiger, "Five Months," 252–53.

Moreover, Freudiger had originated Weissmandl's negotiations with the Germans until Kastner, who had been discussing the "aliya" of six hundred Zionists with Eichmann, persuaded him to replace Freudiger with his own Vaada Group. Rosenfeld, *Tik Plili,* 38–39.

Freudiger not only continued to submit Weissmandl's rescue plans to Saly Mayer and Sternbuch, but also collected the "down payment" of $200,000 on the $2 million demanded by Eichmann, which he gave to the Vaada for Eichmann. See Freudiger, "Five Months," 246–48.

79. Jewish Agency cable, WJCong papers. RG H-10, 1944, AJA.

80. Lichtheim to Grünbaum, June 26, 1944, RG L-22/135. CZA.

81. See Kranzler, "Wise."

6. The Manoliu Mission

1. Besides Mantello's numerous taped interviews, this mission is described in three sources (with further confirmation from Romanian sources in chap. 10). The most important of these is Manoliu's testimony in Werner Rings, *Advokaten des Feindes* (Vienna: Eecon-Verlag, 1966), 140–41, 194–95. The other two are Levai, *Abscheu,* 31–32, and Aron Silberstein, *Schweizer Alarmglocken* (undated, unpublished manuscript), 30–31, MP. There are some minor differences among them, and all of them, as well as Mantello's interviews, ignore a two-week gap in the chronology, which will be dealt with later.

While still in Bucharest, Mantello and his brother, Josef, had already had a long and close relationship with Manoliu, which, no doubt, was primarily financial, because all of Mantello's other high connections involved financial affairs. In Switzerland, Josef was more involved in commercial dealings than George, and thus he had a closer relationship with Manoliu. Moreover, in Josef's position as founder of the Swiss-Romanian Committee, which stressed rescue efforts on behalf of Romanian Jews (see chap. 10), he was closely involved with the liberal members of the Romanian legation, which included Manoliu.

2. Mantello interview.

3. Ibid. See Dr. Scheps's correspondence with me.

4. In *Documents Concerning the Fate of Romanian Jewry During the Holocaust,* ed. Jean Ancel, 5:132.

5. *Advokaten,* 195, 141.

6. Ibid., 195–96; Levai, *Abscheu,* 31–32; *Alarmglocken,* 30–32.

7. Mantello interview.

8. All sources omit a period of about two weeks, either before or after Manoliu's trip to Bistrice. Levai, *Abscheu,* 31, indicates June 3 for his arrival in Bistrice, while *Alarm-*

glocken, 30, cites June 10. Manoliu's own testimony in *Advokaten*, 195, ignores this gap after the time he left Berlin. The most reasonable resolution appears to be the chronology proposed here, although I am open to other evidence.

9. See Levai, *Abscheu*, 32.

10. There is no evidence for the exact date, but Manoliu must have stayed in Budapest for at least one and a half to two days to complete his mission. We also know from Krausz's letter that he left on June 19.

11. Carl Lutz, *Report, Division of Foreign Interests in Budapest* June 1945, 25. RG P-19/III–113. YVA.

12. Ibid., 26.

13. Levai, *Abscheu*, 32.

14. Ibid.

15. Mantello interview. For Krausz's fear of revealing information, see also Bányai to McClelland, June 23, WRB; *Alarmglocken*, 31.

16. Mantello interview. See also Krausz's letter of June 19, 1944, which he attached to the Auschwitz Report.

17. In his interviews, Mantello placed the second meeting of Krausz and Manoliu at a hotel, but the more likely place would be the Romanian legation, as noted by Levai, *Abscheu*, 32.

18. It is highly likely that this five-page copy came from Weissmandl, for it is known that he had incorporated the new testimony into his five-page summary of the Auschwitz Report, and I am unaware of any other five-page summary. This is so despite Riegner's claim that he summarized the Auschwitz Report during the two-week period (June 10–23), that he held the complete copy. There was no reason for Riegner either to summarize the report or to think of "new" suggestions for the Allies to follow, when he had all versions on his desk in front of him. Riegner also claimed that he added the plea to bomb Auschwitz. As is now known, Riegner received both the complete copy of the Auschwitz Report and the summary—which contained the plea to bomb Auschwitz—from Kopecky. Kopecky's copies in turn came from Weissmandl, who had intended the reports for his student, Rabbi Solomon Schonfeld, in London. See Karny, "Vrba and Wetzler," 557.

As for Krausz, in my interview, he claimed that he received the Auschwitz Report from an anonymous member of the Turkish legation. It is more likely that he received both the Auschwitz Report and the Hungarian Report from Freudiger. Among the Hungarian Jewish leaders, Freudiger was the sole recipient of these reports who showed them to all other members of the Jewish Council, and was also the only one to forward them to Horthy Jr., son of the Hungarian regent. Moreover, he dealt with Krausz on other matters relating to the fate of Budapest Jewry. See, for example, Freudiger, "Five Months," et passim. See also Schwartz, *Orthodox*, 113.

19. This Hungarian Report was so detailed and accurate that no Jew could have produced it. According to Dr. Gavriel Bar Shaket, of Yad Vashem, who has studied the transcripts of the highly effective Hungarian Secret Police, it must have been they who composed it.

The statistics used by Veesenmayer indicate a larger Jewish population for the same Jewish towns. See statistics in Levai, *Eichmann,* 115. For the deportations by Apr. 27, 1944, see Schwalb to Mantello, Levai, *Szidórórs,* 46.

Most likely, Freudiger purchased this data from the Hungarians and distributed copies to various circles, including Krausz and Josef Blum of the Joint. (Freudiger never had any hesitancy in purchasing information or ransoming people for rescue; just as he was the only member of the Judenrat to provide copies of reports to his fellow members.)

20. For the various editions of the Krausz letter, see MP. For the Mantello version, see also Levai, *Szidósórs,* 48; Levai, *Abscheu,* 33.

21. Mantello interview.

22. Ibid.

23. Ibid. For a copy of Krausz's letter to Mantello and Berger's note in Yiddish, see below. Copy in MP.

24. See copy in Levai, *Abscheu,* 33. Also in MP.

25. Mantello interview.

26. Bányai-McClelland, June 22, 1944.

27. Mantello interview.

28. Testimony of Taubes, PW Inquiry.

29. Mantello interview.

30. Ibid.

31. Ibid. For the Spanish translation, Mantello had to use a professional translator, for none of the students were proficient in that language. He gave this translator a German-language edition. Mantello interview. Copies of these various translations in MP.

32. See Mantello's version in Levai's two books, as well as in MP. Moreover, articles that mentioned Krausz's letter in more detail cite Mantello's version with these additions.

33. The number 1,715,000 consistently appeared not only in every version of the Auschwitz Report cited in the press throughout the world, but also has influenced the rounding out of the total number to 1.7 million and occasionally even to 1,500,000. The Vatican noticed the discrepancy in one of its reports. See *Le Saint Siège et les Victimes de la Guerre Janvier 1944–Juillet 1945* (Vatican: Libreria Editrice Vaticana, 1980) (Actes et Documents du Saint Siège Relatifs à la Second Guerre Mondiale), 10 Doc. #279, n. 1, 304.

Deborah Lipstadt, in reviewing the appearance of the reports in the American press, noticed the smaller figure of 1,715,000, but is unaware of the basis for this discrepancy. See Lipstadt, *Belief,* 345.

34. Mantello interview. See also Levai, *Abscheu,* 34. The entire episode was detailed by Mr. Mantello.

35. Mantello interview. See also Levai, *Abscheu,* 34, esp. regarding the skeptical Pallai.

36. Bányai to McClelland, June 22, 1944, box 60, WRB.

37. Ibid. I was unable to ascertain Hamori's first name.

38. Ibid.

39. See chap. 7.

40. McClelland to Bányai July 7, 1944, box 60, WRB.

41. For McClelland's dispatch on June 24, 1944, and his skeptical note, see papers of the State Department No. 840.48. Refugees, NA. Kopecky's copy, which most historians ascribe to "the underground," was sent him by Weissmandl, along with a letter intended for his student, Rabbi Solomon Schonfeld of London. See Karny, "Vrba and Wetzler," 557. This information was given Weissmandl by railroad workers.

7. The Beginning of the Swiss Press Campaign

1. Mantello focused on persons in Allied intelligence who were sympathetic and who trusted him. His earlier experience had shown McClelland to be an obstructionist with a negative attitude, so he assigned Bányai to deal with him. Mantello interview.

2. Recent news revealed the existence of numerous Swiss anti-Semitic groups. But this has already been documented in Leni Yahi, "Rescue Efforts in the Neutral Countries," 526–27. See illustration of anti-Semitic newspapers in Häsler, *Lifeboat.*

3. For Swiss censorship, see Levai, *Abscheu,* 57–61. Also see Häsler, *Lifeboat,* 122–23.

4. I have no direct documentation of the details of that meeting other than Mantello's recollection, as well as references in Levai, *Abscheu,* 35, and Rings, *Advokaten,* 144–46. However, I do have solid evidence for certain elements of Mantello's deals on behalf of the British for the chronographs. See above, chap. 3.

Primary evidence for West's cooperation with Mantello's press campaign is found in Garrett's testimony, both in the postwar inquiry (see chap. 12) and in his reaffirmation of that testimony twenty years later in Rings, *Advokaten,* 144–46. The fact that Garrett, head of the British Exchange Telegraph, was a partner in Mantello's daring quest to break through Swiss censorship is sufficient evidence that British intelligence gave its full approval. It would never have become involved, let alone provide approval, for such a radical move unless it had full confidence in the veracity of the reports, and thus in the honesty and reliability of Mantello as a diplomat. This same trust was demonstrated by Allen Dulles of the OSS. Both Dulles and West felt indebted to Mantello because he had helped them obtain chronographs and other goods necessary for the Allied cause from Switzerland, which was surrounded by Axis powers. See chap. 1.

5. Regarding Allied knowledge of Auschwitz, especially the Allies' bombing of its synthetic oil and rubber plants, see Wyman, *Abandonment,* 298–300. For seven illustrations of Auschwitz from Allied aerial reconnaissance missions, including one taken on April 4, three days before Vrba and Wetzler's escape, see Heiner Lichtenstein, *Warum Auschwitz nicht Bombadiert Wurde* (Cologne, 1980), illustrations following p. 96. For recollections of the two Allied bombings (August 20, September 13) of the Buna and other plants manned by Auschwitz inmates, see taped interviews with Rivka Paskus and Rabbi Menachem Rubin. Mrs. Paskus, one of the 999 Slovak girls taken to Auschwitz in the spring of 1942, worked in the Gestapo Bureau in Auschwitz and she witnessed her best friend killed by bombs before her eyes. See Wyman, *Abandonment,* 299; Czech, *Auschwitz Chronicle,* 692, 708.

6. Mantello interview.

7. Ibid. See also Rings, *Advokaten,* 144; Levai, *Abscheu,* 35–36. Although both texts give

June 22 as the date for Mantello's meeting with Garrett, Garrett's immediate postwar letter mentions June 23. I believe that this is not necessarily a discrepancy, because Mantello came to Garrett very late on the night of Thursday the twenty-second, and discussions stretched out until at least two or three in the morning of Friday the twenty-third. Therefore, both accounts are really one and the same.

8. Mantello interview.

9. Ibid. See also Levai, *Abscheu,* 35–36; Rings, *Advokaten,* 144–46.

10. For a copy of the cables, see Levai, *Abscheu,* 39; copies of cables in MP. See also Levai, *Szidósórs,* 68–72. See also appendix. For the Vatican response, see below in this chapter.

11. This is another example of a common confusion between the country, *El* Salvador, and its capital, *San* Salvador. Incidentally, Garrett pointed out here the basis for his and West's trust in Mantello: the Salvadoran papers were useful and distributed without renumeration. See also chap. 12.

12. Compare this sureness with the uncertainty of the Riegner cable of August 28, 1942. See chap. 2.

13. Alternatively, it might have been Baron Gábor Apor, a more recent ambassador to the Vatican.

14. See *SHC. Hungarian Report #6.* (This was one of a series of reports on Hungary collected by the SHC.) In all probability, the SHC was the primary source for such information, for it scanned the Hungarian press and distributed its summaries to various organizations. Another such collection was put together for the WRB by an employee of McClelland named László Hamori. Vogt papers in Zurich, 22. McClelland papers, box 61, WRB.

Later, on July 17, the *Voice of America* aired an appeal by these eight diplomats condemning the Nazi and Hungarian measures. See *Vadirat,* 3, 270, cited in Braham, *Politics,* 811, n. 28.

15. No record exists of a response from either Mayer or McClelland. Bányai to Saly Mayer, June 25, RG #27a, SMP. JDCA.

16. Rings, *Advokaten,* 145–46.

17. Ibid., 146. For Mantello's aid to the Allies, see chap. 1.

18. Ibid., 144–46.

19. See Ankara dispatch on copy of cables in MP. See also Levai, *Abscheu,* 57–59.

Swiss censorship regulations dictated that no anti-German material could appear in the Swiss media unless it had previously been published in another neutral country. Garrett added the dispatch to assure that the cables would bypass this regulation.

20. Copies of Mantello's package can be found among the papers of almost all the Jewish representatives in Switzerland. For examples, see the papers of Dr. Julius Kuhl, Recha and Isaac Sternbuch, Saly Mayer, Natan Schwalb, Gerhard M. Riegner, and Richard Lichtheim.

21. Mantello interview. This was the first of several copies received by the nuncio. He also received a copy accompanied by the letter from the four theologians on July 4. Bernadini first sent the reports to the Vatican on July 28. See *Vatican Docs #279,* 364. See also

below in this chapter for the significance of Bernadini's letter to the pope regarding the difference in the statistics and the Vatican's concern that its inaction, in contrast to the protests of the Protestants, was creating a negative impression in Switzerland.

22. For Scheps's return to civilian life, see his correspondence with me.

23. Scheps and Posner to McClelland, June 24, 1944, WRB. The date of receipt is marked June 27. It is puzzling that they mailed this information rather than handing it that same day to McClelland or his secretary.

24. See chap. 8.

25. Levai, *Abscheu,* 56–57. For more details about Rabbi Silver, see Marc Lee Raphael, *Abba Hillel Silver* (New York, 1989). Many of the Finkelstein papers at the archives of the Jewish Theological Seminary are still closed to researchers. What is available shows Finkelstein's close cooperation with the American Jewish Committee.

26. Levai, *Abscheu,* 56–57.

27. Bányai to McClelland, June 23, 1944.

28. E 2001 (D) 1968/74. Bd. 14. BB.

29. Ibid. For a response to Koechlin and further related rescue efforts, see chapter 8.

30. As will be elaborated below, Pilet-Golaz was one of the seven members of the "ruling clique" who eventually became one of the most active Swiss officials to work on behalf of Hungarian Jewry.

31. See Pehle to Nahum Goldmann, July 20, 1944, box H-320, WJCong, AJA. When I interviewed Dr. Riegner, he explained his delay in forwarding the Auschwitz Report as due to the time he had spent abridging it into a five-page summary. In truth, the version that Riegner claimed as his summary was Weissmandl's short version, which Kopecky had received along with a complete version, and which he had given to Riegner. There was therefore no reason for Riegner to abridge it. For historians' uncritical acceptance of Riegner's claim, see Penkower, *Expendable,* 230, n. 21; Wyman, *Abandonment,* 290; Gilbert, *Auschwitz,* 244–46.

For an analysis of the origin of the report, see also Karny, "Vrba and Wetzler," 557–58. It should be noted that, although Kopecky and Riegner provided McClelland with a copy only on June 23, Kopecky did send this information to London on June 14, where it was received the next day.

32. Karny, "Vrba and Wetzler," 557–59, esp. 559. Riegner incorrectly claimed that he appended these suggestions. In truth, they were the work of Weissmandl, as is quite evident from Weissmandl's May 17 version, which Schwalb distributed on his stationery.

33. Ben-Tov, *IRC,* 151–52.

34. See Levai, *Black Book,* 459. From the censored WJCong collection at AJA (esp. RG H-105, 107, 110, 197, 198, 320), as well as the even more thoroughly sanitized papers of Stephen S. Wise at several archives (including the American Jewish Historical Society Archives, Waltham, Mass., and the American Jewish Archives, Cincinnati, it is apparent that Wise received the report from McClelland through Kubowitzki. It is unclear whether McClelland forwarded the copy of the reports that he had received from

Kopecky and Ullman or whether it was the material that Mantello had given him and Riegner; based on evidence that the information included the Hungarian Report, the copy he forwarded most likely came from Mantello's material. Although he had received the Hungarian Report from a number of people, including Kopecky, Kopecky sent his material to McClelland only on June 23, after Mantello's package had already been widely distributed.

From the statistics cited in the report, one can see that Riegner provided McClelland with Kopecky's version of the Auschwitz Report, as well as Mantello's version of the Hungarian Report.

As noted earlier, to protect the president, Stephen S. Wise did not meet with him, or ask for a meeting with him by a delegation of Jews, to demand the bombing of the rail lines to Auschwitz. See Kranzler, "Wise."

35. Bányai to Saly Mayer, June 25, 1944, SMP. JDCA. When McClelland sent his cable of June 24 to the WJCong in New York, he mentioned a Swiss diplomat returning from Budapest, but did not mention these two Hungarian ambassadors. Also see above, n. 14.

36. This dispatch of the reports was not even sent through the usual cable, a quicker route that would have indicated some concern on his part. Rather, he sent it by surface mail, assuring that the reports he had received in June would not get to Washington until just before the election in November. For the dispatch of October 12, see McClelland to Pehle, Oct. 12, 1944, box 61, WRB. Also in Wyman, *Docs-12,* 75. For the Nov. 1 receipt, see Virginia Mannon to Pehle, Nov. 16, 1944, box 6, WRB. Also in Wyman, *Docs-13,* 108.

37. The story was reported in five major newspapers: *New York Herald Tribune, Louisville Courier Journal, Philadelphia Inquirer, New York Times,* and *Washington Post.* All the other headlines were far more explicit. For example, the headline of the *Philadelphia Inquirer* read: *"1,765,000 Jews Killed with Gas at German Camp."* Lipstadt, *Belief,* 264.

38. See Kranzler, "Auschwitz," 411–17. Sadly, these reports arrived after Roosevelt won an unprecedented fourth term, too late for effective political pressure to be put on his administration. By then, it was also months after the crematoriums in Auschwitz had been shut down. One can readily imagine the pressure that would have been put on Roosevelt, the ultimate political opportunist, to bomb Auschwitz and the rail lines had the same publicity been generated in June, in the heat of the election campaign, when McClelland had obtained Mantello's package; or at least by July 3, when the *New York Times* published the version it received from Pastor Vogt. This, besides the almost daily cables to McClelland by Sternbuch since May 22, conveying Weissmandl's pleas to bomb Auschwitz. See Kranzler, *Thy Brother's Blood,* 104–6. See also below in this chapter. For Vogt's version published in *NYT,* see the issues of July 3 and 6.

39. For the interception of the Hungarian secret police, see Ben-Tov, IRC, 452, n. 57.

40. For a summary of these cables, see Posner papers, RG P-12/41, YVA. *Tawelef* is the Hebrew code for *taw,* 400, and *elef,* 1000.

41. Ibid.

42. Ibid.

43. Ibid.

44. Lichtheim was referring to Krausz's expression of the general mood of despair among the Jews of Budapest, who felt that their end was near. Lichtheim to Grünbaum, June 26, 1944. RG L-22/135, CZA.

45. Posner papers. RG-12/41. YVA.

46. Krausz had shown his copy of the Auschwitz Report to six men: Swedish minister Carl Ivan Danielsson; Per Anger, secretary of the Swedish legation; Swiss minister Maximilian Jäger; Consul Carl Lutz; a member of the Spanish legation; and the papal nuncio, Angelo Rotta. Danielsson forwarded this report to Masur, Lauer, and Olson in Stockholm, and Jäger and Lutz forwarded it to Bern, Switzerland.

47. For details on how Krausz obtained his copy from the Jewish Council and his presentation of it to the diplomats mentioned above, see Levai, *Black Book*, 227–28. See also Braham, "When?," 119, concerning Freudiger's claim that he had received a copy of the Auschwitz Report in early June (although he had received it earlier), and that he first showed it to his fellow members of the Jewish Council. Most likely, Krausz obtained his copies of the Auschwitz Report and the Hungarian Report from Freudiger rather than from an unnamed member of the Turkish consulate, as Krausz claimed to me in an interview. See also Leni Yahil, "Raoul Wallenberg: His Mission and Activities in Hungary," *YVS* 15 (1983):25.

48. See Jeno Levai, *Raoul Wallenberg*, trans. Frank Vajda from the Hungarian (Melbourne: Univ. of Melbourne, 1988), 30–33.

49. See Levai, *Black Book*, 227–28: Yahil, "Wallenberg," 24–27; Levai, *Wallenberg*, 30–33; and Eleanor Lester, "Raoul Wallenberg: The Righteous Gentile from Sweden," in *The Holocaust in Hungary: Forty Years Later* [Lester, "Wallenberg"], ed. Randolph L. Braham and Bela Vago (New York, 1985), 148.

50. Ben-Tov, *IRC*, 150.

51. Yahil, "Wallenberg," 29, n. 35, 30–31. See also Braham, *Politics*, 113–18. Krausz letter, MP. The attitude of the Swiss legation toward rescue of Jews was similar, as Krausz had already noted in his desperate letter of June 19: "The Swiss Legation in Budapest, Department of Foreign Interests [i.e., Carl Lutz], has done its best, but unfortunately, without any success whatsoever . . . [because] this Department does not have sufficient power and authority." By this he meant that it was not supported by Switzerland, and thus was limited in its efficacy.

52. See copy in MP. See also Levai, *Wallenberg*, 33–34.

53. Levai, *Wallenberg*, 36; Yahil, "Wallenberg," 29, n. 35.

54. For the cables from Taubes, see Levai, *Wallenberg*, 33–34; Yahil, "Wallenberg," 25–27. See also Levai, *Black Book*, 227–28. On p. 26, Yahil cites June 23 for Grünbaum's cable to Ehrenpreis. This is an obvious typographical error, because Posner first cabled the information to Grünbaum on June 25, and should read June 27. See Levai, *Wallenberg*, 33. Another typographical error by Yahil on that page gives June 25 as the date of Roosevelt's warning, when in reality it took place the next day. See Levai, *Black Book*, 232–33. See RG L-80, CZA.

For Grünbaum's cable to Ehrenpreis, see RG 048/30a, YVA. For its impact on Ehrenpreis, see State Department note, June 30, 1944, 840.48, National Archives. For Ehrenpreis's poor record in rescue efforts, see Kranzler, *Thy Brother's Blood,* esp. 56–57, 219.

55. The Kultusgemeinde, or official Jewish community, included both Reform and Orthodox factions. This was in distinction to the separatist Israelitische Religions Gesellschaft (IRG) or Austrittsgeinde, which was exclusively Orthodox. This system was based on the German Jewish religious model established during the nineteenth century.

56. Mantello interview. See also article in the Yiddish-language *Morning Journal* of December 7, 1945, MP. For the ancient Jewish custom of interrupting the services for an important, even personal, injustice, see Louis Finklestein, *Jewish Self-Government in the Middle Ages* (New York: Jewish Theological Seminary, 1924), 15–8, 33, text, 119.

57. Häsler, *Lifeboat,* 187–88.

58. Ibid., 297. For the earlier, negative role during this period by Federal Councilor Pilet-Golaz, see 117, 325.

59. Ibid., 201.

60. Levai, *Abscheu,* 39, 55–56.

61. Ibid., 362. For the impact of Koechlin's message, see Braham, *Politics,* 1043–45.

62. Mantello interview. One is hard-pressed to account otherwise for the sudden and deep immersion by Vogt in Mantello's campaign. See also Vogt correspondence with Mantello. MP.

63. Levai, *Abscheu,* 29.

64. Ibid., 40.

65. Paul Vogt, *Soll ich meines [sic] Bruders Hüter sein?* (Zurich, 1944), 5–11.

66. Levai, *Abscheu,* 45.

67. This refers to Sino-Japanese hostilities, which had begun in 1937.

68. *La Vie Protestante,* July 13, 1944.

69. Levai, *Abscheu,* 43.

70. Ben-Tov, *IRC,* 172–74.

71. Levai, *Abscheu,* 41–42.

72. See preface to the first edition, 5. This preface was omitted in the second printing.

73. See Harrison to Huddle, July 4, box 56, WRB.

74. Ibid.

75. I obtained original copies of the first edition of Vogt's book from Mr. Mantello. The reprinted edition was provided me by Dr. Hans Schaffert, Vogt's former assistant. Besides the omission of the preface in the second printing, the only other distinction between the two editions is the announcement on the first edition's title page of the number of copies printed. Schaffert's copy contains a handwritten inscription dated "15 Aug. '44."

76. The publication of this volume stands in sharp contrast to Riegner's publication in October 1944 of a French-language edition of the complete text of the Auschwitz Report. Vogt's book was issued in time to effect rescue, and it prominently displayed

the imprimatur of a major Swiss Protestant Evangelical Church. On the other hand, Riegner's publication, although it must be applauded as an act of courage, appeared anonymously—because, as Riegner pointed out to me, he believed that as a refugee in Switzerland, he would be subject to official repercussions if his name were attached to the book.

77. Levai, *Abscheu*, 41.

78. Ibid., 41. The full text is in Vogt's *Bruders Hüter?*, 5–11.

79. Levai, *Abscheu*, 41–42.

80. Mantello interview. Copies of this letter are found in MP. See also RG M-20/47, YVA. A German-language version of the letter is also found in the WRB.

81. Many copies of this letter are extant, usually along with the rest of the Mantello package. See, for example, McClelland papers, box 60, WRB. Visser't Hooft was a Dutchman who was appointed joint general secretary of the World Council of Churches, which was then in formation. As Prof. John Conway pointed out, it had originally been due to hold its inaugural meeting in 1940, but because of the war, it had to postpone this event until 1948. In the meantime, VIM, as Visser't Hooft was always called, held the fort in Europe, and refused to consider evacuating this body to North America. In effect, Visser't Hooft became the central link between the churches of the free world, and played a notable role in resistance and rescue efforts. Courtesy of Prof. John Conway. See also W. A. Visser't Hooft, *Memoirs* (London: SCM Press, 1973).

82. For Swiss censorship, see above, n. 2. Federal Councilor Eduard von Steiger was in charge of the censorship.

83. Vogt to Mantello, July 6, 1944. MP. Though Max Huber's letter to Horthy on behalf of the IRC had already been written by July 5, this "reluctant" rescuer's epistle was first delivered to Horthy on July 20 or 21 by Dr. Robert Schirmer, the IRC's representative in Berlin. See Ben-Tov, *IRC,* 188.

84. These and several hundred additional articles are part of my collection of the original news clippings found in MP. Mantello's collection includes articles from the following papers: *Berner Tagwacht* (June 28), *Gazette de Lausanne* (June 28 and June 9), *Basler Nachrichten* June 29), *Basellandschaftliche Zeitung* (Liestal, June 29), *Der Aufbau* (Zurich, June 30), and *La Suisse* (July 2). See *The Sixth Report on Hungarian Jews: World Reaction to the Persecution of Hungarian Jews [Sixth Hungarian Report],* 24, compiled by McClelland's office, Geneva, July 7, 1944, 24, McClelland papers, WRB.

85. Levai, *Black Book* (Zurich: Central European Times, 1948), 232.

86. See *Vatican Docs* for the highly selective collection of documents published by the Vatican. For the text of the pope's cable, see Levai, *Black Book,* 232. See also Saul Friedlander, *Pius XII and the Third Reich: A Documentation* (New York: Knopf, 1966), esp. chap. 9. For Horthy's reply, see Levai, *Black Book,* 232–33.

87. Braham, *Politics,* 1070, 1127, n. 50.

88. The *Vatican Docs* indicate that the reports sent by chargé d'affaires Burzio, dated May 22, and Bernadini, dated July 28, reached the Vatican only in October. However, the Vatican must have received many documents on the destruction of European Jewry

earlier than that. See *Vatican Docs* #204, #205, esp. n. 1, and #279. See also Karny, "Auschwitz Report," 556.

So why did the Vatican choose to respond only at this point? This author cannot offer with certainty the reason for the speediness of the Holy See's response to Mantello's press campaign, especially because of the Vatican Docs' deletion of many relevant documents; but the following speculation may be to the point. Garrett's news release contained the phrase "GARRETT ADDS ABSOLUTE EXACTNESS ABOVE REPORT UNQUESTIONABLE AND DIPLOMAT CATHOLIC FUNCTIONARIES WELLKNOWN VATIKAN DESIRE WIDEST DIFFUSION WORLDWIDE END EXCHANGE" (emphasis added). As mentioned earlier, this "diplomat" most likely refers to the influential Catholic György Barcza, the highly respected former Hungarian ambassador to the Vatican, who had sent an urgent, strongly worded cable to the Holy See on June 24 regarding the frightening situation in Hungary. The fact that Garrett's release was distributed on June 23 to all foreign diplomatic posts in Switzerland, including that of the papal nuncio, together with the Vatican's reception of Barcza's urgent cable the next day, must have made it imperative for the Vatican to respond publicly.

In addition, the Vatican was always reacting to the Protestants' activities or public positions on the Jewish question. This is clear from a note Bernadini attached to his tardy dispatch of Mantello's package, which had been handed to him on June 23, but which he did not send to the Vatican until July 28. The appended note read in part: "In the past few days, the Swiss press has carried various reports highlighting the protests of the Protestant Church against the persecution of the Jews in Hungary and their action on behalf of these people. I enclose herewith a clipping from yesterday's [July 27] *Gazette de Lausanne,* which returns to this theme. Evidently, the various Protestant organizations, in agreement with the Jewish communities, wished to give the subjects a high level of publicity. A Hungarian friend [Mantello] brought to my attention the fact that, as nothing has been published about it, *public opinion in Switzerland could be led to the conclusion that the Catholic Church is doing nothing to help save the Jews*" (emphasis added). See *Vatican Docs* #279, 364. See also United States pressure on the Vatican through the WRB: Wyman, *Docs,* v. 8, Doc. #7, 17–18.

89. Levai, *Black Book,* 232–33.

90. Ibid., 232–33. The second cable is mentioned by the British Exchange Telegraph, 7/15/44, Levai, *Abscheu,* 179.

91. Braham, *Politics,* 754.

92. Levai, *Abscheu,* 197; Levai, *Black Book,* 243.

93. Levai, *Black Book,* 243–46. See also Braham, *Politics,* 756–57.

94. Braham, *Politics,* 811, n. 28.

95. Levai, *Eichmann,* 119; Levai, *Black Book,* 228.

96. Levai, *Abscheu,* 126–27. For complete English-language text, see Harvey Rosenfeld, *Raoul Wallenberg* (Buffalo: Prometheus Books, 1982), 282.

97. SHC *Sixth Hungarian Report,* 8–9. See also Wyman, *Docs* 8, Doc. #7, 17–18.

98. Braham, *Docs* 1, Doc. #183, 414.

99. Cable #1826, Veesenmayer to German foreign office [F. O.], 29 June 1944, Inland 2, cited by Ben-Tov, *IRC,* 165.

100. Braham, *Docs-II,* Doc #324, 695.

101. Braham, *Docs I,* Doc. #183, 415. See also Braham, *Politics,* 758.

102. Braham, *Politics,* 1035–36.

103. Levai, *Wallenberg,* 34, for the French text. The English translations are on p. 265. See also Braham, *Politics,* 1131, n.115. Interestingly, according to a cable from the Swiss in Budapest to Bern, Ambassador Jäger handed the Swedish king's cable to Horthy. Perhaps two copies of this message were handed to Horthy. See cable#122, July 4, 1944. E 2001 (D) 1968/74. Bd. 14. BB.

104. Ibid. Levai, *Wallenberg,* 34.

105. Yahil, "Wallenberg," 38. SHC. *Sixth Hungarian Report,* 17. For the earlier request to the king to help the Jews, this report cites as a source "Swiss papers of July 5, 1944," box 61, WRB. For the king's approval of Wallenberg's mission on the thirtieth, see Levai, *Wallenberg,* 38; also see Rosenfeld, *Wallenberg,* 28.

On that same Friday evening, June 30, the day that King Gustav's cable reached Horthy, Eichmann permitted the release of the Kastner Train from Budapest, with twelve hundred Jews who were supposedly on their way to Palestine. The train, however, did not reach Palestine or any other haven of freedom; rather, after a prolonged trip, which included an unexpected stop in Slovakia, it arrived at Bergen Belsen.

Eichmann was not satisfied with the $2 million in jewels that had been guaranteed him in exchange for permitting the departure of the train; nor was he satisfied with the receipt of a letter of credit from the Sternbuchs for the eagerly sought forty tractors. Only Mantello's press campaign, which had made an international impact by June 30, finally impelled him to release the train from Budapest.

106. Levai, *Abscheu,* 54.

107. Ibid., 40. A copy of the letter is found in the MP.

108. *National-Zeitung,* July 23, 1944.

109. Levai, *Abscheu,* 97–106.

110. Ibid.

111. The "basis" for Rothmund's suggestion was a report sent by an informer concerning unknown charges. Very likely it referred to Mantello's issuing of "pre-dated" Salvadoran papers, a charge frequently leveled at Mantello. See internal memo by Rothmund, 6/27/44. E 2001 (D) 1968/74. Bd. 14. BB.

8. The Press Campaign in Full Swing

1. Levai, *Abscheu,* 161. For articles throughout the world, see, for example, Lipstadt, *Belief,* 233–39.

2. Levai, *Abscheu,* 97–106.

3. Ibid., 157.

4. While we are unaware of the specific reaction of the German people to the press

campaign, we do know that some managed to obtain copies of the Swiss papers, paying as much as 100 deutsche marks per copy. See *St. Galler Tagblatt,* Aug. 25, 1945. For the reaction of the German diplomats, see chaps. 10–11.

Although President Roosevelt and Eden had already sent warnings to Horthy in March, after the German occupation of Hungary, they made absolutely no impact and can therefore not be included in the chronology of rescue of Hungarian Jewry.

5. See *Press Comment in Switzerland Concerning the Anti-Jewish Measures in Hungary, June–August, 1944.* McClelland papers, box 61, WRB. Nowhere, however, do we find that these urgent appeals had any impact on his callousness, or that they even entered his consciousness. In fact, he had the audacity after the war to claim at least partial credit for the press campaign, despite his contempt of Mantello and Bányai, and his open indifference to the Jewish plight.

McClelland had the same gall in recent years to claim to have been the first person to transmit Weissmandl's plea, through Sternbuch, to bomb Auschwitz. He had an intense dislike for both Sternbuch and Weissmandl, refusing to transmit their pleas for many weeks until pressed by Kopecky on June 24, even though Sternbuch had made this request almost daily since mid-May. See Kranzler, *Thy Brother's Blood,* 104–5. See also letter by Roswell McClelland to the *Washington Post,* April 27, 1983.

6. *St. Gallen Tagblatt,* June 27, 1944.

7. *National Zeitung,* July 6, 1944.

8. *Volksrecht,* July 6, 1944.

9. *Neue Zürcher Zeitung,* July 7, 1944.

10. *Exchange Telegraph,* July 7, 1944.

11. *Gazette de Lausanne,* July 7, 1944.

12. *Volkstimme,* July 8, 1944.

13. *Basellandischer Zeitung,* July 8, 1944.

14. *Schweizer Republikanische Blätter,* July 8, 1944.

15. *Sandschaeftler,* July 10, 1944.

16. *Der Bund,* July 11, 1944.

17. *Die Nation,* July 13, 1944.

18. *Werkvolk,* July 13, 1944.

19. *Offener Tagblatt,* July 13, 1944.

20. *National Zeitung,* July 13, 1944.

21. *Neue Zürcher Nachrichten,* July 13, 1944.

22. *Bodener Tagblatt,* July 13, 1944.

23. *Der Bund,* July 13, 1944.

24. *Appenzeiler Anzeiger,* July 13, 1944.

25. *Die Nation,* July 13, 1944.

26. *Der Wehnthaler,* July 13, 1944.

27. *Die National Zeitung,* July 14, 1944.

28. *Le Indépendance,* July 14, 1944.

29. *Das Volk,* July 14, 1944.

30. *Oberthurgauer und Arboner Zeitung,* July 14, 1944.
31. *Der Aufbau,* July 14, 1944.
32. *National Zeitung,* July 15, 1944.
33. *Express,* July 15, 1944.
34. *Zürchersee Zeitung,* July 15, 1944.
35. *Basler Volksblatt* (Catholic), July 15, 1944.
36. *Volksrecht,* July 15, 1944.
37. *Exchange Telegraph,* July 15, 1944.
38. *Das Volk,* July 15, 1944.
39. *Volksrecht,* July 15, 1944.
40. *National Zeitung,* July 16, 1944.
41. Ibid.
42. *Neue Zürcher Zeitung,* July 16, 1944.
43. *Volksblatt,* July 16, 1944.
44. Cited in Ben-Tov, *IRC,* 403.
45. *Schweizer Zeitung,* July 18, 1944.
46. *Der Wehnthaler,* July 19, 1944.
47. *Gazetta Ticinese,* July 19, 1944.
48. *Das Volk,* July 19, 1944.
49. *National Zeitung,* July 19, 1944.
50. *Die Nation,* July 20, 1944.
51. *La Sentinelle,* July 21, 1944.
52. *Schweizer Frauenbund,* July 21, 1944.
53. *Limmattaler Tagblatt,* July 22, 1944.
54. *Burgdorfer Tagblatt,* July 23, 1944.
55. *La Sentinelle,* July 25, 1944.
56. *Limmattaler Tagblatt,* July 26, 1944.
57. *Berner Tagwacht,* July 26, 1944.
58. *Neue Zürcher Zeitung,* July 27, 1944.
59. *National Zeitung,* July 27, 1944.
60. *Volksrecht,* July 29, 1944.
61. *Neue Zürcher Zeitung,* July 31, 1944.
62. See, for example, *The Ludwig Report* (1957), *The Lifeboat Is Full* (1969), and most recently, *Die Schweiz und die Juden, 1933–1945* (1994).
63. *Volksrecht,* July 6, 1944.
64. *Neue Zürcher Zeitung,* July 7, 1944.
65. See chap. 7. See also *Exchange Telegraph,* July 7, 1944 and *Sixth Report on Hungarian Jews: World Reaction to the Persecution of Hungarian Jews* (Geneva, July 7, 1944), 2–3. McClelland papers, box 60, WRB.
66. *Badener Tagblatt,* July 12, 1944.
67. *Neue Zürcher Zeitung,* July 9, 1944. Incidentally, Johann Heinrich Pestalozzi

(1746–1827) was a world-renowned Swiss educator who established the basic principles of modern elementary education.

68. Häsler, *Lifeboat,* 286.

69. *Basler Nachrichten,* July 12, 1944.

70. *Sandschäftler,* July 12, 1944.

71. *Züger Volksblatt,* July 12, 1944.

72. *Berner Tagblatt,* July 12, 1944.

73. *Landschäftler,* July 12, 1944.

74. Ibid.

75. *Berner Tagwacht,* July 27, 1944.

76. Ibid.

77. *Züger Volksblatt,* July 12, 1944.

78. *Wervolk,* July 13, 1944.

79. *Schweizer Zeitung,* July 18, 1944.

80. The writer was evidently unaware that Horthy had already quietly halted deportations on July 7, which is why he assumed that the Western protests had been futile.

81. *Zürichsee Zeitung,* July 15, 1944.

82. *Aktion Nationaler Wiederstand,* n.d. (ca. July 1944).

83. *Oltner Tagblatt,* July 13, 1944.

84. Pastor Vogt was known by this epithet because of his concern for refugees.

85. *The Express,* July 15, 1944. See also *National Zeitung,* July 15, 1944.

86. *National Zeitung,* July 15, 1944.

87. Ibid., July 13, 1944.

88. *Basler Volksblatt,* July 17, 1944.

89. *Der Aufbau,* July 14, 1944.

90. Rothmund had also been responsible in October 1938 for persuading the German government to require the placement of a *J* on the passport of every German Jew. See Alexander Grossman, *Nur das Gewissen: Carl Lutz und seine Budapester Aktion Geschichte und Portraet* (Waldgut: Verlag im Waldgut, 1986), 192.

91. See *Ludwig Report,* 293–94; Häsler, *Lifeboat,* 285, 326–27. It stated that "refugees on the ground of race alone are not political refugees," people classified as political refugees were permitted asylum. On July 12, 1944, this regulation was changed to note that "for the present, admission is to be granted to . . . foreigners whose lives and persons are actually in danger for political or other reasons and who have no alternative but flight into Switzerland in order to escape this danger" (328). Ironically, in November 1942, there was a minor flurry of press articles that opposed any further admission of refugees (327). This was somewhat understandable because the Swiss and German borders were open and there was no way of distinguishing the "good Germans" from the unwanted German Jews. Ironically, the Germans at first hesitated to implement Rothmund's suggestion, fearing retaliation in kind; but with Swiss assurance, they willingly approved this pernicious practice. See Hilberg, *Destruction,* 118–20.

In addition, the Swiss regulations were strengthened on December 29, 1942, making a distinction between refugees who were permitted entry and those who were barred. The "political" refugees were the desired ones, and more than 250,000 of these entered legally, including deserters from the German army. On the other hand, "racial" refugees, a euphemism for Jews, were barred unless they were under sixteen or over sixty, or from a family with members in either age-group. See *Ludwig Report,* 204–5. See also Kranzler, *Heroine* (about Recha Sternbuch), and Kranzler, *Thy Brother's Blood.* See Yehuda Bauer, *The Holocaust in Historical Perspective* (Seattle: Univ. of Washington, 1978), 88–91. Von Steiger was not only in charge of censorship, but also was the architect of the anti-immigration attitude known as "The Boat Is Full" mentality. See esp. Häsler, *Lifeboat,* 174–82.

92. When, in late 1938, Rothmund discovered the rescue efforts by Recha's team of Swiss farmers, taxi drivers, and even a police chief (Paul Grüninger), she was arrested and pressured to inform upon her fellow Swiss rescue activists. She admitted everything, yet, despite a threat of a long prison term, she refused to inform on anyone. Although she was released from prison after several weeks, the case continued for three years, after which it was dropped. However, as a result of her incarceration, she suffered a miscarriage.

St. Gallen police chief Paul Grüninger was deposed in 1941 and deprived of his pension by the Swiss government for his part in the facilitating of more than 3,600 refugees into Switzerland. For years, the Sternbuchs helped him earn a livelihood. In 1971, a year before his death, he was honored by Yad Vashem. Only recently (1997) was he fully rehabilitated. See Mordecai Paldiel, "Grüninger, Paul," in *EH,* 627–28. For Recha's arrest, see esp. Kranzler, *Heroine,* chap. four, and Kranzler, *Thy Brother's Blood,* 118–20.

The refugees rescued by Recha Sternbuch were mostly Jews of every political and religious stripe, as well as some non-Jews. She put up all of them in her home until they could be taken care of by various refugee organizations. See the protocols of her interrogation by the prosecutor at her trial. See also Sternbuch correspondence with McClelland of June 22, 27, July 11, 1944, SP, all part of my archives.

93. *The Nation,* July 13, 1944.

94. *Neue Toggenburger Zeitung,* July 14, 1944. Similarly, the *Oberthugauer und Arboner Zeitung,* of this same date, featured an article titled "We Cannot Keep Silent," which was simultaneously reprinted, in its entirety, in two French papers, *L'Indépendance* and *L'Impartial.* Frequently, other important articles manifesting a similar perspective, if not the same originality, were reprinted elsewhere.

95. *National Zeitung,* July 12, 1944. See also the *Schweizer Wochen-Zeitung,* July 12, 1944.

96. See Vogt to the president of the Federal Council, July 14, 1944. McClelland papers, box 58, WRB.

97. *National Zeitung,* July 16, 1944.

98. Ibid., July 24, 1944. See also Levai, *Abscheu,* 154–55.

99. *National Zeitung,* July 24, 1944.

100. Levai, *Abscheu,* 156.

101. See copy in Ben-Tov, *IRC,* 403–4.

102. *Volksrecht,* July 15, 1944.

103. *Das Volk,* July 19, 1944.

104. A similar case involved a conference that had been called to discuss the possibility of declaring Rome an open city, thus sparing it from air raids because of its valuable collection of religious and artistic treasures. Rabbi Abraham Kalmanowitz of the Vaad Hatzalah made a plea to the WRB to see "whether it is not possible to put the saving of Jewish lives and other persecuted people on the agenda" of that conference. See Kranzler, *TBB,* 137.

105. *Das Volk,* Aug. 23, 1944.

106. *Die Nation,* July 20, 1944.

107. Marcus Weiler to Saly Mayer, (covering) July 1944. Dossier 1128, SMP. JDCA.

108. *Burgdorfer Tagblatt,* July 23, 1944.

109. *Neue Zürcher Zeitung,* July 16, 1944.

110. See the July 22 issue of the *Ostschweizerisches Tagblatt.*

111. See Kranzler, "Wise." For the rabbis' march on Washington on Oct. 6, 1943, see Kranzler, *Thy Brother's Blood,* 99–100. The only other protest march was by blacks, organized by A. Philip Randolph in 1941, in a civil rights protest. See John Morton Blum, *V Was for Victory: Politics and American Culture During World War II* (New York: Harcourt, Brace and Javanovich, 1976), 207–8.

112. Even Rothmund, in a letter of May 24, 1948, admitted to former Swiss consul Carl Lutz that "we could have taken in several hundred thousand refugees." Grossman, *Lutz,* 191.

113. *National Zeitung,* July 24, 1944. See also Levai, *Abscheu,* 154–55.

114. Levai, *Abscheu,* 144–45.

9. The Response by the Hungarians, the Germans, and the IRC

1. Ben-Tov, *IRC,* 165.

2. Braham, *Docs-11,* Doc #183, 414.

3. Braham, *Politics,* 753.

4. Braham, *Doc-1,* Doc. #183, 414; Levai, *Eichmann,* 126; Levai, *Abscheu,* 203–4.

5. Levai, *Black Book,* 232–33. See also Levai, *Eichmann,* 122–23. For Horthy's talk with the Swedish ambassador, see Levai, *Wallenberg,* 34, and Anger, *Wallenberg,* 43. Braham, *Docs-1,* Doc. #183, 414; Levai, *Eichmann,* 126; Levai, *Abscheu,* 203–4.

6. Braham, *Politics,* 732–39.

7. Ibid., 761.

8. Levai, *Black Book,* 248.

9. For Horthy's foiling of the coup attempt, see esp. Levai, *Black Book,* chap. 12; Braham, *Politics,* 761–62; and Levai, *Eichmann,* 122.

10. Levai, *Eichmann,* 123.

11. Braham, *Docs-11,* Doc. #186, 420–21.

12. Levai, *Abscheu,* 205–6. See also Braham, *Docs-11,* Doc. #187, 425–27.

13. Levai, *Abscheu,* 207.
14. For the cable, see Braham, *Docs-II,* 426–28.
15. Braham, *Politics,* 762.
16. Braham, *Docs-II,* Doc. #187, 425.
17. Ibid., Doc. #325, 697.
18. Braham, *Politics,* 762.
19. Braham, *Docs-II,* Doc. #189–90, 436–37.
20. Ibid., Doc. #190, 191, 437–40; Levai, *Black Book,* 245.
21. Braham, *Docs-II,* Doc. #188, 430–35.
22. See Levai, *Black Book,* 233, n. 2. In reality, Tahy was not a chargé d'affaires; he was only the representative of Baron George Bakach-Bessenyey, a Hungarian dissident, during the time Baron Karoly Bothmer took over the affairs of the legation in Bern. Tahy acted upon Bakach-Bessenyey's orders.
23. This is part of a report sent to Budapest on July 11, 1944. E 2001 (D) 1968/74. Bd. 14. BB.
24. Ibid.
25. Bányai-McClelland, July 4, 1994, box 60, WRB. Mantello and Bányai kept Imre Tahy informed of every development in the press campaign. Mantello interview.
26. Ben-Tov, *IRC,* 177–78.
27. Ibid., 177.
28. E 2001 (D) 1968/74. Bd. 14. BB. Also cited in Ben-Tov, *IRC,* 176–77. Apparently, Ben-Tov again attributes all the publicity in Switzerland to Koechlin's appeal, unaware of Mantello's role in the press campaign. What is especially interesting about this vignette is the fact that it took place on July 1, during the early stages of the press campaign. The great increase in the number of articles immediately thereafter must have unnerved the one sensitive German in the legation.
29. Levai, *Abscheu,* 430.
30. Braham, *Docs-II,* Doc. #193, 443.
31. Ibid., Doc. #198, 449, July 13, 1944.
32. Braham, *Politics,* 768–69.
33. Levai, *Abscheu,* 219–25.
34. Ibid., 224–25.
35. Levai, *Black Book,* 244. See also Braham, *Politics,* 762.
36. See Kranzler, *Thy Brother's Blood,* 248–50. See also photo of a Spanish Red Cross label on these packages, p. 319. Original in my possession, courtesy of the recipient, Mrs. Rivka Paskus.
37. Ben-Tov, *IRC,* 172.
38. Ibid., 173.
39. Ibid.
40. Ibid., 152.
41. Ibid., 183.
42. Ibid., 182.

43. Ibid., 173.
44. E 2001 (D) 1968/74. Bd. 14. BB.
45. Ben-Tov, *IRC,* 175.
46. Ibid., 183.
47. Ibid., 184. Ben-Tov is fully aware of the Swiss press campaign and the public out-cry in Switzerland, which demanded the end of the government's silence. However, he is totally unaware of Mantello's role as its prime instigator. See p. 448, n.13, where he cites quite a few "sample headlines." He attributes these, however, solely to Koechlin's appeal.
48. Braham, *Docs-II,* Doc. #187, 425, July 6, 1944.
49. Ibid., Doc. #188, 430.
50. See Anger, *Wallenberg,* esp. 32–48.
51. Ben-Tov, *IRC,* 177–78.
52. Wallenberg was precisely the opposite of the legalistic Roswell McClelland, the American representative sent to facilitate rescue during the Allies' winning streak. More-over, unlike Wallenberg, who daily risked his life in pursuit of rescue, McClelland sat securely in Switzerland. For example, see Anger, *Wallenberg.* For additional obstructions by McClelland, see Kranzler, *Thy Brother's Blood,* esp. chap. 8.
53. Ben-Tov, *IRC,* 186.
54. Levai, *Abscheu,* 51.
55. Ibid., 52–53.
56. Braham, *Docs-II,* Doc. #201, 457–58.
57. Vago, "Horthy," 26. Vago is surprised that the same Horthy who only weeks ear-lier had had no compunctions about sending nearly a half million Hungarian Jews to their deaths, and when Hungary was still at the mercy of Hitler's army, should now refuse to complete Hitler's *Aktion.* He is apparently unaware of the enormous impact of the press campaign, the international pressure, and the immediate Swiss threat, all of which were motivating factors for Horthy. Vago prefers to attribute the change to "a combina-tion of political opportunism influenced by Horthy's moderate, anti-Nazi friends and his gentry mentality, which approved of 'humane, conventional' anti-Jewish steps but opposed physical annihilation." He attributes Horthy's sudden change of heart primar-ily to the deteriorating military situation in Hungary, and he apparently ignores the fact that, when Horthy was carrying out Hitler's Final Solution, the Russians were not far from Hungary's borders. By early July, he would have completed the deportations. See also Braham, *Politics,* 762, and Braham, *Docs-II,* 458.
58. Braham, *Politics,* 771–74.
59. Braham, *Docs-II,* Doc. #198, 449. See also Doc. #187, 425.
60. Vago, "Horthy," 26.
61. Ibid., 25–26; Braham, *Docs-II,* 455.
62. Levai, *Abscheu,* 222–23.
63. Vago, "Horthy," 25–26; Braham, *Docs-II,* Doc. #200, 455.
64. Braham, *Docs-II,* Doc. #200, 456.
65. Vago, "Horthy," 25–26; Braham, *Docs-II,* Doc. #200, 455.

66. Levai, *Abscheu,* 232–36. The balance of Tahy's report, cited below, derives from this source. Vago, in his excellent article "Horthy," gives the date of this meeting as the seventeenth. As the report shows, Tahy did go to Geneva on the seventeenth, but first met with the head of the IRC the following day.

67. Ibid., 234–36.

68. Ben-Tov, *IRC,* 195–96, 451, n. 55. See also chap. 7.

69. Levai, *Abscheu,* 236–37.

70. Vago, "Horthy," 28.

71. Ben-Tov, *IRC,* 197.

72. See the correspondence between Pilet-Golaz and various political and nonpolitical Swiss bodies. For example, Koechlin to Pilet-Golaz, June 26, 1944; de Haller to Pilet-Golaz, July 6, 1944; Pilet-Golaz to Ambassador Jäger, July 7, 1944. For Pilet-Golaz's early negative stance, see Häsler, *Lifeboat,* 117, 319.

73. E 2001 (D) 1968/74. Bd. 14. BB.

74. Rothmund memo. July 11, 1944. E 2001 (D) 1968/74. Bd. 14. BB.

75. Braham, *Docs-II,* Doc. #204, 461–463.

76. Before the war, the *Pester-Lloyd* had a reputation as one of the best newspapers in Europe. Copy in my possession. MP.

77. Peretz Szigály to Natan Schwalb July 18, 1944. RG-25. SMP. JDCA. See also minutes, meeting, Hechalutz, July 18, 1944. RG-37a file #187. MLA.

78. Original (in German) in my possession, as part of the MP.

79. Braham, *Docs-II,* Doc. #211, 474.

80. *Das Volk,* July 15, 1944.

81. *Das Volksrecht,* July 15, 1944.

82. *National Zeitung,* July 16, 1944.

83. *Neue Zürcher Zeitung,* July 18. 1944.

84. *Volksblatt,* July 17, 1944.

85. *Das Volk,* July 19, 1944.

86. *Schweizer Frauenbund,* July 21, 1944.

87. *Volksrecht,* Aug. 1, 1944.

88. Ibid.

89. Unidentified article submitted to the Swiss Department of Foreign Affairs, July 20, 1944. MP.

90. An unsigned article in the McClelland papers, box 64, WRB.

91. Braham, *Politics,* 1060–61.

92. Ibid., 1061.

93. *Limmathaler Tagblatt,* July 22, 1944.

94. Schaffert to Mantello, July 24, 1944. MP.

95. *Neue Zürcher Zeitung,* July 27, 1944.

96. Levai, *Abscheu,* 160.

97. The date of the newspaper is not given in the Swiss source listed below, but is based on the obvious reference to the king's public appeal to Horthy.

98. E 2001 (D)/17 Pd. 14. BB.

99. E 2001 (D) 3, BB.

100. The information from Rabbi Hertz was obtained and published through the organization called the Chief Rabbis' Religious Emergency Council [CRREC] run by his son-in-law, Rabbi Dr. Solomon Schonfeld. Rabbi Schonfeld was a former student of Rabbi Weissmandl in the Nitra yeshiva, and a major Jewish rescue activist in Britain. Rabbi Weissmandl was his primary inspiration and they were on some level of communication even during the war. Schonfeld's rescue efforts ran from 1938 through 1948, and by a count based on the Schonfeld papers, he rescued more than 3700 Jews before, during, and after the war. Schonfeld used (with permission) the chief rabbi's prominence to help him open doors in the British government. However, he was the activist. See my *Solomon Schonfeld: His Place in History,* ed. David Kranzler and Gertruder Hirschler (New York: Judaica Press, 1982).

101. Philip Paneth. Notes on the Mantello press campaign. August (?) 1944. MP.

102. Lipstadt, *Belief,* 234.

103. Ibid., 265–66.

104. For a deeper analysis, see Kranzler, "Wise."

105. Lipstadt, *Belief,* 264.

106. In an unofficial survey, I selected at random a dozen Anglo-Jewish and three Yiddish newspapers published after the appearance of the Auschwitz Report. Half a dozen newspapers cited the article on their front pages, three cited it somewhere in the paper, while three omitted it entirely. All three Yiddish papers published the article on their front pages. As noted earlier, for the entire Swiss press campaign, whether appearing in Switzerland, Sweden, England, or the United States, the Mantello version is readily apparent by the use of the statistic of 1,715,000 murdered in Auschwitz, in contrast to the higher and more accurate number of 1,765,000 found in all the other versions. Thus, when the *New York Times* published Vogt's report on July 3 and 6, the statistic used was Mantello's 1,715,000, whereas the WRB-endorsed Auschwitz Report gave the accurate number of 1,765,000. This discrepancy is noted by Lipstadt, without any explanation of why and how the 50,000 Lithuanian Jews were dropped from the former statistic. See Lipstadt, *Belief,* 235, 263–65. Incidentally, the Auschwitz Report publicized by the American press was one of two sent by Weissmandl to Czech ambassador Kopecky, who, in turn, brought it to McClelland.

107. See Josef Mandl to Wilhelm Filderman, Aug. 1, 1944, P-20/46 YVA.

10. Horthy Takes Charge

1. Braham, *Docs-11,* Doc. #201, 457–58. See also Karsai, *Vadirat* 3:81–82; Moshe Y. Herczl, *Christianity and the Holocaust of Hungarian Jewry* (New York: New York Univ. Press, 1993), 216–17.

2. Most Palestine certificates, other than the "Capitalist Certificates," were designated for individuals, and even these had a limit of four members per family. Krausz urged the "creation" of families, as had been done with the Salvadoran papers from the outset. The history of *aliya,* and especially the role of the certificates, has hardly received the

scholarly attention it deserves. One of the few sources is Abraham Edelheit, *The Yishuv in the Shadow of the Holocaust: Zionist Politics and Rescue Aliya, 1933–1939* [Edelheit, *Yishuv*] (Boulder Colo.: Westview Press, 1996); see esp. chap. 6. For Lutz showing Wallenberg his protective papers, see Lutz, *Report—1944*, 5–6.

3. This unit is largely based on Bela Vago's excellent article "The Horthy Offer: A Missed Opportunity for Rescuing Jews in 1944" [Vago, "Horthy"], in *Contemporary Views on the Holocaust*, ed. Randolph L. Braham (Boston: Kluwer Nijhof, 1983), 23–46. See also Braham, *Politics*, 1078–83, esp. 1080, and 1113–17, and Paldiel, "Lutz," *EH*, 925. For the limited protected papers, see Alexander Grossman, *Nur Das Gewissen; Carl Lutz und seine Budapester Aktion* (n.p., im Waldgut, 1986), 54.

4. Braham, *Politics*, 1080–81. Various figures for the number of certificate holders are used: sometimes 7,400, undoubtedly including the hundreds of Swedish exit papers (Vago, "Horthy," 36); sometimes 7,800 (see Braham, *Politics*, 1080); and sometimes 9,000, which most likely included 8,000 people with certificates plus 1,000 children. See Braham, *Politics*, 1082. Robert Rozett, "Horthy Offer," 690, cites the figure 8,243.

5. Vago, "Horthy," 29–30. See also Wasserstein, *Britain and the Jews* (Oxford: Clarendon Press, 1979), 262–64.

6. Vago, "Horthy," 32–34.

7. Ibid., 32–33.

8. Ibid., 35.

9. The number was 7,400, including 400 people with Swedish visas.

10. Vago, "Horthy," 36.

11. David Wyman, *Abandonment of the Jews: America and the Holocaust, 1939–1945* (New York: Pantheon Books, 1985), 239–40. See also FO PRO #371/42822 XC 32688, Nov. 9 and 22. The first document reports the Swiss offer for accepting up to 12,000 Jews. Apparently, this is a combination of the 5,000 children and the approximately 7,000 adults with certificates.

12. Ibid., 239–40.

13. Vago, "Horthy," 34. For the article, see the *New York Times*, Aug. 18, 1944.

14. Vago, "Horthy," 37. See also Josef Mandl to Filderman, Aug. 1, 1944, concerning Romania's policy regarding Jewish transit. Mandl Papers. RG M-20/46. YVA.

15. Vago, "Horthy," 38.

16. Mantello interview. See also PW Inquiry.

17. Mordecai Paldiel and Robert Rozett, "Carl Lutz," *EH*, 924.

18. Carl Lutz, *Report for 1942*. Division of Foreign Interests in Budapest. RG P-19/3-3, 1–2. YVA.

19. Lutz, *Report—1944*, 2. RG P-19/111. YVA. For the labor battalions, see Braham, *Politics*, chap. 10. Lutz had also obtained for Krausz an exemption from the Hungarian Labor Battalion, to which all Jewish men of military age (18–50) had been subject even before the occupation.

20. Lutz, *Report—1944*, 6.

21. Minutes of meeting, Aug. 27, 1944, 1. RG-Administrative-5. SMP, JDCA. See also Paldiel, "Lutz," *EH*, 925.

22. For information on Krausz finally persuading the British to give the Palestine certificates their protection, see Paldiel, "Lutz," 925. For Lutz's remarks about the extraterritorial status, see Lutz, *Report—1944,* 2–4.

23. PW Inquiry, Lutz testimony, 3.

24. Ibid., 4.

25. Ibid.

26. The Orthodox Vaad Hatzalah's efforts in Washington to gain recognition of Paraguayan and other Latin American papers relating to the detention camp at Vittel began in Dec. 1943 and continued through Apr. 1944. See Kranzler, *Thy Brother's Blood,* esp. chap. 7; also Latin American Papers in the index.

27. Levai, *Wallenberg,* 28–30.

28. Ibid., chaps. 1–2. For Rabbi Ehrenpreis's lack of rescue efforts, see Kranzler, *Thy Brother's Blood,* 56–57, 119–20, 219.

29. Levai, *Wallenberg,* 31. See also Yahil, "Wallenberg," *YVS* 15:7–53, esp. 23. For the rescue of 700 Norwegian Jews, see Samuel Abramson, "Norwegian Jewry in the Holocaust," in *EH,* 1067–68.

30. Levai, *Wallenberg,* 47–48. For Sweden's role in relation to Hungary, see Braham, *Politics,* 1083–84. For the history of the Danish rescue, see the excellent book by Leni Yahil, *The Rescue of Danish Jewry,* trans. Morris Gradel (Philadelphia: Jewish Publication Society, 1969).

31. Per Anger, *With Raoul Wallenberg in Budapest,* trans. Mel David Paul and Margareta Paul (New York: Holocaust Library, 1981), 46–47.

32. Levai, *Wallenberg,* 44.

33. Lutz, *Report—1944,* 5–6.

34. Levai, *Wallenberg,* 49–50. For Weissmandl's similar focus on money as the key to rescue, see the cartoon by Andre Steiner, a close associate of Weissmandl, in the Slovakian Jewish underground. This cartoon showed a bearded Weissmandl in the uniform of the seventeenth-century Austrian general Montecuccoli, shooting a cannon spitting out thousands of dollars in bills. See cartoon in Kranzler, *My Brother's Blood,* 311.

35. Levai, *Wallenberg,* 85–86. Mantello interview.

36. Lester, "Wallenberg," 151–52.

37. Ibid.

38. Ibid., 153.

39. Braham, *Docs-II,* Doc. #217, 484.

40. Levai, *Abscheu,* 238–39.

41. Ibid., 239.

42. Ibid.

43. Braham, *Docs-II,* 461–62.

44. Levai, *Abscheu,* 240–41.

45. Ibid.

46. Levai, *Wallenberg,* 68. Because Wallenberg was in close contact with Lutz from the first day, he was most likely the source of this very useful rescue tool.

47. Levai, *Black Book,* 214–20; Levai, *Eichmann,* 139–40. In Colonel Ferenczy's opin-

ion, the deportations were to begin on the twenty-seventh. See also Braham, *Docs-II,*
Doc. #214, 481; Braham, *Politics,* 792–94.

48. Braham, *Politics,* 795.

49. Levai, *Wallenberg,* 69.

50. Ben-Tov, *IRC,* 233–34.

51. Braham, *Politics,* 796. See also Ben-Tov, *IRC,* 213.

52. Ben-Tov, *IRC,* 213.

53. *Die Lage,* Aug. 23, 1944. In Braham, *Docs-II,* Doc. #211, 473.

54. Jäger to Bern, Aug. 26, 1944. E 2001 (D) 3. BB. Braham, *Docs-II,* Doc. #214, 481.

55. For Braham's focus on the geopolitical concerns as the sole basis for Himmler's decision, see Braham, *Politics,* 796–97. For the August 25 date, see also Levai, *Eichmann,* 142.
Braham gives the date as the twenty-fourth. The document itself points to 3 A.M. on the
twenty-fifth. Levai cites the correct date of the twenty-fifth and points out that Kurt
Becher, Himmler's representative in negotiations with Kastner, fooled Kastner with this
cable. Becher told Kastner, who worked with Saly Mayer, to save the remaining Jews of
Budapest, and that it was the result of their joint effort that made Himmler halt deportations. However, as Levai points out, Becher's cable of August 25 to Himmler at his headquarters in Hochwald was sent at nine P.M. and first arrived on the twenty-sixth—i.e.,
thirty-six hours after Himmler's cable was sent. *Abscheu,* 279–280. Yahil cites Braham's
incorrect date of August 24. "Wallenberg," 34. See also Bauer, *American Jewry,* 415. Obviously, Bauer, like most historians, is totally unaware of the Swiss press and church campaigns and their impact. He realizes that Himmler sent his own cable to Becher on
August 25 at 3 A.M., many hours before Becher sent his cable to Himmler, yet he is
unaware of the implications of this thirty-six-hour discrepancy.

56. For Veesenmayer's evaluation of Himmler's halt of deportations, see Braham, *Docs-
II,* Doc. #234, 514, 517. For the August 25 cable, see *Docs-II,* Doc. #214, 481, 483.

57. Braham, *Politics,* 1215.

58. Ibid., 1058–59. In this chapter, I rely to a great extent on Braham's long and important chap. 31, "International Reaction." His sole problem throughout the book is his failure to credit Mantello's role in virtually all aspects of this and other important rescue
efforts by the international community.

59. For a copy of the label on the packages sent to Auschwitz by Mrs. Reichmann under
the aegis of the Spanish Red Cross, one of which reached its recipient, Mrs. Rivka Paskus,
see my *Thy Brother's Blood,* 319. The original of the label in my possession, courtesy of
Mrs. Rivka Paskus.

60. Braham, *Politics,* 1060.

61. General Potamkin was an eighteenth-century Russian officer who tried to impress
the czar by superficially refurbishing a village for inspection purposes.

62. Braham, *Politics,* 1060.

63. Ibid., 1061–62. See the minutes of the meeting of the IRC and the Jewish representatives. RG M-20/47. YVA.

64. Braham, *Politics,* 1062–63. See also n. 5.

65. IRC. Report, *Concerning the Situation of Jews in Hungary,* Dec. 15, 1944, 4. SMP.

JDCA. See also interviews with Samuel Frey and Chaim Roth, two important Jewish leaders who remained in Budapest after the departure of the so-called Kastner Train, on June 30. Frey specialized in caring for Jewish children's institutions. The IRC was very helpful to the very end. He was also helped greatly by Wallenberg, who gave him both the Swedish seal and official consulate paper to permit him to "create" numerous "authentic" Swedish protective papers. Likewise, Chaim Roth obtained original Swedish blank consulate paper to produce such protective papers. An original of such a blank official Swedish paper, part of the original documents, in my archives.

66. See Haim Avni, *Spain, the Jews, and Franco* (Philadelphia: Jewish Publication Society, 1982), esp. chaps. 5–6. See also Avni, "Spain," in *EH*, 1394.

67. See Kranzler, *Thy Brother's Blood*, 247–54.

68. Interviews with Mrs. Renee Reichmann and her daughter, Mrs. Eva Gutwirth. See also the memoirs of Rives Childs, *Foreign Service Farewell*, 116–17; Robert Rozett, "Child Rescue in Budapest," *Holocaust and Genocide Studies* 2 (1987):49–59.

69. Braham, *Politics*, 1061–62, also n. 17. See also Childs, *Foreign Service*, 116–17.

70. Braham, *Politics*, 1062. According to recent research by Robert Rozett, there were more than fifty IRC-protected houses, which would raise the number to as high as six thousand. Dr. Robert Rozett correspondence, with me, Dec. 24, 1997.

71. Braham, *Docs-II*, Doc. #217, 484.

72. See chap. 11.

11. The Nyilas Era

1. Ironically, Horthy's early attempt to achieve independence from the Germans almost doomed the Jews, for the Germans maneuvered a coup and managed to overthrow him.

2. Veesenmayer to Ribbentrop, Oct. 24, 1944, on the Hungarian-Jewish policy as given over to the new Hungarian (Szalasi) government. Oct. 19, 1944. Braham, *Docs-II*, Doc. #234, 514–17. The 7,000 approved by the Germans was for individuals only; they did not approve Krausz's number of 40,000 based on 7,000 families.

3. Braham, *Politics*, 850–58, esp. 854.

4. Levai, *Black Book*, 385–87.

5. Braham, *Politics*, 832–38. Kaltenbrunner was opposed by Gen. Walter Schellenberg, who sought until the end to negotiate with the Allies and Jewish organizations to release Jewish inmates from the camps rather than decimate them. See, for example, Kranzler, *Thy Brother's Blood*, 11–14.

6. This same Hungarian diplomat, who had been expelled from Stockholm, was responsible for a raid on the Swedish legation during the siege in Budapest. Anger, *Wallenberg*, 111.

7. Ibid., 110–11.

8. Levai, *Wallenberg*, 100–1. I have also pointed out earlier (chap. 9, n. 64) that at least two Jewish leaders (whom I interviewed) were provided by Wallenberg with the official Swedish consular paper and seal, with which they mass-produced many hundreds, if not thousands, of additional Swedish protective papers.

9. Perlesca, a rather "unusual" substitute, was in reality an Italian who was sought by his government as an anti-Fascist. He had been a frequent visitor to his friend in the Spanish legation and therefore aroused little suspicion by the Hungarian authorities. Braham, *Politics*, 1090–91. See also Mordecai Paldiel, *The Path of the Righteous* (Hoboken, N.J.: Ktav, 1993), 304, 317. For more details and depositions on Perlesca, see files of the division of "Path of the Righteous," headed by Dr. Mordecai Paldiel. Miguel Angel de Muguiro's earlier reports had been critical of Hungary's anti-Semitic position. See Avni, *Spain*, 170.

10. If we add the 1,500 names reported by Hull to the 1,200 obtained by Mrs. Reichmann, we have 2,700 authorized Jews protected by the Spanish legation. Add several hundred that were added by Sanz-Briz's successor or holders of forged versions or both, and the total comes to approximately 3,000.

11. Braham, *Politics*, 1093–95.

12. *IRC Report*, Dec. 1, 1945, 15–16. SMP, JDCA.

13. Ibid.

14. Braham, *Politics*, 1074–76.

15. Lutz, PW Inquiry, 4. This points once again to the nefarious role of Roswell McClelland, the representative of the WRB, sent to facilitate rescue, who dampened any suggestion to use American interest in the use of Latin American protective papers as rescue tools.

16. Lutz, *Report—1944*, 5–6, YVA.

17. As late as November 1944, Bern was still annoyed by the fact that Mantello had earlier issued thousands of Salvadoran papers, and sought to counteract them. Levai, *Abscheu*, 396.

18. See Rothmund's memo of June 27, 1944. E 2001 (D) 3/277. BB.

19. Bányai to McClelland, Aug. 9, 1944. McClelland papers, box 60, WRB; Mantello to Krausz, Aug. 12, 1944; Levai, *Szidósórs*, 184, 195; Lutz to Mantello, Aug. 16, 1944; Levai, *Abscheu*, 419.

20. Duft-Krausz, Aug. 28, 1944. Levai, *Szidósórs*, 184.

21. PW Inquiry.

22. Levai, *Szidósórs*, 196. See chap. 9 for Lutz's letter to Mantello regarding the press campaign.

23. Riegner to McClelland, Dec. 21, 1944, Riegner papers, WJCong Archives, Geneva. Courtesy of Dr. Riegner.

24. Levai, *Szidósórs*, 207–8.

25. Levai, *Abscheu*, 396. For the Swiss police, even during the war period, Mantello was usually listed as Mandel-Mantello, rather than Mantello.

26. Incidentally, as a sign of the El Salvador government's approval of Castellanos's support of Mantello's rescue efforts, they promoted him a few months later, designating him ambassador to London, one of the most prestigious positions for any ambassador. Levai, *Abscheu*, 399.

27. The lack of sufficient personnel recalls Mantello's earlier offer to McClelland to

send several Swiss citizens to Budapest, at his expense, to handle the matter of the Salvadoran papers. McClelland did not respond to this offer.

28. Copy in Mantello papers. See also Levai, *Abscheu,* 421.

29. Levai, *Szidósórs,* 207–8.

30. Levai, *Abscheu,* 397.

31. PW Inquiry.

32. The Swiss Alien Police report of Feb. 1945 pointed out the following: "Since German party officials realize that the war is lost for Germany, these people try to take measures for their personal safety. Among them are members of the higher echelons of the party, whom the Allies consider war criminals. They planned to obtain traveling passports from neutral states [Spain, Sweden, Switzerland] and go to neutral countries for safety; or, if that should fail, to use these [papers] in Germany as identification papers. . . . There is a conflict, because higher officials of the German Federal Security get such passports, while refusing them to officials of the Gestapo. The manager of the passport office . . . in Berlin received personal authorization from Chief of the German Police Himmler to procure for these people passports of foreign neutral countries."

33. Levai, *Wallenberg,* 78–79.

34. Ibid., 79.

35. Ibid., 101–2.

36. Ibid., 131.

37. Levai, *Szidósórs,* 223.

38. Braham, *Politics,* 1063; Levai, *Wallenberg,* 88–89, 96.

39. Lutz, *Report—1944,* 2, 4, 6.

40. Levai, *Abscheu,* 416.

41. Ibid.

42. A sardonic note concerning the Swiss legation at the Glass House was injected into an IRC report of December 15. At one point, in reference to the approximately 4,500 Jews "employed by" (i.e., hiding out in) the legation, one Nyilas official exclaimed, "A legation could not possibly have need of such a large army." *IRC Report,* 3–4, SMP, JDCA.

43. See esp. Asher Cohen, *The Hehalutz Resistance in Hungary, 1942–1944* (Leiden, Netherlands: E. J. Brill, 1986). See also Lambert, *Hazalah,* 169–70.

44. Lambert, *Hazalah,* chap. 20, esp. 166–70.

45. Ibid., 168.

46. Ibid., chap. 22. See also Braham, *Politics,* 840.

47. Roswell McClelland to Jaromer Kopecky, June 21, 1944; McClelland to Bányai, Aug. 11, 1944, WRB; interview with Maitre Muller.

48. McClelland to Bányai, Aug. 11, 1944. WRB.

49. Lutz, PW Inquiry.

50. Bányai to McClelland, Aug. 2, 1944; McClelland to Bányai, Aug. 2, 1944. WRB.

51. Lutz, PW Inquiry, Jan. 20, 1945.

52. McClelland to WRB, Sept. 9, 1944. WRB.

53. Memo, U.S. legation, Sept. 14, 1944. WRB.

54. McClelland to WRB, Sept. 16, 1944. WRB.

55. Hull to McClelland, Sept. 23, 1944. WRB.

56. Ibid.

57. Ibid., Jan. 1, 1945. WRB.

58. Memo of Benjamin Akzin's talk with Mr. Clattenberg of the State Department, Dec. 11, 1944. WRB.

59. Krausz to Mantello, Dec. 4, 1944.

60. Riegner papers, WJCong Archives, Geneva. Courtesy of Dr. Gerhard Riegner.

61. See, for example, McClelland's memo concerning the Trumpy negotiations, box 58. WRB. Despite Yehuda Bauer's unit in his American Jews on the so-called Kastner Train, this important, but highly complicated effort has not yet received its due, a lacuna I intend to fill soon.

62. Braham, *Docs-II*, Doc. #217, 484. See also three articles by Curt Trumpy in *Sie und Er*, Sept. 14 through Nov. 7, 1961.

63. Rubinfeld had broken with HIJEFS months earlier, as had several other former members. Herman Landau interview. Landau was the secretary of HIJEFS from mid-1942 through the postwar era.

64. Josef Mandl papers. RG M-20/46. YVA.

65. Weissmandl had a Swiss typewriter brought to Slovakia, to be able to write up Roth's messages "in 'authentic' Swiss type." See *Min Hametzar*, 107–9. The tractors were now crucial because they were needed for the fall harvest.

66. Ibid., 134–35. As Kastner and Harrison were to point out (see n. 67), the mere notification of the existence of the trucks prompted the Germans to permit the departure of the train to Bergen Belsen. As I mentioned earlier, I think that the early press campaign had its share of the influence on the departure of the train.

67. See the memo by de Haller of a conversation with Saly Mayer on Aug. 6, 1944, p. 3. E 2001 (D) 1968 /74 BD 14. BB. This primacy of the tractors as a bargaining chip is confirmed by Amb. Lelland Harrison. He echoed letters from Kastner in Budapest, in which he noted: "The affair of the forty tractors which Sternbuch brought to our attention . . . was part of the deal [that Gyula] Link [an Orthodox merchant] with Freudiger of the Orthodox group in Budapest negotiated and relayed to to Sternbuch. . . . On the basis of these offers the Gestapo in Budapest refrained from sending to Auschwitz . . . totaling the following groups, 17,290 souls . . . 1,690 [actually 1,684]. . . . Later sent to the camp of Bergen Belsen . . . approximately 15,000 [actually, closer to 18,000] . . . sent to an unknown destination in Austria to be kept 'on ice' . . . and 600 persons . . . still confined in Budapest." Harrison to WRB. August 11, 1944. WRB.

68. See memo by (Horst) Wagner of Sept. 28, 1944, concerning the basis for the release of the 318 from the Bergen Belsen train on Aug. 21, "which involved the delivery of important military goods for the SS." Braham, *Docs-II*, Doc. #380, 789. Contrary to Bauer's assertion that Sternbuch's tractors were delivered in order to release his "Orthodox clients," virtually none of this group was from the Orthodox group.

69. Edward R. Stettinius (assistant secretary of state) to WRB for Moses A. Leavitt, Aug. 1, 1944. MD, 760:3. See Bauer, *American Jewry,* 420. See also WRB to McClelland, June 27, 1944, where Hull points out to McClelland how much pressure the Union of Orthodox Rabbis put on the WRB for money for the Freudiger Plan. The JDC had already cabled Saly Mayer to confer with Sternbuch concerning this matter. Box 58. WRB. V. 22. See also Kranzler, *Thy Brother's Blood,* 106–9.

70. See Trumpy, *Sie und Er,* 77. See also memos by Saly Mayer, June 27 and 28, 1944, concerning the "Four Rescue Plans," including the Mantello–Trumpy Plan, listed under the "Bányai Committee," Proposition 3. Box 58, WRB.

71. See Kranzler, *Thy Brother's Blood,* chap. 7H.

72. Braham, *Politics,* 850.

73. Levai, *Wallenberg,* 133–36. See also Braham, *Politics,* 838–40, 1074.

74. Braham, *Politics,* 1075–76.

75. Levai, *Wallenberg,* esp. 169–71; Levai, *Black Book,* 392.

76. Levai, *Wallenberg,* 149–50.

77. Anger, Wallenberg, 92–93. See also Levai, *Wallenberg,* 147–52.

78. Paldiel, "Lutz," *EH,* 926.

79. Grossman, *Lutz,* 189.

80. For an incidental and misleading depiction of the Mayer-Becher-Himmler negotiations, see Yehuda Bauer, *American Jewry and the Holocaust* (Detroit: Wayne State Univ. Press, 1981), 420–21. For a somewhat more comprehensive but still inadequate portrayal, see Monty Penkower, *The Jews Were Expendable* (Urbana: Univ. of Illinois Press, 1983), chap. 9. A little more detailed picture is found in my *Thy Brother's Blood,* 109–12 and esp. chap. 7H.

81. Levai, *Abscheu,* 429.

82. Lutz. PW Inquiry, 5–6.

83. *IRC Report,* 3–4, SMP, JDCA.

84. See *IRC Report,* Dec. 1, 1945. See also *IRC Report,* Dec. 15, 1945, 3–4, which cites the figure of 30,000. For details of the 62,000, see 1948 letter from Bernard Joseph of the JA to Lutz, regarding "almost half the Jews saved." Joseph was involved in some aspects of the Salvadoran papers. Rosenfeld, *Wallenberg,* 40–41.

12. Postwar

1. See chap. 11 concerning the Trumpy Negotiations and my forthcoming article on this little-known episode.

2. Chaim Stern to Mantello, Aug. 12, 1976. MP.

3. Mantello interview.

4. Rabbi S. Brom to Mantello, Nov. 13, 1944. MP.

5. Ruth Neuberger (née Munk) interview.

6. Levai, *Abscheu,* 429. Levai gives Stern's first name as Odoen, whereas his secular name was Edmund. See Stern to Mantello, Aug. 12, 1976.

7. Chaim Stern testimony. PW Inquiry. See also Chaim Stern to Mantello, Aug. 12, 1976. MP.

8. Mantello interview.

9. Betar was the youth movement of the Revisionist Zionist Party, founded by Zev Jabotinsky, which had been excluded from the World Zionist Organization in 1935.

10. Elisha Katz to Mantello, Apr. 22, 1945, and Katz to Mantello, Apr. 29, 1945. MP.

11. Chaim Stern testimony, PW Inquiry.

12. Mendel Brach interview. Mr. Brach noted that part of the reason Rabbi Portugal had been successful in his work even under Anna Pauker, the Communist head of Romania, was that he had helped her father emigrate to Israel. After she was deposed, Rabbi Portugal was arrested and jailed for several years before he was allowed to come to the United Sates.

13. Otto Lewin to Mantello, May 20, 1945. MP.

14. Mantello interview.

15. See, for example, Duft to Mantello, Oct. 31, 1946. MP.

16. Griffel's second objective was the rescue of Jewish children who had been left by their parents, before deportation, in the care of gentile homes and Christian institutions. This mission was to occupy him for the rest of his life.

17. In June 1946, there was a pogrom in Kielce, in which forty Jews were murdered and fifty wounded. This tragic incident convinced most Polish Jews that, despite their thousand-year history in Poland, they were not welcome in their homeland. Thousands more sought to leave, but the Communist regime made it very difficult. Poland would permit them to leave only if they had an end-visa to another country.

18. Griffel, *Memoirs,* 94.

19. Based primarily on a taped interview with Bela Vaga. See also article on Vaga about the time he was in Switzerland, in the *Neue Zürcher Zeitung,* Oct. 15, 1947.

20. Although the Communists had less than one-fifth of the 1945 vote, they controlled the Ministry of the Interior, through which they started to arrest anti-Communists even before taking over completely in 1949.

21. See article, "Bela Vaga: Präsident der Ungariaschen Nationalversammlung," in the *Neue Zürcher Zeitung,* Oct. 15, 1947.

22. Mantello interview.

23. Based essentially on taped interview with Bela Vaga. Also, Mantello interview.

24. MP.

25. Stuttgart: Seewald Verlag, 1966. The English-language version was published in New York: A. S. Barnes, 1975.

26. MP.

27. See, for example, 100–2.

28. Kastner, *Bericht,* 22.

29. See Dwork to Kubowitzki, Jan. 16, 1946, and Kubowitzki to Dwork, Jan. 18, 1946, box 318, WJCong Archives. Mr. Kubowitzki later changed his name to Kubovy.

30. Riegner to Kubowitzki, Feb. 12, 1946. WJCong Papers. H-318, WJCA.

31. Hyman to Carlos Bernhard, Mar. 7, 1956. WJCong Papers. RG H-318, WJCA.

32. Mantello to Muller, Nov. 29, 1945. MP.

33. Dr. S. F. Rosing to Maitre Muller, May 3, 1946. MP.

34. MP.

35. Ibid.

36. Grossman, *Lutz,* 191–93.

37. E 2001 (D) 171. BB.

38. Rothmund to Lutz, May 24, 1948, in Grossman, *Lutz,* 191.

39. MP.

40. Although the entire transcript of the inquiry is found in the MP, virtually all of it is found in Levai's compilation, Abscheu, 425–40. Unless cited otherwise, I will rely on the selection in this source.

41. Levai, *Abscheu,* 426. Such cables full of dates were often fifty pages long. Several copies in the MP.

42. Silberschein testimony, PW Inquiry. Also in Levai, *Abscheu,* 426–27.

43. Levai, *Abscheu,* 428.

44. Ibid., 427–28.

45. Ibid., 430–31.

46. Ibid., 431–32.

47. Ibid., 427.

48. Ibid., 436.

49. Ibid.

50. Max Cahn to the PW Inquiry panel, May 13, 1946. MP.

51. Mantello interview. Copy of the visa in MP.

52. Mantello interview.

53. The Kastner trial focused prominently on the very issues in which Mantello had been directly involved during the war: the receipt and dissemination of the Auschwitz Reports. He had been exhorted by Kastner to stop his press campaign, because the Germans had told Kastner that this would endanger his own negotiations with Eichmann to save as many Jews as possible. Mantello disregarded this warning, correctly believing that the campaign was the only means of alerting the world to the horrors of Auschwitz and saving the rest of Hungarian Jewry.

Some Israeli officials informed Mantello that, if Kastner lost the trial, it might seriously affect the Israeli government itself, for Kastner represented the Jewish Agency, which was essentially the predecessor of the Mapai Labor Party organization, in Budapest. They also told him that Shmuel Tamir, the brilliant young lawyer defending Malkiel Greenwald, Kastner's original accuser, was a Revisionist Zionist, and was interested not only in showing Kastner to be a traitor to Hungarian Jewry, but also in undermining the labor government itself. In accusing Kastner, he was essentially accusing the Mapai Party, especially because Kastner was put up as a candidate for election to the Knesset. This even though he had been an admirer and supporter of the Revisionist Zionists. Under these circumstances, it took great effort for Mantello to refrain from testifying at the trial. For a detailed description and analysis of the trial, see Rosenfeld, *Tick Plili*.

13. Afterword

1. The article was entitled "The U.S. Board Bares Atrocity Details: Told by Witnesses at Polish Camps," and appeared on Nov. 26, 1944. Incidentally, after this article appeared, Pehle asked once again, in a much more forceful way, for the bombing of Auschwitz. This despite the opposition of other American officials, who did not even want the report to appear in the newspaper.

2. Lipstadt, *Belief*, 239.

Bibliography

Books

Anger, Per. *With Raoul Wallenberg in Budapest.* Translated by Daniel Mel Paul and Margarita Paul. New York: Holocaust Library, 1981.

Aschenauer, Rudolf. *Ich. Adolf Eichmann: In Historisches Zeugenbericht.* Augsburg: Druffel Verlag, 1980.

Avni, Haim. *Spain, the Jews, and Franco.* Translated by Emanuel Shimoni. Philadelphia: Jewish Publication Society of America, 1982.

Bauer, Yehuda. *American Jewry and the Holocaust.* Detroit: Wayne State Univ. Press, 1981.

———. *Jews for Sale? Nazi-Jewish Negotiations, 1933–1945.* New Haven: Yale Univ. Press, 1994.

Ben-Tov, Arieh. *Facing the Holocaust in Budapest: The International Committee of the Red Cross and the Jews in Hungary, 1943–1945.* Geneva: Henry Dumont Institute, 1988.

Berman, Aaron. *Nazism, the Jews, and American Zionism, 1933–1948.* Detroit: Wayne State Univ. Press, 1990.

Blet, Pierre, et al. *Le Saint-Siège et les Victims de la Guerre, Janvier 1944–Juillet 1945 (Actes et Documents du Saint Siège Relatifs à la Second Guerre Mondiale) v. 10.* Vatican, Vaticana: Libreria Editrice, 1980.

Bolchover, Richard. *British Jewry and the Holocaust.* Cambridge, England: Cambridge Univ. Press, 1993.

Braham, Randolph L. *The Destruction of Hungarian Jewry: A Documentary Account.* 2 vols. New York: World Federation of Hungarian Jews, 1963.

Braham, Randolph L., and Bela Vago, eds. *The Holocaust in Hungary: Forty Years Later.* New York: Institute of Holocaust Studies of the City Univ. of New York, 1985.

Braham, Randolph L., ed. *Hungarian Jewish Studies.* 3 vols. New York: World Federation of Hungarian Jews, 1966, 1969, 1973.

Braham, Randolph L. *The Politics of Genocide: The Holocaust in Hungary.* 2 vols. New York: Columbia Univ. Press, 1981.

Bibliography

Braham, Randolph L., ed. *The Tragedy of Hungarian Jewry: Essays, Documents, Depositions.* New York: Institute for Holocaust Studies of the City Univ. of New York, 1986.

Cohen, Asher. *The Halutz Resistance in Hungary, 1942–1944.* Leiden, Netherlands: E. J. Brill, 1986.

Czech, Danuta. *Auschwitz Chronicle 1939–1945.* New York: Henry Holt, 1990.

Del Fuego. *Sephardim and the Holocaust.* Edited by Solomon Gaon and Mitchel Sereles. New York: Sepher-Hermon Press, 1995.

Edelheit, Abraham. *The Yishuv in the Shadow of the Holocaust: Zionist Politics and Rescue Aliah, 1933–1939.* Boulder, Colo.: Westview Press, 1996.

Encyclopedia of World War II. Edited by Thomas Parrish. New York: Simon & Shuster, 1978.

Favez, Jean-Claude. *Une Mission Impossible? Le CICR, le Déportations et les Camps de Concentration Nazis.* Lausanne: Payot Lausanne, 1988.

Feingold, Henry. *Bearing Witness: How America and Its Jews Responded to the Holocaust.* Syracuse, N.Y.: Syracuse Univ. Press, 1995.

Fenyo, Mario D. *Hitler, Horthy, and Hungary.* New Haven: Yale Univ. Press, 1972.

Friedenson, Joseph. *Dateline Istanbul: Dr. Jacob Griffel's Lone Odyssey Through a Sea of Indifference.* New York: Mesorah Publications, 1984.

Frieder, Emanuel. *To Deliver Their Souls: The Story of a Young Rabbi During the Holocaust.* (Heb.) Jerusalem: Yad Vashem, 1986.

Friedlander, Saul. *Pius XII and the Third Reich: A Documentation.* New York: Knopf, 1966.

Fuchs, Abraham. *Unheeded Cry.* New York: Mesorah Publications, 1984.

Gaon, Solomon, and Mitchel Serels. *Sephardim and the Holocaust.* New York: Yeshiva Univ. Press, 1987.

Grossman, Alexander. *Nur Das Gewissen: Carl Lutz und Seine Budapester Aktion.* Geneva: Im Waldgut, 1986.

Grünhut, Aron. *Katastrophenzeit des Slowakischen Judentums.* Tel Aviv: published privately, 1972.

Gutman, Yisrael, and Michael Berenbaum, eds. *Anatomy of the Auschwitz Death Camp.* Bloomington: Indiana Univ. Press, 1994.

Handler, Andrew. *The Holocaust in Hungary: An Anthology of Jewish Response.* University, Ala.: Univ. of Alabama Press, 1982.

Häsler, Alfred A. *The Lifeboat Is Full: Switzerland and the Refugees, 1933–1945.* New York: Funk and Wagnalls, 1969.

Herczl, Moshe. *Christianity and the Holocaust.* Translated by Joel Lerner. New York: New York Univ. Press, 1993.

Hilberg, Raul. *Documents of Destruction: Germany and Jewry, 1933–1945.* Chicago: Quadrangle Books, 1971.

Historiography of the Holocaust Period, The. Jerusalem: Yad Vashem, 1983.

Kastner, Rudolph. *Der Kastner Bericht.* Munich: Kindler Verlag, 1961.

Korff, Baruch. *Flight from Fear.* New York: Elmar Publishers, 1953.

Kranzler, David. *Heroine of Rescue.* New York: Mesorah Publications, 1984.

———. *Japanese, Nazis, and Jews: The Jewish Refugee Community of Shanghai, 1938–1945.* New York: Yeshiva Univ. Press, 1976.

———. *Thy Brother's Blood: The Orthodox Jewish Response During the Holocaust.* New York: Mesorah Publications, 1987.

———. *To Save a World: Profiles of Holocaust Rescue.* 2 vols. Lakewood, N.J.: CIS, 1991.

Lampert, Giles. *Operation Hazalah: How Young Zionists Rescued Thousands of Hungarian Jews in the Nazi Occupation.* New York: Bobbes-Merrill, 1974.

Laqueur, Walter. *The Terrible Secret: Suppression of the Truth about Hitler's Final Solution.* Boston: Little, Brown, 1980.

Levai, Jeno. *Abscheu und Grauen vor dem Genocid in aller Welt.* New York: Diplomatic Press, 1968.

———. *Black Book on the Martyrdom of Hungarian Jewry.* Zurich: Central European Times, 1948.

———. *Raoul Wallenberg: His Remarkable Life, Heroic Battles, and the Secret of His Mysterious Disappearance.* Translated by Frank Vajda. Melbourne: Univ. of Melbourne Press, 1989.

———. *Eichmann in Hungary: A Documentary.* Budapest: Penonia Press, 1961.

———. *Papst Pius XII Hat nicht geschwiegen.* Cologne: Verlag Wort und Werk GMBH, 1966.

———. *Zsidósórs Europaban.* Budapest: Magyar Teka, 1948.

Lichtenstein, Heiner. *Warum Auschwitz nicht bombadiert wurde.* Cologne: Bund-Verlag, 1980.

Lipschitz, Chaim U. *Franco, Spain, the Jews, and the Holocaust.* New York: Ktav Publishing House, 1984.

Lipstadt, Deborah. *Beyond Belief: The American Press and the Coming of the Holocaust, 1933–1945.* New York: Free Press, 1986.

Lookstein, Haskel. *Were We Our Brother's Keeper: The Public Response of American Jews in the Holocaust, 1938–1944.* New York: Hartmore House, 1985.

Lucas, Noah. *History of Modern Israel.* New York: Praeger, 1975.

(Ludwig, Carl.) *Die Fluechtlingspolitik der Schweiz Seit 1933 bis zue Gegenwart.* Bericht an den Bundesrat, n.p, n.d. (1955).

Morse, Arthur. *While Six Million Died.* New York: Random House, 1967.

Nazi Concentration Camps, The. Jerusalem: Yad Vashem, 1984.

Papanek, Ernest. *Out of the Fire.* New York: William Morrow, 1975.

Pat, Emanuel, and Edward Linn. *In Gerangel: Yaakov Pat un Zein Dor* (Yid.). New York: Jacob Pat Family Fund, 1971.

Penkower, Monty N. *The Jews Were Expendable.* Urbana: Univ. of Illinois Press, 1983.

Picard, Jacques. *Die Schweiz und die Juden, 1933–1945.* Zurich: Chronos, 1994.

Porat, Dina. *The Blue and the Yellow Stars of David: The Zionist Leadership in Palestine and the Holocaust, 1939–1945.* London: Harvard Univ. Press, 1990.

Bibliography

Raphael, Marc Lee. *Abba Hillel Silver: A Profile in American Judaism.* New York: Holmes & Maier, 1987.

Rescue Attempts During the Holocaust. Jerusalem: Yad Vashem, 1977.

Rings, Werner. *Advokaten des Feindes.* Vienna: Econ-Verlag, 1966.

Rosenfeld, Harvey. *Raoul Wallenberg: Angel of Rescue.* Buffalo, N.Y.: Prometheus Books, 1982.

Rosenfeld, Shalom. *Tik Plili 124* (Heb.) (re Kastner trial). Tel Aviv: Karni, 1955.

Ross, Robert W. *So It Was True: The American Protestant Press and the Nazi Persecution of the Jews.* Minneapolis: Univ. of Minnesota Press, 1980.

Rothkirchen, Livia. *The Destruction of Slovak Jewry: A Documentary* (Heb.). Jerusalem: Yad Vashem, 1961.

Safran, Alexander. *Resisting the Storm: Romania, 1940–1947: Memoirs.* Jerusalem: Yad Vashem, 1987.

Selwyn, Ilan I., and Benjamin Pinkus. *Organizing Rescue: Jewish National Solidarity in the Modern Period.* London: Frank Cass, 1992.

Shelley, Lore. *Secretaries of Death: Accounts by Former Prisoners Who Worked in the Gestapo of Auschwitz.* New York: Shengold, 1986.

Shulman, Abraham. *The Case of Hotel Polsky.* New York: Holocaust Library, 1982.

Suhl, Yuri. *They Fought Back: The Story of the Jewish Resistance in Nazi Europe.* New York: Schocken Books, 1975.

Urofsky, Melvyn I. *A Voice That Spoke for Justice: The Life and Times of Stephen S. Wise.* Albany: State Univ. of New York, 1982.

Visser't Hooft, W. A. *Memoirs.* London, SCM Press, 1973.

Vogt, Paul. *Soll ich meines [sic] Bruder's Hüter Sein?* Zurich: Evangelischer Verlag, 1944.

———. *Ich war ein Mensch wie Du! Schicksale verfolgter Menschen.* Zurich: Schweiz Zentralstelle für Flüchtlingshilfe, n.d. (ca. 1945).

Wasserstein, Bernard. *Britain and the Jews of Europe, 1939–1945.* Oxford: Clarendon Press, 1979.

(Weissmandl, Michael Ber). *Min Hametzar* (Heb.). N.p., n.d.

Wyman, David S. *Abandonment of the Jews.* New York: Parthenon Books, 1985.

Wyman, David, ed. *America and the Holocaust: A Documentary.* 13 vols. New York: Garland Publishing, 1990.

Yahil, Leni. *The Holocaust: The Fate of European Jewry, 1932–1945.* New York: Oxford Univ. Press, 1990.

———. *The Rescue of Danish Jewry.* Philadelphia: Jewish Publication Society, 1969.

Articles

Bauer, Yehuda. "When Did They Know?" *Midstream* 14, no. 4 (Apr. 1968), 57–63.

Braham, Randolph L. "The Holocaust of Hungarian Jews in Light of the Research of." In *Yad Vashem Studies* 25 (1996):361–82.

————. "The Kamenets-Podolsk and Delvidek Massacres: Prelude to the Holocaust in Hungary." *Yad Vashem Studies* 9 (1973):133–56.

————. "The Official Jewish Leadership of Wartime Hungary." In *Patterns of Jewish Leadership in Nazi Europe, 1933–1945.* Jerusalem: Yad Vashem, 1979.

————. "The Uniqueness of the Holocaust in Hungary." In *The Holocaust in Hungary: Forty Years Later.* Edited by Randolph L. Braham and Bela Vago, 177–90. New York: Institute for Holocaust Studies, City Univ. of New York, 1985.

————. "What Did They Know and When?" In *The Holocaust as Historical Experience.* Edited by Yehuda Bauer and Natan Rotenstreich, 109–31. New York: Holmes and Maier, 1981.

Cohen, Asher. "The Halutz Resistance and the Anti-Nazi Movements in Hungary, 1944." In *The Holocaust in Hungary: Forty Years Later.* Edited by Randolph L. Braham and Bela Vago, 139–46. New York: Institute for Holocaust Studies, City Univ. of New York, 1985.

————. "Li-Demutah shel Va'adat Ha-ezra ve-Hatzalah beBudapest Bereshit Darkah" (Heb.). *Yallkut Moreshet* 15 (1980) : 143–57.

————. "Pétain, Horthy, Antonescu, and the Jews, 1942–1944: Toward A Comparative View." In *Yad Vashem Studies* 18, 163–98.

————. "Protocol Auschwitz, the Deportation of Hungarian Jewry in the Swiss Press" (Heb.). *Dafim leHeker Tekufat haShoah* 8 (1990):203–10.

Eck, Nathan. "The Rescue of Jews with the Aid of Passports and Citizenship Papers of Latin American States." In *Yad Vashem Studies* 1 (1957):125–52.

Erez, Zvi. "The Jews of Budapest and the Plans of Admiral Horthy-August—Oct. 1944." *Yad Vashem Studies* 16 (1984):177–203.

————. "Six Days in July 1944 in Hungary" (Heb.). *Yalkut Moreshet* 20 (Dec. 1975):78–89.

Fox, John. "The Jewish Factor in British War Crimes Policy in 1942." *English Historical Review* 92 (Jan. 1977):1–15.

Freudiger, et al. "Hungarian Report." In *Hungarian Jewish Studies* 3. Edited by Randolph L. Braham, 75–146. New York: World Federation of Hungarian Jews, 1973.

Gelber, Yoav. "The Free World and the Holocaust." In *Comprehending the Holocaust.* Edited by Asher Cohen, Yoav Gelber, and Charlotte Ward, 107–23. Frankfurt am Main: Verlag Peter Lang, 1988.

Genizi, Haim, and Naomi Blank. "The Rescue Efforts of Bnei Akiva in Hungary During the Holocaust." *Yad Vashem Studies* 23 (1996):173–212.

Karny, Miroslav. "The Vrba and Wetzler Report." In *Anatomy of Auschwitz.* Edited by Yisrael Gutman and Michael Berenbaum, 553–68.

Kranzler, David. "The Mantello-Trumpy Negotiations" (forthcoming).

————. "Orthodox Ends, Unorthodox Means: The Role of the Vaad Hatzalah and Agudath Israel During the Holocaust." In *American Jewry During the Holocaust.* Edited by Seymour Maxwell Finger, Appendix 4-3. New York: American Jewish Commission on the Holocaust, 1984.

Bibliography

———. "The Role in Relief and Rescue During the Holocaust by the Jewish Labor Committee." In *American Jewry During the Holocaust.* Edited by Seymour Maxwell Finger, Appendix 4-2. New York: American Jewish Commission on the Holocaust, 1984.

———. "Stephen S. Wise and the Holocaust." In *Reverence, Righteousness, and Rahamanut: Essays in Memory of Rabbi Dr. Leo Jung.* Edited by Jacob J. Schacter, 155–92. Northvale, N.J.: Jason Aronson, 1992.

———. "Why Auschwitz Was Really Never Bombed." In *Proceedings of the Tenth World Congress of Jewish Studies,* 411–17. Jerusalem: World Union of Jewish Studies, 1990.

Kubovy, Arieh.. "The Silence of Pope Pius XII and the Beginning of the 'Jewish Question.'" *Yad Vashem Studies* 6 (1967):7–25.

Kulka, Erich. "Escapes of Jewish Prisoners from Auschwitz-Birkenau and Their Attempts to Stop Mass Extermination." In *Nazi Concentration Camps,* 401–16. Jerusalem: Yad Vashem, 1980.

Lewin, Isaac. "Attempts at Rescuing Jews with the Help of Polish Diplomatic Missions During World War II." *Polish Historical Review* 22, no. 4 (1967):4–16.

Ofer, Dalia. "The Activities of the Jewish Agency in Istanbul in 1943." In *Rescue Attempts During the Holocaust.* Edited by Yisrael Gutman and Efraim Zuroff, 435–50. Jerusalem: Yad Vashem, 1977.

Paldiel, Mordecai, and Robert Rozett. "Carl Lutz." In *Encyclopedia of the Holocaust.* Edited by Yisrael Gutman, 924–25. New York: Macmillan, 1974.

"Rescue Efforts with the Asssistance of International Organizations—Documents from the Archives of Dr. A. Silberschein." *Yad Vashem Studies* 8 (1969):60–80.

Rothkirchen, Livia. "Hungary—An Asylum for the Refugees." *Yad Vashem Studies* 7 (1968):127–46.

Rozett, Robert. "From Poland to Hungary: Rescue Attempts, 1943–1944." *Yad Vashem Studies* 24 (1995):177–94.

———. "Jews and Hungarian Armed Resistance in Hungary." *Yad Vashem Studies* 19 (1989):269–88.

Stern, Samu (Samuel). "A Race Against Time." In *Hungarian Jewish Studies* 3. Edited by Randolph L. Braham, 1–47. New York: World Federation of Hungarian Jews, 1973.

Vago, Bela. "Budapest Jewry in the Summer of 1944—Otto Komoly's Diaries." *Yad Vashem Studies* 8 (1970):81–106.

———. "The Destruction of Hungarian Jewry as Reflected in the Palestine Press." In *Yad Vashem Studies* 3: 291–323.

———. "The Horthy Offer: A Missed Opportunity for Rescuing Jews in 1944." In *Contemporary Views on the Holocaust.* Edited by Randolph L. Braham, 23–46. Boston: Kluwer-Nijhof, 1983.

———. "The Intelligence Aspects of the Joel Brand Mission." *Yad Vashem Studies* 10 (1974):111–28.

————. "Political and Diplomatic Activities for the Rescue of the Jews in Northern Transylvania." *Yad Vashem Studies* 6 (1967):155–74.

Yahil, Leni. "Raoul Wallenberg—His Mission and His Activities in Hungary." *Yad Vashem Studies* 15 (1983):7–54.

Taped Interviews

Bein, Rabbi Jacob, 1966–67, oral.
Brach, Mendel, Mar. 19, 1985.
Frey, Samuel, May 20, 1985.
Gottesman, Lajos, Jan. 19, 1980.
Hecht, Reuven, Jan. 16, 1980.
Krausz, Moshe (Miklós), Jan. 28, 1980.
Landau, Herman, Jan. 26, 1983.
McClelland, Roswell, Oct. 26, 1989.
Mantello, George Mandel, Jan. 1980–89 (80 hours).
Muller, Maitre, Jan. 10, 1980.
Neuberger, Ruth, Jan. 6, 1987, oral.
Riegner, Dr. Gerhard, July 18, 1989.
Roth, Chaim, Feb. 2, 1982.
Schaffert, Dr. Hans, July 13, 1989.
Schwalb, Natan, Jan. 22, 1994.
Springman, Sámuel, Jan. 23, 1980.
Stern, Brudi, Aug. 22, 1980; Mar. 13, 1982.
Stern, Shloime, Aug. 22, 1978.
Sternbuch, Eli, July 10–11, 1989.
Sternbuch, Guta, Jan. 19, 1994.
Sternbuch, Renee, Jan. 20, 1994.
Varga, Monsignor Bela, May 26, 1989.

Index

Abwehr, 46, 52–53, 270nn. 16, 17

Agudath Israel: components of, 262n. 13; factions within, 25; ideological differences with other organizations, 24; Latin American papers for friends and relatives of, 27; and Mantello's trust fund proposal, 6, 7; and McClelland on Salvadoran papers, 219; Muller's papers project funded by, 31; Rosenheim, 19, 20, 21–22, 36, 72; Swiss operations of, 15, 17, 18

Akzin, Benjamin, 219

American Jewish Committee, 99

American Jewish Congress, 16

American Jewish Joint Distribution Committee (the Joint): Hungarian branch of, 44, 270n. 7; ideological differences with other organizations, 24; and the Kastner Train, 222; and Mantello's joint trust fund proposal, 6, 7, 246; papers as closed, 262n. 8; rescue operations supported by, 23; and the SHC, 63; and Swedish plan to provide refuge, 105; Swiss operations of, 15, 16; on the "visa business," 27. *See also* Mayer, Saly

American Jews: early information about Hungarian Jews reaching, 56–58; Madison Square Garden rally, 57, 141, 176; Morgenthau, 37, 181, 182, 222, 268n. 39; Orthodox rabbis demonstrate at White House, 141; Roosevelt not pressured by, 57, 58, 72, 73, 80, 176. *See also* Wise, Stephen S.

Anger, Per, 200, 290n. 46

Antonescu, Ion, 82

Apor, Gábor, 98

Apor, Vilmos, 161

Arrow Cross. *See* Nyilas

atrocity reports. *See* Auschwitz Report; Hungarian Report

Auschwitz: bombing of, 72–73, 286n. 5; enlarged to accommodate Hungarian Jews, 68; ghettoization as first step to, 53; Hungarian Jews deported to, xvii–xviii, 1; plan to bomb railroads to, xviii, 23, 43, 69–72, 102, 147, 252, 269n. 2, 279n. 41, 280n. 46, 293n. 88; Rosin and Mordowicz escape from, 87; Swiss press campaign revealing facts about, 123, 130–32; Vittel inmates deported to, 38; Vrba and Lanik escape from, 68–69

Auschwitz Report (Auschwitz Protocols), 68–73; Freudiger discloses to the Judenrat, 48; Freudiger receives from Weissmandl, 272n. 28; Garrett and authenticity of, 124; Garrett summarizing, 97; International Red Cross receiving, 101–2, 103, 156; Kastner receiving, 52; at Kastner trial, 313n. 53; Krausz receives from Freudiger, 104, 290n. 47; Krausz sends to Danielsson, 104, 290n. 46; Manoliu bringing from Hungary, 82, 87; Mantello discloses to the Press, xix, 95, 98; Mantello guarantees for Vogt, 109; McClelland sends to United

Index

Auchwitz Report (*continued*)
States, 94, 102, 175; *New York Times*
publishes, 175, 252, 303n. 106; Riegner's
French-language edition of, 291n. 76;
and Schwalb asking Bernadini to intercede with Holy See, 269n. 3; skepticism
regarding, 112; summary version of, 87,
101, 284n. 18, 288n. 31; Swiss-Hungarian
students' translation of, 91–92, 285n. 33;
the Vatican receives, 116, 292n. 88; Vogt
distributes, xx, 112, 113, 114, 115; West
presented with, 96

Bakách-Bessenyey, György, 102, 300n. 22
Baky, László: attempted coup against Horthy, 146–47; attempt to deport Kistarcsa
Jews, 161; dismissal of, 162; Horthy abdicating his power to, 145; Horthy calling
for removal of, 117; Horthy's policy
change opposed by, 155; SHC monitoring statements of, 63, 64
Bányai, C., 59
Bányai, Michael (Mihály): American legation asked to cable State Department by,
62–63; and Barcza, 98; and McClelland,
76, 92–94, 100, 286n. 1; Protestant theologians contacted by, 66; and recognition of Salvadoran papers, 204–5; Red
Cross asked to transmit Salvadoran
papers by, 64; on rumors about deportation of Hungarian Jews, 79; SHC as
represented by, 81; in SHC's founding,
59; War Refugee Board informed of
Hungarian confiscations by, 66
Bányai Committee. *See* Schweizerisches
Hilfskomitee fuer die Juden in Ungarn
baptismal certificates, 202–3
Barcza, György, 98, 102, 117, 293n. 88
Barlas, Chaim, 23, 25, 75, 103–4, 180
Bar Shaket, Gavriel, 284n. 19
Barth, Carl, xx, xxv, 100–101, 114, 152, *153*,
166
Barthe, Ferenc, 201–2
Batisfalvy, Nandor, 224

Bauer, Margaret, 224
Bauer, Yehuda, 306n. 55, 310nn. 61, 68
Bavier, Jean de, 276n. 59
Becher, Kurt, xxiv, 55, 166, 223, 306n. 55
Bein, Jacob, 275n. 57
Ben–Gurion, David, 70, 248
Ben–Tov, Arieh, 75, 300n. 28, 301n. 47
Berg, Mary, 35
Berger, Ignaz (Yitzchok), 88–89
Bernadini, Filippe: atrocity reports received
by, 287n. 21; Bányai meeting with, 63;
Jewish organizations interceding with,
43; Mantello delivering atrocity reports
to, 99; on Protestant rescue activities,
293n. 88; Schwalb asks him to intercede
with Holy See, 269n. 3; Sternbuchs
obtaining information from, 36
Bernhard, Carlos, 237
Bethlen, Istvan, 145
Bieler, Victor, 119
Bindlinger, Otto, 220
Biss, Andre, xxiii, 55, 235–36
Bistrice (Romania), 83, 84, 89
Bloom, Sol, 118
Blum, Josef, 76, 270n. 7, 285n. 19.
Boden, Max Otto, 220
Bona, B., 65
Born, Friedrich: attempts to visit detention
camps, 194–95; Budapest Jews working
through, 168; on danger to Budapest
Jews, 80–81; in International Red Cross
rescue efforts, 197; letter to Huber on
Budapest situation, 75; Nilson and
Bauer saved by, 224; Pillaud's message
to, 159; protective papers distributed by,
196; Schwartzenberg given Auschwitz
Report by, 156
Bothmer, Karoly, 190, 300n. 22
Brach, Mendel, 231, 312n. 12
Braham, Randolph L., 48, 197, 273n. 31,
274n. 49, 275n. 57, 306nn. 55, 58
Brand, Joel: as aware of impending invasion
of Hungary, 52; Brand Mission, 54–55,
221, 275n. 55; family members on the

324

Index

Davis, Elmer, 175
de Andrade, Narciso Freire, 39, 40–41
DeGaulle, Charles, 193
Diamant, Alexander, 47, 270n. 9
Dobkin, Eliyahu, 25, 70, 265n. 55
Donnebaum, Hugo, 76
Dragenescu, General, 4, 5, 10, 13, 14
DuBois, Josiah, 182
Duft, Johannes, 119–20, 205, 220, 240
Dulles, Allen: atrocity report summaries
    cabled to Washington by, 98; Horthy
    pressured by, 117, 147; Mantello assisted
    by, xxv, 9, 74, 260n. 10, 286n. 4; and
    Spellman's radio address, 118

Eck, Nathan, xxiv
Eden, Anthony, 98, 182
Ehrenpreis, Marcus, 105–6, 187, 188
Ehrmann, Solomon, 60, 277n. 7
Eichmann, Adolph: attempt to deport
    Kistarcsa Jews, 161, 171, 195; and Bandi
    Grosz mission, 54; Himmler removes
    from Hungary, 194; Horthy pressured
    by, 191–92; Horthy's policy change
    opposed by, 155; and the Kastner Train,
    55, 294n. 105; as pressing to complete
    Final Solution in Hungary, xvii, xviii,
    xxi, 50, 145, 191, 198, 200; returns to
    Budapest, 200; SS contingent as too
    small to carry out final solution in Hun-
    gary, 144; and Vajna deporting Jews to
    Germany, 223
Eis, Yisroel Chaim, 7, 18, 27, 31
Eisenzweig, Guta, 27, 35, 264n. 44, 267n. 34
Eisenzweig, Sara, 35, 267n. 34
El Salvador: breaks off relations with the
    Axis, 3; Castellanos, xxii, xxv, 2, 28, 42,
    206, 253, 308n. 25; Castro, 253; Guer-
    rero, xxii, xxv, 28, 247, 253; Manoliu dis-
    tributing, 83; Mantello as consul for,
    xxii, 2, 6, 206; Enrico Mantello having
    diplomatic passport from, 40, 42;
    Switzerland representing interests of,
    203, 204–5. See also Salvadoran papers

Emergency Visitors' Visas (above–quota
    visas), 17
Endre, László: attempted coup against Hor-
    thy, 146–47; attempt to deport Kistarcsa
    Jews, 161; dismissal of, 162; Horthy abdi-
    cating his power to, 145; Horthy calling
    for removal of, 117; Horthy's policy
    change opposed by, 155; on Jews as
    threat to Hungary, 121; SHC monitoring
    statements of, 63–64
Entjuden, 112
Erny, Dr., 111
Esterhazy, Moric, 145
Europa Plan, 52, 53, 54, 270n. 17
"Exposé" (Mantello), 62

"Fate of the Hungarian Jews, The" (news-
    paper article), 115
Federation of Swiss Jewish Communities
    (Schweizer Israelitische Gemeinde;
    SIG), 5, 8, 16, 242–43
Federation of Swiss Women's Organiza-
    tions, 120, 137–38
Ferency, Laszlo, 189
Filderman, Wilhelm, 2, 83, 176, 177, 270n. 9
Final Solution: Eichmann as having too few
    troops to carry out alone, 144; Eich-
    mann as pressing to complete in Hun-
    gary, xvii, xviii, xxi, 50, 145, 191, 198,
    200; Germans keeping secret, xix, 84;
    Jewish leaders despairing of halting, 74;
    the Riegner cable on, 19–20; the Stern-
    buch cable on, 20–22; Veesenmayer's
    role in, xvii, 3, 145, 178–79, 191, 198–99;
    Weissmandl warning Hungarian Jews
    about, 51; Wise announcing, 22
Finkelstein, Louis, 99, 288n. 25
Fischer, Theodore, 230
Fischer, Wilhelm, 243
Fleischmann, Gisi, xviii, 16, 23, 265n. 48
Flüchtingshilfe, 106
Franco, Francisco, 155, 194
Frankel, Shabse, 268n. 39
Frankfurter, Felix, 20

French Maquis, 231
Freudenberg, D. A., 109, 113, 151
Freudiger, Philip: Auschwitz Report obtained by, 69; Auschwitz Report sent to Krausz by, 104, 284n. 18, 290n. 47; Auschwitz Report shown to Judenrat members by, 48, 272n. 28, 280n. 45, 284n. 18; as head of Budapest Orthodox community, 47; and the Hungarian Report, 270n. 9, 284n. 18, 285n. 19; on Judenrat, 48, 53; and the Kastner Train, 55, 276n. 58, 310n. 67; on Keresztes–Fischer, 49; report on deportation of Hungarian Jews, 76, 282n. 78; and Stern, 229; Swiss attaché informed about fate of Hungarian Jews by, 79, 80; and Weissmandl, 272n. 23; in Wisliceny negotiations, 53, 54, 274n. 52
Frey, Arthur, 108
Frey, Samuel, 196, 307n. 65

Gafencu, Grigore, 82, 84, 177
Garrett, Walter: British press on role of, 174; at inquiry into Mantello's activities, 245–46; and Mantello's chronograph procurement, 74, 260n. 10; press release on atrocity reports prepared by, xxv, 96–98, 115, 117, 123, 293n. 88; in Swiss press campaigns, 123, 124, 127, 191; and West's involvement with Mantello, 286n. 4
Gautier, Claude, 242
Germany: Abwehr, 46, 52–53, 270nn. 16, 17; consent to Horthy agreement, 165, 167, 182, 199; Goebbels, 167, 168, 193; Hitler, 50, 151, 161, 162, 181, 226; Hungary occupied by, xvii, 43, 44, 48, 49–55; propaganda film on Hungarian brutality, 162; Salvadoran papers sought by Nazis, 210, 309n. 32; SS, 52–53, 144, 147, 191–92, 193; Swiss press campaign affecting, 151. *See also* Eichmann, Adolph; Himmler, Heinrich; Veesenmayer, Edmund
ghettoization: Budapest Jews fearing, 78; of

Carpatho–Ruthenian Jews, 62, 64, 85, 87; as first step to Auschwitz, 53; SHC possessing only rumors of, 79; Weissmandl on Jews fighting their way out, 51
Glass House, 212, 213–16, 309n. 42
Goebbels, Joseph, 167, 168, 193
Goldmann, Nahum, 20, 103, 104
"Goods for Blood" ("10,000 Trucks for One Million Jews"), 54, 78, 181, 222, 269n. 1, 310n. 66
Gottesman, Lajos, 275nn. 56, 57
Great Britain. *See* Britain
Greenwald, Malkiel, 313n. 53
Grell, Theodore H., 85
Griffel, Jacob, 23, 58, 231–32, 275n. 55, 312n. 16
Grosz, Bandi, 54
Grumsinger, Germaine, 235
Grünbaum, Yitzchok, 72, 80, 104, 105
Grüninger, Paul, 17, 298n. 92
Guerrero, José Gustavo, xxii, xxv, 28, 247, 253
Guggenheim, Paul, 243
Gulden, Gyula, 202
Günther, Christian, 106
Gurny, Max, 243
Gustav V (king of Sweden), 105, 106, 119, 146, 188, 294n. 105

Häsler, Alfred A., 108
Haller, Edouard de, 75, 158, 165, 222
Hámori, László (assistant to McClelland), 93
Hapoel Hatzair, 215
Harrison, Lelland, 43, 62, 310n. 67
Hashomer Hatzair, 16, 46
Hehalutz, 15, 16, 24, 265n. 52
Held, Adolph, 17
Hertz, Joseph H., 174
Herzog, Isaac, 116
HIJEFS (Relief Organization to Help Jewish Refugees in Shanghai), 15, 17–18, 19
Himmler, Heinrich: deportations halted by, 193–94, 306n. 55; and Grosz mission, 54; Sternbuch–Musy–Himmler negotia-

Index

Himmler, Heinrich (*continued*)
tions, 223, 226–27; Winkelman informs
that Veesenmayer could no longer handle situation, 159
Hirschmann, Ira, 54
Hitler, Adolph, 50, 151, 161, 162, 181, 226
Hoddel, Florence, 80
Holy See. *See* Vatican, the
Horthy, Madame, 120, 137–38
Horthy, Miklós: abdicating power to pro-
Nazi ministers, 145; on anti–Jewish
measures, 182, 273n. 33; attempt to
defect from Axis, 198; and the Auschwitz
Report, 69, 280n. 42; Baky–Endre coup
attempt against, 146–47; de Andrade
visits, 39; deportations to Auschwitz
halted by, xviii, xxi, 103, 105, 117, 120,
144, 145, 148, 159, 163, 179, 301n. 57;
deposed by the Nazis, xviii, 198; Eichmann pressuring, 191–92; Germans
acquiesce in agreement of, 165, 167, 182,
199; Hitler summons, 50; the Horthy
offer, xxiv, 125, 138, 148, 179–85; Huber's
letter to, 156, 158–59, 182, 292n. 83;
Hungarian Jews as confident in policies
of, 47; intended letter to Hitler, 151, 161;
International Red Cross's letter to, 292n.
83; Judenrat entreats to stop deportations, 77; Pius XII's open letter to, 116;
reasserting his authority, xviii, 147, 155,
193; relative independence of, xvii; Roosevelt's warning to, xviii, 116–17, 151,
164–65; Spellman's radio address to, 118;
standing up to Hitler, 161; Swedish King
Gustav's cable to, 105, 106, 119, 146, 187,
294n. 105; Swiss press campaign influencing, 120, 122, 124, 146
Huber, Max: Born describes conditions in
Budapest to, 75; on detention camps,
195; Horthy deplores anti–Jewish measures in note to, 182; International Red
Cross policy defended by, 66, 156;
Koechlin's plea to, 112, 155–56; letter to
Horthy of, 156, 158–59, 182, 292n. 83; letter to Koechlin of, 158; photograph of,

157; Swiss press campaign influencing,
158; Sztojay asked to end deportations
by, 170–71
Huddle, Klahr, 62, 112
Huegly, Mr., 18
Hull, Cordell, 37, 98, 117, 268n. 39
Hungarian Alien Police (KEOKH), 188,
205, 210
Hungarian Church: deportations finally
condemned by, 119; Serédi, 63, 119, 161;
SHC asks Vatican to use its influence
with, 63; as unable to manage an appeal
to the government, 81, 85
Hungarian Jews: American press on, xvii,
175; Auschwitz enlarged to accommodate, 68; beginnings of Swiss press campaign on behalf of, 95–121; deportation
to Auschwitz, xvii–xviii, 1; early information about reaches the West, 56–58;
on the eve of the occupation, 44; Horthy halting deportation of, xviii, xxi,
103, 105, 117, 120, 144, 145, 148, 159, 163,
179, 301n. 57; Jewish rescue efforts for,
43–58; Kallay's benign policy regarding,
49; as last reservoir of European Jewry,
xvii; Mantello's early rescue efforts,
59–81; men drafted into labor battalions,
44, 259n. 1, 304n. 19; nonnationals
deported to the Ukraine, 44, 269n. 6;
organizations of, 44–48; as relatively
secure before German occupation,
47–48; Romania permitting entry of
refugees, 100; Sweden permitting entry
of refugees, 165; Swiss press campaign in
full swing, 122–43; Weissmandl warning
about the Final solution, 51, 274n. 43.
See also Budapest Jews;
Carpatho–Ruthenian Jews; Judenrat
Hungarian Red Cross, 81, 85
Hungarian Report: authors of, 270n. 9; Garrett summarizing, 97; Hungarian Secret
Police as composing, 284n. 19; Krausz
giving to Manoliu, 87; Krausz receives
from Freudiger, 284n. 18; Mantello dis-
closing to the press, xix; Mantello guar-

Index

Mizrachi, 46, 215

Moetza, 23, 52, 54

Mordowicz, Czeslaw, 87

Morgenthau, Henry, Jr., 37, 181, 182, 222, 268n. 39

Muguiro, Miguel Angel de, 201

Muller, (Matthieux) Maitre: and Cahn, 247; at inquiry into Mantello's activities, 244; Mantello's letters on denial of visas, 237–39; and McClelland in recognition of Salvadoran papers, 217; and Munk, 229; in Salvadoran papers project, 18–19, 31; in SHC founding, 59; as source for this study, xxiii–xxiv

Munk, Elie, 228

Musy, Jean–Marie, xxiv, 223, 226

Nazi Germany. *See* Germany

Nef, Clara, 137–38

Neolog, 45; on Judenrat, 48, 53; relief provided to Jews by, 44

Neufeld, Miss, 209–10

Neumann, Oscar, 69

Nilson, Asta, 224

Nobi, Ernst, 100

Norwegian Jews, 188

Nuremberg trials, 21

Nyilas (Arrow Cross), 198–227; Germans blaming cruelties of deportation on, 162; Hungarian government on role in deportations of, 190; Lutz on difficulties with, 186. *See also* Szalasi, Ferenc

Obuda brickworks, 214, 223

Offenbach, Sándor, 55

Olson, Ivor, 104, 105, 187, 188, 290n. 46

Operation Hatzalah, 215

Operation Tiyul, 45

Orgaz, Luis, 196

Orthodox Jews: false papers made available by, 45, 270n. 9; on the Judenrat, 48, 53; relief provided to Hungarian Jews by, 44

Palestine Certificate Office (Palestina Amt; Palamt): Germans close office of, 185;

and Mantello's trust fund proposal, 6, 7; Posner in temporary charge of, 261n. 2; Scheps, 7, 15, 60, 83, 99, 261n. 2; as Zionist organization, 15, 46. *See also* Krausz, Moshe (Miklós); Posner, Chaim

Palestine certificates, 46; "capitalist certificates," 46, 303n. 2; for families, 303n. 2; in Horthy offer, 165, 180, 182, 200; Krausz in distribution of, 46, 271n. 22; and Lutz providing refuge for Krausz, 86; as protective papers, 186, 205, 210; as sole means of rescue for Budapest Jews, 103; Swiss as hesitant to provide protection for holders of, 65; Switzerland taking responsibility for, 185

Pallai, Geza, 59, 60, 92, 277n. 5

Paneth, Philip, 174

Paraguay, 35, 36, 37

Paskus, Rivka, 72, 286n. 5

Pat, Jacob, 17

Pawiak Prison (Warsaw), 35, 267n. 35

Pehle, John, 72, 175

Peney, Jules, 240–41

Penkower, Noam, 263n. 30

Perlasca, Giorgio (Jorge), xxv, 201, 308n. 9

Perlzweig, Maurice, 20

Pestalozzi, Johann Heinrich, 128, 296n. 67

Pilet–Golaz, Marcel: de Haller meeting with, 158; Koechlin's appeals to, 101, 156, 166; report on steps taken to help the Jews, 174; in Swiss "clique" working for Hungarian Jews, 288n. 30; on Swiss failure to protest treatment of Jews, 136, 137; and Tahy on the Swiss press campaign, 164; transformation in views of, 165–66

Pillaud, Claude, 159

Pinkerton, L. C., 72

Pius XII, Pope, 115–16

Polish Jews: Latin American papers for, 27, 35; reports on slaughter of, 17; in Vittel detention camp, 36; Warsaw Ghetto, 19, 21, 27, 28, 35

Porat, Dina, 275n. 55

Portugal, 39, 40, 123, 145, 183, 201–2

Index

Rothmund, Heinrich (*continued*)
  Jews as danger to Switzerland, 108;
  Mantello arrested by, 73, 74; and Enrico
  Mantello's entry into Switzerland, 40,
  42; postwar harassment of Mantello,
  241; and recognition of Salvadoran
  papers, 204; and *refoulement* policy, 134,
  241, 268n. 46, 297n. 91; Sternbuch
  arrested by, 298n. 92
Rothschild, L., 140
Rotta, Angelo, xxv, 161, 192, 200, 290n. 46
Rubin, Menachem, 73
Rubinfeld, Leo (Leibish), 221
Rubinstein, William D., 253

Sagalowitz, Benjamin, 20
Sajo, Eli, 78
Salvador, El. *See* El Salvador
Salvadoran (citizenship) papers: counterfeit,
  214–15; early papers, 26–42; the Glass
  House for processing, 212, 213–16; International Red Cross and delivery of, 32,
  64–66, 185, 208; Mantello issuing,
  xxi–xxii, xxiv, 18, 29, 61, 74, 83, 183–84,
  186–87, 197, 204, 211–12, 217, 227,
  231–32; McClelland's legalistic attitude
  toward, 216–20; as model for all protec-
  tive papers, 180, 186; Nazis seeking, 210,
  309n. 32; non-Jews seeking, 231; postwar
  use of, 231–32; recognition of, 203–12
Sanz–Briz, Angel, xxv, 192, 197, 201
Sarrossy, Bela, 148–49, 151–52, 154–55
Schaffert, Hans, 108, 171–72, 291n. 75
Schellenberg, Walter, xxiv, 223, 307n. 5
Scheps, Samuel, 7, 15, 60, 83, 99, 261n. 2
Schirmer, Robert, 159, 170–71, 182, 195,
  292n. 83
Schlesinger, Ferenc, 59
Schmidt, Joseph, 52, 53
Schmidthuber, General, 225
Schonfeld, Solomon, 71, 284n. 18, 303n. 100
Schulte, Eduard, 19, 263n. 30
Schutzpaesse, 201, 210
Schwalb, Natan: and Abwehr couriers,
  270n. 17; asking for citizenship papers
  but not providing information, 61; and

the Auschwitz Protocol, 69, 70, 280nn.
  41, 46; Bernadini asked to intercede
  with Holy See by, 269n. 3; as cooperating only with certain individuals, 25;
  courier system of, 16; desperate letters
  from Budapest to, 74, 76, 78; as Hehalutz head, 16; Jewish organizations providing information to, 24; McClelland
  supporting, 24, 265n. 52; papers of,
  261n. 6, 281n. 48; Weissmandl and
  Fleischmann communicating with,
  23, 71
Schwartz, Zahava, 272n. 28
Schwartz, Joseph, 222
Schwartzenberg, Jean, 66, 101–2, 156
Schwarzbart, Ignacy, 19, 22
Schweizerisches Hilfskomitee fuer die Juden
  in Ungarn (SHC; Bányai Committee),
  59–68; emergency meeting of June 21,
  1944, 90–91, 92; formation of, 59; Hungarian reports of, 287n. 14; as lacking
  information on deportation of Hungar-
  ian Jews, 79; Mantello staying in back-
  ground of, 81; Salvadoran papers
  distributed by, 31
Schweizer Israelitische Gemeinde (SIG;
  Federation of Swiss Jewish Communi-
  ties), 5, 8, 16, 242–43
Schweizer Rabbinerverband (Swiss Rabbis'
  Committee), 7–8, 92, 99
Seidman, Hillel, 27, 35, 267n. 34
Serédi, Jusztinián, Cardinal, 63, 119, 161
SHC. *See* Schweizerisches Hilfskomitee fuer
  die Juden in Ungarn
Sherer, Emanuel, 16
Shertok, Moshe, 104
SIG (Schweizer Israelitische Gemeinde;
  Federation of Swiss Jewish Communi-
  ties), 5, 8, 16, 242–43
Silberschein, Abraham: at inquiry into
  Mantello's activities, xviii, 243–44; Kuhl
  providing information to, 18; and Latin
  American passports, 27; Josef Mandl
  appealing for aid to, 279n. 35; and Man-
  tello's trust fund proposal, 7; as
  RELICO head, 7, 15; Riegner as not